Robert Manning Strozier Library

JAN 30 1986

Tallahassee, Florida

STUDIES IN SEVENTEENTH-CENTURY ENGLISH LITERATURE,
HISTORY AND BIBLIOGRAPHY

Photograph by Phil Hyams

STUDIES IN SEVENTEENTH-CENTURY ENGLISH LITERATURE, HISTORY AND BIBLIOGRAPHY

FESTSCHRIFT FOR PROFESSOR T.A. BIRRELL ON THE OCCASION OF HIS SIXTIETH BIRTHDAY

EDITED BY

G.A.M. JANSSENS AND F.G.A.M. AARTS

Amsterdam 1984

NEW SERIES   VOLUME 46

COSTERUS

*Soc
DA
440
S73*

CIP-GEGEVENS KONINKLIJKE BIBLIOTHEEK, DEN HAAG

Studies

Studies in seventeenth-century English literature, history
and bibliography / ed. by G.A.M. Janssens and F.G.A.M.
Aarts. — Amsterdam : Rodopi. — (Costerus. New Series ;
vol. 46)
ISBN 90-6203-736-4
SISO enge 853 UDC 820"16"
Trefw.: Engelse letterkunde ; geschiedenis ; 17e eeuw.

©Editions Rodopi B.V., Amsterdam 1984
Printed in The Netherlands

CONTENTS

Preface	VII
A.F. Allison, *The "Mysticism" of* Manchester Al Mondo. *Some Catholic borrowings in a seventeenth-century Anglican work of devotion*	1
A.G.H. Bachrach, *General Othello's Service*	13
F.J.M. Blom, *Lucas Holstenius (1596-1661) and England*	25
J.M. Blom, *A German Jesuit and his Anglican Readers: The case of Jeremias Drexelius (1581-1638)*	41
Hans Bots, *Jean Leclerc as Journalist of the* Bibliothèques. *His contribution to the spread of English learning on the European continent*	53
D.E.L. Crane, *Richard Stanyhurst's Translation of Vergil's* Aeneid *(1582)*	67
A.I. Doyle, *The Library of Sir Thomas Tempest: Its origins and dispersal*	83
Mirjam M. Foot, *Some Bindings for Charles I*	95
Johan Gerritsen, *A Jonson Proof-Sheet —* Neptunes Triumph	107
Wytze and Lotte Hellinga, *Between Two Languages: Caxton's translation of Reynaert de Vos*	119
F.J.M. Korsten, *Thomas Baker's* Reflections upon Learning	133
Hans Pörnbacher, *English Virtue in Bavarian Baroque Literature: Mary Ward and her biographer Marcus Fridl*	149
J.G. Riewald, *The English Actors in the Low Countries, 1585 - c. 1650: An annotated bibliography*	157
David Rogers, *Antony Batt: A forgotten Benedictine translator*	179
Irène Simon, *Stillingfleet's Sermon Preached Before the King on the Anniversary of the Execution of Charles I (30 January 1668/9)*	195
Anna E.C. Simoni, *John Wodroephe's* Spared Houres	211
D.R.M. Wilkinson, Sospetto d'Herode: *A neglected Crashaw poem*	233
J. Anthony Williams, *No-Popery Violence in 1688: Revolt in the provinces*	245
A Checklist of the Writings of T.A. Birrell	261
Tabula Gratulatoria	269

Preface

This Festschrift was presented to T.A. Birrell, Professor of English and American literature at the Catholic University of Nijmegen, on the occasion of his sixtieth birthday in the summer of 1984. The essays in this book, written by friends, colleagues and former students, all reflect Professor Birrell's major field of research: the seventeenth century. As his bibliography shows, his writings testify to a wide range of interests. It has proved impossible to do justice to all of them.

The idea of this Festschrift arose in conversation with three of Professor Birrell's former students, now themselves professors at the Catholic University of Nijmegen: J. Aarts, W. Bronzwaer and F. Diekstra. Some of his English friends, notably Antony Allison, Ian Doyle and David Rogers were also in on this venture from the very start. We wish to thank all of them for their advice and support. Our thanks also go to Eric Kellerman for his valuable suggestions on matters of language and style. We wish to thank Elly Kersjes for the meticulous care with which she typed the manuscripts and for the assistance she gave us with the proofs and the bibliography.

G.J.
F.A.

THE "MYSTICISM" OF *MANCHESTER AL MONDO*. SOME CATHOLIC BORROWINGS IN A SEVENTEENTH-CENTURY ANGLICAN WORK OF DEVOTION

A.F. Allison

A few years ago Professor Birrell published in the *Downside Review* a series of three articles entitled "English Catholic Mystics in Non-Catholic Circles".[1] Their main drift was to show that the mystics, both of the mediaeval period and later, were widely known and admired outside the Catholic circles for which they wrote and that their spiritual influence has persisted till modern times. Professor Birrell also touched upon the theme that some Protestant religious writers looked to Catholic mysticism as a source of inspiration lacking in their own spiritual tradition. Such writers, he pointed out, were for the most part members of non-conformist groups for whom the essential feature of true religion was the cult of an immediate, experimentally perceived knowledge of God which they substituted for the sacramental system and traditional ecclesiastical forms of institutional Christianity. It was the fact that the Catholic mystics claimed to have immediate personal experience of the divine presence that struck an answering chord in their hearts. Needless to say, while they borrowed (and sometimes bowdlerised) the texts that suited them, they repudiated the Catholic position that this experience is perfectly reconcilable with institutional religion. Among high-church Anglicans, where there was not the same emphasis on the personal element in religion, the influence of the Catholic mystics seems to have been less marked, though there were some exceptions, the best-known being perhaps that of the seventeenth-century community at Little Gidding. Further investigations might well reveal that their influence among Anglicans was more widespread than has up till now been thought. Much work remains to be done in the field. As a small contribution to this *Festschrift* in honour of Professor Birrell I should like to offer a note on one Anglican spiritual writer of the early seventeenth century, Henry Montagu, first Earl of Manchester, the author of a work generally known by the title of its third edition, *Manchester al mondo*.

1 *Downside Review*, 1976, pp. 60-81, 99-117, 213-28.

This work contains borrowings from at least two contemporary Catholic sources. I shall try to answer the question whether they indicate a genuine spiritual influence or one that is merely literary.

Henry Montagu was born c. 1563 of a Northamptonshire family of strong Protestant leanings. His paternal grandfather, Chief Justice Sir Edward Montagu (d. 1557) had played a major role during Edward VI's reign in drafting the legislation designed to secure the succession to the throne of Lady Jane Grey. Henry was educated at Cambridge and the Middle Temple and quickly rose to prominence as a lawyer and politician. In 1601 he was elected M.P. and two years later was made Recorder of London and knighted. Thereafter he consistently showed himself a staunch upholder of the royal prerogative. In 1618 he was rewarded by James I with the office of Chief Justice of the King's Bench in succession to the disgraced Sir Edward Coke. In 1620 James appointed him Lord High Treasurer and raised him to the peerage as Baron Montagu of Kimbolton and Viscount Mandeville. Though compelled soon afterwards to resign the Treasurership at Buckingham's instance, he retained James's favour and continued to occupy high office during the remainder of the old King's reign and afterwards under Charles I. In 1626 Charles created him Earl of Manchester. He was one of the King's most loyal adherents and trusted advisers throughout the long political struggle leading up to the Civil War. In 1641, during Charles's absence in Scotland, he was one of the Guardians of the Realm. He died on 7 November 1642, just over two months after Charles raised his standard at Nottingham.[2]

In religion Manchester was an Anglican of the school of Hooker, a firm upholder of the established church and the royal supremacy. Catholics and Puritans alike he regarded as defectors from true religion, the former because of what he considered their misuse of tradition, the latter because they attached too little weight to it. He has left a statement of his religious convictions in a letter that he wrote in 1635 to his second son, Walter, who had just become a Catholic.[3] In this he sets out the Anglican position very clearly. The Church of England, he says, is no mere creation of the Reformation as Catholics maintain. It is grounded in Christ and follows the scriptural teachings held by the primitive church, teachings which, he says, the Roman Church has corrupted in the course

---

[2] The biographical particulars are taken from the article by J.M. Rigg in DNB and from J.E. Bailey's introduction to his edition of *Manchester al mondo* published in 1880 (See note 6).

[3] There is an account of Walter Montagu in DNB. For his conversion to Catholicism see Gordon Albion, *Charles I and the Court of Rome*, 1935, pp. 204 *et seq.* His letter to his father announcing his conversion, together with his father's reply, was printed in 1641 (Wing N2472).

of centuries. The true church of Christ has no need to prove visible succession from the Apostles or to be able to point to visible professors at all times: the links in the chain have sometimes been broken and the truth has from time to time lain hidden. What gives a church authenticity is the agreement of its doctrine with that taught by the Apostles and handed down by the early church in the centuries before it became corrupted. These deeply held Anglican convictions have a bearing on questions that I want to consider later in this article.

For all his lifelong involvement in affairs of state Manchester was a man of a contemplative turn of mind. He is chiefly remembered today as the author of the work of English prose that forms the subject of this article. There seems to be little contemporary evidence concerning the circumstances of its composition. No manuscript of it has so far been discovered. It first appeared in print in 1631 when Manchester was sixty-eight and just entering the last decade of his life. Two separate editions appeared in that year under the title *Contemplatio mortis et immortalitatis*. Though neither of them gives the author's name or identifies him in any way, both bear internal evidence of having been seen through the press by Manchester himself.[4] The second contains a number of authorial alterations and additions. In 1633 a third edition appeared with the amended title, revealing the author's identity, *Manchester al mondo. Contemplatio mortis et immortalitatis.* This edition, which makes the somewhat conventional claim that earlier editions were published without the author's consent, contains further authorial alterations and additions. The new title was retained in most editions from 1633 onwards. A fourth (calling itself the third) appeared in 1635, and a fifth (also calling itself the third) in 1636. A sixth (calling itself the fourth), with more authorial alterations and additions, was printed in 1638-9. A seventh, printed in 1642, the year of Manchester's death, reprints the text of the sixth. After his death the work continued to enjoy popularity for another fifty years: by 1690 at least eight more editions had appeared, all (to judge by those of which copies have survived) based on the text of 1638-9. From 1655 onwards most editions included an English translation of the numerous Latin passages with which Manchester intersperses his text. In the second half of the century the work came to be looked upon as a kind of prayer-book to be distributed among guests at funerals. In at least one of the later editions the text is accompanied by prayers for the dead and dying. But by the end of the century the class of writing to

---

4 The first has an *errata* list at the end in which directions to the reader are given in Latin, which strongly suggests that it was drawn up by the author himself. In the second, the mistakes of the first have been corrected. The textual changes in the second edition are plainly by the author.

which it belonged had passed out of fashion. As far as is known, there were no further editions after 1690 for nearly two hundred years.[5] It was not until the late nineteenth century, when a growing interest among Anglicans in their own spiritual tradition caused many early works to be reprinted, that it was rescued from the neglect that had overtaken it. In 1880 J.E. Bailey published an edition based on the text of 1638-9 but in modern spelling and with the translations first published in 1655 added.[6] Since then there have been three further editions based on that of 1638-9 and a facsimile reprint of the second edition of 1631.[7] In none of these is there an adequate editorial commentary on the text.

Manchester al mondo is a Christian meditation on the last things. Its form is conventional. It has four main divisions. The first contains general reflections on the meaning and inevitability of death and on the nature of man and the freedom God has given him to decide his own destiny. The second treats of man's natural fear of dying and argues that this will fade away if he will only reflect on the joy, the "regeneration of the soul", that death will bring. The third deals with preparation for death: the best preparation is settlement in religion, repentance for sin, detachment from the things of this world and a determination to live always with one's final end in mind. The fourth is on what a man's last thoughts should be before he dies and on the soul's entry into paradise. What distinguishes *Al mondo* from most other contemporary works of its kind is the author's serene and detached handling of his subject. The great mysteries of sin and redemption are here seen through the eyes of a philosopher rather than a preacher. There is no fanaticism of any kind, no rabid insistence on orthodoxy, no dwelling on the torments of the damned, that theme so beloved of religious writers of the time. Manchester keeps his eyes fixed on the end for which man was created, the enjoyment of the beatific vision in paradise which can be attained by all who genuinely seek to do God's will in this life. It is surely significant that

---

5 The editions printed between 1631 and 1638-9 are listed in New STC, nos. 18023.5 - 18028.5. Editions printed between 1642 and 1688 that are known to have survived are listed in Wing, nos. M.404-410. Wood (*Athenae*, 1691-2, vol. 2, col. 837) cites an edition of 1690; it is not recorded by Wing and may be a "ghost". Bailey (See note 6), pp. xliii-lvii, gives an account of some of the seventeenth-century editions which is still useful though in need of revision.

6 *Manchester al mondo. A contemplation of death and immortality*, ed. John E. Bailey. London, Pickering, 1880. It has a long biographical introduction and a few textual notes.

7 One, edited by J.A.L. Riley, forms part of *The Little Book of Death and Rest Eternal*, London, Rivingtons, 1899; one was published by the Oxford University Press in 1902; and one, edited by Elizabeth Waterhouse, appeared in *Methuen's Library of Devotion*, 1906. The facsimile reprint was published by Theatrum Orbis Terrarum, Amsterdam and New York, 1971 (*The English Experience*, no. 337).

the authors whom he quotes most frequently are the ancient philosophers, especially Plato, Cicero and Seneca, and the early church fathers, particularly St. Augustine. He also cites with approval some of the early mediaeval writers but he scarcely so much as mentions the theologians of the Reformation or of his own time. It seems as though he wants at all costs to avoid anything that might savour of disharmony or vexation of spirit.

To the exposition of his theme Manchester brings a style that has some of the qualities of Sir Thomas Browne's some twenty or so years later. For both of them prose serves not merely to express rational thought but also to provoke in the reader the imaginative and emotional response to it that the author intends. There is a continual counterpoint between thought and emotion. To achieve this Manchester presses into service a number of literary devices. Carefully contrived rhythms and cadences match the solemn mood induced by the thought of death; aphorisms skilfully placed create the impression of sudden shafts of light penetrating the surrounding gloom; imagery drawn from different, and sometimes disparate, aspects of human experience gives concrete embodiment at the level of the imagination to the concept of a world in which all things are interrelated because they exist to serve God's purpose; homely comparisons and simple words of Anglo-Saxon origin juxtaposed with abstract ideas and sonorous Latin expressions jolt the mind and sharpen its responses. I shall cite two short passages to illustrate these characteristics. One, taken from the section headed "What Death is" (1638 edition, p. 14),[8] exemplifies Manchester's use of aphorism, Biblical allusion and quotation, and metaphors drawn from sources that to the modern mind might seem disparate:

> To die is to be no more unhappy. If we consider death aright, it is but a departed breath from dead earth, enlivened at first by breath cast upon it. *Mors tinea est*, saith Job: *ex veste oritur tinea, ex corpore mors*. It is but a point of time interjected betwixt two extremes: a parenthesis which interposed breaks no sense when the words meet again.

The other example, taken from the section headed "The Name of Death" (1638 edition, pp. 21-2), is one of the most eloquent passages in the work. Here, abstract conception and homely image, aphorism, metaphor and literary allusion, find expression in sentences exquisitely modulated and a vocabulary in which the Latin and the native elements are carefully balanced:

> Death is but a dormitory for a day . . . The night savours of mortality and sleep: that *Mors brevis* is but the shadow of death; and where the shadow is, the body cannot be far off . . . Let her [Death] be styled Lady, Mistress of the world, that will

---

[8] In all quotations from seventeenth-century texts I have modernised the spelling.

not be courted, nor yet cast off: yet is she but *vox tantum* a thing next to nothing, *solo timenda sono*. Better is it called a transfiguration or transmigration from life by death to life again. *Exitus, non transitus; transitus quem ire non intelleximus, transisse sentimus.* The grave is but a withdrawing room to retire in for a while, a going to bed to take rest sweeter than sleep.

As these extracts show, Manchester's prose is highly self-conscious. He is always thinking of the imaginative impact that it will have on the reader. This is also apparent in the textual changes he made in successive editions of the work: they are seldom introduced to extend the thought or clarify the meaning but almost always to elaborate the imagery. I shall return to this point later.

Manchester al mondo is not a mystical treatise, at least not in the theological sense of a work concerned with the progress of the soul from simple to advanced states of prayer. It does, however, contain one or two passages that might suggest that the author had experienced some of the spiritual favours described by the mystics. Geraldine Hodgson, in her *English Mystics*, published in 1922,[9] was so convinced of this that she placed him among the mystics of the Anglo-Catholic tradition. She cited two passages in justification. One occurs in the introductory section where, having announced his subject, Manchester distinguishes between meditation and contemplation, the other almost at the end, immediately following the section on what a man's last thoughts should be before he dies, describing the extasy of a soul in communion with God. I shall give both passages (using the text of the first edition of 1631 which is a little fuller for the first passage than that of the later editions) and then comment on Miss Hodgson's interpretation of them:

1. [*Manchester al mondo*, first edition, pp. 4-5]. Meditation or recogitation, I saw, was but a reiterated thought, proper to production either of good or evil. *Day and night have I meditated on thy law*, saith David in one Psalm: in another, *Why have they meditated vain things?* But divines do now dedicate contemplation to divine mysteries. Which affecting our souls and exciting our wills, produceth some holy resolution. We meditate, saith one, to know God; we contemplate to love God. Meditation is the mother, contemplation the daughter. Yet as Joseph was the crown of his father, and brought him increase of honour and contentment: the like doth contemplation to her mother meditation. When God himself had seen the things created in several pieces, he said they were good. But when he considered the universe (as it were in contemplation) then he said, Lo, they were exceeding good. For meditation considers her objects piece by piece; but contemplation sums them up all together, and sees, as in a gross, all the several beauties of meditation's objects. Meditation is with a man as he that smells the violet, the rose, the jessamie and the orange flowers, one after the other, distinctly. But contemplation is a sweet water compounded of them all, wherein you shall smell all these odours together, extracted from the several scents, which before you smelt dividually. Which extract is far more fragrant

9 Geraldine E. Hodgson, *English Mystics*, London, Mowbray, 1922, pp. 210-15.

than were any of the simples, though every one was sweet alone. This is more elegantly denoted in the Canticles; where the Spouse plaits up her hair, trussing it up in one knot, to show that we should not diffuse our thoughts into variety of considerations, but recollect them by contemplation.

2. [*Ibid.*, pp. 119-22.] *Rapitur anima, cum coelestia contemplatur, et contemplando iucundatur.* And because sight increases delight; therefore rapture would fain ascend to vision. *Videre illa, non quae videntur, sed quae non videntur.* But that's a privilege for Saint Paul; it so divinely ravishes as it raises in man towering thoughts, irradiates his soul with high apprehensions; yea, so it elevates man's soul to God, as it takes him out of himself to live above himself. The soul being thus powerfully by the fair inducements of so divine delight, she on her part corresponds, and with a willing ascent glides after these attracts; and as a vapour exhaled by the sun she goes out of herself, would willingly draw the body with her, but that substance is too sad; wherefore she quits it as not agile and spriteful enough to soar so high. It is an admirable thing to consider that the eye of a man, so weak a creature, should look up every day to heaven, so wonderful in height, and yet never be tired by the way. But by this I see, that heavenly contemplation, if it be strong enough, and not over-clogged with earthy thoughts, is able to carry us with ease to heavenly extasy; but then there must be application of the will and understanding, from things sublunary to things heavenly. For the will takes pleasure to perceive the understanding taken into rapture; and whenas the faculties both of will and understanding do intercommunicate their ravishments, then are we sweetly brought into divine extasy. Of this sacred extasy the seraphical divines make divers sorts: one of understanding, a second of affection, a third of action. Action is well added, for a man is not to be above himself in contemplation and under himself in conversation. The first of the three is in *Splendore*, the second in *Fervore*, the third in *Labore*. The one caused by admiration, the other by devotion, the last by operation. In these raptures the Fathers who were styled saints had such a complacency, as they strove to act this as the way of a new life, some time before their death, insomuch as the votaries would say: Never was saint but had extasy and ravishment of life before his death. They laboured by a liquefaction of their souls into God to insoul themselves in God, to put their souls out of the natural comportment of the body, and so to live in divine extasy, without living in the body. Some so lived, as it was doubted whether they were living men dead or dead men living: nay, some with fervency of spirit were transported into such extasy that, their souls being wholly conversant in divine contemplation, they cared not to afford common assistance to nature, and so have died through exinanition and want of strength . . .

Miss Hodgson evidently thought that the sentiment and language of these passages were Manchester's own. In fact, the whole of the first and much of the second are lifted almost word-for-word from the sixth and seventh books of the *Traité de l'amour de Dieu* of S. François de Sales, where S. François treats of the exercises of love in prayer and the union of the soul with God which is perfected in prayer. Manchester may have known the *Traité* in the original French. It was first published in 1616 and went into many editions in the next few years. On the other hand, he may have used the English translation by the Catholic priest, Miles Pinckney (alias Thomas Carre),[10] which was published in 1630, the year before *Al mondo* first appeared in print. The closeness of Pinckney's version to the original makes it difficult to decide the question with any certainty. I shall give the relevant extracts as translated by Pinckney:

1. [Pinckney's translation, p. 323.] This word [meditation] is frequent in the holy Scripture and imports no other thing than an attentive and reiterated thought, apt to bring forth good or evil affections. In the first Psalm the man is said to be blessed whose will is in the way of our Lord and in his law will meditate day and night; but in the second Psalm: Why did the gentiles rage and people meditate vain things. Meditation therefore is made as well for evil as for good ends . . . [p. 330] And in the beginning we consider the goodness of God to excite our wills to love him; but love being formed in our hearts, we consider the same goodness to content our love, which cannot be satiated in seeing continually what it loves. In conclusion, meditation is the mother of love, but contemplation is her daughter . . . As the ancient Joseph, who was the crown and glory of his father, did greatly increase his honours and contentment . . . so contemplation doth crown its father, which is love . . . [p. 339] He saw, sayeth Moses, all that he had made, and all of it was very good. The sundry parts considered severally by manner of meditation were good, but beheld in one only look together in form of contemplation, they were found very good . . . [pp. 336-7] Meditation considereth by piecemeal the objects proper to move us, but contemplation beholds the object it loves in one simple and recollected look . . . Meditation is like to him that smells a pink, a rose, rosemary, thyme, jasmine, or the orange flower, distinctly one after another; but contemplation is like to one smelling the sweet water distilled from all these flowers. Hence it is that the heavenly Spouse . . . [has] her hair so well tressed, that it seems to be but one hair . . . And what is it to have her hair thus folded but not to scatter her thoughts in the multiplicity of considerations?

2. [*Ibid.*, p. 368.] But how is this sacred liquefaction of the soul into the well-beloved practised? An extreme complacence of the lover in the thing beloved begets a certain spiritual impotency which makes the soul not find any more power to remain in herself; and therefore . . . she permits herself to slide and run into the thing beloved; for she neither casteth herself by way of jaculation nor locks herself by way of union but lets herself gently glide, as a liquid and fluent thing, into the Divinity . . . [p. 407] As touching sacred extasies, they are of three kinds; the one belongs to the understanding, the other to the affection, and the third to the action: the one is in splendour, the other in fervour, the third in the work: the one is made by admiration, the other by devotion, and the third by operation . . . [p. 410] Amongst purely corporal creatures there is neither goodness nor beauty equal to that of the sun . . . he gains unto himself all the appetites and inclinations of this corporal world: for he doth extract and draw up all the exhalations and vapours . . . [p. 425] Love is strong as death; death doth separate the soul of him that dies from the body and from all earthly things: sacred love doth separate the lover's soul from the body and all earthly

10 A&R 343. STC 11323.

things; nor is there any other difference, saving that death doth that in effect which love ordinarily do in affection . . . [p. 432] The soul powerfully drawn by the divine sweetness of her Beloved, to comply of her part with his dear allurements forcibly springs out and to her power tends towards her desired attracting friend, and not being able to draw her body after her, rather than to stay with it in this miserable life, she quits it and gets clear . . .

When we compare the two passages from *Manchester al mondo* with the texts in the *Traité de l'amour de Dieu* from which they are taken, it becomes clear at once that Manchester is not trying to express an experience of his own. Both passages are completely derivative in sentiment and language. Moreover, the use to which he puts the borrowings shows that he is not describing a mystical experience of any kind. The sixth and seventh books of the *Traité* contain well over a hundred pages of spiritual analysis in which the terms and figures used are explained and extasy is defined in relation to the progress of the soul in prayer which alone gives it significance. But Manchester is not here concerned with prayer, at least not in the sense used by S. François: he is simply indulging in philosophical reflections on death. In this altered context, the borrowed imagery, though it loses none of its imaginative appeal, ceases to have mystical significance. When S. François uses the word contemplation, for example, he is speaking of a gift freely given or withheld by God by which the mind is infused with an understanding that it could not reach by its own unaided efforts. In other words, he is describing a truly mystical experience. But when Manchester uses it in the first passage to denote the way in which he intends to consider the subject of death, it appears to mean no more than a state of philosophical apprehension attainable by an effort of the imagination. Thus employed, the word has no mystical connotation at all. Again, when S. François speaks of rapture or extasy he means (as do all the mystics) a transitory state experienced during this life on earth, a foretaste of paradise which God may grant at his pleasure to souls advanced in prayer. Manchester, in the second of the two passages quoted, borrows the language which S. François uses to describe this state but adapts it to a different purpose. He places the passage, without explanation or introduction of any kind, immediately after his section on what our last thoughts should be before we die. In this position, even though the language borrowed refers quite clearly to a transitory experience, the passage seems to be intended to serve as a description of the joys of paradise, the perfect and everlasting bliss which crowns a life lived according to God's will. The eternal felicity of the saints is not a mystical experience.

It seems plain from the evidence that Manchester's use of mystical terminology is really a literary device. He is not seeking words to express a personal, experimentally perceived knowledge of God, as the non-conformists are. For him, as for many other Anglicans, that kind of knowledge, attested though it is by many of the early Fathers of the Church, is to be treated with circumspection, for the pursuit of it can lead to dangerous delusions. Whatever extraordinary graces it may please God to bestow on certain chosen souls in this life, the ordinary Christian should keep to the well-trodden paths, fixing his hope on the joys of heaven. For Manchester, the *Traité de l'amour de Dieu* is a literary quarry from which to draw splendid imagery for his own verbal tableaux. The impression left on the reader is that he has skimmed through S. François' work, pencil in hand, jotting down a passage here, some colourful phrase or metaphor there, to be worked into his own essay together with similar pickings from other sources. In fact, it is probable that this is exactly what he did. Bailey, in his edition of 1880, cites the sentence (in the section headed "The Fears of Death"): "Groans, convulsions, discoloured faces: these show death terrible" (1638 edition, p. 69), pointing out that it is taken almost *verbatim* from Francis Bacon's essay "Of Death" published in 1625. A thorough investigation would undoubtedly reveal many more such borrowings. I shall cite one which, as far as I know, has not previously been noticed. It is from a contemporary Catholic devotional work of a non-mystical character. In 1630, Jean Puget de la Serre, librarian to Gaston d'Orléans and prolific writer of plays, novels, histories and moral pieces, published a meditation on death entitled *Les douces pensées de la mort*. It is a conventional Counter-Reformation treatment of the theme, in florid prose and full of elaborate Baroque conceits. An English translation by the Jesuit Henry Hawkins was published at the English College press, S.Omer, in 1632.[11] When Manchester published the sixth edition of *Al mondo* in 1638-9, he introduced at the end of the section headed "Death Desirable for Three Respects" a conceit drawn from mediaeval cosmology, describing the attraction by which God draws the soul heavenwards in terms of the universal tendency of all created things to seek their centre. The added passage is taken almost word-for-word from Puget de la Serre's work. I shall cite it in full together with the relevant extract from Hawkins's version of *Les douces pensées*. Certain words and phrases used by Manchester suggest that he is copying from Hawkins rather than directly from the French original. I shall draw attention to these by italics, giving the French in a note at the end:

> [*Manchester al mondo*, 1638-9 edition, pp. 32-3.] All things tend to their centre, the stones tossed from the earth borrow wings to their weighty nature to descend beneath *where they have their look* [a]: rivers are touched with amorous curiosity to *revisit* [b] their mother the sea, the pyramidal flames of fire witness they burn but with desire *only of joining themselves with their first beginning* [c]. Heaven is our

11 A&R 441. STC 20492.

centre, why should we not be ravished to be there to join as atoms to their unity, and as rays to the body of their light? To show us the way from aloft, those torches of the night *gallantly show us their twinkling baits* [d], they shine not to us but to show us the way of their azure vaults, as being the only place of our repose.

[Puget de la Serre, *The Sweete Thoughts of Death*, translated by Henry Hawkins, p. 11.] All things tend to their centre; the stones being raised from the earth, do borrow wings to their weighty nature, to descend down beneath, *where they always have their look* [a]. The rivers, though insensible, are touched with this amorous curiosity to *revisit* [b] continually their mother. And the pyramidal flames of fire do witness they burn but with desire *of joining themselves with their first beginning* [c] . . . The heaven is our centre; with what more violent passions may we be quickened than with that of being ravished from ourselves, to join as atoms to their unity and as rays to the body of their light? Those torches of the night, whose number is infinite and beauty incomparable, not so *gallantly show us their twinkling baits* [d] but to show us the way of their azure vaults, as being the only place of our repose.

[a. *ou elles visent toujours.* b. *de revoir.* c. *de se joindre à son principe.* d. *font parade de leur brillant appas.*]

This borrowing is plainly of a literary character. Manchester evidently discovered Puget de la Serre's work after the publication of his own earlier editions. When he came to this passage he saw that it could be adapted to expand an idea that he had touched upon but not fully developed in his original text, so he appropriated it. His use of it, in fact, is much the same as his use of the sentence from Bacon that Bailey notes. Both are instances of literary quarrying. Once we recognise that this is a common practice with him it becomes easier to see that the mystical terminology that he takes from S. François de Sales falls into the same category: S. François supplies him with an exceptionally rich source on which his poetic imagination can draw. To say this does not mean that Manchester is lacking in genuine inspiration. His achievement, like that of Sir Thomas Browne, with whom he has much in common as a writer of English prose, is to have woven the different strands of his materials into a satisfying whole. The reason for inquiring into his sources and the way he handles them is simply to enable us to avoid drawing false conclusions from a use of language that is essentially poetic.

GENERAL OTHELLO'S SERVICE

A.G.H. Bachrach

The tragedy of *Othello, the Moor of Venice* ends in a speech before a large assembly of dignitaries and their entourage. The protagonist, the hero fallen from his high estate and found to be an ordinary wife-murderer, claims the customary privilege of a final message. Disarmed — to all intents and purposes — he takes his chance unopposed and turns it into a dramatic attempt to justify himself in a mini-apology *pro vita sua*. It is his ultimate effort at creating for himself a pattern into which he once more may fit, an order that may prove to belie the emotional chaos in which he had earlier seen himself all but engulfed. And he opens this supreme statement by declaring:

> I have done the State some service . . . (V,ii,303)

On the whole, the introduction of that "word or two before you go" has not been deemed worthy of much comment. Its patently false modesty has been recognized for what it was, its meaning taken to be crystal-clear, and the pathos of the ensuing train of thought — so like and so unlike Hamlet's, Coriolanus's, or even Anthony's curtain lines — has always been considered as meant to completely exhaust what is left by then of an average audience's capacity for expending spirit in a waste of shame. In fact, the speaker's "Soft you . . . " has in one sense proved effective beyond the grave.

However, by the 1980s this may no longer suffice. In the age of the self-service petrol station and at a time when even the very idea of "after-sales service" has practically become a mockery, the correspondence of Government agencies may still be conveyed in buff-coloured envelopes marked "O.H.M.S.", but what these initials stand for, if at all recognized, does not carry any appreciable connotation any longer. They or their equivalent, even in the few monarchies left to-day, indicate no more than that the document thus dispatched is official and therefore exempt from postage dues; the notion that it is being delivered "On Her Majesty's Service" has almost totally evaporated.

Yet, for centuries, "Service" with a capital S has stood for "armed service" based on an oath of allegiance and automatically understood to comprise a devotion to duty which would not stop short at laying down one's life in the discharge of the same. "Service", in other words, and "potential death" were at one time inextricably linked; it was a link that had been, from the first, forged and kept intact by the associated concepts of honour and reputation, and by the special social position this entailed. Hence its heroic overtones — hence also their opposite.

In the tragedy under consideration, Othello's closing speech is not the only context in which he uses the term. In the very scene in which he first appears in person and is being warned that the irate father of the young woman he has allegedly eloped with may well threaten his position and worse, his deep-voiced rejoinder is:

> My Services . . . shall out-tongue his complaints. (I,ii,20-21)

The two situations, marked off each time by the Moor's placing such a peculiar emphasis on the value of his Service, bracket as it were the course of the entire drama; this lends the two statements an importance all of their own.

Curiously enough, although the phenomenon has been noted before, the real implications seem to have escaped most critics. Not only do they lightly pass over the fact that thereby Othello's military "occupation" is deliberately thrust into the limelight in strategically crucial positions in the play, but they also ignore the fact that this is done in a strictly non-military context centred round the nature of his relationship with Desdemona. Indeed, it is as if a banner is twice being waved by invisible standard-bearers, pointing to the way in which — on the strength of their "Word" — this relationship should be read.

Of course, we may well ask: have we not been offered enough readings of the plight of the Moor? Do not both students of the text and producers of the play know only to their disadvantage of the rivers of ink poured out in discussing character and motive, structure and imagery, language and tone? Is not for them to try and make sense of even a fraction of the theories advanced a hopeless task? But this type of question only provides an alibi to allow basic issues to remain unsolved. And although it is being demonstrated all the time that "you can't kill Shakespeare", one such basic issue where *Othello* is concerned is the fact that criticism of this play has been constantly characterized by uneasiness, mental reservations and even actual distaste — while no-one has been able to deny its compelling stature.

At the present moment, to be sure, everybody is falling over backwards to argue how utterly untenable has become any suggestion of racial or sexual inequality, not to speak of social inequality for which there does not seem to be a carpet big enough to cover all that has been swept under it on that count. But what is being overlooked throughout is the question of the origin of the uneasiness, reservations or distaste, and whether those who are upset by the play may not perhaps have missed the essence of what and whom the poet of the Moor of Venice had intended to portray. In other words, what would seem to have been neglected almost consistently is viewing the protagonist's position not simply as a black man in a white society, but as a professional soldier and General Officer — that is as C.-in-C. V.E.F., Commander-in-Chief Venetian Expeditionary Forces — launched into a civilian orbit.

Admittedly, we shall probably never know exactly why in 1604 Shakespeare chose the third tale of one of those popular collections of Italian short-stories sold at every book-stall in St. Paul's Churchyard to dramatize — and dramatize as a tragedy and not as a comedy. When we consider the climate of the times, recent public events, and what may be deduced about the playwright's frame of mind from the general tenor of his work at this juncture, we may perhaps guess. But such is not our concern here. What has prompted the present reflections is the urge to discover "some special human trait" (as Joseph Conrad put it in *Under Western Eyes*) "that is beyond the ken of mere professors"[1] — even if it meant to start all over again at the beginning, i.e. at the source in the *Hecatomithi*.

Cinthio's story, it may be recalled, concerns a high-ranking Moor (unnamed), his wife Disdemona (*sic*), an ensign (likewise unnamed) with wife and little daughter, and a captain (again unnamed). The ensign does not hate the valiant and respected Moor but covets the wife and it is her chastity that causes the ensign to plot her undoing. The means hit upon is the fabrication of an alleged affair between her and the captain, and bringing this to the notion of the Moor. Convinced by a stolen handkerchief, the Moor slaughters his wife with the help of the ensign who has nearly killed the captain. But the latter lives and succeeds in bringing the Moor to justice, the ensign meeting a gruesome fate in the end as well.

A comparison between this tale and Shakespeare's version usually yields as a conclusion that it shows how a skilful dramatist tightens up a rambling plot and heightens the psychological colours of the main characters. But this is only half the truth. What Shakespeare actually achieves besides is to offer his audience the first full-length portraits of a regular Commanding Officer and his Aide-de-Camp! It is true, in the Comedies, Histories and Tragedies he had written before this date, military types have figured on divers levels. In their evident descent from the Capitano of the Commedia dell'Arte, his *milites gloriosi* had gladdened the hearts of countless spectators, partly because they were so pre-eminently recognizable. After all, ever since 1572 when they first landed

---

1. Joseph Conrad, *Under Western Eyes*, 1911, p. 1.

at Flushing the Low Countries had offered for decades practical employment and scope for advancement to British soldiers of fortune — as well as glory to the scions of noble houses. As examples of the former could be cited Sir Humphrey Gilbert or Sir Thomas Morgan, with their bands of volunteers, and of the latter the Sidneys and the Cecils.

It is not, however, only in connexion with the contemporary credibility of Shakespeare's army personnel that the war in the Netherlands should be borne in mind. In addition to the land-war (fought and paid for by that Venice-of-the-North, the Dutch Republic, with the aid of foreign mercenaries and British auxiliary troops), there was also the war at sea with the repeated threat of invasion. Towards 1604 the memory of the dispersal of the Spanish Armada by the forces of nature rather than by military prowess alone, may have faded somewhat but would surely have been a good deal more alive in the minds of audiences than that of the Battle of Lepanto, as artificially resuscitated on the occasion of James's coronation. To Shakespeare's compatriots, therefore, an amphibious enemy operation directed against a garrisoned port would hardly have been a figment of the imagination.

But all this is merely circumstantial evidence of the contemporary audiences' receptivity. For us, once again, the point is the credibility of the military themselves, in this play, and to what extent the playwright must have relied on the shock of recognition, as generated in the militarily aware among his audiences when confronted with this particular sight in the mirror held up to nature. In fact, the real problem would seem to be the amount of amplification we need to improve to-day's reception of signals which, when first transmitted more than three-and-a-half centuries ago, must have been "loud and clear".

What seems to be elementary is to realize that General Othello is presented to us both in his military and in his civilian context, but that, with one exception, he is in uniform throughout. In a world of civilians, the man-in-uniform is an outsider, is a stranger. He is, or at any rate used to be, both envied and resented. The much-decorated officer in his flattering dress-uniform, invited to civilian households in order to be pampered and shown off, is not a phenomenon limited to 20th-century society. Nor is it only on stage and screen that the battle-scarred can be observed being "caressed" till sleep can no longer be fought off, their leave liable to be curtailed at any time, their entertainment forever the same. Considered as a patriotic gesture, moreover, the generosity of starry-eyed girls (providing that poignant contrast to the camp-followers or whores, normally available) would as wholeheartedly be there for the battered veteran as for the raw recruit, provided the country's situation was critical enough. As to the effect of a suitably dramatic narration of

Amanda Harris as Desdemona and Ruddy L. Davis as Othello in a 1982-production of the Cheek and Jowl touring company which "allowed the modern military setting to pay uniquely rich dividends: the officers looked as though they had stepped straight out of the Pentagon and the precision of their bearing, a parade-ground smartness, matched the overall line of approach", as reviewers put it. Up to a point the present writer was agreeably surprised—but only up to a point: his Othello would never strike the audience as "modest of stature . . . a gentle little teddy-bear".

dangers overcome — and a judicious display of newly-healed wounds — as infallible aphrodisiacs, this was not a Shakespearean invention either. And thereby we are back at the behaviouristic picture of the military and at the central question of the difference between their conduct and that of the average civilian.

In order to get to the bottom of this, perhaps the most promising point of departure is the realization that the professional soldier's life, even more than that of his "temporary" brother-in-arms, is really a double life. In the above we have only touched upon certain aspects of this life outside barracks and beyond the battlefield. Our next target for evaluation must be what is inextricably woven into the Service itself, viz. the relationship between officer and N.C.O., between commander and A.D.C.

From the very beginnings of modern armies, and certainly in Shakespeare's time, this relationship was not merely the consequence of the chain of command and the hierarchy of rank built into the functioning of regimental organization.[2] It is also the immediate result of often traumatic experiences shared. Having regularly been under fire together, having in combat successfully achieved impossible-seeming objectives together, having also committed together actions which in their ugliness would probably have been unthinkable under peace-time conditions, having, in addition, been prisoners-of-war together, tortured and humiliated and physically as well as spiritually all but destroyed, and having eventually been ransomed or liberated and miraculously rehabilitated and reinstated together . . . , in every one of such circumstances an officer and his adjutant (or "ancient") learn to depend on each other in a way infinitely more basic than the majority of civilian relationships of an ordinary hierarchic nature will ever afford.

That is why, underneath the well-groomed features of his glittering superior on victory parade, certain veteran regimental sergeant-majors (in fact, any N.C.O. who has been in the same "show") will happily or bitterly remember the unshaven, hollow-cheeked mask of their then captain in sodden trench or behind rusty barbed wire, feverish, half-starved and filthy — and not, after all, so very long before successive promotions had exalted him to his present lofty rank.

For the professional soldier, promotion in rank is of immense importance — again, in a very different way from what it is to a civilian. It is not only a matter of the increase in pay and privilege. A major factor in the intensity of his feelings about promotion is connected with the fact that rank is visible openly and to all the world all the time in the chevrons, pips, stars, crowns or badges on sleeves, shoulders, collars, caps and helmets — and audible in the forms of address used. The salute, moreover, as a sign of recognition and respect, is to uniform and rank, as has been dinned into him from his first day in the Service, not to person. And this in turn takes us to the matter of that perennially needed personal compensation for the special constraints and risks inherent in army-life, which in their all-pervading implications are, again, hardly conceivable to the average civilian.

2. In Elizabethan times anybody who commanded a number of men, whether a handful of horsemen or a few archers or an army of several thousand was a captain. A general, if not the Prince himself, is merely another captain, appointed to serve for the duration of a campaign as "High Captain". The company was the only administrative unit in the army, the captain being responsible. Noblemen and gentlemen doubled as captains and as staff-officers, leaving the day-to-day business in connection with their companies to their lieutenants. After the middle of the 16th century an intermediary between general and captains first appeared: the sergeant-major. Systematic drill was only introduced after Prince Maurice had shown its effectiveness in the Low Countries, but the increasing number of military books printed towards the latter quarter of the century was mostly read among civilians. Equating "ancient" with "ensign" and A.D.C. is a deliberate anachronism. (See J.A. Dop, *Eliza's Knights*, 1981, pp. 130, 137, 139.)

In the social context, one such compensation is the soldier's attitude to looting and stealing, two phenomena far more closely connected with his ways than is on the whole suspected. Of course, since time immemorial, looting and stealing has almost automatically been associated with active service, both on garrison duty and in the field. It has even been a major incentive for enlistment, first of all in the other ranks, but not as rarely as one would like to think among officers seeking a regular commission. For a long time, moreover, loot and ransom were the only means for the non-aristocrat to quickly make his fortune. Governments have turned a blind eye to this state of affairs, the proper and unquestioning execution of orders being their prime concern. Up to the present day, the spectacle may be observed how, without the stiffening and buckram of his regimental pride, without the little belts and straps of custom, of tradition and of comradeship, the cocksure tends to blink uncertainly, to look around in astonishment, to bluster and occasionally even to weep; one has to know how vulnerable this male animal is, this corporate piece of flesh addicted to sudden rages, unpredictable tenderness and fleeting nobilities, when separated from his herd. Booty, prize-money and loot are part of the system and form the "compensation mechanism" which can be seen to manifest itself in individual or combined operations any day to an extent ranging from the most ridiculously petty to the most impressively brazen. And, strikingly enough, this has never necessarily needed to detract from the perpetrators being otherwise model soldiers and clearly capable of staunch loyalty and remarkable feats of valour and endurance.

Besides, all this does not merely concern the professional. There is also the Army as a temporary career notoriously for the younger son wanting to escape from the fetters of convention and "widen" his horizon. Being faced, every waking hour, with unaccustomed standards of values, where property, indeed where morality as such, is concerned — especially state-owned property and "bourgeois" morality — has at once a profoundly unsettling effect. As a result, the pattern in which he has to function is naturally ambivalent, also because his functioning is frought with unwritten caste-rules and snobberies impenetrable to the outside world. It is still one of the stranger anomalies of that formidable military bible, the *Queen's Regulations*, that one of the commonest charges in bringing an officer before a Court Martial is for "behaviour unbecoming to an officer and gentleman". But then, *Queen's Regulations* had its predecessors even in the Earl of Leicester's Forces, way back in the 1580s, in the Revolted Provinces.[3]

Needless to say, Shakespeare's *Othello* has gradually come to be seen as

---

3. See Thomas and Leonard Digges, *An Arithmeticall Militare Treatise named Stratioticos*, 1579, 1590, *passim*, about good officers and bad.

more than a tragedy of jealousy. But even where the play is recognized as first and foremost a tragedy of social insecurity, the grounds for this insecurity have remained vague or peripheral or distorted. Commentators have gone out of their way to show that in turning Cinthio's novella into drama, the principles of the Commedia dell'Arte were observed in structure and characterization, as well as conflict pattern.[4] From being regarded as a re-incarnation of the medieval Vice, Iago was presented as really a Zanni in Elizabethan garb. Brabantio was identified with Pantalone, Desdemona with the Amorosa or Inamorata, Bianca with the Courtesan, and so on. As to the personal tragedy of Othello himself, this was declared to be rooted in his constitutional incapacity to come to terms with the world. If Othello's status was mentioned at all, it was so no more than in passing. Again, none have wondered whether in his dramatization of that Italian story, Shakespeare had not deliberately set out to show how fatally the dice, whose throw decided the fate of his protagonists, would have been loaded, once the lead used was of the "condition militaire".

If we view the play in this light, starting at the beginning of the relationship between Othello and Desdemona as the outcome of the meeting of a veteran General and a prominent Government official's young daughter, with Iago as regular N.C.O. and Cassio as well-born subaltern in the offing, what had actually gone on before mobilization — and what was actually to follow after mobilization? For an answer we have to return to the observation that next to pillage, looting and stealing, the function of women in the life of a professional soldier is a "compensation-target" *par excellence.* The issue is not merely that easy availability of patriotic girls for soldiers on leave in war-time or near-war situations, it is also connected with the automatically produced coarse ribaldry and persistent obscenity in every-day army-life, which to the sheltered civilian has really to be seen (and heard) to be believed. And it is finally the evermore compelling need for the senior regular officer, who has reached the top and tasted its "joys" to the full, to withdraw for at least part of his existence into a safe haven of emotional security.

For this there are a number of reasons. The obvious one resides in the regular soldier's social isolation in an — up to our own age — all-male world. But there are also far more insidious ones. These have to do with the very nature of the military profession and the way in which it can warp a man's reactions to fundamental matters of life and death.

---

4. See " 'Othello' a Tragedy built on a Comic Structure" by Barbara Heliodora C. de Mendoça in *Shakespeare Survey*, 21, 1970, pp. 31-46.

The various manifestations of the attitude to women, as touched upon above, are inevitably not exactly the same among the different ranks in the Services. If not entirely or under all circumstances, they are essentially bound up with the prevailing hierarchy. But the point held in common by all soldiers is that on principle their functioning is from first to last bound up with the dealing and receiving of death on order, i.e. with what is by definition an anti-natural existence. No beast of prey will kill beyond its physical needs; the society of man, as we all know, works differently. The development from armed bands under feudal chiefs to standing armies under professional leaders is a long story in itself. Up to a point, it is symbolized in the transition from "retainer" to "service-man". But that is neither here nor there in the present context in which what counts is the combination of factors turning a commissioned killer of national enemies into a private killer of a woman, while in a state of utter confusion about "the cause".

Earlier on, the regular soldier's attitude to women in general has been described as polarised by a deep-seated need of compensation for the constraints and risks of army-life. The constraints can be seen as embodied in the compulsory wearing of uniform and in the perennial guards at the gates of barracks or camp; the risks in the perennial liability to become what is so disarmingly called "a casualty". Physical constraint in the military profession and sexual restraint in a civilian context are intrinsically linked in the sense that the harshness of the former produces the flaunting of the latter, as far as circumstances allow and temperaments prompt. But there is more. To the human being pressed or conditioned to live for death, the human being physically and emotionally conditioned to live for life and giving birth becomes the great antagonist; even the act devised by nature to lead to parturition thus becomes endowed with an almost neurotic overtone close to one of revenge. In this perspective, the practically obsessional use of the four-letter word for copulation, to which the continuative -ing has been attached, falls into place. So does rape and any other form of sexist violence — so does sudden marriage between social opposites who even lack "sympathy in years".

If all this is brought to bear on the characters and actions as well as on the speech of General Othello, Ensign Iago and Lieutenant Cassio, it will appear that each of the features outlined above can be found to colour or even determine them. First there is the relationship between General and A.D.C.; viewed from the present angle there is nothing in this General to warrant a simplistic dubbing him "gullible" or "simple-minded". No matter how many "dishonesties" Iago may have committed outside this relationship, to any fellow-veteran he could not but be "honest". But then, he is true to type all over, as an evaluation of every relationship he has — or suggests he has — may prove.

If we take his speech, in it Iago strikingly illustrates that strange, inseparable mixture of real, almost instinctive obedience and covert, largely futile disobedience which long army service in the ranks so often creates; it is a mixture with which any field officer is familiar. The way the civilian Roderigo is addressed and treated is exactly what could be expected. Also, Iago's conversation with the wife of his Supreme Commander in Cyprus, i.e. at the front before any cease-fire has come into effect, is not really outrageous or overly impertinent. Nor is Desdemona's reaction *infra dignitatem* at the time and place concerned: even Field-Marshalls' wives have been known to speak in such vein and use the language of the troops under similar circumstances.

As for Iago's handling Othello and Othello's infatuation, it would seem that he only acts out what in such situations is more often than not dreamt of — and suppressed. The motive in Cinthio's ancient was clearly only camouflaged in Shakespeare's. Besides, why should he, who deemed himself so much more intelligent and worldly wise than this General, not use his intelligence to show up what his own experience as a soldier had taught him to be mere stupid illusions about what does and what does not bind man to man and man to woman in a civilian society which he despised and envied as much as it did him? What did civilian society understand about the military society in which any General might at any time from high-flown bombast revert to barrack-room usage when suitably prodded?

Shakespeare endowed his protagonist with the capacity to display all the attributes of feudal heroics found in knightly epic and courtly romance. He gave him the bearing, the (alleged) lineage, the war-record, and the organ-music. But he also bestowed on him two insuperable handicaps: the colour of his skin and the nature of his profession. Singly, either might have been overcome; together they merely reinforced each other. After this, the additional handicap of his years is no more than the unkindest cut of all, making his self-degradation in the end even more pathetic than it would have been if the generation-gap had not existed. But, when all is said and done, Othello's trap is sex — as it is for Desdemona. For, what were his terms of reference as a professional soldier? To him it is precisely her "downright violence and storm" that testify against her, as they would never have done so easily and so fatally if the General had been a high-placed civilian, foreign, middle-aged or both.

In the case of the aristocratic Cassio, newly appointed to the General's staff according to the rules of the feudal network, both his words and his actions are no less in keeping with the picture so far painted of the military mind where women are concerned, although the courtly veneer is somewhat thicker in appearance. This makes him no better than he should be. In fact, it is he who has avoided marriage as a "circumscription" to his "unhoused free condition" — as his superior has not. But in Cyprus he in turn is degraded in his attitude not only to Bianca, but also to Desdemona and to Emilia; he even pulls rank when drunk, insisting that at heaven's gate "the Lieutenant is to be saved before the Ancient". And although he does not lose his life at the end of the tragedy, he is condemned to remain alone and loved by none, no matter how honourable his preferment to the Governorship of Cyprus may be, no matter how welcome his campaign-ribbon. He will naturally wear cravat and cavalry twills off duty and his shame in the scene where he is held vomiting over a bucket by a khaki-shirted squaddie has to be almost unbearable to watch.

As always, then, Shakespeare has worked on many levels. Perhaps in *Othello, the Moor of Venice* we have been given an object-lesson in "fair is foul, and foul is fair", more impressive than in *Macbeth* or any other play in the canon. After that mythic pair of Siamese twins, Marlowe's Faustus and Mephistopheles, that of Shakespeare's Othello and Iago can touch audiences to the quick as few comparable dramas will — even in our own day and age, provided we allow all the ingredients that went into the play's making to carry their weight. If the unease provoked by the play — and so often rationalized by presenting it as a product of Shakespeare's "bad conscience" supposedly symbolized in the black stranger — threatens to remain, perhaps it may at least slightly be allayed by a homeopathic application of De Vigny's remarkably suggestive phrase of *Servitude et Grandeur Militaire*.[5] Once again, Shakespeare clearly knew what he was doing, whether he ever trailed a pike in the Low Countries or not. As with beautiful notions such as Kingship or Courtly Love, he knew that the notion of Service and the ideals it embodied were not really of this world.[6] But then, was not one of the most harrowing needs in the Renaissance the need of new discoveries to "save appearances"? Black,

---

5. De Vigny's "prose epic of disillusion" was composed in 1835 and is quoted here as another deliberate anachronism.

6. In 1572, Sir Roger Williams was in an action which he subsequently described in a passage starting with:

> This piece of service was one of the best and worthiest encounters that our men had from that time to this hour in all their wars of the Lowe Countries ... (Williams, *Works*, p. 116).

In an epitaph in verse, glorifying one of the officers slain in this engagement, George Gascoigne wrote:

middleaged, alien General Othello never had a chance, it would seem, precisely because he had "done the State some Service ...". There lies the pity of it.

    And mark the courage of a noble heart,
    When he in bed lay wounded wondrous sore,
    And heard alarm, he soon forgot his smart,
    And called for arms to show his service more:
    I will to field (quoth he) and God before.
    Which said, he sailed into more quiet coast,
    Still praising God, and so gave up the ghost.

Gascoigne, *A Hundreth sundrie Flowres bound up in one small Poesie*, 1573 (Works, I, 73-74), both as in Dop, *op.cit.*, pp. 150-1. Even if read as an instance of the "il n'y a qu'un pas" between the sublime and the ridiculous, the use of the term "service" is self-evident.

LUCAS HOLSTENIUS (1596-1661) AND ENGLAND

F.J.M. Blom

As librarian of the Barberini Library (1636) and of the Vatican Library (1641 second custodian; 1653 first custodian) Lucas Holstenius worked in one of the centres of the seventeenth-century world of learning. It was through him that scholars could get access to the rich and often unique resources contained in these libraries and it is therefore not surprising that Holstenius had many contacts all over Europe: friends, acquaintances and correspondents. Since Holstenius was a Catholic convert and occupied a position at the headquarters of the Catholic Church it is not surprising that many of these contacts are found in the Catholic parts of Europe. Yet Holstenius's scholarly relations were not limited to his fellow Catholics and he had quite a few correspondents in the Protestant countries of Europe including England. The aim of this article will be to throw some light upon Holstenius's English friends and correspondents. They form an interesting group of scholars, librarians and booksellers and show that friendly relations, scholarly cooperation and business connections did not stop at religious and geographical boundaries. In the following pages we will try to give a brief account of Holstenius's visit of more than two years to England and to present a survey of his relations with Englishmen in the years afterwards. This survey is mainly based on published material, but use has also been made of some manuscripts, notably Holstenius's album amicorum. It does not seem unlikely that a thorough examination of unpublished letters in the Vatican Library may yield further results.[1]

Lucas Holstenius (or Holste, as was his original German name) was born in Hamburg in 1596 of Lutheran parents.[2] Having finished his

---

1 Although many of Holstenius's letters have appeared in print in various collections (a well-known early collection is e.g. I.F. Boissonade, ed., *L. Holstenii Epistolae ad diversos*, Paris 1817), both the *Neue Deutsche Biographie*, IX, 548-550, and L. Pastor in his *History of the Popes*, XXIX, 440, state that the many unpublished letters in the Vatican Library would well reward fresh study.

2 Unless indicated otherwise the biographical facts in this article can be found in *Neue Deutsche Biographie*, IX, 548-550, *Biographie Universelle* (Michaud), XIX, 560-564, and N. Wilckens, *Leben des Gelehrten Lucae Holstenii*, Hamburg 1723. Other information has been derived from Holstenius's album (see note 3).

studies at the academic "Gymnasium" in Hamburg, he decided after some deliberation to continue his studies at Leyden. In May 1616 he left for Holland, together with Erycius Santmann, the son of a Hamburg physician, and matriculated at Leyden University. He applied himself mainly to the study of medicine and the classical languages but very soon displayed interest in other fields as well, especially the study of ancient geographers. As with so many German students of that period he had acquired an album amicorum at the outset of his tour. This album or "Stammbuch" was a small, oblong book with blank pages in which autographs of scholars and of other interesting people were collected.[3] The album forms an interesting and useful source of information, since it gives a good idea of the contacts and the whereabouts of the owner (although Holstenius apparently did not take it along on all his trips and after a time seems to have lost interest). In Leyden Holstenius managed to acquire the signatures of many of the great scholars attached to this famous university. Gerhard John Vossius, Daniel Heinsius, Thomas Erpenius, Everhardus Bronchorst, Petrus Cunaeus, Petrus Scriverius and Johannes Meursius could be mentioned here.[4] Lucas Holstenius stayed with Johannes Meursius and the latter became a good friend and important correspondent. During a period of about six years Holstenius spent most of his time in Leyden, although he certainly did not confine his activities to this place. During the summer-vacations he paid visits to the Spanish Netherlands and called on people such as Erycius Puteanus at Louvain, Andreas Schottus S.J. at Antwerp, and Janus Lernutius at Bruges, visits which could have played a role in Holstenius's conversion to Catholicism. The Jesuit Jacques Sirmond, the man who received him into the Catholic Church in Paris in 1624, was a friend of Schottus.

One of Holstenius's friends at Leyden was Philip Cluver (1580-1622), geographer and historian. As part of the preparations for his work on classical geographers, Cluver planned to make a tour of Italy and he asked Holstenius to be his companion. The two of them left for Italy in December 1617 and during the greater part of 1618 they travelled together through Italy on foot. After this interlude Holstenius again took up his studies at Leyden, although further trips were made to his native town Hamburg in 1620 and to Denmark in 1621. On the latter trip he

---

3 Holstenius's album amicorum is among the collection of the Oesterreichische Nationalbibliothek in Vienna (Sign. Cod. 9660). A survey of the album, containing a list of all the contributors, can be found in an appendix to this article. Otto Mazal in his article "Stammbücher von Studenten aus dem Besitz der Österreichischen Nationalbibliothek" in *Österreichischen Hochschulkunde* I, 1965, pp. 59-68, refers briefly to Holstenius's album (pp. 61-62).

4 Dates and other brief data regarding the people mentioned in the text and also occurring in Holstenius's album are given in the appendix.

accompanied Gaspar van Vosbergen, a Dutch diplomat, on a mission to Copenhagen.

In June 1622 Lucas Holstenius finally left for England. His good friend Philip Cluver wrote a farewell entry in Holstenius's album (in which he refers to their common tour of Italy) on 10 June 1622 and by 27 June 1622 Holstenius had arrived in Oxford where he was admitted to the Bodleian Library.[5] Inspired by his friend Philip Cluver Holstenius had taken up the plan to edit a number of Greek geographers and he intended to collect material in England. It is quite likely that Cluver had suggested this research visit to England. Cluver himself had spent a considerable time in England and had married an English girl. The rich resources of English libraries were well-known to him and he could provide introductions to leading scholars.

Although Holstenius arrived in Oxford in June, the first Oxford entries in his album date from November 1622, towards the end of his Oxford period. It looks as if Holstenius made a final round of friends and acquaintances before he left for London. On 23 November we find the name of Thomas James, who had been librarian of the Bodleian Library from 1602 till 1620. Six days later it is Henry Briggs, Savilian Professor of Mathematics, who fills a page in Holstenius's album. On 2 December 1622 Holstenius collected the autographs of two other Oxford men, John Prideaux, Regius Professor of Divinity, and John Rouse, James's successor as Bodley's librarian. All these people express their friendship towards the German visitor and in his later correspondence Holstenius often sends his best wishes to them. It is perhaps worthwhile to quote from John Rouse's entry since it contains more than the usual stock phrases:

> Habe Doctissime Luca qualecunque amicitiae nostrae perpetuo uti spero duraturae symbolum; sed cum hoc, ut memor Bodleyanae quae te cultorem nobilem et assiduum per aliquot menses habuit lenias aliquando nobis desiderium tui, illuis operis editione quod hic foeliciter meditatus es. Hoc a te reipub. literaria nomine peto
> Jo. Rous inclytae Bodleyanae apud Oxon. Custos
> Decemb. 2° 1622

This entry confirms that Holstenius worked for some time in the Bodleian Library (from June till December), gathering material for his planned edition of Greek geographers.

It was not only Englishmen who filled the pages of Holstenius's album during his stay in England. There is an interesting Oxford entry by a Greek clergyman, Metrophanes Critopulus, probably written on 25 November 1622. This young presbyter had been sent to England for

---

5 See Bodleian MS. Wood E5, f. 94.

further education and theological training by the patriarch of Alexandria, Cyrillus Lucaris. Through the kind offices of Archbishop Abbot of Canterbury Metrophanes was admitted to Balliol College, Oxford. From 1617 onwards the Archbishop paid for his fees, board and lodging. Metrophanes stayed in Oxford for five years until he was called back to Constantinople in the autumn of 1622.[6]

Soon after the collection of these autographs Holstenius moved to London for the second stage of his English period. The first conclusive evidence of Holstenius's presence in London is an entry in his album by Meric Casaubon, son of the well-known classical scholar Isaac Casaubon and himself a scholar of note. Holstenius's friend Philip Cluver was well acquainted with Meric Casaubon and we may assume that this was Holstenius's introduction. Meric Casaubon's entry is dated 5 March 1623 and since it speaks of love and friendship it seems likely that the first meeting had taken place some time earlier. Another London entry, dated 1 April 1623, shows the name of Robert Ashley (1565-1641), a proficient linguist and miscellaneous author. This looks more like a chance acquaintance. Ashley's name never crops up in Holstenius's correspondence and the text of his entry is rather formal and does not express anything approaching friendship.

The final three entries in the album show dates in April and May 1623 and are by non-Englishmen. We find the names of Otto van Bueren, judging from his name of Dutch origin (or perhaps from the Spanish Netherlands since he gives a Spanish motto), Karl Baner, a student from a well-known Swedish aristocratic family on his Grand Tour, and Jacobus Hunter, another Swede. An interesting point about the latter is that he was converted to Roman Catholicism round about this time (1623) while he was in England and subsequently left for France.[7] Holstenius was going through the same process. There is evidence that even before he went to England, as early as 1620, Holstenius was in spirit quite near the Catholic Church, although his official conversion did not take place before the end of 1624 in Paris.[8]

The last English entry (which is also the last entry in the album) does not indicate the end of Holstenius's English period. On the contrary, he stayed in England for another seventeen months, till October 1624.

---

6 For an extensive account of Metrophanes and of his relations with the librarian Patrick Young, see J. Kemke, *Patricius Junius: Mitteilungen aus seinem Briefwechsel*, Leipzig 1898 (repr. Wiesbaden 1969), pp. 124-130. This work (hereafter Kemke) also contains a number of letters from and to Holstenius.

7 See P.C. Molhuysen, ed., *De Briefwisseling van H. Grotius*, IV, 399note (Rijksgeschiedkundige Publicatiën, Grote Serie, Deel 113).

8 See R. Almagià, *L'Opera Geografica di Luca Holstenio*, Vatican City 1942, p. 5 and L. Pastor, *op. cit.*, XXIX, 440.

Neither can we say that everyone of his English friends and acquaintants was asked to fill a page in the album. It seems more likely that he grew out of it and did not bother to ask any more people for their autographs. This at least is the conclusion one could draw from the fact that the names of some prominent friends of Holstenius's are lacking. Everything, for instance, seems to point at Patrick Young, librarian of the Royal Library, as the most intimate acquaintance of Holstenius's in England, yet his name does not occur in the album. Patrick Young became Holstenius's host and gave him a great deal of assistance in his work. The two of them would keep in touch till 1652, the year of Young's death.

In a letter of 4 January 1624 to Johannes Meursius in Leyden[9] Holstenius speaks about his stay in England, mentions Patrick Young's role in procuring for him entrance to the Royal Library, and states that he feels so enchanted by the delights of England that his position could be compared to that of the Lotus eaters:

> Post meum a vobis discessum Britannia suis deliciis ita me detinuit ut ad Lotophagos accessisse videar. Delitui ut plurimum in Oxoniensium bibliothecis veteres codices Graecos latinosque Sedulo excutiens quibus nemo isthic locorum negotium facessit. Descripsi nonnulla, quaedam contuli, quibus rem literariam juvari posse sperabam. Nunc Londini haereo: ubi regia bibliotheca Cl. viri Patricii Junii beneficio semper mihi patet.

In the Oxford libraries he has examined and copied a number of unknown Latin and Greek manuscripts, and in London, where he is at that moment, the Royal Library is always open to him, thanks to the benevolence of Patrick Young (Patricius Junius). Holstenius goes on to say that he is in doubt whether to return to Holland or to go on to France: he does not seem to like either possibility. Yet in order to find a publisher for his Syntagma of Greek geographers he will have to go to the Continent, and France or Holland seem the best choice.

In an extensive footnote Holstenius refers to the complications surrounding the planned Spanish marriage of Charles and he also asks Meursius to pass on his very best wishes to Heinsius, Vossius, Scriverius, Jacchaeus, Heurnius and Bronchorstius. Finally he adds some gossip about common acquaintances. Peregrine Hoby, the natural son of Sir Edward Hoby, has inherited the whole of his father's estate and Peter Courten has been created a knight and has married a rich woman of noble birth. In 1617 this Peter Courten had been a student at Leyden, where he and Holstenius were acquainted, as is clear from Holstenius's album. The address given by Lucas Holstenius is "To inquire at Mr. Fetherstoons shop in Pauls Churchyard". This same address is often given by Patrick Young in his later correspondence with Holstenius and

---

9 See Boissonade, *op. cit.*, pp. 6-22.

forms an indication of the close links between the bookseller Henry Featherstone and Patrick Young, a fact of considerable importance for Holstenius's future relations with Englishmen.

During the rest of the year 1624 (until his departure for France in October) Holstenius and Meursius kept in touch and exchanged letters regularly.[10] Recurring features of these letters are references to Richard Montagu (1577-1641) and Henry Spelman (1564?-1641). They are personal acquaintances of Lucas Holstenius and pass on their best wishes to Meursius. In a letter of 22 September 1624[11] Holstenius asks Meursius to find out whether the Elzeviers are willing to publish his work on the Greek geographers; if not, he will try to find a publisher in France. In the same letter Holstenius states that he has finished the text itself, but is still working on the notes and emendations.

Through Holstenius Patrick Young and Johannes Meursius get in touch and become correspondents. The name of their common friend Lucas Holstenius crops up frequently in their letters and also Henry Spelman and Richard Montagu are often referred to.[12]

Shortly after writing his letter of 22 September Holstenius left England for France. On 2 November 1624, when he had been in Paris for some time, he wrote a letter to Patrick Young showing himself very grateful for the hospitality received during his stay in London.[13] He is also glad that, thanks to Young's letters of introduction, he immediately got in touch with the Puteanus brothers (Christoph Dupuy [1580-1654] and Pierre Dupuy [1582-1651]), Nicolas Rigault (1577-1654) and Salmasius (Claude de Saumaise, 1588-1653). They obtained admittance for him to public and private libraries. Holstenius did not lose much time in continuing his study of the ancient Greek geographers: he has already copied from the Royal Library Agathemerus and other Greek geographers. He lives near Clermont College and the Sorbonne, a very convenient place, not far from the Royal Library. Only two days later Holstenius sent another letter, mainly to ask for some books from Mr. Featherstone's shop.[14] It took some time before Young replied: till April 1625.[15] His letter is full of self-pity: Holstenius must be very happy to be in Paris whereas he himself has to perform his dreary tasks in London. At the end of his letter he asks Holstenius to send his regards to the Jesuits Ducaeus (Fronton du Duc [1558-1624]), Jacques Sirmond (1559-1651) and Petavius (Denis Petau

10 See Boissonade, *op. cit.*, pp. 6-29.
11 The letter is mentioned by R. Almagià, *op. cit.*, who discovered it in the Vatican Library (Cod. Barb. Lat. 2179, ff. 123-4).
12 See Kemke, e.g. pp. 50, 51 and 55.
13 See Kemke, p. 52.
14 See Kemke, p. 53.
15 See Kemke, p. 54.

[1583-1652]), and also to Rigault, Morellus (this must be either Claud Morel [1574-1626] or Charles [1602-1640], both of them printers) and the Puteanus brothers. Shortly afterwards, in May, Young wrote again and enclosed a letter from Henry Briggs, an old Oxford acquaintance of Holstenius's.[16]

It looks as if after this last letter Patrick Young lost track of Holstenius for some time. In July 1626, more than a year later, we find Patrick Young writing a memorandum for A. Alexander, a servant of Henry Featherstone's, who is going to Paris.[17] Young asks him to find out Lucas Holstenius and to remind the latter of his earlier requests to recover some manuscripts he lent to Ducaeus (who died some time before), Petavius, and Puteanus (it is not clear which of the two brothers is meant here).

> Alexander, if you love me, soone after you come to Paris, enquyre for one Lucas Holstenius, Hamburgensis, he liveth with one of the presidents in that toune. If none of his contrimen schollers can tell you of him, the keeper of the king of France his librarie, M. Rigault, who is an advocate of the court of Parleament there, into whom no doubt he often doth resorte, will find him out.

At the end of his memorandum he asks Alexander to urge Holstenius to write back soon. The message got through because immediately afterwards, in August 1626, Holstenius replied.[18] He informs Young of the whereabouts of his precious manuscripts and in his turn asks Young for a favour: Could you ask our Oxford friends to have a look at some books in the library of Lincoln College? And could you lend me your Strabon[19] for a couple of months? When I was in England I did not have time enough to copy or extract everything. Young was willing to lend the work but Holstenius's promise of a speedy return was not kept. As late as 1646 (twenty years later!) Patrick Young was still trying to reclaim his valuable Strabon.

During the following years (1626 till 1629) Young and Holstenius kept in touch at regular intervals, exchanging news about work in progress and new scholarly editions.[20] After his Paris period and a stay of about a year in Auxerre where he was the guest of bishop Gilles de Souvré, Holstenius was invited to Rome by Cardinal Francesco Barberini. He

---

16 See Kemke, p. 55.
17 See L.G. Pélissier, "Les amis d'Holstenius", *Revue des Langues Romanes*, Quatrième Serie, Juillet-Août-Septembre 1891, pp. 321-378 and pp. 503-547. The article (hereafter Pélissier) contains a series of letters addressed to Holstenius. The letters are numbered and the memorandum in question is letter 23, pp. 366-367.
18 See Kemke, p. 56. The presence of Young's memorandum in the Vatican Library also confirms that Alexander managed to find Holstenius.
19 A geographical work by Strabon of Amaseia, philosopher, historian and geographer (fl. first century B.C.). Holstenius does not give the title of the work.
20 See Kemke, pp. 59-64.

had met Cardinal Barberini in Paris, where the latter was Papal Nuncio. Some time after his arrival in Rome Holstenius wrote once more to Patrick Young.[21] He gives an account of his first period in Rome and also sends some copies of *Themistoclis Epistolae* (Romae, 1626) to Young, asking him to present a copy to the Bodleian. He ends his Latin letter surprisingly in English:

> I entreat yow of all my heart, to remember my love and most humble service unto all good friends, principally Academics Oxoniensibus, Mr. Briggius [Henry Briggs], D. Bembridge [John Bainbridge][22] and Mr. Rouse [John Rouse], and to excuse me that I write by a strange hand. I assure yow my love and affection is not the less; neither shall be as long as I live; and if I can do any service unto you, or the least of your friends in these parts, I will endeavor to show me your most willing and affectionate servitour.

In 1629 there is one more letter from Patrick Young to Holstenius, the last one for the time being.[23] The letter is written "Ex Officina Fetherstoniana" and also in the letter itself the name of Henry Featherstone crops up again. References to booksellers and printers which are quite frequent in these early years of the correspondence between Young and Holstenius (1624-1629), are even more striking in the second period of their correspondence (1646-1652) during which years there are also direct contacts between Holstenius and English booksellers. Before we will discuss this period, however, mention should be made of another important English connection.

In the years 1638 and 1639 John Milton, then a young poet aged thirty, made a tour of the Continent, especially of Italy, where he spent about a year (summer 1638 — summer 1639). Milton paid two visits to Rome and it looks as if Lucas Holstenius was his chief contact there. Milton testifies to his important association with Holstenius in a long letter written from Florence to Holstenius in Rome.[24] This letter of 30 March 1639, written about five months after his introduction to Holstenius, is full of gratitude for the reception he received and for his introduction to Cardinal Barberini:

> I am quite ignorant, most learned Holstenius, whether I am the only one of my country who has found you so friendly and hospitable or whether, in respect of your having spent three years in study at Oxford [not quite correct, F.B.] it is your express habit to confer such obligations also on all Englishmen. If the latter, truly, on your part, you are paying back finely to our England the benefits of your schooling there, and you eminently deserve equal thanks, both on private grounds

---

21 See Kemke, pp. 61-62.
22 John Bainbridge (1582-1643), physician and astronomer, professor at Oxford.
23 See Kemke, pp. 63-64.
24 D. Masson in his *The Life of John Milton*, 7 vols., London 1859-1880, gives an English translation of this letter (I, 749-751, 770-771) from which we quote. The original letter is printed in Milton's *Epistolarum Familiarum Liber Unus*, 1674, pp. 25-28.

from each of us, and on public grounds for our country. If the former is the case, then that I should have been accounted by you distinguished beyond the rest and should have seemed worthy so far that you should wish to form a bond of friendship with me, I both congratulate myself on this opinion of yours, and at the same time point your good nature in the place of my merit.

Holstenius showed Milton his collection of books and manuscripts and he asked Milton to have a look for him at some Medicean Codex in the Laurentian Library at Florence, a commission which Milton proudly accepted but could not carry out due to the rules of the library which forbade copying without special permission.

In May 1646, after an excessively long period, Patrick Young again writes to Lucas Holstenius.[25] The occasion is the plan of the bookseller George Thomason (d. 1666) to send one of his servants to Rome. This servant is not mentioned by name but he later turns out to be James Allestree (d. 1670). One of the things Thomason is interested in is to find unedited material in the Vatican and Barberini libraries suitable for publication. At the end of his letter Young inquires discreetly after his Strabon. It was the work borrowed by Holstenius some twenty years before, when Holstenius had promised to return it within a couple of months. It is hardly surprising that after such a long period Young wants to know how things are and whether anything has come of it.

Seven months later, in December 1646, Holstenius replies and confirms the arrival of James Allestree whom he calls "your bookseller".[26] He is afraid that he cannot be of much service to Allestree; there is not much available in the Roman bookshops and he can suggest only one codex in the Barberini Library. He finishes his letter by sending his best wishes to his friends in England, among whom is John Selden.

A couple of months later Allestree's employer, George Thomason, writes to Holstenius.[27] He thanks Holstenius for the favours done to his servant and states that Mr. Samuel Bonnel at Leghorn, to whom he refers as his agent, will help in procuring books. Thomason says that he is glad that he can be of help to Holstenius and Cardinal Barberini and that he is willing to send any books they may require:

> You may remember at your being here we are generally better furnished with books from all parts than in any part of Christendome besides.

After this proud advertisement he orders some books from Rome and asks Holstenius to send them to Mr. Bonnel at Leghorn. Finally he adds that Patrick Young and John Selden send their best wishes.

There cannot be any doubt that it was through Young that Thomason

---

25 See Kemke, pp. 105-106.
26 See Kemke, p. 106.
27 See Pélissier, letter 25, pp. 368-369.

and Holstenius got in touch. Moreover, the fact that George Thomason was one of the executors of Henry Featherstone's will also points to this relation finding its origin in the old links between Holstenius, Young and Featherstone.

As far as George Thomason's servant James Allestree is concerned it is interesting to note that in H. Plomer's *A Dictionary of the Booksellers etc. (1641-1667)* nothing is known about him till the year 1652 when he is found in business in The Bell in St. Paul's Churchyard.[28] Plomer states that details of his early life are wanting but it is obvious from Holstenius's correspondence that James Allestree travelled about in the service of George Thomason over a period of several years, visiting Italy at least twice, in 1646 and 1650. We have already mentioned his first visit in 1646, but four years later, in 1650, there is again proof of Allestree's presence in Italy. This time it is Allestree himself who writes to Holstenius from Florence.[29] The reason for his writing is that he is in trouble with the Inquisition. Four Italian bibles in his possession were confiscated and Allestree asks Holstenius, who is his only acquaintance in Rome, to use his influence and interfere on his behalf. Mr. Bonnel is again referred to as George Thomason's agent to whom letters are to be sent. Shortly afterwards, on 23 July 1650, when Allestree is in Venice, he writes a second time to Holstenius.[30] Besides mentioning the still unsolved problem of the confiscated bibles he says:

> Also I expect with much earnestness your letters to Mr. Patricius Junius, and Mr. Edward Bis, and Mr. Rodius in Padova and a catalogue of those greeke and latine manuscripts you have ready for the presse, and a note of such books as you desire out of Holland and England, which I shall be very diligent in procuring for you or any other things those parts will afford.

Allestree concludes by informing Holstenius that he will remain in Venice for another three weeks, then proceed to Milan and subsequently return to England. A year and a half later, when Allestree is back in England, there is another letter to Holstenius.[31] Having stated that he has been busy in France, Holland and Germany he asks for permission to print new editions of *De Vita et Scriptis Procli* and *De Vita Pythagorae*, earlier works by Holstenius, and inquires after other manuscript texts that could be printed. He continues:

> Mr. Selden is very well and desired mee to remember his respects to you. He hath lately had a very great fortune, viz. three score thousand pounds sterling, left him

---

28 H.R. Plomer, *A Dictionary of the Booksellers and Printers Who Were at Work in England, Scotland and Ireland from 1641 to 1667*, The Bibliographical Society 1968 (first printed 1907), pp. 2-3.
29 See Pélissier, letter 26, pp. 369-370.
30 See Pélissier, letter 27, pp. 370-372.
31 See Pélissier, letter 28, pp. 372-374.

by the death of the countesse of Kent. Mr. Bish, likewise, who extreamely honour[s] and admires you, is much your servant, and hath sent you the enclosed manuscript out of Jo. Antiocheni Historia, which is now upon the press here.

Then he asks information about books printing and finally, giving free play to his bookseller's instinct, adds:

> If you know of any good greeke books to be sold proper for England, give them to Sign. Casione [Allestree's Italian agent] and he will send them to me.

It is clear from these extracts that English booksellers were very interested in contacts with Holstenius from a business point of view. They were always looking for manuscript texts that could be published, for interesting books which they could buy in Italy and sell elsewhere or even interested in Holstenius simply as a prospective customer.

Patrick Young, in the meantime, had not forgotten about Holstenius, although he must have had some doubts about Holstenius's willingness to cooperate in his projects. Young was about to finish his work on a new edition of the Septuagint. Only some years before, in 1646, Holstenius had offered to put at Young's disposal a collation of a Barberini Codex of greater and minor prophets, but so far Young had not received anything.[32] James Allestree had returned to England without the required alternative readings of the text and Young was very worried. Young wrote several times to Holstenius[33] and especially his last letter shows in a rather pathetic way his urgent need for the required information:

> The last year about this tyme, I wrote twice unto yow, expressing how much I was troubled that Mr. Allastree returned hither without the fragments of Aquila and the rest and the diverse readings of the text of the Prophets out of the manuscript copie in your Cardinalle librarie. Which now (because by Godshelpe I intend after a moneth to begin the edition of the Septuagint, casting the diverse readings and the notes at the end of the whole), I desire and long for, with great earnestnesse may be, assuring myself that you, who are readie to help all others in this kynde, will not be backward in so just a request and suitable to your noble disposition to pleasure your ancient acquaintance and most faithful friend Patricius Junius.

The required text never arrived and hardly more than half a year later, on 7 September 1652, Young died. Holstenius's conduct seems rather ungrateful. The explanation could be that in this matter the question of religious differences, an element that so far seemed not to have played a major role in Holstenius's dealings with Englishmen, became important and that Holstenius perhaps received instructions from his superiors not

---

32 See Kemke, p. 106.
33 See Kemke, p. 115 and Pélissier, letter 24. Kemke prints two letters by Young dated respectively 12 and 25 February 1651. He interprets this as 1652 (English style of dating) but this does not seem very likely considering a third letter (Pélissier, letter 24, 6 Febr. 1652, pp. 367-368) from which we quote.

to give his cooperation to a project which was to substitute the Roman edition of the Septuagint for a Protestant one.

Although the above account of Holstenius necessarily had to be limited to some broad outlines, it ought to be clear that this librarian of the Vatican Library deserves our attention, not in the last place because of the surprising light he sheds on the intricacies of the literary relationships between England and the Vatican. A Lutheran convert to Catholicism who introduces to the Vatican one of the most prominent English Puritans must be an intriguing figure.

Appendix
The album amicorum of Lucas Holstenius

Below a complete list is given of the entries in the album of Lucas Holstenius. The entries have been arranged in chronological order. The name and dates of the contributor are followed by the place and date of the entry and the relevant folio in the album. In most cases some very brief biographical information is given in order to identify the man in question and to give some idea of his background.

Nicolaus Santman (d.1621) Physician	Hamburg	24-3-1616	(f.122r)
Geverhart Elmenhorst (1580-1621) Philologist and theologian	Hamburg	27-3-1616	(f.117r)
Petrus Lauremberg (1585-1639) Professor at various schools and universities	Hamburg	5-4-1616	(f.127r)
Georg Ludwig Frobenius (1566-1645) Bookseller and printer	Hamburg	5-4-1616	(f.182r)
Erycius Santmann (d.1616) Son of Nic. Santman; Holstenius's companion to Leyden	Hamburg	24-4-1616	(f.269)
Hieronymus Praetorius (1560-1629) Organist and composer	Hamburg	4-5-1616	(f.225r)
Jacobus Praetorius (1586-1651) Organist and composer	Hamburg	4-5-1616	(f.225v)
Johannes Praetorius Son of Hier. Praetorius	Hamburg	4-5-1616	(f.226r)
Heino Lambeck (1586-1661) Mathematician	Hamburg	5-5-1616	(f.223r)
Paulus Sperling (1560-1633) Rector of the Johannis-Schule	Hamburg	7-5-1616	(f.166r)
Johannes Wetken (d.1616) Local official from Hamburg, on a mission to The Hague	Leyden	20-6-1616	(f.75r)
Janus Rutgersius (1589-1625) Lawyer, diplomat	Leyden	23-6-1616	(f.99v)

Erycius Puteanus (1574-1646)	Louvain	30-8-1616	(f.97r)
Professor at Louvain			
Fredericus Lindenbrog (1573-1648)	Leyden	4-9-1616	(f.114r)
Lawyer			
Vincentius Moller (d.1625)	Leyden	1616	(f.76r)
Physician and local government official from Hamburg			
Johan Caspar Gevartius (1593-1666)	Leyden	22-6-1617	(f.103r)
Philologist and neo-latin poet			
Andreas Schottus S.J. (1552-1629)	Antwerp	30-8-1617	(f.96r)
Philologist			
Janus Lernutius (1545-1619)	Bruges	5-9-1617	(f.98r)
Neo-latin poet			
Johannes Meursius (1579-1639)	Leyden	13-11-1617	(f.116r)
Historian and philologist			
Daniel Heinsius (1580-1655)	Leyden	23-11-1617	(f.100r)
Historian and Graecist			
Gerhard John Vossius (1577-1649)	Leyden	8-12-1617	(f.115r)
Philologist			
Petrus Scriverius (1576-1660)	Leyden	10-12-1617	(f.109v)
Philologist and poet			
Petrus Courten (c.1597-1625)	Leyden	1617	(f.207r)
Cr. bart. in 1622, son of Sir William Courten			
Gaspar Schoppe (1576-1649)	Milan	10-9-1618	(f.136r)
Polyhistor			
Fortunatus Sprecher (1585-1647)		11-9-1618	(f.54r)
Swiss historian and statesman			
Johann Guler von Weineck (1562-1637)	Chur	Sept. 1618	(f.52r)
Historian, soldier, diplomat			
Salomon Neugebauer (fl. early 17th c.)	Leyden	Nov. 1618	(f.161r)
From Prussia, author, state official in Brieg			
Otto Heurnius (1577-1652)	Leyden	27-2-1619	(f.134r)
Professor of Medicine at Leyden			
Everhardus Bronchorst (1554-1627)	Leyden	6-3-1619	(f.66r)
Professor of Law			
Petrus Cunaeus (1586-1638)	Leyden	6-3-1619	(f.67r)
Lawyer, classical scholar			
Everhardus Vorstius (1565-1624)	Leyden	6-3-1619	(f.84r)
Professor of Medicine			
Gilbertus Jacchaeus (1578-1628)	Leyden	6-3-1619	(f.130r)
Physicist, philosopher			
Thomas Erpenius (1584-1624)	Leyden	7-3-1619	(f.85r)
Orientalist, hebraist			
Willebrord Snellius (1580-1626)	Leyden	8-3-1619	(f.107v)
Mathematician			
Simon Episcopius (1583-1643)	Dordrecht	28-3-1619	(f.147r)
Arminian theologian[34]			

34 Holstenius visited Dordrecht at the time of the famous Synod of Dordrecht. One of the main points of discussion was the conflict between the Remonstrants and the Contra-Remonstrants. When we go by the signatures Holstenius acquired we must

Rodolphus Goclenus (1547-1628) Philosopher, envoy to the Synod of Dordrecht	Dordrecht	1619	(f.154r)
Ludovicus Crocius (1586-1653) Theologian, envoy to Dordrecht	Dordrecht	29-3-1619	(f.157r)
Matthias Martinus (1572-1630) Philologist and reformed theologian	Dordrecht	29-3-1619	(f.160r)
Martinus Ruarus (c.1588-1657) Socinian theologian	Leyden	1-6-1619	(f.167r)
Theodorus ab Alefeldt (c.1596-?) Student at Leyden[35]	Leyden	5-9-1619	(f.198r)
Benedictus ab Alefeldt (c.1598-?) Student at Leyden	Leyden	5-9-1619	(f.199r)
Albertus Crucius (c.1594-?) Student at Leyden (from Hamburg)	Leyden	9-9-1619	(f.180r)
Bernardus Sutholt (fl.1625) Catholic convert from Giessen	Leyden	13-9-1620	(f.213r)
Henricus Vagetius (1587-1659) Philosopher, diplomat, lawyer, from Hamburg	Leyden	24-9-1620	(f.214r)
Theodorus Rigemannus From Riga (Lithuania)	Leyden	1620	(f.210v)
...?[36]	Hamburg	2-10-1620	(f.215r)
Johann Hesse (c.1620-?) A student tutored by L.H.	The Hague	3-3-1621	(f.209r)
Philip Cluver (1580-1622) Geographer and historian	Leyden	10-6-1622	(f.101r)
Thomas James (c.1573-1629) Bodley's librarian 1602-1620	Oxford	23-11-1622	(f.155r)
Metrophanes Critopulus (d.1639) Greek clergyman, later patriarch of Alexandria	Oxford	25-11-1619	(f.105v)
Henry Briggs (1561-1630) Mathematician	Oxford	29-11-1622	(f.156r)
John Prideaux (1578-1650) Theologian	Oxford	2-12-1622	(f.168r)
John Rouse (1574-1652) Bodley's librarian 1620-1652	Oxford	2-12-1622	(f.177r)

conclude that his sympathies were clearly on the side of the Remonstrants. The first entry in Dordrecht is written by Simon Episcopius, the spokesman of the Remonstrants, and also the other people who signed the album at Dordrecht (representatives of reformed churches in Germany) inclined towards the Remonstrant side. One of the reasons given for Holstenius's conversion to Catholicism is his antipathy against the internal conflicts among Protestants (see *Neue Deutsche Biographie* and N. Wilckens, *op. cit.*).

35 The first of a number of students from aristocratic families who signed Holstenius's album. Holstenius probably acted as their tutor (see *Neue Deutsche Biographie*, IX, 548).

36 The name is illegible.

Meric Casaubon (1599-1671) Classical scholar	London	5-3-1623	(f.195r)
Robert Ashley (1565-1641) Miscellaneous author, linguist	London	1-4-1623	(f.139r)
Otto à Bueren	London	18-4-1623	(f.140r)
Jacobus Hunter	London	21-5-1623	(f.282r)
Carolus Baner (1598-1632) Student from a well-known Swedish aristocratic family	London	27-5-1623	(f.151r)

A GERMAN JESUIT AND HIS ANGLICAN READERS
THE CASE OF JEREMIAS DREXELIUS (1581-1638)

J.M. Blom

Within the context of 17th- and 18th-century bookproduction one tends to characterize the relationship between Roman Catholics on the one hand and Anglicans and Non-Conformists on the other in terms of fierce controversial writing. Examples abound of vitriolic pen-and-ink battles fought out by means of pamphlets entitled *An answer to a late book..., A reply to the answer of..., The vindication of an answer of..., A defence of the reply to the answer of...,* etcetera. It is perhaps due to the dramatic appeal of these controversies that some other aspects of the literary relationship between Catholicism and the other religious persuasions in England have received relatively scanty attention. If one concentrates on the literature of private devotion rather than on the works of theological swordsmanship, the picture that emerges is radically different.

A survey of the publishing histories of some of the popular Roman Catholic devotional compilations such as the 17th-century *Primer, or Office of the Blessed Virgin Mary,* the *Manual,* the *Key of Paradise* and John Austin's *Devotions,* and Challoner's 18th-century *Garden of the Soul,* reveals both that the number of editions was astonishingly high and that these books were continually being revised in order to meet changing tastes and needs.[1] In the period 1600-1800 the average number of editions of these pious volumes taken as a group is almost one a year.[2] And although it seems fashionable nowadays to dismiss the language and contents of these and similar Catholic products as characteristic of Recusant provinciality and outmodedness,[3] it is hard to overstate their

---

1 For the *Primer,* the *Manual,* the *Key of Paradise* and *Devotions* see *The Post-Tridentine English Primer,* Catholic Record Society Publications, Monograph 3, 1982. For the *Garden of the Soul* see E.H. Burton, *The Life and Times of Bishop Challoner* (London, 1909) and M. Trappes-Lomax, *Bishop Challoner* (London, 1936).

2 The *Primer* had 42 editions, the *Manual* at least around 85, the *Key* at least 12, *Devotions* 6 and the *Garden* around 25.

3 See, e.g., J.C.H. Aveling's *The Handle and the Axe* (London, 1976). Aveling speaks of *Primers* and *Manuals* in terms of "old semi-monastic, superstitious devotional accompaniments to the Latin liturgy" (p. 310). Elsewhere (p. 352) he speaks

contemporary importance. As opposed to controversial pamphlets these works with their individual mixtures of traditional ritual, instructions and practical devotion were meant to be used daily and thus show us something of the most basic elements of the spiritual life of the past. Furthermore any estimate of the number of copies that these editions represent would result in the conclusion that one or more of these books found their way to the bookshelf of every Roman Catholic reader during these two centuries, however small that shelf might have been, and to those of a good many readers who did not have recusant allegiances. When there are so many editions in a given case, one cannot but assume that the editions themselves were sizeable: it would be commercial stupidity on the part of the publishers to go on producing editions consisting of a few copies when they had to produce a new printing every one or two years.

The influence of Roman Catholic devotional literature on non-Roman Catholics is not only testified by the quantity of copies of the above books that could apparently be marketed, but also by the existence of frequent Anglican and Non-Conformist "pirated" editions. John Cosin's *A Collection of Private Devotions*[4] (based on the post-Tridentine *Primer*) and Dorrington's and Susannah Hopton's adaptations of John Austin's work[5] are only two examples. Thus in the midst of hectic religious dispute Catholic books of private devotion tended to bridge a gap that in many ways seemed insurmountable.

One of the authors exemplifying this Roman Catholic influence on English non-Catholic devotional practice is the German Jesuit Jeremias Drexelius (1581-1638).[6] The publishing history and spread of his works of private devotion represents one of the most outstanding success stories of the Counter Reformation. Drexel was born in Augsburg of Lutheran parents, but nevertheless received his schooling at the Jesuit St. Salvador

---

of the "undeserved reputation" of English R.C. devotional writers and his description of 17th-century Catholic devotional practice (pp. 191-2) can only be intended to suggest that 17th-century pious Catholics were hopelessly old-fashioned and out of touch with their time.

4 First edition 1627. See STC 5816-9, Wing C 6352-7.

5 See Wing D 1946-9 for five 17th-century editions of Dorrington's *Reformed Devotions*. A further 4 editions were published in the first quarter of the 18th century. Susannah Hopton's adaptation of John Austin's book was edited by Dr. George Hicks and had at least 8 18th-century editions. See E. Hoskins, *Horae Beatae Mariae Virginis* (London, 1901), GK III and NUC for the editions during the 18th century.

6 The standard work to date on Jeremias Drexelius's biography and bibliography is K. Pörnbacher, *Jeremias Drexelius. Leben und Werken eines Barockpredigers* (München, 1965).

Gymnasium. In these decades before the outbreak of the Thirty Years' War Augsburg was a city of mixed religion and the reputation of the Society of Jesus in the field of education quite often constituted a strong inducement for non-Catholic parents to place their children in the able hands of the Jesuits. Jeremias proved susceptible to their influence. He became a Roman Catholic during his schooldays and decided to proceed to the noviciat of the order at Landsberg. He entered there on 25 July 1598, and after studying at Landsberg and at other places was ordained priest on 18 December 1610. In the service of the order he fulfilled various functions, but his most important post came when he was appointed as preacher to the court of Kurfürst Maximilian at Munich. He would occupy this influential position for 23 years till the end of his life in April 1638. By 1615 he had already begun to write and from that date onwards till his death he published 21 works, while another 9 were brought out posthumously. With one exception they were all written in Latin, although German translations, made with the author's approval, generally appeared within a few years after the first editions of the Latin versions. Translations into other languages—Dutch, English, French, Italian and even Welsh, Polish and Hungarian—quite often soon followed.

Anyone interested in 17th-century bibliography is bound to come across Drexel's name with a great deal of regularity and it does not make much difference whether one is researching in Protestant countries such as England or Holland, or in predominantly Catholic areas such as France. Karl Pörnbacher, who has listed the Latin and German editions, basing himself on German and Austrian sources, has counted close to 300 editions in these two languages during the 17th century and his data could be further supplemented if one took the holdings of libraries in other countries into consideration. The number of copies that these many editions represent is proportionally high. Drexel's oeuvre is one of the rare cases in the history of early 17th-century printing about which definite figures as to the sizes of the editions are available. In the preface to *Noe, Architectus Arcae* (1639) the publisher states that in the period from 1620 to 1639 158.700 copies of Drexelius's books were marketed. From the foreword to the second edition of the same book, three years later, we learn that during the past three years another 12.000 copies of various Drexel volumes were produced.

In spite of the traditionally very bad name which the Jesuit order had in England, this country did not form an exception with regard to the general popularity of Drexel. One must immediately add here that the story of Drexelius in England is too long and many-sided for one brief article, so that the following account must be considered as a preliminary study.[7] Latin copies were offered for sale in the catalogues of English booksellers and can be frequently found in 17th- and 18th-century auction sale catalogues and in the published catalogues of private libraries. Thus the Edinburgh bookseller David Trench[8] stocks copies of *Gymnasium patientiae, Nicetas, seu triumphata incontinentia* and *Horologium auxiliaris tutelaris angeli* in 1667 and 10 years earlier Octavian Pulleyn[9] advertises no less than 25 works by Drexel. In the 1682 Smith sale[10] a 25 volume edition of Drexel's *Opera omnia* changed hands. Edward, 2nd Viscount Conway (1594-1655) owned a copy of *Aeternitatis prodromus*,[11] Sir Simonds D'Ewes (1602-1650) had a copy of *Nicetas*[12] and in the catalogues of the libraries of Robert Leighton (1611-1684) and John Byrom (1692-1763)[13] we even find no less than 13 and 9 different Latin works by Drexelius, respectively. Byrom also possessed a number of English translations, one of which—a translation of *Zodiacus Christianus*, entitled *The Coelestial Prospect, or Eternity decyphered in twelve Emblems*, 12°, London, 1658—is not recorded in Wing, not even in the latest edition.[14] This neatly brings us to the subject of English Drexel translations and the difficulties surrounding a thorough investigation of them.

The number and spread of translations of an author writing in Latin are of course an even more telling measure for his popularity in a given country than the amount of copies or references to copies of the Latin editions that can be found in national or local libraries or booklists. The existence of a translation provides clear contemporary evidence that there was a market for a given book and that at least one commercial mind

---

[7] The author hopes to complete a longer study of "Drexelius in England" some time in the future, which will attempt to answer a number of queries that are necessarily glossed over in the course of the present article.

[8] See *Catalogus Librorum venalium apud Davidem Trench* (Edinburgh, 1667).

[9] See *Catalogus librorum in omni genere insignium, quorum copia suppetit Octaviano Pulleyn* (London, 1657).

[10] See *Bibliotheca Smithiana sive Catalogus Librorum Richardus Smith* (London, 1682).

[11] See the forthcoming study on Conway's library by Mrs. M.A.E. de Wit-Stevens of Nijmegen University.

[12] See *The Library of Sir Simonds D'Ewes* (London, 1966) by Andrew G. Watson.

[13] See T.A. Birrell, "English Catholic Mystics in Non-Catholic Circles" in *The Downside Review*, XCIV, 1976, pp. 60-81, 99-117, 213-231 for Robert Leighton and John Byrom and their libraries. Their library catalogues were published as *Catalogue of the Leightonian Library Dumblane* (Edinburgh, 1843) and *Catalogue of the library of the late John Byrom* (Manchester, 1848).

[14] The other translations listed in the catalogue of Byrom's library are copies of STC 7239, STC 7240 and a second edition of Robert Samber's *The Devout Christian's Hourly Companion* (London, 1717; see below).

thought that the work might be of interest to the less educated reading public who did not read Latin. It goes without saying that these conclusions gather more weight as the number of translated editions goes up. Of the 30 tracts that Drexelius wrote 12 were translated into English: *De Aeternitate Considerationes, Zodiacus Christianus, Horologium, Nicetas, Recta Intentio, Aeternitatis Prodromus, Gymnasium Patientiae, Infernus Damnatorum, Aurifodinae Atrium, Coelum Beatorum Civitas, Rosae Selectissimarum* and *Heliotropum*. It is hard to generalize about this body of translations: for some of the books English versions appeared within a decade of the publication of the Latin original, while in the case of *Heliotropum* English readers had to wait till the second half of the 19th century before they could peruse it in their mother tongue. Similarly there were Catholic and Protestant translations, versions that were published only once and others that had a whole series of reprintings, verbatim renderings and adaptations. Moreover, the reference in the Byrom catalogue to the *Coelestial Prospect* might be used to underline the fact that not all editions of English "drexeliana" are extant (or known to be extant) at the present time.

The one thing that is clear is that Drexel translations were both popular and respectable. The present author counted 32 English editions of Drexel books in the 17th century (from 1630 onwards), 13 in the 18th and another 22 after the beginning of the 19th century. In the *Catalogue of the Most Vendible Books in England* for the years 1657, 1658 and 1660 Drexel is represented by translations of four of his tracts. The bookseller David Trench, to whom reference was made above, offers for sale "Right intention" and "On Eternity"; Conway (see above) had a copy of STC 7235; and in the early 18th century "Dunster's Drexelius" formed part of the regular stock of the parochial libraries that Thomas Bray set up.[15] With regard to "respectability", there were, of course, Roman Catholic translations published abroad for importation into England, or printed more or less secretly in England itself, but the majority of translations were made by Anglicans or Non-Conformists and published without any conscious attempt at concealment concerning publisher or place of publication. On the contrary, English versions of works by this German

---

15 *The Catalogue of the Most Vendible Books in England* (reprinted as vol. 2 of the *English Bibliographical Sources Series 2*) lists copies of STC 7235, Wing D 2184, Wing D 2185 and STC 7239 (or possibly other editions of these translations). The books that Trench had were probably translations of *De Aeternitate Considerationes* and *Recta Intentio*. For Thomas Bray and his library scheme see T.A. Birrell, *op.cit.*, and Bodley MS Rawl. D.834 (the MS contains inventories of Bray libraries). For "Dunster's Drexelius" see below.

Jesuit received official imprimaturs from the bishop of London[16] and were dedicated to unsuspected peers of the realm.[17] The obscurity surrounding the identity of quite a few of the Protestant translators is due more to the conventions of the 17th-century publishing trade than to the dangers inherent in the dissemination of Roman Catholic books at the time.

The beginning of the publishing history of Drexelius in England dates to the early 1630s. In 1632 the Cambridge scholar and translator Ralph Winterton (1600-1636) brought out his *The Considerations of Drexelius upon Eternitie*[18] (a translation and part adaptation of *De Aeternitate Considerationes*), more or less at the same time that at Rouen Roman Catholic translations were published of three other Drexelius works, *The Angel-Guardian's Clock, The Christian Zodiack* and *Nicetas*.[19] Winterton's translation was to prove the most widely read Drexel book in England, which may be partly due to his well-considered choice of text. There were at least 15 reprintings of his book throughout the rest of the 17th century,[20] and in any case 3 more during the 18th.[21] While early 18th-century editions of Winterton's translation were still coming out, Samuel Dunster (1675-1754) tried his hand at the same tract that Winterton had chosen. His translation appeared in 1710 under the same title as Winterton's rendering. Later on during the 19th and 20th centuries at least one more edition of Dunster's version appeared and two new translations, one of them making use of Winterton's version.[22]

---

16 E.g. STC 7240 and Wing D 2185.

17 E.g. STC 7239 and Wing D 2181 A.

18 STC 7235.

19 STC 7234, NSTC 7234.5 (the proofs of this vol. of NSTC were consulted in the BL) and STC 7238.

20 STC 7235-7, Wing D 2169-81. Pörnbacher, *op.cit.*, mentions also a 1685 edition, not in Wing.

21 There were further editions in 1705 (BL 4400.g.12), 1716 (BL 4404.b.74) and 1724 (NUC D 0375821). Note that for reasons of space 18th-century and later editions will be identified in the present article by reference to GK III or NUC, or if necessary to other library catalogues.

22 Dunster's *The considerations of Drexelius upon eternity* first appeared in 1710 (BL 854.f.12). According to DNB there was a second edition in 1714 and mention is made of "subsequent editions". The present author could only locate an 1844 revision of Dunster's translation made by Henry Peter Dunster and published as *Reflections on eternity* (BL 1361.c.11). The two new translations referred to are *Nine Considerations on Eternity from the Latin of 1629* by Father Robert Trent (London, 1856; BL 4404.b.75) and *Considerations on eternity*, translated by Sister Marie José Byrne and edited by Rev. Ferdinand E. Bogner (New York, 1920; NUC D 0375795). Bogner also edited a translation of another Drexel tract (see below). In the preface to the Trent translation, the translator's debt to Winterton's version is acknowledged.

The three early Roman Catholic translations were obviously part of a Jesuit-inspired scheme to introduce the works of their brother Jesuit, which were so popular abroad, into England. The translations of *Zodiacus Christianus* and *Horologium* were published by the Rouen bookseller John Le Cousturier and the Rouen printer Nicholas Courant, respectively, and the English version of *Nicetas* can be assigned on typographical grounds to the press of the widow of the latter.[23] All three were actively involved in the production of Roman Catholic books for the English market and links can be established both between the three publishers/printers themselves and between them as a group on the one hand and the Jesuit English College Press on the other.[24] Even if these three presses did not produce reprints of the above editions as far as is known, the scheme itself—the large-scale introduction of Drexelius into England—did not flounder. In 1647 the Cousturier translation of *Zodiacus* was published in London with only a minimal amount of variant readings,[25] and in the same year an independent Protestant translation of this tract appeared.[26] Thirty years later, in 1676, again a new version of *Zodiacus Christianus* was brought out under the title *A Spiritual Repository*.[27] This last translation is clearly an Anglican effort,[28] although, curiously enough, it contains (by mistake?) the official permission which Drexel received from his Jesuit provincial to publish the book. Of the other two Rouen choices the *Horologium* appeared in a new English version at the beginning of the 18th century entitled *The Devout Christian's Hourly Companion*, and had at least 5 subsequent reprintings.[29]

---

23 The information that the widow of Nicholas Courant was responsible for the printing of *Nicetas* (STC 7238) derives from Dr. D.M. Rogers, one of the compilers of *A Catalogue of Catholic Books in English Printed Abroad or Secretly in England 1558-1640*. Dr. Rogers also established that *The Angel-Guardian's Clock* (STC 7234) ought to be dated "1630", i.e. 2 years before the appearance of Winterton's translation of *De Aeternitate Considerationes*.

24 For these links see the *Catalogue* by A.F. Allison & D.M. Rogers, referred to above. Good examples of this collaboration are A&R 54,55,56,57 and 58, or A&R 215 to 222.

25 *The Christians Zodiake* (London, 1647, Wing D 2168).

26 *The Hive of Devotion* (London, 1647, Wing D 2184).

27 Wing D 2186.

28 The translator every now and then adapts Drexel's text in ways such as the following: "We find a story among the Popish legends of which we may make some use. It is of Bertoldus a Franciscan..." (p. 319). However, in the main he sticks remarkably closely to Drexel's original.

29 The first edition was published in London in 1716 (Cambridge University Library, pressmark 1.51.34), the second edition came out in the same year (BL 4404.aaa.31), the third in 1719 (BL 1606/865), the fourth in 1728 (BL 3456.e.21), the

The man responsible for the *Hourly Companion* signs himself "Robert Samber" at the end of the Dedication in the first and subsequent editions. It is typical of the lack of scholarly interest in 17th- and 18th-century translators, particularly of this type of book, that Samber's name has remained not much more than a name. GK III cannot provide his dates and there is obvious confusion as to which books ought to be assigned to him. He was in fact born in 1682 as the son of the presumably Catholic Samuel Samber and Sussanah Legg.[30] He went to the English College Rome in 1705, but left there a year later to enter upon a very chequered life as hack writer, renegade Freemason, renegade Catholic and pornographer. He exploited his masonic connections in order to make money by first courting the favour of his wealthier brethren and by later ridiculing them.[31] He made use of his Catholic background and education in a variety of ways: his translation of *Roma Illustrata*[32] testifies to his knowledge of Rome and Catholic art; his adaptation of Drexel to his knowledge of Catholic devotional stuff and its attractions among English non-Catholics; and his translation of *Venus in the Cloister*[33] to his shrewd eye for the contemporary interest in smutty stories about the secrets of the convent. It is a nice irony that his role in Edmund Curll's publication of the latter book is Samber's only literary activity that has been noticed in the 20th century.[34]

---

fifth in 1759 (BL 1507/1153) and a later one in 1889 (BL 4401.o.8). See also note 14 for a reference to a second edition in 1717.

30 See Catholic Record Society, Records Series, Vol. 40, *The Liber Ruber of the English College Rome*, p. 137, entry 1204. "Robertus Samber, Hamptoniensis, annorum 23, filius Samuelis Samber et Sussanae Legg, habens Confirmationem venit ad Collegium 11^{mi} Julii 1705 et inter Alumnos Sm. Domini nostri Clemens 11^{mi} admissus a R.P. Rodulpho Postgate Rectore nullo existente E^{mo} Protectore venit ad Physicam nullo accepto iuramento dicessit 15 April 1706". For Samber and his masonic connections, see also Edward Armitrage, "Robert Samber" in *Ars Quator Coronatorum*, 1898. Samber's papers are preserved in Bodley MSS Rawl poet.11,131-133, 134^a, 134^b and 135 and MS Rawl C 640. These letters and papers give a fascinating and by no means unsympathetic picture of the life of an impecunious hackwriter. Samber's date of death has not been established, but he must have died some time after 1735.

31 In the dedication of *Long Livers* (London, 1722; Bodl. 8° Rawl 313, written under the pseudonym "Eugenius Philalethes") Samber eulogizes his masonic brethren. In his *Ebriëtatis Encomium or The Praise of Drunkenness* (London, 1723) he gives a rather slanderous account of the same brethren.

32 *Roma Illustrata* (London, 1723; Bodl. Douce S 659). A translation of François Raguenet's *Les Monuments de Rome* (Amsterdam, 1701).

33 *Venus in the Cloister* (E. Curll, London, 1725; BL P.C. 25.a.63) translated from Abbé Du Pratt's *Venus dans le cloître*.

34 See Ralph Straus, *The Unspeakable Curll* (London, 1927) and David Foxon, *Libertine Literature in England 1660-1745* (New York, 1965).

From his letters and manuscripts in the Bodleian Library Samber emerges as a man particularly short of cash and always on the look-out for ways to turn one of his many literary projects to profit. Even within the scholarly context of this *Festschrift* one cannot help remarking that God works in mysterious ways when he uses a lapsed Catholic pornographer to spread a papist book on guardian angels written by a Jesuit in Protestant England.

A similar observation about the mysteriousness of God's ways can be made, albeit with a different application, to another Roman Catholic attempt at promoting Drexelius in Great Britain, this time relating to *Coelum Beatorum, Infernus Damnorum* and *Aeternitatis prodromus*. The project as such failed, but Drexelius kept on being translated and published by others. The scheme referred to can be distilled from the 17th-century Bodley manuscript Tanner 109. It contains clearly Roman Catholic translations of the three tracts. The texts are copied out neatly for the printer and instructions for the typesetter can be found in the margins, but as far as can be ascertained, none of them ever appeared in print. However, two different Anglican translations came out of *Aeternitatis prodromus*, one in 1642 by the mysterious W. Croyden,[35] *Forerunner of eternity*, and another one in 1699, *Considerations upon eternity*,[36] while both an independent Roman Catholic translation was published of *Infernus Damnatorum*, appearing in 1667 under the title *A pleasant and profitable treatise of hell*,[37] and an early 18th-century non-Catholic one, entitled *Considerations of Drexelius on the eternity of hell torments*.[38]

A translation that was in all probability a Jesuit success is *The School of Patience* (a tr. of *Gymnasium patientiae*) which was published in 1640 by somebody who signs himself "D.L.".[39] Halkett & Laing III[40] venture the guess that we have to do here with Donald Lupton (d. 1676), but this seems unlikely in view of the Catholic nature of the translation, the phrase "permissu superiorum" in the preliminary matter and the Jesuit warcry of "Ad majorem Dei gloriam" at the end. In the same year another translation appeared, this time from a non-Catholic angle,[41] and

---

35 Wing D 2183.
36 Wing D 2181 A (erroneously called another edition of the translated *De Aeternitate Considerationes*).
37 Not in Wing (NUC D 0375918). Wing mentions a 1668 edition, D 2184 A.
38 London, 1703 (BL 874.f.26). GK III erroneously states that this is another edition of the Winterton translation of *De Aeternitate Considerationes*.
39 STC 7239.
40 *A Dictionary of Anonymous and Pseudonymous Publications in the English Language* (3rd edition), edited by John Horden, London, 1980.
41 *The School of Patience* (London, 1640; STC 7240).

19 years later in 1659 again a new version of *Gymnasium patientiae* came on the market.[42]

"A most eminent Anglican preacher of his time", John Dawson (1605-1641),[43] Vicar of Maidenhead in Berkshire, was responsible for the first English translation of *Recta intentio*, published in 1641 as *A right intention of the Rule*.[44] A reprint of his work came out in 1655[45] and a reverend colleague of his, L.M. Dalton, tried to give this work by Drexel a new lease of life by means of his *Amussis. A right intention the rule of all human actions* in 1903.[46]

The Dalton translation fits in with the revival of interest—or should one say "the continuing interest"—in Drexelius during the 19th and early 20th centuries. Around the beginning of the 19th century G.M. Horne, Bishop of Norwich (1730-1792), decided that Drexel's *Aurifodina Atrium* should form part of every scholar's spiritual education and his English abridgement of this book was included in William Jones's (1726-1800) compilation *The Scholar Armed*.[47] With a very select audience in mind—the participants of retreats—the Reverend W.H. Cleaver published Miss Trench's translation of *Rosae selectissimarum virtutum* (*Spiritual readings from Drexelius*) in 1885.[48] However, the most curious instance of Drexel's popularity is the explosion of editions of the translated *Heliotropum* that appeared between 1863 and the 1920s. By 1890 the translation of the Anglican Reverend Reginald Shutte, first published in 1863 as *The Heliotropum or Conformity of the human will to the divine* had had at least 8 reprintings.[49] In 1912 it was brought out in America, edited by the Catholic Reverend Ferdinand Bogner and had a

---

42 *The School of Patience* (London 1659; NUC D 0375942; not in Wing).
43 See Anthony Wood's *Athenae Oxoniensis*.
44 Wing D 2185.
45 Wing D 2185 A.
46 BL 04403.eee.4.
47 *The Scholar Armed* (1795; BL 224.g.7). There was another edition in 1800 (BL 495.f.9) and the abridged Drexel tract can also be found in Horne's *Diary* (1814; BL 11825.i.28).
48 London; BL 4400.aaa.42.
49 First edition London 1863, BL 4403.i.27. Other editions in 1881 (London; NUC D 0375863), 1883 (Portsmouth; BL 1608/2496), 1884 (fourth edition, London; BL 4401.n.8), 1884 (Portsmouth 6th edition; NUC D 0375867), 1886 (London; BL X. 108/1455), 1888 (London; NUC D 0375868), 1890 (second edition, London; BL 1608/5580). From this series it will be obvious that there were more editions than the ones listed above. With regard to the popularity of the book, the preface to the fourth edition states that the third edition sold out within 6 months.

run of at least 6 American editions within the next 12 years.[50] The 4th edition of Shutte's translation mentions in the imprint that one of the partners in the publication of this book was "Smith & Son, Railway Book Stalls".

From the presses of Nicholas Courant in 1630 to a place among the popular novels of the day in Mr. Smith's railway stalls: it is a considerable journey that Jeremy Drexel would have appreciated.

50 Editions in 1912 (New York; NUC D 0375870), 1917 (New York; NUC D 0375871), 1918 (New York; NUC D 0375872), 1919 (New York; NUC D 0375873), 1920 (New York; NUC D 0375874), 1924 (New York; NUC D 0375875).

JEAN LECLERC AS JOURNALIST OF THE *BIBLIOTHEQUES*. HIS CONTRIBUTION TO THE SPREAD OF ENGLISH LEARNING ON THE EUROPEAN CONTINENT

Hans Bots

Among the many scholarly journals published all over the European continent in the decades around 1700 Jean Leclerc's *Bibliothèques*, which appeared in Amsterdam, occupied a special place. In editing his first periodical, the *Bibliothèque Universelle et Historique* (1686-1693), this theologian, a refugee from Geneva, was alternately assisted by Jean Cornand de La Crose, Charles Le Cène and Jaques Bernard. For the next two periodicals he published, the *Bibliothèque Choisie* (1703-1713) and the *Bibliothèque Ancienne et Moderne* (1714-1727), he was the sole editor, however.[1] Thanks to Jean Leclerc's journalistic activities, we now have an excellent picture, covering a period of approximately thirty years, of contemporary scholarship in the Republic of Letters, the more so since, in the Republic of the Seven United Provinces, the editor did not need to worry so much as his colleagues in the surrounding countries about all kinds of repressive measures resulting from sometimes strict censorship. The editors of several other periodicals that were published in the Republic at the time, such as Pierre Bayle and Jaques Bernard's *Nouvelles de la Republique des Lettres*,[2] also possessed this open-mindedness and journalistic independence, but this does not alter the fact that, among these periodicals, Leclerc's *Bibliothèques* occupied a place all their own.

One aspect in which Jean Leclerc's periodicals distinguished themselves in particular from others requires special attention here: his great interest in England and in English scholarship. In an age in which more and more European scholars began to take an interest in the intellectual

---

1 For the *Bibliothèque Universelle et Historique* (BUH), see H. Bots, et al., *De Bibliothèque Universelle et Historique (1686-1693). Een periodiek als trefpunt van geletterd Europa*, Amsterdam 1982. This book also contains a great deal of information on Jean Leclerc, see especially pp. 1-26. For the next two *Bibliothèques*, see Sam. A. Golden, *Jean Leclerc*, New York 1972, pp. 55-104. Many biographical data in this paper derive from my own study.

2 *Nouvelles de la République des Lettres*, Amsterdam 1684-1689; 1699-1710; 1716-1718. See also H.J. Reesink, *L'Angleterre et la littérature Anglaise dans les trois plus anciens périodiques français de Hollande de 1684 à 1709*, Paris 1931.

activities in Great Britain, Leclerc, more than any other non-English journalist around 1700, was well-equipped to make scholarly publications accessible to a wide public, notably those that were not written in Latin or French. Unlike many of his contemporaries who had been born and bred on the continent, Leclerc possessed a good passive knowledge of the English language, with which he had familiarized himself during a stay in London, where he had gone in April 1682 in order to find a suitable permanent position. However, since it would be some time before he would be able to preach in English and above all because of the heterodoxy of some of his theological views these attempts failed in the end. During this short period, however, Leclerc had acquired a great and lasting love for England.

Ten years later, in 1691-1692, he made another attempt via John Locke to find employment in England. Considering his salary, life in the Republic was expensive and he was only moderately happy with it. He was even prepared, he told the English philosopher, to become a member of the Anglican Church and he would be satisfied with an allowance of £ 100, "sine cura animarum", in some small English town.[3] During the next few years Gilbert Burnet and Lord Pembroke were also approached in vain by Leclerc, who very much wanted to move to England for good.[4] But even if Leclerc did not succeed in turning his back upon his Remonstrant employers in Amsterdam, whom he often wrongly despised, he had made many contacts in England in the course of the years and his knowledge of English had become more and more thorough. So thorough indeed that in 1688, when reviewing a work by Robert Boyle, the journalist did not shrink from passing judgement on the author's stylistic qualities: "Ceux qui entendent l'Anglois pourront voir que l'élégance du style répond à la beauté du sujet".[5] In May 1689 the same Boyle expressed himself in the most laudatory terms about Leclerc's journalistic abilities and about his knowledge of English: "After so many judicious extracts you have made of English books, I think I may presume, that so great a

---

3 Cf. his letter to John Locke of 1 April 1692, published by E.S. de Beer (ed.), *The Correspondence of John Locke*, Vol. IV, Oxford 1979, no. 1486, p. 436. Cf. also nos. 1446 (pp. 354-355) and 1381 (p. 248).

4 For his attempts to settle in England via Pembroke and Burnet, see A. Barnes, *Jean Leclerc (1657-1736) et la République des Lettres*, Paris 1938, pp. 163 and 164.

5 His review of *The Martyrdom of Theodora and Didymus* . . ., Londres 1687, BUH, X (1688), p. 543. Cf. also BUH, XV (1689) pp. 35-36, where Leclerc ventures a comparison between English and French: "sa langue maternelle (English) qui pour la richesse surpasse la Françoise; quoi qu'elle ne soit pas si nette, ni si douce dans la prononciation. On en voit des preuves assez considerables dans les Lettres, et dans les Poësies d'Howel".

linguist as Monsieur Le Clerc, is not unacquainted with the language of this country . . .".[6]

In this way Leclerc was able to render a great service to all those members of the Republic of letters who were "less acquainted" with the English language, "cette langue étant peu connue hors de l'Angleterre".[7] Was not he even obliged, from 1710 onwards, to translate all the English titles of books into French at the request of his readers?[8] As late as 1718 Leclerc came to the conclusion that outside England there were but few people who had a command of English: "Combien peu de gens y a-t-il deçà la mer, qui sachent l'Anglois? Cependant il y a une infinité de bons Livres dans cette Langue, qu'on n'a point traduits, et qui ne le seront apparemment jamais; dont il est néanmoins très-avantageux au Public d'avoir au moins quelque connoissance".[9] It was only in the course of the 18th century that knowledge of English was to increase on the continent, as Leclerc himself seems to observe in his *Bibliothèque Ancienne et Moderne* of 1726.[10] However, the majority of European scholars who, around 1700, wished to acquaint themselves with scholarly achievements in England, had to rely almost completely on translations or on scholarly journals in which these works were reviewed. That the distribution of English books across Europe was not always satisfactory naturally formed another complicating factor. As a result it repeatedly happened that Leclerc was too late (in his own opinion) in drawing his readers' attention to a certain publication. Thus in 1715, on the occasion of the publication by George Cheyne in 1705 of *Philosophical Principles of Natural Religion*, he wrote that this work was still completely unknown on the continent: "Cet ouvrage n'a guère été vû deçà la Mer, où l'on n'apporte que très peu de Livres Anglois; sur tout de matiéres philosophiques ou mathématiques",[11] while three years later, in reviewing a publication by Daniel Whitby, he was obliged to state: "Je ne savois pas

---

6 Letter from R. Boyle to J. Leclerc of 30 May 1689, in *The Works of the honourable Robert Boyle*, VI, London 1772, p. 61.

7 BUH, IX (1688), p. 196: "Celui qu'on va lire est en Anglois, et cette Langue étant peu connue hors d'Angleterre, en comparaison de la nôtre, on a cru que le public seroit bien aise de le voir ici (. . .). Le voici donc mot pour mot autant que le genie de la langue Angloise et celui de la nôtre l'ont pu permettre".

8 *Bibliothèque Choisie* (B.Ch.), XXI (1710), avertissement.

9 BUH, XXVI (1718), avertissement to part of register.

10 *Bibliothèque Ancienne et Moderne* (BAM), XXV (1726), pp. 331-332: à propos of J. Selden's *Opera Omnia*: "Il y avoit long-temps que le monde savant souhaitoit de voir tous les ouvrages de Selden dans un seul corps (. . .). Comme il y a aujourdhui beaucoup plus de gens qu'il n'y en avoit autrefois, qui entendent la langue Angloise, sur tout en Allemagne, il se trouve plus d'acheteurs des livres Anglois".

11 BAM, III (1715), p. 41.

même, qu'il fût publié, à cause du peu de commerce que nos Libraires font de livres Anglois".[12]

As far as the translations were concerned that appeared of English books, Leclerc was well aware that unfortunately they were not always reliable. In his review of Robert Boyle's *De Specificorum Remediorum*, which had been translated into Latin, he observes that the translator had been rather careless.[13] His review of the translation of Richard Steele's *Spectator*, on the other hand, is very favourable, since it had been rendered "avec autant de fidélité et d'exactitude que la différence des langues l'a pu souffrir". Leclerc shows that he knows exactly how to evaluate the translation, when he observes: "La langue angloise est si abondante en termes et si hardie, qu'il est fort difficile qu'on l'égale en François, et les Versions ne paroissent jamais si vives que les originaux, à moins qu'on ne prenne trop de liberté; ce qu'on ne doit jamais faire, et sur tout en des livres de cette nature".[14]

Being equipped with a thorough knowledge of the English language, Leclerc was able to provide his reading public with reliable information about the state of English learning. If this was one of the conditions that had to be met for him to carry out his task adequately, it was just as important for a reviewer that he should always have enough books at his disposal to make a selection from for his *Bibliothèque*. In this respect Leclerc depended primarily on his publishers of course.[15] For the *Bibliothèque Universelle et Historique* this was the Amsterdam Compagnie of Wolfgang, Waesberghe, Boom and Van Someren, who kept up excellent relations with the London bookseller Samuel Smith. Henri Schelte, who had published Pierre Coste's translation of Locke's *Essay Concerning Human Understanding* in 1700, subsequently published the *Bibliothèque Choisie* from 1703 till 1713. Finally, the *Bibliothèque Ancienne et Moderne* was published by David Mortier (1714-1719), who for many years had had a bookshop in London, by the Wetstein brothers (1719-1726) and by the librarian Pierre Husson from The Hague (1727-1728).[16] Even if all

---

12 BAM, VI (1716), p. 109.

13 BUH, II (1686), p. 276: "On y trouve non seulement plusieurs barbarismes, mais encore des mots pris dans un sens fort éloigné de leur signification".

14 BAM, V (1716), p. 420. Cf. also BAM, VIII (1717), p. 453: "L'Angloise est si hardie et si énergique, comparé à la nôtre qu'il est très difficile de rendre par tout beauté pour beauté. On est obligé d'y laisser bien des traits, qui se ressentent encore du terroir".

15 Cf. H. Bots, "Recueil des Informations dans deux périodiques hollandais à la fin du XVIIe siècle", in: P. Rétat (ed.), *Le Journalisme d'Ancien Régime. Questions et propositions*, Lyons 1982, pp. 55-68.

16 Cf. H. Plomer, *A Dictionary of the Printers and Booksellers who were at work in England, Scotland and Ireland from 1668 to 1725*, s.l. 1968, p. 276 and I.H. van Eeghen,

these booksellers may be assumed to have had extensive business contacts and to have regularly bartered their books for recent publications published by their English colleagues, for a keen journalist like Leclerc, who did not want to adopt a waiting attitude, this was not enough, especially since books from England, as we have already observed, were usually distributed late on the continent and then only in a limited selection.

This is the reason why, during the first few years of his journalistic activities, Leclerc made grateful use of the friendships he had managed to establish with John Locke and Gilbert Burnet, who were staying in the Republic at the time.[17] In those years both of them were engaged in preparing a number of publications, which Leclerc not only reviewed but for which he also offered them all kinds of other services. Leclerc translated Burnet's answer to Varillas' attack: *la Critique du IXe livre de l'Histoire de M. Varillas*, as well as the reply to the *Réponse de M. Varillas*, which this *Critique* had provoked.[18] As early as 1686, Locke, who reviewed several books for the *Bibliothèque*, was given an opportunity by Leclerc to publish an original contribution in his journal, "contenant une Methode nouvelle et facile de dresser des Recueils . . .". For the first time Locke was also able to publicise his ideas about the theory of knowledge when he published in the same *Bibliothèque* the *Extrait d'un Livre Anglois qui n'est pas encore publié, intitulé Essai philosophique concernant l'Entendement ...*[19]

Yet Leclerc the journalist was to profit even more from the services of the English philosopher, when the latter had returned to England in the spring of 1689. He had asked Locke, just before his departure, not to forget his *Bibliothèque*.[20] On 19 April 1689 he explicitly asks him to send lists of book-titles to Amsterdam: "Lorsque vous aurez le loisir de me marquer seulement les noms des livres qui viendront à vôtre connoissance, et que vous jugerez passables, j'aurai soin de les faire venir par la voie de nos libraires qui ont des correspondances à Londres".[21] Apart from books and lists of titles the philosopher had also sent him two

---

De Amsterdamse Boekhandel 1680-1725, t. III and IV, Amsterdam 1965 and 1967, passim.

17 Cf. C.L. Thijssen-Schoute, "De Nederlandse Vriendenkring van John Locke", in: *Uit de Republiek der Letteren*, 's-Gravenhage 1967, pp. 90-103.

18 A. Barnes, *op. cit.*, pp. 160-161.

19 BUH, II (1686), pp. 315-340 and BUH, VIII (1688), pp. 49-142.

20 Letter of 12 February 1689, *Correspondence of John Locke, op. cit.*, III, no. 1103, pp. 547-548: ". . . que, lors que quelques uns de vos amis auront quelque piéce, qu'ils veuillent faire connoître deça la mer, vous ayez la bonté de vous ressouvenir de nôtre Bibliotheque".

21 *Ibidem*, no. 1126, p. 595.

BIBLIOTHEQUE UNIVERSELLE
ET
HISTORIQUE
DE L'ANNÉE
M. D. C. LXXXVI.
TOME PREMIER.

A AMSTERDAM,
Chez Wolfgang, Waesberge, Boom, & van Someren.
M. D. C. LXXXVI.

BIBLIOTHEQUE CHOISIE,
POUR SERVIR DE SUITE
A LA
BIBLIOTHEQUE UNIVERSELLE.
Par Jean Le Clerc.
Année MDCCIII.
TOME I.

A AMSTERDAM,
Chez Henry Schelte,
M DCC III.

BIBLIOTHEQUE ANCIENNE
ET
MODERNE.
Pour servir de suite aux
BIBLIOTHEQUES
Universelle et Choisie.
Par Jean Le Clerc.
TOME I.
POUR L'ANNÉE MDCCXIV.
Partie Premiere.

A AMSTERDAM,
Chez David Mortier Libraire
MDCCXIV.

periodically published works: the *Mercurius Librarius or a Catalogue of Books printed and published in Michaelmas Term* and the *Philosophical Transactions*.[22] From the latter periodical containing accounts of the Royal Society in London Leclerc took over no fewer than six articles between 1686 and 1688.[23] That Leclerc did not like having to do without the *Transactions* appears from his letter of December 1689, in which he asks whether this periodical, whose publication had been interrupted between December 1687 and February 1691, had meanwhile appeared again. The *Term Catalogues* were naturally also excellent sources for Leclerc to keep abreast of what was being published in England.

Via Locke Leclerc also made the acquaintance of the 3rd Earl of Shaftesbury, with whom he became close friends and who helped him on several occasions in his work as a journalist.[24] Thus, together with Lady Masham, he provided a great deal of biographical material for the *Eloge* which Leclerc published after Locke's death in the *Bibliothèque Choisie* of 1705.[25] The letters that Leclerc sent to Shaftesbury clearly show how interested he was in English culture and manners: "Il y a longtemps, Mylord, que je suis tout acquis à la nation anglaise, et en particulier à des personnes de votre caractère. On me raille même quelquefois ici, à cause de cela; mais il faut rendre justice à ceux à qui elle est due, quoi que les gens de mauvais goût en puissent dire".[26] Unfortunately, as he informed Shaftesbury a few months later, it was not always possible to adequately fulfil his task as a reporter on the state of English learning on the continent, for English books were expensive and were but seldom bought in his circles, so that he could not borrow them from anybody.[27] Precisely because of the large number of books that were offered for sale and the fact that they were so expensive, the journalist had to be able to count on good advisers and friends, who could alleviate his task. It goes without saying that Shaftesbury's services were highly appreciated by Leclerc and it is no wonder, therefore, that it was Leclerc who, in several lengthy

---

22 Cf. *ibidem*, nos. 1216 and 1234, letters of 7 November 1689, 13 December 1689 and 21 January 1690.

23 R. Boyle, *A free inquire* . . ., BUH, II (1686), pp. 277-280; D. Papin, *Expérience d'un Mousquet à vent*, BUH, II (1686), pp. 477-479; E. Halley, *Des regles que l' on peut donner de la hauteur du vif argent, dans le Barometre* . . ., BUH, II (1686), pp. 479-499; E. Halley, *Relation Historique des Vents reglez* . . ., BUH, IV (1687), pp. 66-93; M. Brotherton, *L'accroissement des arbres*. . ., BUH, IX (1688), pp. 186-195; E. Halley, *Estimation de la quantité des Vapeurs* . . ., BUH, IX (1688), pp. 195-203.

24 Cf. A. Barnes, *op. cit.*, pp. 168 ff.

25 Amsterdam, University Library, MS. J. 20 and J. 57a, letters of 8 February 1705 and 12 January 1705. See also A. Barnes, *op. cit.*, pp. 169-171.

26 Letter from J. Leclerc to Shaftesbury of 27 February 1705, published in A. Barnes, *op. cit.*, pp. 170-171.

27 *Ibidem*, p. 172, letter of 17 September 1705.

articles, gave more publicity to Shaftesbury's *Characteristics*.[28]

Locke, Shaftesbury and Gilbert Burnet all died long before Leclerc was to finish his editorial activities for the last *Bibliothèque*. It was fortunate, therefore, that his circle of correspondents in England had gradually increased in the course of the years. For example, he corresponded with several scholars in Cambridge, such as John Davies, William Wotton, Joseph Wasse and Peter Needham, to whose philological work he paid attention in his *Bibliothèque Choisie*. Leclerc was also on friendly terms with the Archbishop of Canterbury, the Unionist William Wake, as well as corresponding with, among others, John Sharp and Joseph Addison.[29] However, it would be beyond the scope of this paper to deal with all the correspondents that Leclerc had in England. That would require much more extensive research, which would otherwise be quite justifiable. However, we already know for a fact, particularly thanks to the research carried out by Annie Barnes, that Leclerc had enough channels of information in Amsterdam to be able to offer the European world of scholars, via his *Bibliothèque*, a good anthology of the books that were produced in England.

In comparison with the other contemporary learned journals the *Bibliothèques* thus gave the best impression of England and of the state of learning in that country. The *Bibliothèque Universelle et Historique* is clear proof of this. Almost 25 per cent of the total number of pages of this first periodical are devoted to publications about England and English scholarship or to books written by English authors, that is to say by authors who were born in England, Scotland or Ireland or who had later settled there permanently (refugiés). What is immediately striking is that theological and philosophical works predominate. No less than 70 per cent is devoted to this category, while another 15 per cent deals with historical and philological works. Leclerc's interest in England manifests itself even more strongly in the *Bibliothèque Choisie*, where 35 per cent of all pages are devoted to this subject. About half of them deal with theological and philosophical works and almost 40 per cent of the pages in this journal are devoted to historical and philological works, a field in which Leclerc has clearly begun to take a greater interest. This tendency is even more obvious in the *Bibliothèque Ancienne et Moderne*. Whereas contributions dealing with England cover over 38 per cent of the contents of this periodical, the theological and philosophical works that are discussed cover only about 35 per cent, while this percentage goes up to approximately 52 per cent for historical and philological works.

---

28 Cf. S.A. Golden, *op. cit.*, pp. 87-90; see B.Ch., XIX (1710), pp. 427-438; XXI[1] (1710), pp. 177-197 and XXIII[1] (1711), pp. 89-168.

29 Cf. A. Barnes, *op. cit.*, pp. 178-182 and 166-168; S. Golden, *op. cit.*, pp. 91-92.

It is hardly surprising, of course, that Leclerc, who was a theologian himself, should pay a great deal of attention in his three successive periodicals, to the Anglican Church and to English theology in general. As a true follower of Locke and as a theologian who, first in Geneva, but also later on, had personally experienced how much evil and damage intolerance could cause, Leclerc made a continuous plea in his *Bibliothèques* for liberty of conscience and for ecclesiastical tolerance. As long as the most essential foundations of Christianity were not affected, "modération théologique" was required.[30] That is why, in his review of Selden's *Table Talk* Leclerc says explicitly: "Il ne faut pas imposer, comme Loi Divine et comme Article de Foi, ce qui ne l'est pas et punir de peines civiles ceux qui sont d'un autre sentiment, lors qu'ils vivent bien d'ailleurs et qu'ils s'acquitent des devoirs de bon citoyens".[31] In his view Christians should be prepared to forgive each other, if the basic tenets of the faith are not to be betrayed.

Within the category of historical and philological works almost three-quarters was devoted to history, the writings of William Temple, Lord Clarendon and Thomas Rymer receiving the most attention.[32] The work of the last historian was abbreviated by the French Huguenot Paul Rapin de Thoyras and published in the *Bibliothèque Choisie* and the *Bibliothèque Ancienne et Moderne*. These writings were reviewed very favourably by Leclerc: Rapin not only knew English very well and had studied the best English historiographers, he had also analyzed numerous documents "qu'on ne trouve que dans le Recueil de feu Mr Rymer; il a amassé ses materiaux depuis long tems, et les a digerez en maniere qu'il n'est guere possible que son Histoire ne soit la meilleure, ou l'une des meilleures de celles que l'on ait déjà vues ou qui puissent paroître à l'avenir".[33] What is remarkable is that in Leclerc's last *Bibliothèque* more space is devoted to contemporary English literature, even if this is only a fraction of the whole (about 1,5 per cent). In the *Bibliothèque Choisie* an article had already been devoted to *Remarks on several parts of Italy* . . . (London 1705) by Addison, "un des meilleurs poëtes Anglois qu'il y ait à present".[34] In Leclerc's last periodical we find lengthy reviews[35] of

---

30 BAM, XVI (1721), p. 428; where Leclerc makes a plea for "moderation théologique, qu'on entend une disposition d'esprit, par laquelle on n'outre rien, en matières de controverses, qui sont entre les chrétiens; mais on pardonne et tolère, autant qu'il est possible, sans trahir la verité, ce qui lui est opposé, en ceux qui sont dans l'erreur".
31 *Ibidem*, VI (1716), p. 273.
32 Cf. S.A. Golden, *op. cit.*, pp. 93-94.
33 BAM, XVIII (1722), p. 332.
34 B.Ch., XI (1707), pp. 198-217.
35 BAM, I (1714), pp. 383-451; V (1716), pp. 418-426; VIII (1717), pp. 453-458.

Addison and Steele's *Spectator Papers*, "un ouvrage qui ne fût seulement pour les jeunes gens ou pour les dames, qui ne cherchent souvent qu'à se divertir, mais pour une infinité de personnes plus avancées en âge qui veulent qu'on les entretienne de quelque chose de sérieux et de solide".[36] Leclerc also paid attention to Steele's *Ladies Library*,[37] as well as devoting some articles to Pope, Jonathan Swift and Daniel Defoe.[38]

Science occupies only a minor place in the attention Leclerc pays to England, although Newton's *Philosophiae Naturalis Principia Mathematica*, which had appeared in London in 1687, was reviewed in the *Bibliothèque Universelle et Historique* as early as March 1688.[39] If Leclerc himself was probably not yet able to grasp the importance of Newton's theory of gravity in all its consequences, it was certainly to his great credit that he published the article, which had been edited by Locke, in its entirety. In 1706 Leclerc reviewed another work by the English mathematician and physicist: *Optics or a treatise of the Reflexions, Refractions, Inflexions of Leight . . .*, published in 1704. The journalist is then firmly convinced that Newton is the greatest mathematician and physicist of all times, as also appears from remarks in the first instalment of the *Bibliothèque Ancienne et Moderne* in which Newton's work is mentioned a number of times.[40] This was on the occasion of the publication in 1711 of *Analysis per Quantitatum, Series, Fluxiones ac Differentias cum enumeratione Linearum tertii Ordinis*, of the publication of a reprint in 1713 of the *Principia* and of an article from the *Philosophical Transactions* of 1711. In these articles and in several others Leclerc clearly shows that he has definitely done with Descartes' hypothetico-deductive approach and that nature could only be revealed via the empirico-inductive method.

As has already been observed, it was Locke who had edited Newton's article on the *Principia* and who had for years helped Leclerc in editing

---

36 *Ibidem*, I (1714), p. 384.
37 *Ibidem*, VI (1716), pp. 225-228 en XI (1719), pp. 414-417.
38 For Pope, see BAM, VII (1718), pp. 234-236 (*Essai sur la Critique imité de l'Anglois de Mr Pope*); for Swift, see BAM, XV (1721), pp. 441-449 (*A Tale of a Tub*); for Defoe, see BAM, XIII (1720), pp. 461-462; XV (1721), pp. 440-441 (*Robinson Crusoe*). On this work Leclerc observes: "Ceci n'est qu'un Roman, mais un Roman instructif et digne par consequent d'attention" (BAM, XIII, p. 462).
39 BUH, VIII (1688), pp. 436-450. See J.K. van der Korst, "Natuurwetenschappen en geneeskunde in de 'Bibliothèque Universelle et Historique' ", in: H. Bots e.a., *De Bibliothèque . . ., op. cit.*, pp. 352-354.
40 B.Ch., IX (1706), pp. 245-319; BAM, I (1714), pp. 58-61, 69-96. In this last instalment, where he discusses an article from the *Philosophical Transactions*, he observes (p. 64): "M. Newton le plus grand physicien, aussi bien que le plus grand Mathematicien, qui nous soit connu, a suivi une méthode toute differente. Il n'établit rien, que ce que l'Experience et les Observations nous ont appris . . .". See also BAM, XII (1719), pp. 433-462 (an article on Newton's *Optics*).

his *Bibliothèque*.[41] For this reason it seems justified to examine here the English philosopher's presence in Leclerc's periodicals. What follows is a list of all the works that relate to John Locke and that were reviewed in the three *Bibliothèques*.

1. Méthode Nouvelle de dresser des Recueils. Communiquée par l'Auteur, BUH, II (1686), 315-340.
2. Extrait d'un Livre Anglois qui n'est pas encore publié, intitulé Essai Philosophique concernant l'entendement, où l'on montre quelle est l'étendue de nos connoissances certaines, et la manière dont nous y parvenons. Communiqué par Monsieur Locke, BUH, VIII (1688), 49-142.
2a. *An essay concerning humane Understanding. In four books . . .*, London [T. Basset] 1690, in fol., BUH, XVII (1690), 399-427.
2b. *Essay concerning Humane Understanding, in four books, written by John Locke, gentleman, the fifth Edition with large Additions*, London [A. et J. Churchill] 1706, in fol., BCh, XII (1707), 80-123.
2c. *Abrégé de l'Essai de Mr. Locke sur l'entendement humain. Traduit de l'Anglois par Mr. Bosset*, Londres 1720, in-8°, BAM, XIII (1720), 225-227.
3. *Epistola de Tolerantia ad clarissimum virum T.A.R.P.T.O.L.A.* [Ph. van Limborch] *scripta a P.A.P.O.I.L.A.*, Goudae [J. ab Hoeve] 1689, in-12°, BUH, XV (1689), 402-412.
3a. *A second Letter concerning toleration. Licensed, June 24, 1690*, London [A. et J. Churchill] 1690, in-4°, BUH, XIX (1690), 365-391.
4. *Two treatises of government: in the former, the false principles, and foundation of Sir Robert Filmer, and his followers, are detected and overthrown. The latter is an essay concerning the true original, extent, and end of civil government*, London [A. et J. Churchill] 1690, in-8°, BUH, XIX (1690), 559-591.
4a. *Du gouvernement civil où l'on traitte de l'origine, des fondemens, de la nature du pouvoir et des fins des sociétéz politiques, traduit de l'anglois* [par D. Maze], Amsterdam [A. Wolfgang] 1691, in-12°, BUH, XX² (1691), 263-265.
5. *Que la Religion chrétienne est très-raisonnable telle qu'elle nous est représentée dans l'Ecriture Sainte*, 2° partie Traduite de l'Anglois [by Pierre Coste of the Reasonnableness of Christianity], Amsterdam [H. Schelte] 1703, BCh, II (1702), 284-305.
5a. *Le Christianisme Raisonnable tel qu'il nous est représenté dans*

---

41 Cf. the letter from J. Leclerc to J. Locke of 16 April 1693, *Correspondence of John Locke, op. cit.*, t. IV, no. 1621, pp. 666-667.

l'*Ecriture Sainte. Traduit de l'Anglois de Mr Locke* [par M. Coste]. *Sec. édition revüe et corrigée et augmentée d'une dissertation, où l'on établit le vrai et l'unique moyen de réunir tous les Chrétiens malgré la différence des sentimens. On a joint à cette Edition la Religion des Dames*, t. I-II, Amsterdam [chez l'Honoré et Châtelain] 1715, in-8°, BAM, IV (1715), 230-232.

6. Eloge de feu Mr Locke [par Jean Leclerc], BCh, VI (1705), 342-411.

7. *Posthumous Works of Mr John Locke, viz. I of the conduct of the Understanding. II An Examination of P. Malebranche's opinion of seeing all things in God. III A Discourse on miracles. IV Part of a fourth Letter on Toleration. V Memoirs relating to the Life of Anthony first Earl of Shaftesbury. To which is added VI His new method of a Common placebook, written originally in French and now translated into English*, London [A. et J. Churchill] 1706, in-8°, BCh, XII (1707), 123-170.

8. *An Essay for the Understanding of St Paul's Epistles by consulting St Paul himself. A combined edition of the Paraphrase by John Locke entitled respectively: A Paraphrase and Notes on the Epistles of St Paul to the Galathians, to the Corinthians, to the Romans and to the Ephesians . . .*, London [A. et J. Churchill] 1707, in-4°, BCh, XIII (1708), 37-178.

9. *De l'Education des Enfans, traduit de l'Anglois de Mr Locke par Pierre Coste sur la dernière édition revue, corrigée et augmentée*, Amsterdam [chez H. Schelte] 1708, in-8°, BCh, XVI (1708), 420 (annonce).

9a. *De l'Education des Enfans traduit de l'Anglois de Mr Locke par Mr Coste sur l'Ediction Angloise, publiée après la mort de l'Auteur qui l'avoit revüe, corrigée et augmentée de plus d'un tiers*, Amsterdam [chez Steenhouwer et Uytwerf], 1721, in-12°, BAM, XV (1721), 449-452.

10. *Some familiar Letters between Mr Locke and several of his Friends*, London [A. et J. Churchill] 1708, in-8°, BCh, XVII (1709), 234-241.

11. *Oeuvres Diverses de Mr Jean Locke.* [Précédées d'un Eloge Historique de l'Auteur par Jean Leclerc], Rotterdam [chez Fritsch et Böhm] 1710, in-12°, BCh, XXI[1] (1710), 228 (annonce).

12. *A Collection of Several Pieces of Mr John Locke, never before printed or not extant in his Works. Publish'd by the Author of the Life of the ever memorable Mr John Hales etc.*, London [by J. Bettenham for R. Franklin] 1720, in-8°, BAM, XIII (1720), 444-459.

This list clearly shows that virtually all the major works of John Locke were reviewed by Leclerc in his *Bibliothèques*. Only *A Third Letter for Toleration* (1692), in which Locke continued his controversy with Jonas Proast over the question whether the worldly authorities were justified in supporting the true religion with their power and whether this religion had an intellectual foundation, was not dealt with in the *Bibliothèques*.[42] Though Locke's work had been sent to Leclerc himself, he no longer reviewed it, because, since 1691, from volume XX onwards, he had left the editorship of the *Bibliothèque Universelle* almost completely to Jaques Bernard. However, thanks to the review of the *Second Letter*, readers of the *Bibliothèque* were not entirely ignorant of this controversy. Moreover, the European reading public could easily follow the continuation of this controversy in the *Histoire des Ouvrages des Savans*, edited in this same period by Henri Basnage de Beauval, who made a detailed summary of the *Third Letter*. Yet, as a friend and confidant of the English philosopher, Leclerc was more qualified than Basnage (who also reviewed a large number of Locke's works in the *Histoire*) to assess the significance and import of Locke's ideas. Indeed all his reviews testify to a critical and balanced approach.

During Locke's lifetime Leclerc hardly ever expressed any negative opinions on his work. Also shortly after his death he described him in the *Eloge* as "un des plus excellens Philosophes de nos jours, qui après avoir pénétré presque toutes les parties de la Philosophie, et en avoir developpé les mystères les plus cachez, avec une finesse et une exactitude peu commune, tourna heureusement son esprit du côté de la Religion Chrétienne, qu'il examina dans sa source, avec la même liberté qu'il avoit fait les autres sciences et qu'il trouva si raisonnable et si belle, qu'il lui consacra le reste de sa vie . . .".[43] The *Eloge*, incidentally, has a predominantly biographical character and unfortunately is not an in-depth study of the contents of the great philosopher's works. Where Leclerc does deal with them, he is always full of praise.

Nevertheless Leclerc was not entirely uncritical of Locke's ideas. Thus he believed that, in his *Essay*, Locke had failed to express himself clearly and without ambiguity about the idea of freedom (Book II, chapter XXI).[44] However, the criticisms he made in his review of the 5th edition of this work did not, as he himself said, detract from the respect and admiration he had always felt for the Englishman. As he testifies in the

---

42 For Locke's polemic with Jonas Proast, see Maurice Cranston, *John Locke, a biography*, London 1968[4], pp. 366-368 and J. de Vet, "John Locke in de Histoire des Ouvrages des Savans", in: H. Bots (ed.), *H. Basnage de Beauval en de Histoire des Ouvrages des Savans 1687-1709*, t. II, Amsterdam 1976, pp. 194-199. The *Third Letter* was reviewed in Basnage's periodical in HOS, September 1693, pp. 24-39.
43 B.Ch., VI (1705), p. 401.
44 *Ibidem*, XII (1707), pp. 80-123, esp. pp. 81 and 99.

same article, Locke's ideas had also greatly benefited his own philosophical work. Leclerc is again critical of Locke, and this time not only because of a detail, in the review of his own *Opera Philosophica* (1700). Locke, according to Leclerc, had not given enough thought to his "methode": "Cet habile homme ne paroît pas avoir jamais fait assez de réflexion sur la Méthode; puisqu'il n'y a guere de chapitre de son Ouvrage qui ne soit un peu confus, quoi que les parties de l'Ouvrage en général soient en très-bon ordre. Je pourrois même citer d'habiles gens, qui ont crû que j'avois exprimé quelques uns de ses sentimens plus clairement, que lui même. L'ontologie et la pneumatologie sont pleines de matières qu'il n'a jamais touchées".[45] It is not so surprising, incidentally, that a philosopher like Leclerc, who had always preferred the ontological approach, always remains a little disappointed when confronted with a way of thinking that does not meet the requirements of the philosophical method as formulated by Descartes. After reminding his readers that in volume XII of the *Bibliothèque Choisie* he had already used the concept of "freedom" to illustrate that Locke was occasionally obscure, he again concludes his remarks on a positive note: "Cela soit dit, avec le respect dû à la mémoire de cet habile homme, que j'ai estimé, honoré et loué, autant qu'il le méritoit; mais sans m'entêter de sa simple autorité, non plus que de celle des autres Philosophes".

There is one final occasion, in his last *Bibliothèque*, when Leclerc takes the liberty of expressing a less than favourable opinion on Locke's occasionally somewhat tedious style.[46] The question in how far these few less laudatory remarks of Leclerc's are justified cannot be dealt with here. What is certain is that he regarded Locke as an authority, without falling into servile docility. Nor can there be any doubt that Leclerc's three *Bibliothèques* made a major contribution to the spread on the Continent of English learning in general and of Locke's ideas in particular. Thanks to his good command of the English language, his philosophical and theological interest and his friendly relations with Locke and several other English contemporaries, Leclerc was better qualified than anyone else to inform the European reading public about the best things that were being produced in England.

---

45 *Ibidem*, XXI¹ (1710), pp. 217-218.
46 *Ibidem*, XXV² (1712), pp. 399-400: "Je n'approuve pas tout ce qui est dans le livre du *Christianisme Raisonnable*; j'y retrancherois bien des choses, et j'y en ajouterois d'autres; outre que j'en changerois l'ordre, si c'étoit mon ouvrage (...). Feu Mʳ Locke croyoit qu'elles étoient nécessaires, les répétitions, pour faire mieux entendre ce qu'il vouloit dire; mais je ne suis pas de son sentiment, en cela".

RICHARD STANYHURST'S TRANSLATION OF VERGIL'S
AENEID (1582)

D.E.L. Crane

Stanyhurst's translation into English hexameters of parts of Vergil's *Aeneid*[1] is some of the strangest poetry in the language. When not wholly neglected, it has attracted largely contemptuous notice:

> Master *Stannyhurst* (though otherwise learned) trod a foule lumbring boystrous wallowing measure, in his translation of *Virgil.*[2]

> he tooke upon him to translate *Virgill*, and stript him out of a Veluet gowne, into a Fooles coate, out of a Latin Heroicall verse, into an English riffe raffe.[3]

> As Chaucer has been called the well of English undefiled, so might Stanihurst be denominated the common sewer of the language.[4]

One turns to Stanyhurst, after such comment, expecting little, and yet it is rapidly apparent that he was not a fool, a vulgarian or an incompetent. There is an intensity of perverse inspiration about his performance that is well beyond foolishness or incompetence, and which produces not only breathtakingly grotesque results but also on occasion verbal effects successful, and successful in rendering Vergil, beyond anything any other of the English translators have been able to manage.

The first thing to notice about Stanyhurst's language is its energy. He makes the most that could be made of the capacity English has for sharp

---

1. R. Stanyhurst, *Thee first foure bookes of Virgil his Aeneis translated intoo English heroical verse*, Leiden, 1582 (RSTC. 24806); London, 1583 (RSTC. 24807). Stanyhurst was born in Dublin in 1547, where his father was recorder of the City of Dublin; he went up to Oxford in 1563 where he became acquainted with the future Jesuit and martyr, Edmund Campion, who was greatly impressed by his abilities. After leaving Oxford he became a Catholic and went to live in the Low Countries, where his translation of Vergil was first printed. He became a priest about 1607 and died in Brussels in 1618. The most recent edition of his *Aeneid* is by Dirk van der Haar, Amsterdam, 1933; references to Stanyhurst's text in this article are from this edition. More recently a full biography has also appeared, by Colm Lennon, *Richard Stanihurst the Dubliner, 1547-1618,* Irish Academic Press, 1982.
2. *The Works of Thomas Nashe*, ed. R.B. McKerrow, rev. ed. F.P. Wilson, 1958, vol. 1, p. 299.
3. Barnaby Rich, *The Irish Hubbub*, 1617, p. 2.
4. Robert Southey, *Omniana*, 1812, i, 193.

variety of consonantal sound, the sound accompanying, mocking, swamping, screeching in the ears of the meaning. One is reminded at times of various Elizabethan pamphleteers in this use of the language with its sound quality uppermost, but Stanyhurst outmarprelates Marprelate:

> Now doe they rayse gastly lyghtnings, now grislye reboundings
> Of ruffe raffe roaring, mens herts with terror agrysing.
> With peale meale ramping, with thwick thwack sturdelye thundring.
> Theyre labor hoat they folow: toe the flame fits gyreful awarding.
> And in an od corner, for *Mars* they be sternfulye flayling
> Hudge spoaks and chariots, by the which thee surlye *God*, angerd,
> Hastye men enrageth, too wrath towns bat'ful on eggeth.
> And they be fresh forging toe the netled *Pallas* an armoure,
> With gould ritchlye shrined, wheare scaals be ful horriblye clincked
> Of scrawling *serpents*, with sculcks of poysoned *adders*.
> In brest of the Godesse *Gorgon* was cocketed hardlye,
> With nodil vnioyncted, by death, light vital amoouing.
> Voyd ye fro these flamfews, quoa the *God*, set a part the begun wurck.[5]

The full bellied pleasure in emphatic sound in this version of Vergil's description of the forging of iron in the cave of the Cyclops shows Stanyhurst with a grip on the language at its earthiest and most ruffianly level, at the level of the carter yelling or the shrew scolding. Here is the very reverse of the attempt made by some other sixteenth-century poets to produce a highly vocalic and almost stressless movement in imitation of Italian or French, in which the consonantal energies of the English words were attracted towards, and almost absorbed by the pools of vowel sound. Such soft and smooth verses[6] were the civilised direction for sixteenth-century poetry; Stanyhurst clearly chose deliberately to move in the reverse direction, towards a cultivation of the consonantal energies of the language, and especially of the harder and less dissolvable consonant sounds, and towards the highly stressed context which such sounds evoke and require. In a set piece of the kind just quoted, where the poet is "aduauncing at ful thee loftines of his veyne",[7] he is not content even with the consonantal sound he can urge out of the words needed to carry the sense of the Latin, but supplements it with "ruffe raffe's" and "thwick thwack's" to increase the volume.

---

5. The first editions of Stanyhurst's translation, of 1582 and 1583 included, beside the first four books of the *Aeneid*, various fragments of translation from other parts of Vergil's poem, and a small number of original pieces. Most of this matter was omitted by van der Haar, but appears in Edward Arber's edition of 1895. The passage quoted here is a translation of *Aeneid* viii. 431-39 (Arber, p. 138).

6. Walton in *The Compleat Angler* says of Donne's "The Bait" that it was "made to shew the world that hee could make soft and smooth Verses" (John Donne, *The Elegies and The Songs and Sonnets*, ed. Helen Gardner, 1965, p. 156).

7. Arber, p. 137.

What is interesting about Stanyhurst is that the man who chose deliberately this ruffianly direction for his poetic style adopted a grotesquely odd orthography for the most learned of reasons;[8] chose also to write, and to write pretty accurately, in the most pedantic of metres, the English hexameter; and was concerned as a learned man might be with the problems of rendering the nuance of Vergil's Latin. In his dedication of the translation to his brother, Lord Dunsanye, Stanyhurst comments on the version his would have to compete with. He is not by any means ungenerous to Thomas Phaer's translation,[9] but introduces examples of the kind of care with which he has himself considered Vergil's meaning with these words:

> More ouer in soom poinctes of greatest price, where thee matter, as yt were, doth bleede, I was mooued too shun M. *Phaer* his enterpretation, and clinge more neere too thee meaning of myne authoure, in slising thee husk and cracking thee shel, too bestow thee kernel vpon thee wyttye and enquisitiue reader.[10]

He is intent upon reaching the heart of Vergil's meaning, especially at points where its very life blood is to be found, and he gives examples of the sort of advance he has attempted to make upon Phaer's version. There is a clear impression given of a translator concerned in detail with the relation between Vergil's Latin and his English.

That is not the kind of concern apparent in Phaer's version. The earlier translator demands of himself a less detailed fidelity, and in constructing his own English poem gives less attention at the level of the word than of the line to its relation with the original. He writes in well filled fourteeners, with individual words used not only vitally to convey the sense but also as a kind of metrical polyfilla. Phaer's assumption seems to be, as Stanyhurst remarks, that Vergil worked in the same way:

> Againe *Virgil* in diuerse places inuesteth *Iuno* with this epitheton, *Saturnia*, M. *Phaer* ouerpasseth yt, as yf yt were an idle woord shuffled in by thee authoure too dam vp thee chappes of yawning verses. I neauer, too my remembraunce, omitted yt, as in deede a terme that carieth meate in his mouth, and so emphatical, as thee ouerslipping of yt were in effect thee chocking of thee poet his discourse, in suche hauking wise, ac yf hee were throtled with the chincoughe.[11]

This attitude of fiercely detailed attention to translation clearly en-

---

8. See his lengthy and perhaps wrong-headed but not foolish discussion of quantity in English (van der Haar, pp. 58-61). One notices often how in other circumstances a feeling for the learned direction and a feeling for the grotesque coincide in Stanyhurst.

9. I mention various versions of the *Aeneid* other than Stanyhurst's in this article: versions by Phaer (1558-62); Dryden (1697); Pitt (1740); William Morris (1876); Conington (1881); Rhoades (1893).

10. van der Haar, p. 54.

11. van der Haar, p. 55. Stanyhurst's memory has failed him; he is not so reliable about translating "Saturnia" as he claims.

couraged Stanyhurst to choose a quantitive metre for his English version. It is easy to suppose that the whole attempt to introduce quantitive metres into English poetry in the late sixteenth century was a piece of hilariously foolish pedantry, but Stanyhurst's reasons do arrest the attention:

> For in thee one [quantitive verses] euerye *foote*, euerye *word*, euerye *syllable*, yea euery *letter* is too bee obserued: in thee oother [rhyme] thee last *woord* is onlye too bee heeded...What *Tom Towly* is so simple, that wyl not attempt, too bee a *rithmoure*?[12]

The development of critical awareness in the last four hundred years has provided us with elaborate and acute ways of seeing how much else there is in a good rhymed poem beside the rhyme, and of discriminating between good and bad. We would accept Stanyhurst's insistence that the poetic transformation should affect every part of a poem and his observation that a preoccupation with rhyme as the essentially poetic thing is likely to produce nothing much more than rhymed prose or doggerel, but the *formality* of his demand for transformation throughout the line now seems to us excessive. To write English in Latin hexameters is to set before oneself at the beginning of each line the task of converting each foot, word, syllable and letter into a poetic scheme. Poetry is thus rescued from being minimally shaped doggerel, and made to tread an elaborate and intricate measure, but that intricate measure itself may inhibit the appearance of some shape yet more subtle. It is true that Vergil himself wrote within the hexameter measure and yet produced subtlety and delicacy as much as one could wish for, but the English language is not the Latin, and English with its tyrannical stress must stamp through the steps of the dance that Latin moves almost imperceptibly in.

The case against the English hexameter is strong, even though the case for it is not negligible. For Stanyhurst the hexameter is the only possible metre in this poem, and it contributes largely both to his strangely energetic success and to his ludicrous failure. The hexameter made him attend fiercely to every foot, word, syllable and letter of his English verse; that kind of attention was at one with the attention he thought desirable to every nuance and detail of Vergil's Latin; and was at one, too, with the cultivation of consonantal sound which made of each word a separate and undissolvable experience, so that no word is lost in the line, and many words are strangely used or newly created. You cannot let Stanyhurst flow over you, as you can Phaer and most other English translators of Vergil; word after word arrests the attention, looming awkwardly, impressively, oddly out of the line. The urbanely smooth

---

12. van der Haar, pp. 56-7.

reader will find this laughably, unbearably rustic, like a road full of gates; but once consent to stop at every gate and one begins to see the countryside differently. Vergil is urbane as Stanyhurst is not, but it is part of Vergil's greatness that his easy, unobtrusively subtle forward movement does not impede more local intensities, so that the reader even as he is carried past also fixes upon moments of grotesque horror, or pity, or quiet, disorder or collapse.[13] Almost every English translator of Vergil reproduces in some way his urbanity while virtually missing these more local intensities, but Stanyhurst's characteristic style is one that will always stop for some local reason, even if the range of local effects is nothing like so extensive as with Vergil. This is not fundamentally Stanyhurst *influenced* by a certain understanding of Vergil; it is more an accidental coincidence between the English and the Latin poet, for Stanyhurst's instincts remain robustly undisturbed by Vergil. If there is evidence from his introduction and elsewhere of a concern to render the Latin accurately, if there is a precise piety about his adoption of the metre Vergil used, then these links which are established between himself and the earlier poet are not allowed to invade and damage the closer link between himself and his own native tongue; indeed, the hexameter, as I have suggested, is at least in part adopted because it can give effective help in expressing that native instinct. In translating the famous set piece on Rumour at *Aeneid* iv. 174-88,[14] Stanyhurst can be latinate and pedantic in vocabulary and speak of the "graund Gods celical anger", but this pedantry is set within the context of a dominating physicality (Rumour is "lyke a shrimp squatting", she is "a foule fog pack paunch", the earth "litterd this leueret") which has nothing to do with Latin. Nevertheless, we notice that a very conscious and English idiosyncracy ("to the skyes shee flickereth, howling/Through the earth shade skipping") often vibrates with an element in the Latin, as here to "nocte... stridens";

> nocte volat caeli medio terraeque per umbram
> stridens.

The notion "nocte...stridens" threads its way as a dark force through a beautifully constructed balanced line, and with "howling" and especially "flickereth" Stanyhurst has caught the resonance of it, as for instance Dryden has not:

> She fills the peaceful universe with cries.

It is really in his refusal of tributary status, then, that Stanyhurst comes

---

13. One is reminded of the way in which, at a thematic level, the providential onward thrust of the epic story of Aeneas and the triumph of Rome is counterpointed by local loyalties and tragedies (Dido, Deiphobus, Palinurus, and so on) which cannot for long be allowed to impede the onward movement.

14. van der Haar, p. 122.

closest to Vergil. A passage from a slightly later point in the fourth book illustrates very well, especially in the use of the hexameter, his brand of fidelity and independence. Dido turns in fury upon Aeneas at the news that he must sail for Italy:

> nec tibi diva parens, generis nec Dardanus auctor,
> perfide; sed duris genuit te cautibus horrens
> Caucasus, Hyrcanaeque admorunt ubera tigres.
> nam quid dissimulo? aut quae me ad maiora reservo?
> num fletu ingemuit nostro? num lumina flexit?
> num lacrimas victus dedit, aut miseratus amantem est?
> quae quibus anteferam? iam iam nec maxima Iuno,
> nec Saturnius haec oculis pater aspicit aequis.
> nusquam tuta fides. eiectum litore, egentem
> excepi, et regni demens in parte locavi;
> amissam classem, socios a morte reduxi.
> heu foriis incensa feror![15]

Dido's passion of anger cuts across the hexameter in a way which emphasises rather than damages the form. She speaks like a queen in the grip of naked emotion: the formalities of a highly wrought rhetoric are so natural to her that they will serve her for the most direct communication of unpremeditated fury. No English translator of Vergil can reproduce the intensity of balance between anarchic, unbridled passion and self-conscious literary formality. The pattern of the hexameter is broken into by abrupt pauses, changes of mood and tone, and changes of speed, and yet it survives resiliently and evidently. The pressure of meaning and stress on the individual words is very varied, ranging from the lightly burdened "aut quae me ad" to "perfide" or "nusquam tuta fides"; and yet these words fit harmoniously together.

Dryden renders the harmonious quality of the Latin well; he gives us a satisfying completeness of structure, with an extended and shapely rhetorical power, but at the expense of the more jagged energies of the original. The tone he catches is that of:

> iam iam nec maxima Iuno,
> nec Saturnius haec oculis pater aspicit aequis

but not of:

> sed duris genuit te cautibus horrens
> Caucasus.

Dryden begins, significantly, with a line having no equivalent in the original. In the Latin, Dido goes to the heart of the matter with her scorn of Aeneas' parentage; but Dryden has a good deal of rhetorical padding before, at the end of his second line, we reach Vergil's starting point, by this time with rather less sting than it had:

15. *Aeneid* iv. 365-76.

> False as thou art, and more than false, forsworn:
> Not sprung from noble blood, nor goddess born,
> But hewn from hardened entrails of a rock!
> And rough Hyrcanian tigers gave thee suck!

The whole of Dryden's first line is to be found in Vergil's single explosive word "perfide", but the movement of Dryden's verse would not allow, or survive, so intense a concentration. Again, Dryden makes two lines of Vergil's "nusquam tuta fides":

> Faithless is earth, and faithless are the skies!
> Justice is fled, and truth is now no more!

Some other English translators of this passage make better, or different, attempts at parts of the Latin, but it is fair to suggest that in one way or another they all settle upon an unvarying tone. In some cases it is that kind of extensive rhetorical rant which goes easily with an emphatically shaped metrical structure:

> *Pitt*: (translating "nusquam tuta fides")
> Guilt, guilt prevails; and justice is no more.
> *Conington*:
> No goddess bore you, traitorous man:
> No Dardanus your race began:
> No; 'twas from Caucasus you sprung,
> And tigers nursed you with their young.

In other cases, the broken up quality of Vergil's lines is echoed, but little variation of tone or emphasis emerges:

> *Rhoades*:
> Now, now no more
> Juno, great queen, nor the Saturnian sire
> Looks on these things with equal eyes. Nowhere
> Can faith be trusted. Cast upon my shore
> A beggar, I welcomed him, and, mad the while,
> Set on my throne to share it.

A superficial variation, with the pattern of line endings countered by natural syntactic pauses, is accompanied here by no deeper variety of emotional colour, and the syntactic breaks in mid-line succeed only in largely destroying the formality of metrical shape, where Vergil's success is to produce a deeply resonant variety which yet does not destroy the metrical formality. A slightly subtler version of this point emerges from a comparison of Vergil's "demens" (in the penultimate line) with Rhoades' "mad the while". Vergil's word is located with absolute firmness in the main body and movement of the syntax of his sentence, and yet it is also centrally placed in the line to assist it in turning sharply away from its emotional context. Without "demens", Dido is simply remembering in those two and a half lines at the end of the passage the chivalrous and romantic beginning of her love for Aeneas; "demens" twists into the tormented present, bringing the rest of the sentence with it as it is fully part of its syntactic structure, leaving behind the rest of the sentence as it is a conscious departure from the pattern set by it. Pattern is violated and survives; and we might add that the placing of "demens" in the mid-point of the line is evidence both of Dido's passion breaking uncontrollably forth, and of her careful rhetorical formality.

Of course, the syntactic grip that Latin has upon the words in its sentences is flexible and tenacious beyond anything that English could manage, and Vergil is exploiting fully a resource that is not so much available to Rhoades, and yet "mad the while" is a very poor thing. In place of Vergil's word which is both the keystone of his sentence and the lone voice in a crowd of different words, we have a feeble parenthesis, not concentrated or poised for maximum effect on its surroundings, nor yet for the maximum of haughty withdrawal from them.

Morris, like Rhoades, tries to catch the balance of metrical formality and abrupt pause:

> Traitor! no Goddess brought thee forth, nor Dardanus was first
> Of thine ill race; but Caucasus on spiky crags accurst
> Begot thee; and Hyrcanian dugs of tigers suckled thee.
> Why hide it now? why hold me back lest greater evil be?
> For did he sigh the while I wept? his eyes — what were they moved?
> Hath he been vanquished unto tears, or pitied her that loved?

The metrical swing of the lines, however, prevails steadily upon everything else. By line four the line is established as the unit of shape which is not thereafter disturbed. In line two and three there are indeed unbridgeable pauses after "race" and "thee"; but in line four the pause is bridged easily by the repetition of "why", in line five there is almost no break after "wept" and what break there might have been after "eyes" is bridged by the metrically necessary but otherwise redundant "what", while an extra "the" slipped in before "while" further emphasises the metrical shape.

Stanyhurst has fully the declamatory energy of Morris, but not running in the easy channel of rant:

> No Godes is thye parent, nor th'wart of Dardanus ofspring,
> Thow periurde faytoure: but amydst rocks, Caucasus haggish
> Bred the, with a tigers soure milck vnseasoned, vdderd.
> What shal I dissemble? what poincts more weightye reserue I?
> At my tears showring dyd he sigh? dyd he winck with his eyelyd?
> Ons dyd he weepe vanquisht? dyd he yeeld ons mercye toe loouemate?
> What shal I first vtter? wyl not graund Juno with hastning,
> Nor thee father Saturne with his eyes bent rightlye behold this?
> Fayth quite is exiled: fro the shoare late a runnagat hedgebrat,
> A tarbreeche quystroune dyd I take, with phrensye betrasshed

> I placed in kingdoom, both ships and coompanye gracing.
> Woa to me thus stamping, sutch braynsick foolerye belching.[16]

The first thing to notice about Stanyhurst here, by contrast with the other versions we have just looked at, is the weight he is able to load upon individual words:

> but amydst rocks, Caucasus haggish
> Bred the, with a tigers soure milck vnseasoned, vdderd.

The flexible word order of Latin in part accounts for Vergil's success in using individual words as emotional angles, turns and pauses. Stanyhurst's violation of English order in "Caucasus haggish bred the" separates the noun from the adjective, allowing the voice to concentrate separately on each word; the taking up of an expected and familiar syntactic order with the verb after "haggish" encourages the reader to move on rapidly and ignore any pause for the line ending. By these means, though at the price of a grotesqueness exacted by the violation of the word order, Stanyhurst comes near to the effect of the Latin. Neither the metre nor the syntax is allowed to capture or reduce the words; by contrast Conington's Caucasus sings in its chains:

> No; 'twas from Caucasus you sprung.

Again at the end of the line, as against Conington's "And tigers nursed you with their young", we have:

> with a tigers soure milck vnseasoned, vdderd.

At the end of the line, in Latin fashion, two words drawn from quite different syntactic points in the sentence structure are put next to each other. The line shudders to a halt with a deliberate turning from the expectation invited that the last word will be an easy rhetorical addition to "vnseasoned". The expectation is taken up by the chime of the first syllable of "vdderd", but ground into nothing as the meaning of the word becomes clear, as we have to reach with effort not ease for its syntactic context, and as the final stress on "-erd" comes heavy and ungainly on the ear. The last two words, and especially the last, concentrate within themselves Dido's passion of hatred; rhetorical and syntactic ease are abandoned for it. Like a skilful dancer, Vergil at his most abandoned can recover to suggest that the unshapely move was always part of a subtler pattern; Stanyhurst does not really recover here, but he has an emotional grip upon the situation that Conington's line is nowhere near. In general, Stanyhurst's version of this passage gives us a fundamental varying of emotional tone that the other translators make little attempt at. After "vdderd" there is the scornfully rapid "dyd he winck with his eyelyd?/ Ons dyd he weepe vanquisht?"; then the grandly filled movement of:

---

16. van der Haar, p. 127.

> wyl not graund Juno with hastning,
> Nor thee father Saturne with his eyes bent rightlye behold this?

followed by the quiet "Fayth quite is exiled".

In a passage such as this we see clearly the advantages of the hexameter for Stanyhurst's purposes. We have noted already the kind of attention to every detail of the line encouraged by the use of this quantitive metre. We are used by now to the notion that Stanyhurst's poetic choices are influenced by his feeling for what is latinate and Vergilian, but also and more evidently by his feeling for what will natively suit him. Now, although it would be possible, just about, formally to scan the lines of this passage in a classical way, the use Stanyhurst is here making of the hexameter is English. The stress groupings encouraged in English by the use of a line so long as the hexameter are inherently unstable and the effort of most English poets who have tried hexameters has been to stabilise the movement of the verse into these large groupings, with strangely wooden results. Stanyhurst in this passage precisely exploits the fissiparous quality of this long line in English. Although, as in the eighth line, he can urge the movement to a full line's length, it is the opportunity provided by the tendency of lengthy movement to break down that he chiefly makes use of. So we have dramatically abrupt pause and resumption, and a variety of speed within the line and running across lines. The smaller lines and verbal units hatched out of the hexameters can be particularly tough and indissoluble nuclei ("sutch braynsick foolerye belching") or simply shorter lines held together less fiercely ("with phrensye betrasshed I placed in kingdoom"). The result really is free verse:

> No Godes is thye parent,
> nor th'wart of Dardanus ofspring, thow periurde faytoure:
> but amydst rocks, Caucasus haggish bred the,
> with a tigers soure milck vnseasoned,
> vdderd.

This is not really an appropriate metrical style for a long poem, as Vergil's hexameter is. There is an extensive metrical reliability about Vergil though not the awful predictability of some of his English translators. Stanyhurst, by contrast, is excited by the hexameter at the point of breakdown, and this is a very *local* kind of enthusiasm.

This point might be clarified by being extended somewhat. Stanyhurst's passion for individual words, especially new and strange words whose singularity is more marked, overwhelms any desire he may have had to fit words carefully together with each other, smoothly in a metrical pattern, decorously in an overall semantic and tonal pattern. Where the passage he is translating is itself starkly "local", as here, then the English translator's style does very well. Dido's curse is a point of breakdown for her. I have suggested already that Vergil keeps a savagely energetic formality of shape and tone in the midst of Dido's uncontrolled fury; but that it is the uncontrolled quality that Stanyhurst chiefly conveys. Dido as queen, as foundress of a city, as a woman moving in accord with the extensive and secret forces of destiny is discernible amid the fury in Vergil's passage, but in Stanyhurst we have *this* uncontrollably furious woman at *this* moment of fury, all position, decorum, history and social place forgotten. Stanyhurst is good at the word grotesquely inappropriate in the mouth of a queen addressing a hero:

> runnagat hedgebrat; tarbreeche quystroune; with phrensye betrasshed; sutch braynsick foolerye belching.

So Dido screams, and in Stanyhurst's imagination, though not Vergil's, she stamps her foot as well, a ludicrously undignified and inadequate gesture:

> Woa to me thus stamping.

The passage, then, suits Stanyhurst's strange strengths well; but there are times when his resolute refusal to admit the claims of context, especially the tonal claims, produces very odd and unsuccessful results. Puttenham complains of him:

> as one, who translating certaine bookes of *Virgils Æneidos* into English meetre, said that AEneas was fayne to trudge out of Troy [Stanyhurst: i.7]: which terme became better to be spoken of a beggar, or of a rogue, or a lackey.[17]

Puttenham's defence of decorum is often myopic, but it must be allowed that Stanyhurst's tremendous innovatory energies sometimes lead to disaster. Puttenham in the passage I have quoted from argues essentially that words which are socially inappropriate to the dignity of the characters referred to are unacceptable. I want to attempt to elaborate a more satisfactory distinction between success and failure at the local level of word formation and use in Stanyhurst; and to try to account for the fact that, although his imagination is extraordinarily "verb"-like, having to do with vigorous noise and movement, his failures seem more often to be with verbs than with nouns or adjectives. That vigorous imagination, full of physical activity, is overwhelmingly attracted towards the noun and noun phrase, perhaps because of Stanyhurst's feel for the exciting tension between the activity of his imagination and the static character of the noun, perhaps also because of an instinctive feeling that the noun phrase would undergo better the kind of transformation of the language he was drawn to.

---

17. George Puttenham, *The Arte of English Poesie* (1589), Scolar Press facs. ed., 1968, sig. Hh1 (III. xxiii).

Here Dido pleads with Aeneas to stay in Carthage:

>   yf yeet soom progenye from me
> Had crawld, by the fatherd, yf a cockney dandiprat hopthumb,
> Prittye lad AEneas, in my court, wantoned, ere thow
> Took'st this filthye fleing, that thee with phisnomye lyckned,
> I ne then had reckned my self for desolat owtcaste.[18]

These lines seem to illuminate Stanyhurst's strengths and weaknesses in the use of strange words. What is essential for success is first the casting off of any extended conventional contextual restraint and then the consequent establishing of a sudden unexpected rightness for the word or phrase in the place in which it occurs, a complete though short-lived and local justification for it. The kind of focussed local intensity which will produce this result is the same as that commended by Stanyhurst in the metrical aspect of poetry.[19] In this passage the verb "crawld" is the first word to make a bid for our special attention. We can see quite clearly that the essential action in the context for this verb is something colourless like "come forth", but that emphatic tonal colour has been added. The verb is very isolated in the line (and verbs tend not to gather to themselves reinforcement from other elements in the sentence, as nouns do), but to a reader aware of the emotional complex at this point in the *Aeneid* it seems possible at first that a strange and violent loathing of the wished for but unconceived child could appear and grow suddenly from "crawld". It is only when one realises that nothing further is made of the tone introduced by it that the verb seems a failure, and the more grotesque for its emphatic quality. The verb has brought focussed attention upon itself but has failed to attract enough in the way of reinforcement to produce an intense though short-lived justification of itself. In marked contrast is the immediately following noun phrase. We have here a fine example of the way in which nouns can command support from other sentence elements, so that they are better for this poet's purposes:

>   a cockney dandiprat hopthumb,
> Prittye lad AEneas.

A gentle and affectionate tone is so emphatically established in this phrase as to obliterate "crawld"; and what is more, a whole world of an innocent, petted ("cockney"), tumbling, tiny urchin ("dandiprat") of a child, small enough to hop over my thumb, is brought into being in despite of the grave and adult emotion of the general context. The noun "AEneas" has been taken over from this adult context, and is made part of a dancing group of noun, adjective and verb elements, all drawn powerfully towards noun status. This little noun world appears suddenly,

18. van der Haar, p. 126.
19. See pp. 69-70.

utterly establishes itself, and as suddenly disappears. It is hedged about very evidently by the adult figures of Aeneas ("by the fatherd") and Dido ("in my court"), and the dancing unconcern for all but itself, once past, makes a paler, more distant and formal appearance in that adult world in the verb "wantoned".

A final passage from Stanyhurst's *Aeneid* illustrates how his strange freedom with English word order contributes to the substantival quality of his poetic style. His treatment of word order has clear affinities with what is more naturally possible in Latin but, characteristically, seems chiefly an exploration of what natively the English language might be made to do. It is not the pedantic attempt to latinise English, but the attempt to draw on energies lying dormant in the English language itself. Anna tries to revive her dying sister:

> Speedelye bring me water, thee greene wound swiftlye toe souple;
> And yf in her carcasse soom wind yeet softlye be breathing,
> With lip I wil nurse yt: thus sayd shee climd toe the woodpile,
> Claspt in her arms bracing thee panting murtheres haulfquick,
> With grunt wyde gasping: thee blackned gellyeblud, hardning,
> Shee skums with napkins;[20]

In the first line, the verbs are positioned at the edges so that "me water, thee greene wound" can form an undiluted substantival cluster in the middle of the line. The consequent close association of "water" and "greene", it should be noticed, draws out of "greene" something more than the sense "raw, fresh" formally demanded by the context. The adjective as used of young green shoots, growing things needing water, also intrudes upon the reader, adding its almost Jacobean force to the grotesque horror of the passage as a whole, for the wound is made a green living thing needing nourishment, a parasite in Dido's flesh, and the sense too of the *colour* green thus vividly introduced brings with it the image of flesh corrupted.

In the second part of this passage, the finite verbs "shee climd" and "shee skums" operate also at the periphery of a poetic shape. It is true that "claspt" at the beginning of the fourth line is finite, but the subject "shee" is a little removed from it, and any reader well used to Stanyhurst's style will feel that verb modulating into a participle adjectivally linked to "murtheres". The verbal presence in the rest of the passage between the two finite verbs is participial, the four participles relating to the three players in the scene: Anna ("bracing"), Dido ("panting", "gasping"), the wound ("hardning").

The first of these is awkwardly placed as a present participle or an adjective qualifying "arms"; but it is strongly and effectively placed if we

20. van der Haar, p. 135.

take it as a noun, with "arms" as a genitive. It seems clear that the general shape of these two lines will hardly allow that "bracing" is a verbal substantive rather than a participle, but it is exactly for this reason that the substantival quality of the word is interesting. Stanyhurst's treatment of the surface order of the language, in placing that participle, has released or attracted a substantival energy.

The central and largest block of words in the two lines, equipped with a participle at beginning and end, naturally refers to Dido, "thee panting murtheres haulfquick,/With grunt wyde gasping". The chief action of the lines is Dido panting and gasping for life, but this action has been slowed, congealed; "panting" and "gasping", like the verbs "climd" and "skums" round the larger passage, are given peripheral status, and are made adjectival, so that we have a run of adjective, noun, adjective ("haulfquick"), noun, adjective/adverb ("wyde"), adjective. The important fact that Dido is still half alive is principally conveyed by the static adjective "haulfquick" with its two noun supports. The word "wyde" could either be an adjective qualifying "grunt" (in which case "grunt wyde" almost becomes a single rather grotesque noun) or an adverb modifying "gasping" and giving that participial adjective some verbal force. The third possibility cannot be ruled out, perhaps, that we are to take "grunt wyde" as a compound adjective and "gasping" as a gerund. The whole phrase, in fact, oscillates densely in our understanding, the verbal impetus sublimated into a set of possibilities, rather than cleanly and simply running on forward, as it would if the phrase read "gasping with wyde grunt", each word then firmly set in a single syntactic role.

Lastly the wound: "thee blackned gellyeblud, hardning". Although the noun is formally the object of "skums" in the following line, it can almost as well be taken as an absolute phrase making up part of the near static tableau of Anna, Dido, wound in the two lines we have been considering. The line break after "hardning" is used to insulate the cluster of words somewhat from the motion it comes to be involved with as we get to "skums"; the end of the previous line, too, with its adjective/noun/adjective shape, naturally attracts towards itself a similarly constructed phrase. What verbal motion there is about "hardning" is slowed by its association with the perfective "blackned", and these two verbal adjectives are directed and organised by the compound noun between them, which conveys to the reader substantivally almost all that the two adjectives have to convey.

The observation that the two lines we are discussing consist of three centrally placed nouns, "arms, murtheres, gellyeblud" flanked by adjectives leads one to a final speculation about "with grunt wyde gasping". I have already suggested how one might take "wyde" as adjective, adverb, or almost part of a compound noun; there is the further possibility of "wyde" as a noun by itself, occurring in the place the pattern of the two lines would suggest. The adjective "wyde" thus used in this absolute substantival sense would refer to the wound opened in Dido's body, and the phrase, if understood as referring to the wound, would separate itself from the previous phrase about Dido herself, "thee panting murtheres haulfquick", so that the tableau became Anna, Dido, wound, blood.

It might seem that we have reached an extreme of absurdity in the reading of this passage when we have a wound grunting and gasping; but it is just at this point of grotesque extremity that we may turn again to Vergil:

> infixum stridit sub pectore volnus.[21]

These words come just after the passage Stanyhurst is translating here, and when he comes to them he gives them a rather anodyne rendering:

> thee deadlye push yrcks her.[22]

This is perhaps because he had already, two lines previously, allowed into his version Vergil's strident wound. What sound quite Vergil imagined as he wrote "volnus stridit" is unclear; but it is clear that he imagined the wound as a living thing in Dido's flesh uttering its sounds. There is no doubt, too, that the living wound which consumes her at the end of Book IV links with the wound she fed with her blood in the first lines, and that the whole of Book IV is encompassed by the energetically grotesque double image.

Vergil is deep in strange imaginings here and is followed, no doubt clumsily, but followed by Stanyhurst. By contrast Dryden, for example, will not venture so far as living wounds, either at the beginning of Book IV or at the end. His version of this passage about Dido's death is *respectably* horrific. He has none of Vergil's malevolently black blood, none of the sense of hopelessly disgusting mess which threatens to overwhelm the civilised movement of the Latin, and which in Stanyhurst breaks free of all restraint as Anna soaks up the foul scum of blood with napkins. It is difficult for us to acknowledge that all the dignity of life is so close to nauseous physical corruption and mess, and Dryden is easier reading as he makes something literary and rhetorical of the disgusting scene:

> "Bring, bring me water; let me bathe in death
> Her bleeding wounds, and catch her parting breath".
> Then up the steep ascent she flew, and prest
> Her dying sister to her heaving breast;

21. *Aeneid* iv. 689.
22. van der Haar, p. 135.

> With cries succeeding cries her robes unbound,
> To stanch the blood that issu'd from the wound.

One's last word about Dryden's strange precursor might be that none of the literary considerations, for tone, metre, syntax, which would normally bear down from outside upon the imagination expressing itself at this or that moment and make it fit together with many other things, respond to many other expectations, both inside the work and outside, is allowed much weight by Stanyhurst. Instead, the *moment* prevails, in a single sound, a word, a clump of sounds or words, an arrangement of clumps, so that the *innate* characteristic of the moment's imagination spreads out into the three thousand or so lines of his poem. There is, then, the irresponsible trusting of the moment's imagination; and indeed the whole of Stanyhurst's poem is, in comparison with his life as a whole, a moment having no regard to anything but itself. The fourth book of the poem, Stanyhurst tells us himself, was ten days' work, and the earlier books were done by fits and starts, "as my leasure and pleasure would serue mee".[23] The whole of his poetic output is contained in the little 1582 volume and the rest of a long life was passed unpoetically. He became a Catholic priest and no doubt that was then the business of his life and not poetry. In this respect he is as different as possible from a more famous sixteenth-century priest and poet, St. Robert Southwell, for whom poetry was one of the weapons in the battle for souls, and whose poetry is written in the shadow of that vital external consideration.[24]

Perhaps he does not differ so much, however, from Southwell's fellow Jesuit and poet, Hopkins, whose poetic attitudes seem to oscillate uneasily between the extremes represented by the two earlier poets, and whose style has an abandoned idiosyncracy at times that seems to resemble Stanyhurst's:

> How to kéep — is there ány any, is there none such, nowhere
>   known some, bow or brooch or braid or brace, láce, latch
> or catch or key to keep
> Back beauty, keep it, beauty, beauty, beauty,...from
>   vanishing away?[25]

> Thee gates of warfare wyl then bee mannacled hardly
> With steele bunch chayne knob, clingd, knurd, and narrolye lincked.[26]

---

23. van der Haar, p. 56.
24. See Southwell's preface to a group of short lyrics addressed "to his loving Cosen" (*The Poems of Robert Southwell*, ed. by James H. McDonald & Nancy Pollard Brown, Oxford, 1967, p. 1).
25. Gerard Manley Hopkins, "The Leaden Echo and the Golden Echo", lines 1-2.
26. van der Haar, p. 69.

THE LIBRARY OF SIR THOMAS TEMPEST:
ITS ORIGINS AND DISPERSAL

A.I. Doyle

Fourteen medieval manuscripts in the British Library have an inscription of ownership which led the late Dr C.E. Wright to ask, after tracing the path by which they apparently entered the Harleian collection, "And how did Sir Thomas Tempest of Stella, co.Durham, obtain so many manuscripts from the library of Durham Priory?".[1] Not all of them (twelve certainly) came from the Cathedral Priory but he could have added, if he was aware, that many more books, most of them printed, with the same inscription "Sir Thomas Tempest Bart" have been found in a number of other libraries, and that the majority of them had also belonged to the medieval Benedictine monastery at Durham and its monks or former monks.[2] It appears that they had been kept together until that inscription was made in them, supposed from the style of writing to be in the time of the fourth baronet of the family, i.e. 1662-92,[3] and that they were dispersed in groups, chiefly by gift or loan, in the course of the following century or so. Dr Wright noted that the son and heir of Sir Thomas dying abroad in 1698 was succeeded by his sister Jane who married Lord Widdrington and after her death in 1714 he was induced to give or sell

---

1 C.E. Wright, *Fontes Harleiani: a Study of the Sources of the Harleian Collection of Manuscripts . . . in the British Museum* (London 1972), pp. xx, 325; cf. *The Diary of Humfrey Wanley 1715-26*, eds. C.E. & R. Wright (London 1966), vol. I, p. 73.
2 E. Bonney, "Some Durham Abbey books in the College Library", *Ushaw Magazine*, vol. XV (1905), pp. 247-63; B. Payne, "More Durham Abbey books in the Library", *ibid.* LXII (1952), 41-7; those certainly from Durham are listed by N.R. Ker, *Medieval Libraries of Great Britain*, 2nd. ed. (London 1964), pp. 61-76, within which all 30 Ushaw entries were Tempest's. Dr Ker, to whom the present account is indebted for his list of Tempest books in other places, at the time of his death was preparing a supplement to *Medieval Libraries* which will include a number more, at least eight at Ushaw. I owe notes of other books there to Mgr B. Payne and Dr J. Rhodes.
3 This identification, made independently by Bonney and Wright, is also supported by comparison of his grandfather's signature (Durham County Record Office, D/Lo/F.718 of 1623, D/X487/1/122 of 1626) and his own (D/Lo/F.136 of 1666, D/Lo/F.721 of 1670), which excludes the former, yet leaves it doubtful if the inscriptions in the books were actually written by or for the latter.

I. Upper half of title-page of Durham Cathedral Library Inc. 3: Bartholomeus Anglicus, Strassbourg 1491, with medieval Durham Priory classmark A8 and inscription of Stephen Marley as a gift from Thomas Swalwell, both monks of Durham, 1537.

II. Upper half of title-page of Durham Cathedral Inc. 25: Antonius de Rampengolis, Venice 1496, with inscription of Nicholas Marley, monk of Durham, 1536, 'ex dono nullius sed care emptus'.

those manuscripts to Lord Harley, between 1720 and 1731.[4]

The answer to Dr Wright's question lies in the antecedents of this branch of the Tempest family.[5] Their forebears were settled at Lanchester, co.Durham, and Holmside Hall, just north of it, from the fifteenth century and at Stanley, in the same north-west quarter of the county, from early in the sixteenth. Nicholas Tempest of Lanchester and Stanley who died in 1538 or 1539 had married Anne Marley of Gibside and one of her brothers was Stephen, a monk of Durham who was sub-prior at the suppression of the monastery in 1539.[6] A somewhat younger monk, Nicholas Marley, was most likely another brother.[7] Their names as owners, either as monks or later as canons of the new Cathedral Chapter, occur on many of the books which were later Sir Thomas Tempest's, though by no means all. Other monks whose names occur, however, are also found as previous owners of the Marleys' books and often as donors to them.[8] And none of the Marleys' books seem to survive which did not pass through Tempest hands. The latest date of publication or acquisition found in any of Stephen's books is 1537 but for Nicholas 1560. It is clear from many other books from the Cathedral Priory, and from other monastic communities, that before their abolition monks were allowed to have books for their individual use, and to buy and give them, though to members of their own community only;[9] after its dissolution and their secularisation they felt free to keep anything they had, including items marked more specifically as from the institutional collections, and even from the chained library, which must have been broken up.[10]

4 The possibility was first mentioned in 1720; one manuscript was bought through a bookseller in 1725 and another was given by Lord Widdrington in 1731, but the dates and terms for the remainder are uncertain: see Wright, *Diary*, ut supra, n.1.

5 R. Surtees, *History & Antiquities of the County Palatine of Durham*, vol. II (Durham 1820), pp. 271, 325-7; E. Blanche Tempest, "Tempest of Holmeside, County Durham", *The Northern Genealogist*, 1895, pp. 5-14; British Library MS. Add. 40670, fol. 18.

6 Surtees, II, 229-30, 253, 256; T.W. Marley, *The Marleys of . . . County Durham*, 2nd ed. (London 1921), p. 6.

7 Their names occur in a list of nine members of the family, after the two parents and separated from three more of the name, in the Priory's *Liber Vitae*, facsimile ed. A.H. Thompson (Surtees Society 136, 1923), f.82v.

8 Ker, *Medieval Libraries*, 256-7; cf. A.B. Emden, *Biographical Register of the University of Oxford 1501-40*, p. 379, whose Nicholas Marley senior, incidentally, is in fact unconnected with Durham.

9 See Ker, pp. xxvi-vii; it may be noted here that more printed books can thus be connected with Durham than any other British medieval community, and that is largely though not wholly owing to the Tempest collection.

10 Harley MS.3858 has the desk-numbers of the chained library and most of the other manuscripts have catalogue identifications: cf. A.J. Piper, "The libraries of the monks of Durham", in *Medieval Scribes, Manuscripts & Libraries: Essays presented to N.R. Ker*, eds. M.B. Parkes & A.G. Watson (London 1978), pp. 213-49.

Stephen and Nicholas Marley having been appointed, like most of their fellow-monks, canons in the new Cathedral Chapter in 1541, so continued through the accelerating reformation under Henry VIII and Edward VI and then the return of the old order under Mary, but on its reversal by Elizabeth they and a number of their colleagues refused to accept the new articles of religion in 1559, had their benefices sequestrated and were compelled to give sureties for £200 each that they would appear in London before the royal commissioners when required. Stephen Marley's sureties were Thomas Tempest of Lanchester, his nephew, and William Hogeson of the same, probably his sister's second husband; while Nicholas Marley's were Thomas Tempest and Robert Tempest of Holmside, Thomas's cousin and former guardian.[11] Stephen may have subsequently temporised, for he was not apparently replaced till 1572, but Nicholas, whose answers to the visitors had been more uncompromising, lost his canonry and vicarage of Pittington in 1560.[12] It was in that year that one book was given *to* him *by* Thomas Tempest,[13] and in 1562, described by the royal visitors as "unlearned" (though he and his fellow Robert Dalton were, as the late Canon Greenslade remarked, both B.D.s of Oxford!) he was "confined to the Bishoprick of Durham, but not to come within eight miles of the city" — the distance almost exactly of the Tempest seats of Holmside and Stanley and Lanchester.[14] Despite this, in 1563 he matriculated at the University of Louvain and is said to have been recommended for a pension from the King of Spain.[15] He does not appear in lists of Catholic exiles of 1577-80, however, by which time he would have been in his 70s, nor do we know when Stephen Marley died, presumably after 1571.[16] Thus it seems likely that Nicholas took his books with him to a Tempest house in 1560 and left them there on going abroad, while Stephen's books, and other Durham ones not certainly connected with either, could have been taken then or somewhat later if he

---

11 *The Royal Visitation of 1559: Act Book for the Northern Province*, ed. C.J. Kitching (Surtees Society 187, 1975), pp. xxiv, 24-5, 109.

12 P. Mussett, *Lists of Deans & Major Canons of Durham* (Durham 1974), pp. 50, 69.

13 Ricardus de S. Victore, *De Trinitate* (Paris 1510), Bodleian Library, Oxford, Broxb.29.13/R 1327.

14 H. Gee, *The Elizabethan Clergy and the Settlement of Religion 1558-1564* (Oxford 1898), pp. 79, 157, 181; S.L. Greenslade, "The last monks of Durham Cathedral Priory", *Durham University Journal*, vol. XLI (1948-49), pp. 107-13.

15 Emden, ut supra; A.M.C. Forster, "An outline history of the Catholic Church in North East England from the sixteenth century", *Northern Catholic History*, no. 2 (1975), p. 5.

16 A replacement in his canonry would presumably be recorded as by deprivation even if he had died in the interval. As he was ordained deacon in 1517 he must have been about 80 by 1572.

did not have to find another home so soon. The inventory of Thomas Tempest at Stanley, 1569, mentions "Mr Marlees chamber", for which Stephen is a good candidate, unless Nicholas had come back.[17] Thomas's cousin Robert, of Holmside, with his son Michael, in the same year, 1569, was deeply involved in the rising of the northern earls, and on its collapse the two escaped to Belgium with another son who became a secular priest, as later did one of Michael's; both Robert and Michael lost their lands or life-interests by attainder.[18] Though Thomas and his immediate family were not implicated, others of their kin were, and it would hardly be surprising if this line of Tempest should have also remained attached to the ancient faith and have kept the books which embodied the monastic tradition of theological learning, still of potential utility to clergy with a scholastic training, as well as representing family alliances. Nicholas, Thomas's first son, who seems to have settled at Stella first by 1582, although he only bought the manor in 1600,[19] was in fact conforming to the established church and claimed to be bringing up his many children likewise in 1594, when his wife had been imprisoned for her recusancy, in which she persisted nonetheless;[20] it may have been her rather than him whom Bishop Matthew of Durham in 1598, reporting on the members of an active group around Lanchester, meant by "that great recusant".[21] His eldest son, Thomas, who inherited in 1626 the baronetcy his father had acquired in 1622, was firmly declared to be "no Recusant" in a composition of 1632 for a widow who was,[22] and his son, Sir Richard, who succeeded in 1641, by his own confession in *A discourse touching choyce of religion*, addressed to his mother and printed in the 1640s, most probably, had wavered in his beliefs before becoming convinced of the Catholic faith.[23] He sent his first son Thomas to the English College at

17 *Wills and Inventories from the Registry at Durham*, ed. W. Greenwell, vol. III (Surtees Society 112, 1906), p. 48.
18 C. Sharp, *Memorials of the Rebellion of 1569* (London 1840), pp. 33, 229, 264; G. Anstruther, *The Seminary Priests: a Dictionary*, vol. I (Durham 1968), pp. 348-50; M.E. James, *Family, Lineage and Civil Society... in the Durham Region 1500-1640* (Oxford 1974), p. 206.
19 His second son was baptised at Ryton in 1582 and another buried in 1587 (Surtees, II, 270); the letters patent for the sale, 1 March 1600 (n.s.) are Sheffield City Libraries Archive Dept 3287 and also include the chapel of St Edmund in Gateshead and land at Lanchester.
20 *Memoirs of Ambrose Barnes*, ed. W.H.D. Longstaffe (Surtees Society 50, 1867), pp. 295-6, a letter to Lord Burghley from her kinsman Ralph Eure; *Miscellanea*, ed. C. Talbot (Catholic Record Society 53, 1961), p. 52, recusants presented 1595: "Isabell Tempest, wife of Nicholas Tempest late of Stelloe and nowe of Newcastle uppon Tyne gent an housholder". Did he move to evade her prosecution, and perhaps his own?
21 Surtees, II, 322; it is grammatically ambiguous.
22 *Miscellanea*, ed. Talbot, p. 401.
23 The only known copies of the book (not in Wing or Clancy) are at Ushaw and

Douai which he left on completing the humanities in 1661, six months before his father's death, with the commendation "Iuvenis magnae expectationis, discretus et valde pius".[24] This must have been the man whose name was inscribed in the books which had come down to him, chiefly yet not exclusively from the Durham monks and canons.[25]

Even amongst the earliest books there are some certainly from other sources: a Serapion (Venice 1479) in a contemporary continental blind-stamped binding and with foreign ownership inscriptions, which might well have been bought in northern France or in Belgium;[26] a Burley (Venice 1500) in a contemporary London binding, with only English secular owners up to 1520 and no evidence of Durham ones;[27] and a Lefèvre d'Étaples (n.p. 1521) in an English panel binding which belonged to a Franciscan friar.[28] A Sarum pocket breviary (Paris c.1506) with many manuscript obits must have belonged to one of the clergy of the college at Lanchester or of the chantry founded at Holmside by the Tempests as late as 1540.[29] Others probably or certainly post-date the Marleys' collections: e.g. Nicholas Sander, *The supper of our Lord set foorth according to the truth of the gospell and catholike faith* (Louvain

the British Library from the Hassop Inner Library. As the author is called Baronet it cannot be before 1642, it must be before 1660 and probably precedes his other book, *An Entertainment of Solitariness* 1648, dedicated to his brother from Amsterdam, on which he is called Knight and Baronet. He was a royalist commander in the civil war. Cf. *Records of the Committees for Compounding etc. 1643-60*, ed. R. Welford (Surtees Society III, 1905), pp. 356-7.

24 *Douai College Documents 1639-1794*, ed. P.R. Harris (Catholic Record Society 63, 1972), p. 16.

25 And who may have justified Surtees' statement (II, 270) that the Tempests at Stella "resided here in catholic loyalty and splendour".

26 Newcastle upon Tyne, Literary and Philosophical Society; the manuscript index, annotations and three early ownerships are not in English hands; the late Dr W.S. Mitchell was not able to localise the binding tools, but they are of a north European type. It has a late 18th- or early 19th-century bookplate of Thomas Davidson of Newcastle.

27 Bristol, University Library; it belonged to Christopher Falowfeld before 21 March 1503 (when the witness Ralph Tracy, prior of Sheen Charterhouse, was murdered) and was acquired from him in 1520 (n.s.) by John Huchynson; Emden, *Biographical Register... Oxford to 1500*, vol. II (Oxford 1958), p. 665, says Falowfeld died by August 1512. It belonged to Cosmo Gordon in 1906.

28 Ushaw College XVII.E.5.5, from Yealand Conyers: "frater Gyllsonus", "boniventura ora pro nobis". It is of course not impossible that this and the preceding item came into the hands of Durham monks before the Dissolution but one would expect a superseding claim.

29 Ampleforth Abbey C.V.144: see A.I. Doyle, "Two medieval servicebooks from the parish of Lanchester", *Transactions of the Architectural & Archaeological Society of Durham & Northumberland*, new series, vol. VI (1982), pp. 19-21.

1566);³⁰ Luis de Molina, *Commentaria in primam Divi Thomae partem* (Cuenca 1592);³¹ *Orationes funebres* (Hanover 1613), which had belonged to Thomas Swinburne, one of a north-eastern family as mixed in their religious allegiances as the Tempests and as repetitive of the same Christian names;³² and T. Farnaby, *Systema grammaticum* (London 1641), which one may guess had fed the studies of the fourth baronet, born the year after its publication.³³

There is not, however, enough evidence to show that Sir Thomas or his forebears were very notable book-collectors in their own time, and it is fortunate that his interests were presumably conservative, not fashionable, pride in his inheritance perhaps, for the remarkable proportion of the fifteenth and sixteenth-century volumes which retain their early bindings (and even more did before the nineteenth century) could easily have been eliminated by a wish for neat rows of gilded spines and elegant covers, and with the old endpapers would have disappeared much of the pedigrees of provenance. When Sir Thomas died in 1692 the detailed inventory of Stella Hall's contents mentions simply "The Library of Books" but values it, at £60, more highly than any head other than the owner's clothes and money in hand, out of a total of £406 for house and farm goods.³⁴ If the books had been, for a large part, earlier at Stanley, it may have been when they were moved to Stella that they were inscribed, and it may have been done for the benefit of a resident chaplain (though there is understandably no word in the inventory about a chapel), or to protect the collection for and from his successors, as its subsequent treatment proved to be apposite.³⁵ By 1700, when Sir Thomas's daughter

---

30 R. Waterfield, Oxford, catalogue 11, no. 550, said to have marginal notes by Sir Thomas Tempest.

31 Ushaw College V.B.4.5.

32 I owe the note of this, formerly in the Hassop library, to Mr J.C.H. Aveling; the second baronet was godfather along with Sir Thomas Swinburne at the baptism of Thomas son of Mr Thomas Swinburne at St Oswald's church, Durham, in 1627: *Parish Registers 1538-71*, ed. A.W. Headlam (Durham 1891), p. 74; John Swinburne of the Capheaton (Northumberland) strongly recusant family, who married Sir Thomas Tempest's daughter about 1631, had access to MS. Harley 4843 about 1638 (Bodleian Library, Oxford, Dodsworth MS. 45, f.57v); and John Cosin, Canon of Durham, appears to have annotated it sometime before the Civil War, to judge from the writing (f.16r).

33 Sotheby & Co., New Bond Street, London, auction catalogue, 29 January 1973, lot 43.

34 Durham University Department of Palaeography, Probate Records, 15 August 1692. Durham Cathedral Library Raine MS. 2, p. 271, has a large engraved armorial bookplate (not in the Franks collection, British Library) of "Sir Thomas Tempest of Stella in the Bishoprick of Durham Bart the 199 Bart in Creation", which I have not found elsewhere. There is no indication of its provenance.

35 Stanley seems to have been occupied by younger sons of the family from early in

Jane had succeeded her brother in the family estates and had married Lord Widdrington, there was a Benedictine chaplain, and the hall was served by members of that order until 1732, followed by secular priests and a Jesuit.[36] It was in the Benedictine period, and after Jane's death in 1714, that Widdrington (who had in law lost his title by attainder for his involvement in the Jacobite rising of 1715) disposed of the batch of medieval manuscripts to the Harleian library, presumably on behalf of their son Henry, though he came of age in 1722 and could have been styled Lord Widdrington even in the life of his father.[37]

Jane had left an endowment for the permanent maintenance of a priest at Stella[38] and when, on Henry's death in 1774, the family estates went to Thomas Eyre of Hassop (Derbyshire), his nephew, the latter appointed a kinsman and namesake, the Rev. Thomas Eyre to the mission there, where he served until 1792,[39] the year of his patron's death. The latter must have felt free to remove books to Hassop, where he established an Inner and Outer Library, the former being bequeathed by his will and private instructions to the Bishop of the Midland District "for the joint use of the Priests at or near Hassop and at Hathersage", with money for a library room in a house to be built for the priest at Hassop.[40] He seems to have taken a comparatively small number of those inscribed with the fourth baronet's name, but he may have given others informally for similar purposes in the Northern District, through his namesake, and when, by the will, the contents of Stella Hall were sold (for the purpose of building a separate chapel), the books were not obviously meant to be included, though a few may have escaped that way.[41] Some, besides the

the 17th century. The standard inscription appears to have been done by one hand at one time.

36 Northumberland County Record Office, RCN 4/31 includes the Rev. T. Eyre's list of the clergy serving Stella 1700-93; RCD 6/4 has transcriptions of those originals by the Rev. W. Vincent Smith.

37 G.E. Cokayne & V. Gibbs, *Complete Peerage*, vol. XII, part ii (1959), pp. 629-30, say that he did not do so before his father's death in 1743.

38 Northumberland C.R.O., RCN 4/31 and RCD 6/4.

39 Anstruther, *The Seminary Priests*, vol. IV (Great Wakering 1977), pp. 99-100, has him at Stella only 1775-80 but by his own account, ut supra, n.36, he was there till 1792.

40 R. Meredith, "The Eyres of Hassop from the Test Act to Emancipation", *Recusant History*, vol. 9 (1968), pp. 273-4; Northumberland C.R.O., RCD 6/4, p. 341, copy of private instructions, 12 Oct. 1788.

41 It may be a coincidence, but in a letter from Minsteracres, 4 June 1793, Northumberland C.R.O., RCN 4/3 (Stella mission papers), Henry Rutter writes to the Rev. T. Eyre, "When at Newcastle I enquired for the books you had marked in Charnley's Catalogue, but was told by his son that they were dispos'd of: however I suspect he did not know much about them & the old man was not in the shop". This may relate to the incunabula bought from Charnley by the Dean & Chapter of

Harley manuscripts, had gone earlier: a fourteenth-century manuscript of Durandus, *Rationale divinorum officiorum*, from Durham Priory, belonged to John Jackson, citizen of London, by 1781, whether by purchase or gift unstated.[42] The Sarum breviary now at Ampleforth Abbey could have been taken by one of the Benedictine chaplains, earlier in the century,[43] but one of the books at Downside Abbey has an early nineteenth-century inscription of Brother Maurus Hodgson (a Tyneside family) which suggests it was acquired then.[44] Some scattered items may have migrated with individual members of the clergy or of families connected with Stella: G. Reisch, *Margarita philosophica* (Basle 1517), in a contemporary panel binding, bought by Stephen Marley as monk of Durham for 3s.4d. in 1530, came back to the Cathedral Library in 1970 from an auction of books belonging to the Welds, a Catholic family with marriage ties to many others, including owners and occupants of Stella.[45]

The great majority of Sir Thomas Tempest's inscribed books (over 80 volumes against over 40 known elsewhere) are however now at Ushaw College, assembled at different times and from different sources since its foundation in 1808 with the Rev. Thomas Eyre as its first President. A number he is known to have brought with him, from Crook Hall, a temporary residence in the county of the students from the English College, Douai, belonging to the north, of whom he had taken charge after their escape from the French Revolution.[46] A few have a late eighteenth-century ex-libris of the library of the secular clergy of Durham and Northumberland "apud Os Vedrae" (i.e. Wearmouth, now Sunderland), which seems to have been moved to the residence of the Vicars Apostolic at Old Elvet, Durham, and in 1848 broken up, with the pick coming to Ushaw.[47] Either as a result of this or earlier dispersal from Stella, others have come subsequently to Ushaw from the missions at Hexham and Esh. Some bear the names of local clergy, chiefly that of

---

Durham in 1838 (see n. 53 below); they do not occur in W. Charnley's *Catalogue ... 21 Jan. 1793* (Newcastle Central Library) but there could have been a later catalogue which I have not traced.

42 John Forbes of Boyndlie collection, deposited in Aberdeen University Library, recorded by Dr N.R. Ker in 1968: *Catalogi Veteres Librorum Ecclesiae Cathedralis Dunelm.* (Surtees Society 7, 1838), p. 76, in the 1395 catalogue, identified by *secundo folio*.

43 See n.29 above.

44 Ker, *Medieval Libraries*, p. 62; I owe descriptions and reproductions to the kindness of Dr D.M. Rogers. This is 970, Jerome, 1497.

45 Durham Cathedral Library P.X.40, lot 105 in Christie, King St, auction 24 July 1970.

46 B. Payne, "The Ushaw Library", *Ushaw Magazine*, vol. 44 (1934), pp. 199-214, esp. p. 202.

47 Bonney, *Ushaw Mag.*, XV, pp. 256-7.

Henry Rutter, who from 1785 to 1822 was chaplain to the Silvertop family at Minsteracres (Northumberland), then priest at Yealand Conyers (Lancashire) until 1834 and at Dodding Green (Westmorland) 1834-38.[48] The Silvertops had risen through Stella, and continued to be closely concerned with the hall and estate for its absent owners in the later eighteenth century, and in the establishment of public chapels in both places.[49] Rutter was on respectful terms with the Rev. Thomas Eyre and it must have been with his consent that he removed a large number of Sir Thomas Tempest's books, first to Minsteracres, where he left a few, and then to Yealand, but giving some to Ushaw. In 1952 three volumes were found in the remains of the Minsteracres library and 37 at Yealand Conyers, and deposited at Ushaw College.[50] It is possible others remain in ecclesiastical and family libraries, in the north or south,[51] but the scope for discovery shrinks fast, as *aggiornamento* takes its toll, except through the book-trade.

In 1974 the Inner Library of Hassop, which had been deposited for a number of years at St Hugh's College, Tollerton Hall (Nottinghamshire), was sold by auction at Sotheby's as the property of the Roman Catholic Diocese of Nottingham, despite last-minute protests from the Catholic Record Society and individuals who knew its history and contents.[52] The Dean and Chapter of Durham Cathedral, which in or before 1838 had bought at least six incunabula, five of them Durham monks', with Tempest and Widdrington inscriptions, from Charnley the Newcastle bookseller, by whom they may have been got at the sale of Stella contents or through an intermediary,[53] and which had subsequently purchased

48 Anstruther, IV, 16-17.

49 E. Mackenzie & M. Ross, *An Historical . . . View of the County Palatine* (Newcastle upon Tyne 1834), vol. I, pp. 189-93.

50 B. Payne, *Ushaw Mag.*, LXII, pp. 41-47.

51 Dr Ker had recorded ones at Blairs College (now deposited in the National Library of Scotland), the London Oratory, Hawkesyard Priory and Mount St Bernard, besides those at Ampleforth and Downside already mentioned.

52 Sotheby, New Bond Street, catalogue, 7 October 1974, with introductory historical note and facsimile of bookplate 1792. A contemporary manuscript catalogue of the Hassop library from the Old Elvet mission or Vicars Apostolic residence is now deposited at Ushaw College.

53 Durham Cathedral Library Inc. 2, 3, 35, 44, 45 as listed in Ker, *Medieval Libraries*, pp. 71-72. Among papers on library history is a list of them by G.T. Fox, 1838, mentioning their repair in London. I am grateful to Mr P. Mussett for finding a payment of 12 guineas to Charnley in the year 1837-38 for books, but there is a possibility the incunabula had been acquired by Charnley in 1792-93: see n. 41 above. One, Inc. 4, Caracciolus, *Sermones* (Strasbourg, 1497), with no Durham monastic connections, bears the name of Henry Brandling, who was mayor of Newcastle (d. 1578), from a part-recusant family, before Sir Thomas Tempest's inscription. Another, Inc. 49, Turrecremata, Quaestiones (1484), is said by Fox to have been Lord Widdrington's though no evidence is now visible.

and was given two more,⁵⁴ besides the Reisch of 1517 already mentioned, was able (with the help of the fund administered by the Victoria and Albert Museum) to secure the two Hassop books known to have Durham monastic as well as Sir Thomas Tempest's inscriptions, an incunable of 1494 and Erasmus's edition of St Jerome's letters (Basle 1524), the latter with annotations of great interest.⁵⁵ Since the sale later books of Sir Thomas have consequently reappeared in various booksellers' catalogues, to reach appreciative homes, one hopes, and it is clear that some books from Hassop, the Inner as well as the Outer Library, had been sold, legitimately or not, before.⁵⁶ Early Tempest books which came from Durham Priory certainly or possibly, and some certainly not, are now in academic libraries as far afield as Los Angeles and Toronto as well as Cambridge, London and Oxford, and possibly in many other ownerships. One manuscript and one incunable which have been offered for sale more than once are at present untraced (at least by me).⁵⁷ Not every book whose location is known has yet been thoroughly inspected for signs of its provenance before or after Sir Thomas Tempest Baronet; when it can be done the proportionate contributions of the several sources of the collection and of the different agents in its dispersal ought to become clearer. It must have been a special *pietas* towards the last monks of Durham and their church which preserved what is predominantly their collection so well and so long, and, as study of their annotations advances, more of the books without explicit inscriptions can be recognised as theirs from the individualities of handwriting alone. Although clear evidence of comparable value is even more dispersed than in this case of the Tempests, there can be little doubt, from the later sympathetic annotation of many manuscripts, incunabula and post-incunabula, that recusant or church-papist owners were responsible for an exceptionally important share of the preservation of our medieval literature, liturgy and theology, to the benefit of subsequent study and judgment.

54 Inc. 21b and 25, both in Ker, the former given by Sir Stephen Gaselee in 1928, the latter having the bookplate of Joseph Beard, Alderley (19/20th century).

55 *Repertorium in postillam N. de Lyra* now Inc. 15a; Jerome is D.VI.37 and instead of the standard inscription has a large and current one, without "Bart", which looks more like a signature.

56 Chicago University Library MS. 156 has the Inner Library plate: the catalogue at Ushaw has items which did not occur in the auction.

57 G. de Tignonville, *Dits moraux de philosophes*, with miniature, 15th century, with bookplate of J. Borthwick, sold at Sotheby's, 3 June 1946, no. 198: B. Quaritch Ltd, cat. 699, no. 55 & cat. 716, no. 304. J. Lathbury, *Liber moralium* (Oxford 1482), from Chatsworth Library, sold at Christie's 1977 and Sotheby's 24 Sept. 1979, lot 186A: C.W. Traylen, Guildford, cat. 81 (1974), no. 19; cat. 95 (1983), no. 23.

SOME BINDINGS FOR CHARLES I

Mirjam M. Foot

The bindings from Charles I's library, now in the British Library, present a confused picture. Most, though not all, came with the Old Royal Library in 1757, and can be identified by the presence of the Museum Britannicum stamps[1] and the successive press-marks showing their places in Montagu House and in the stacks of the British Museum Library before they were moved to the cases where they are kept to-day. Most can be traced in the Montagu House alphabetical author catalogue of the Old Royal Library[2] and a substantial number can be identified in the inventory of the Royal library drawn up by Patrick Young in 1650 (C.120.h.6).[3] All have the royal arms stamped on both covers.[4]

Five different arms blocks and two different large blocks showing the Prince of Wales's feathers were used for Charles I when he was Prince of Wales, all of which had been in use previously for Prince Henry. A large number of arms blocks, varying both in size and shape were used after Charles's accession. Several of these blocks had been employed on bindings for James I and a few were still in use after the restoration of King Charles II to the throne in 1660.

These arms blocks can be divided into five types: a large block without supporters but with decorative scroll work, frequently used for James I;[5] a large block with mask and claw handles of which at least 16 variants are known, some also used for James I and Charles II; a large block with lion and unicorn supporters and garlanded with vine branches, used oc-

---

1 S. Jayne and F.R. Johnson, *The Lumley Library*, London 1956, p. 25, note 1.
2 *Ibid.*, p. 23, p. 295, note 6.
3 *Ibid.*, pp. 20-21. See also J. Kemke, *Patricius Junius*, K. Dziatzko (ed.), *Sammlung Bibliothekswissenschaftlicher Arbeiten* XII, Leipzig 1898, pp. xxv-xxvi. The combinations of letters and figures quoted in brackets throughout this article are the current British Library press marks of the books discussed.
4 Royal arms do not necessarily denote royal ownership. However, most of the bindings discussed here are either elaborately decorated presentation copies or belong to the Old Royal Library, or both.
5 Used during Charles I's reign in two variants on: *The Book of Common Prayer* [and] *Psalmes,* London 1630 (not from the Old Royal Library, possibly made for a member of the royal household; C.82.b.9) and on J. de Bie. *La France metallique*, Paris 1634 (dedicated to Charles I, from the Old Royal Library; 603.k.3).

casionally for James I and at least once for Charles II; and several kinds of round blocks without handles or supporters in roughly two sizes, the smaller of which is often found on small books in vellum bindings. The type with the mask and claw handles is the most common. In the British Library binding files it has been called the Stuart Royal Arms (SRA) and its 16 variants have been numbered.

The first two variants, SRA I and II, were mainly used for James I. John Bill's binder used SRA I.[6] It is just possible that J. Norden's *England. An intended Guyde*, London 1625 (C.77.d.16) was bound after James I's death, but though it has the SRA I arms block it did not belong to the Old Royal Library and it may well have been made for a member of the royal household. The one binding from Charles I's library decorated with SRA II that I have found covers T. Harriot, *Artis analyticae praxis*, London 1631 (C.74.e.4).[7]

SRA III was used almost exclusively[8] for Charles I. It is found on R. Crakanthorp, *Defensio Ecclesiae Anglicanae*, London 1625 (C.82.d.3), possibly bound before Charles's accession, as well as on L. Guicciardini, *Description de touts les Pays-Bas*, Amsterdam 1625,[9] H. Isaacson, *Saturni Ephemerides*, London 1633 (C.77.i.4),[10] and G. Sandys, *A Paraphrase upon the Devine Poems*, London 1638 (C.83.i.7).

Of SRA IV only one example is known used for James I. SRA V (fig. 1A) I have found on three bindings for Charles I. The *Speculum Romanae magnificentiae*, [Rome 1519-75] (C.77.i.11) tooled in gold with this arms block and the initials CR may well have been the "very great book in fol. of prints being of several antiquities of Statutes and Roman buildings . . . given to the King by the Earl of Exeter".[11] The other two bindings with this arms block cover Thomas Morton, *The Institution of the Sacrament*,

---

6 H.M. Nixon, *Five Centuries of English Bookbinding*, London 1978, n.28.

7 An example of this block used on a binding for James I is illustrated in H.B. Wheatly, *Remarkable Bindings in the British Museum*, London 1889, pl. XLVIII.

8 A binding with this block, probably made for James I, covers a very elaborately tooled *Book of Common Prayer* [and] *Holy Bible*, London 1616, at the John Rylands University Library, Manchester. The binding was made by the same shop that bound A. Thevet, *Pourtraits et vies des Hommes illustres*, Paris 1584, for James I (C.22.f.4, illustrated in W.Y. Fletcher, *English Bookbindings in the British Museum*, London 1895, pl. XXXIV).

9 B. Quaritch, Catalogue, 1921, *35*, pl. X. There is no copy of this book in the Old Royal Library.

10 The large corner pieces found on this binding are closely similar to but not identical with those used by the Lord Herbert/Squirrel bindery. Identical corner pieces occur on a *Book of Common Prayer*, London 1639 [and] *The Whole Booke of Psalmes*, London 1640 with SRA VIII (C.61.k.5).

11 Mentioned in a list of books "kept in his Maj:^{tys} Cabinet rome at Whitehall" in Landsdowne MS. 1050, fol. 23^v. This MS. is one of several copies of a "Catalogue of Pictures, Books, . . . belonging to King Charles I . . . drawn up by Vander Doort".

London 1635 (C.47.k.4)[12] and J. Woodall, *The Surgeons Mate; or, military and domestic surgery*, London 1639 (C.77.h.18).

SRA VI is again known in only one example on a binding probably from James I's library.

SRA VII and VIII were used almost exclusively for Charles I. SRA VII has been found on five or six bindings made during his reign, as well as on a rather plain binding from the library of James I (C.83.k.1). Two cover music books, the first of which, a "Collection of English and Italian Songs with Music" written in the 18th century in what was originally a blank book ruled for music and bound in gold-tooled black morocco (Add. MS. 27932), may have belonged to James I.[13] The second is the "Music Book of William Lawes" written in the first half of the 17th century and bound in gold-tooled brown calf (Add. MS. 31432).[14] Four bindings with the SRA VII block come from the Lord Herbert/Squirrel bindery.[15] The presentation copy to Charles I of M. Raderus, *Bavaria Pia*, Munich 1628 (C.24.c.4), elaborately tooled with a border built up of separate tools, large leafy corner blocks and the arms on a semis of thistles and fleurs-de-lis was illustrated by H.M. Nixon in *Royal English Bookbindings in the British Museum*, London 1957 (pl. 8). The other three bindings cover copies of the same work: John Davies, *Antiquae linguae Britannicae*, London 1632. One copy (C.47.k.11) belongs to the Old Royal Library and has the same leafy corner pieces that are found on the Raderus. One was the author's presentation copy to the first Earl of Bridgewater; it has an inscription dated 18 June 1632, is bound in olive-brown morocco decorated with the same corner pieces and is now in the H.E. Huntington Library in San Marino (60976). The third, in a light brown binding elaborately tooled with fleurons, the leafy corner blocks and a semis of thistles, is at Knole House.

SRA VIII occurs on two bindings, covering G. Williams, *The Right*

---

12 This binding has a vine roll also used by the Lord Herbert/Squirrel bindery (see below).

13 This manuscript came to the British Museum with the Slade Bequest. Illustrated in H.B. Wheatly, *op. cit.*, pl. XXII. The corners that decorate this binding also occur on R. Brooke and A. Vincent, *A Discoverie of Errours*, London 1622, with the arms of Charles, Prince of Wales (Maggs, Catalogue 665, *4*); H. Briggs, *Arithmetica Logarithmica*, London 1624, for Charles, Prince of Wales (C.82.f.8); and Matthew Locke, "Compositions for Consorts", autograph manuscript presented by Locke to Charles II in 1672 (Add. MS. 17801). The sun tool also occurs on G. Coperario, "Instrumental Fantasias", an early 17th-century manuscript with the same royal arms as occur on Locke's "Compositions" (R.M. 24.k.3).

14 See J.P. Cutts, "British Museum Additional MS. 31432", *The Library*, 1952, pp. 225-34.

15 M. Foot, *The Henry Davis Gift. A Collection of Bookbindings*, vol. I, London, 1978 [1979], section 4.

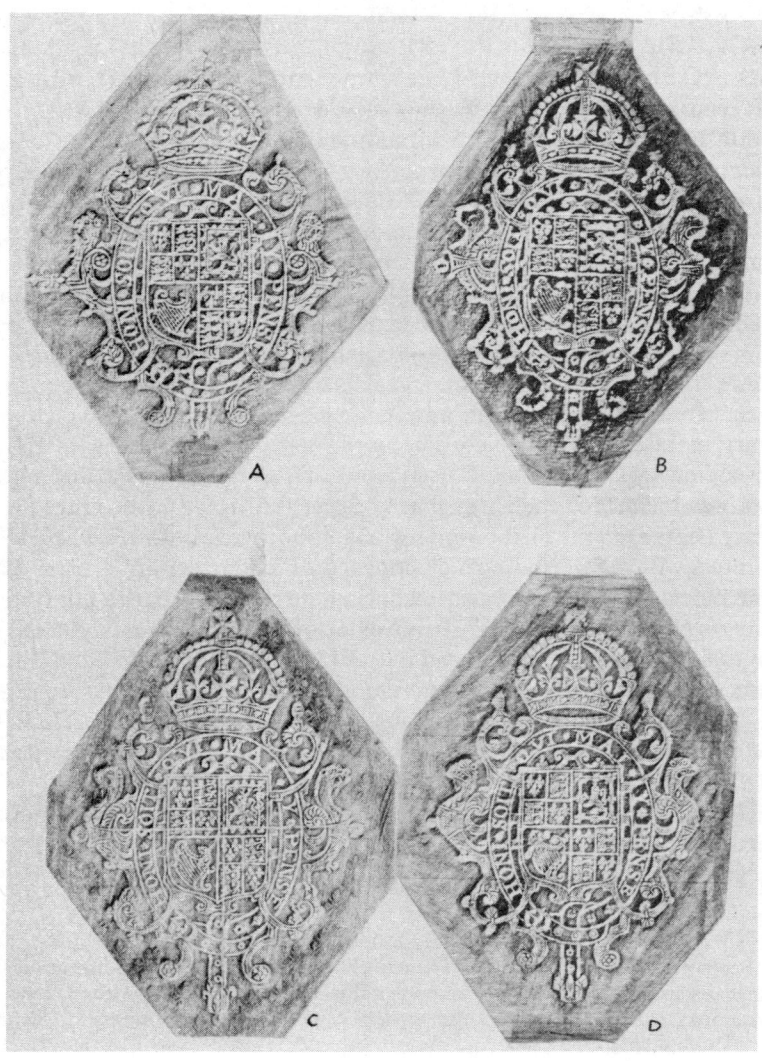

Fig. 1. Rubbings of Stuart Royal Arms blocks not illustrated elsewhere: A. SRA V, B. SRA VIIID, C. SRA IX, D. SRA XII (reduced).

Way to the best Religion, London 1636 (C.21.e.14, fig. 2), to which I will return later, and a *Book of Common Prayer*, London 1639 [and] *The Whole Booke of Psalmes*, London 1640 (C.61.k.5).[16] Of the two examples of SRA VIIIA in the Old Royal Library, one occurs on a binding for James I (C.81.i.4), the other on one from Charles II's library (C.75.c.19). G.D. Hobson, in *English Bindings 1490-1940 in the Library of J.R. Abbey*, London 1940 (pl. 19), illustrates a binding on G. Williams, *Seven Golden Candlestickes*, London 1627, probably made for Charles I, which is decorated with this arms block.[17]

Of SRA VIIIB there is only one example in the Old Royal Library. This block was used by Daniel Boyse on the presentation copy for Charles I of Mercator's *Atlas*, Amsterdam 1613 (C.18.e.15, now Maps C.3.d.8) bound in murray-coloured velvet and tooled in gold and silver.[18] The same block occurs on two elaborately gold-tooled copies of J. Selden, *Mare Clausum*, London 1635, in black morocco, one in the Henry Davis Gift to the British Library,[19] the other in an identical binding in the Sydney Jones Library in Liverpool (H.75.2). The book is dedicated to Charles I and both copies look like presentation copies but there is no evidence as to which was meant for the King. The copy of this book in the Old Royal Library (C.77.h.11) is also bound in black morocco, but rather sparsely decorated with a narrow border and a different royal arms block.

This block, SRA VIIIC, was used during the reign of Charles I only and occurs on three more bindings, covering J.J. Boissard, *I-VI pars Romanae urbis topographiae et antiquitatum*, Frankfort 1627, 28, 1597-1602 in 6 volumes (C.79.c.3), *Corpus Statutorum Universitatis Oxon.*, Oxford 1634 (C.24.d.6)[20] to which I will return later, and J. Puget de la Serre, *Histoire de l'Entree de la Reyne Mere ... dans la Grande Bretaigne*, London 1639 (C.37.l.9).[21]

Of SRA VIIID (fig. 1B) I have found only one example, on a binding covering the manuscript of T. Gardyner's "Theological Tracts", 1627, dedicated to Charles I (Arundel MS.3).

---

16 See note 10. This binding also shows a fleuron which links it with the group of bindings discussed on pp. 103-4. The book belonged to Isaak Walton (see J. Bevan, "Some Books from Isaak Walton's library", *The Library*, 1980, p. 260) and only reached the British Museum in 1897.

17 There is no copy of this edition in the Old Royal Library.

18 Illustrated in H.M. Nixon, *op. cit.*, n.29

19 M. Foot, *op. cit.*, vol. II, London, 1983, n.86; illustrated in B. Quaritch, Catalogue, 1921, *36*, pl. XI. '

20 Illustrated in W.Y. Fletcher, *op. cit.*, pl. XLVII.

21 This book came to the Old Royal Library with the library of John Morris and was probably issued in this binding. See T.A. Birrell, *The Library of John Morris*, London 1976, n. 1277.

Fig. 2. G. Williams, *The Right Way to the best Religion*, London 1636: upper cover with SRA VIII (B.L., C.21.e.14).

SRA IX (fig. 1C) was probably used for James I as well as during the reigns of both Kings Charles. The binding with Charles I's arms covers a *Book of Common Prayer*, London 1629 together with the *Bible*, London 1630 and *Psalmes in Meeter*, London 1629 (C.47.f.13). It is made of brown calf tooled in gold with a semis of fleurons and large corner pieces.[22]

SRA X does not occur on any binding in the Old Royal Library in the British Library, but has been found on J. Smith, *The Generall Historie of Virginia*, London 1624 in the Folger Shakespeare Library in Washington (22790).

Of SRA XI there is only one example in the British Library. It occurs on Vanderdoort's manuscript "Catalogue of Pictures belonging to Charles I" (Add. MS. 10112). It is bound in brown sprinkled calf and has the initials CR as well as the arms block and the date 1639. An identical binding on another copy of this manuscript is illustrated in R.R. Holmes, *Specimens of . . . Bookbinding, selected from . . . Windsor Castle*, London 1893 (pl. 26).

The last variant, SRA XII (fig. 1D), has also only been found once. It decorates a 1636 London *Booke of Common Prayer* (C.36.1.1) in red morocco, tooled in gold with a sun-roll border, fleurons and the initials CR. This book does not belong to the Old Royal Library; it reached the British Museum in 1857.

Frequently the same block was used by more than one binder and it is probable that the library bindings as well as the bindings for the royal household were ordered through the King's printer or the King's stationer who were issued with or had access to a variety of arms blocks owned by the Palace, and who gave them with the books to be bound to the binder of their choice. In the Wardrobe accounts for the reign of Charles I there are several entries of payment to John Harrison, stationer, for binding books, mostly Bibles, Psalters and Service books, as well as for providing stationery.[23] The King's printer is also paid on occasion for providing bound books, often unspecified, and again mainly Bibles and Service books.[24] Though John Bateman was still Royal Binder during Charles I's reign—he was last issued with a livery in 1639/40—[25]

---

22 A third variant of the leafy corner pieces used by the Lord Herbert/Squirrel bindery, see also note 10. This book does not come from the Old Royal Library and may well have been bound for a member of the royal household.

23 P.R.O., LC 5/38, pp. 57, 106, 124, 157; see also pp. 65, 67, 116; LC 9/102, fols 13, 22v; LC 9/103, fols. 5, 17v, 20.

24 See Add. MS. 5756, fols. 141 and 144. One more easily identifiable work, Fox's *Book of Martyrs* "in three Volumes bound in redd Leather & filletted", "Received from the King's Printer this 24th of December 1641" (fol. 144) is not the copy in the Old Royal Library (C.78.i.3) which is bound in dark brown morocco.

25 P.R.O., LC 9/103, fols. 41-41v; see also M. Foot, *op. cit.*, vol. I, pp. 40-43.

no bindings made by him for the King survive and only three bindings decorated with his tools carry the insignia of Charles as Prince of Wales. One of these is the presentation copy for Prince Charles of Sir Robert Dallington's *Aphorismes Civill and Militarie*, London 1613 (C.46.i.11), bound in gold-tooled olive morocco with Charles's arms and initials in the centre.[26] The other is a *Booke of Common Prayer* with *The Whole Booke of Psalmes*, London 1615, recently acquired by the British Library (C.183.a.18), bound in gold-tooled brown calf, decorated with the Prince of Wales's feathers.[27] The third, now in a private collection, covers James I, *Workes*, London 1616 and is bound in gold tooled olive morocco, also with the Prince of Wales's feathers. This feathers block was also used by Bateman on bindings for Prince Henry and it was still in use when the future King Charles II was Prince of Wales.[28] It occurs on one other binding for Charles I as Prince of Wales in combination with his initials, the date 1623, and a tiny rosette tool, covering Albrecht Dürer, *Hierinn sind begriffen vier Bücher von menschlicher Proportion durch Albrechten Dürer von Nürerberg erfunden und beschriben*, n.p. 1528 (C.82.g.9). This is almost certainly the book that was "given to the King when he was prince by his Servant Vanderdort . . . a book in fol. of Wood Prince of Albardure [transcription error for "prints of Albrecht Durer"] being the inscription in high dutch of the proportions of men", mentioned in a list of books "kept in his Maj:^{tys} Cabinet rome at Whitehall".[29]

Very little is known of John Bateman's son Abraham, who shared the office of Royal Binder with his father. Except in the original grant of the office of bookbinder to the King of 1604, Abraham is not separately mentioned. He presumably worked with his father, but only the elder Bateman appears to have been issued with a yearly livery and to have been paid regularly for binding or providing books.[30] Abraham was apprenticed to his father and freed by patrimony on 13 April 1607. He took his first apprentice on 27 June 1608 and two more apprentices have been recorded.[31] He may have been the "Master Bateman" who went to the Lord Mayor's dinner on 29 October 1610 and who was mentioned as

---

26 Illustrated in W.Y. Fletcher, *op. cit.*, pl. XXXVII. The same arms were also used by Bateman on bindings for Henry, Prince of Wales (see M. Foot, *op. cit.*, vol. I, p. 46, n. 18, p. 48, n. 42).

27 Illustrated in E.P. Goldschmidt, Catalogue 163, *211*.

28 R.R. Holmes, *Specimens of Royal Fine and Historical Bookbinding, selected from the Royal Library, Windsor Castle*, London 1893, pl. 32.

29 Landsdowne MS. 1050, fols. 22^v-24^r, for this entry see fol. 23^v.

30 See M. Foot, *op. cit.*, vol. I, pp. 40-43.

31 D.F. McKenzie, *Stationers' Company Apprentices 1605-1640*, Charlottesville 1961, pt. II (Bateman).

Renter Warden on 6 May 1618.[32] The last of his apprentices was freed in 1624, but by Thomas Johnson. It is useless to speculate whether Abraham died early or moved away, or whether he used a completely different set of tools so that his work cannot be connected with that of John. The last "Bateman" binding covers a book printed in 1635[33] and the name Bateman is not found in the records after 1640.

The binder who worked for John Bill, the King's printer, and who bound at least 15 books for James I[34] made two bindings for Charles. One, on A. Gil's *Logonomia Anglica*, London 1619 (C.21.b.8),[35] was made for Charles as Prince of Wales. The arms block that decorates this binding was previously used for Prince Henry and it occurs on four more bindings for Charles.[36] The other binding covers William Lithgow's *Totall Discourse*, London 1632.[37]

Two London shops seem to have been responsible for a fair number of presentation bindings for Charles I and both used a number of different blocks for the royal arms.

The smaller group comprises six bindings mostly elaborately tooled with curls, fleurons, pointillé tools, and four different arms blocks. Three of these are variants of the Stuart Royal Arms type: SRA VIII, SRA VIIIB, and SRA VIIIC.

G. Williams, *The Right Way to the best Religion*, London 1636, dedicated to Charles I, bound in brown morocco elaborately tooled in gold to a panel design with tall fleurons in the outer border, small fleurons, curls of various kinds, and flower vases, has the SRA VIII block in the centre (C.21.e.14). A *Book of Common Prayer*, London 1639 [and] *The Whole Booke of Psalmes*, London 1640, also with SRA VIII in the

---

32 E. Arber, *A Transcript of the Registers of the Company of Stationers of London 1554-1640*, London/Birmingham 1875-94, III, 692, 695.

33 M. Foot, *op. cit.*, vol. I, p. 49, n. 66.

34 H.M. Nixon, *op. cit.*, n. 28; also M. Foot, *op. cit.*, vol. I, p. 54 (the binding referred to in note 44 was made for Charles, not for Henry, Prince of Wales).

35 Illustrated in W.Y. Fletcher, *op. cit.*, pl. XL.

36 G. Primerose, "Panegyrique a tres-grand et tres-puissant Prince Charles Prince de Galles", 17th-century manuscript in gold-tooled white vellum (Add. MS. 27936). It has the same corner blocks, as well as the same arms blocks, as England — [Laws and Statutes], *Anno regni Jacobi, Regis ... 21° ... At the Parliament begun ... the 19. day of February* (a fragment containing two acts), London 1624 in gold-tooled vellum (C.77.h.17). M. Du Val, *Rosa Hispani-Anglica seu Malum punicum Angl'Hispanicum*, [Paris 1622?] in gold-tooled olive morocco (C.46.f.1). Also probably on E. Grimstone, *The Imperiall Historie*, London 1623, in gold-tooled olive morocco (Quaritch, Catalogue, 1921, *34*, pl. IX: the plate is not sufficiently clear to identify the arms block with certainty. The Old Royal Library copy of this book, 591.h.8, has been rebound).

37 Maggs, Catalogue 665, *5*. Neither of the two British Library copies of this edition belong to the Old Royal Library.

centre, has large leafy corner pieces of the type used by the Lord Herbert/ Squirrel bindery and one fleuron tool found on other bindings of this group (C.61.k.5).[38] The two lavishly tooled copies of Selden's *Mare Clausum*, London 1635 with the arms block SRA VIIIB which I have mentioned already come from this same bindery, and so does the presentation copy of *Corpus Statutorum Universitatis Oxon.*, Oxford 1634, printed on vellum with a manuscript dedication to Charles I from the Chancellor, Masters and Scholars of Oxford University (C.24.d.6). It is bound in black morocco and tooled in gold to a panel design with various curls, tall fleurons and smaller fleurons around the arms block SRA VIIIC. The other binding from this group came to the British Library with the Henry Davis Gift. It covers *The Book of Common Prayer*, London 1639 [and] *The Holy Bible*, London 1639 [and] J. Downame, *A briefe Concordance*, London n.d. [? 1633] [and] *The Way to true Happinesse leading to the Gate of Knowledge*, London n.d. [? 1640] [and] *The Whole Book of Psalmes*, London 1639, all bound together in gold-tooled brown morocco decorated with curls and fleurons surrounding a round arms block.[39]

This same block was used by a shop responsible for nine or possibly ten bindings with Charles I's arms, the Lord Herbert/Squirrel bindery. It occurs on two bindings, both probably presentation copies to the King, one on A. Freitag, *L'Architecture militaire*, Leiden 1635 in brown morocco tooled in gold to a panel design with large corner and centre pieces built up of curls and fleurons,[40] the other on Charles Lodowick, Count Palatine's *Manifest . . . concerning the Right of his Succession*, London 1637 (C.81.b.18) in dark olive morocco, tooled in gold to a panel design with small rolls and fleurons at the corners. A different round arms block was used on a similar binding of brown morocco also decorated with small rolls and a fleuron, covering W. Parks, *The Rose and Lily*, London 1639, 38 (C.82.a.17).[41]

An entirely different arms block with large lion and unicorn supporters, frequently used by John Bateman on bindings for James I,[42]

---

38 See notes 10 and 16.

39 M. Foot, *op. cit.,* vol. II, n. 93. There is no evidence that this book was bound for Charles I and it could have been bound for a member of his household. Other non-royal bindings from this shop are: *The Book of Common Prayer*, London 1633/4 (C.130.i.2) and [Bible—Job], *Catena Graecorum Patrum in Beatum Iob*, London 1637 (St. John's College, Oxford, D.2.22).

40 M. Foot, *op. cit.*, vol. I, pp. 50 and 53 (illus.); vol. II, n. 71.

41 This book does not belong to the Old Royal Library. The same arms block that was used on Parks is found on P. Heylyn, *Ecclesia Vindicata*, London 1657. According to a manuscript note this is the author's presentation copy to Charles II (C.73.b.10).

42 M. Foot, *op. cit.*, vol. I, section 3, appendix.

occurs on a semis of thistles and fleurs-de-lis and in combination with the triangle tools and the large leafy corner pieces that belong to the Lord Herbert/Squirrel bindery on a 1630 London *Book of Common Prayer* in brown morocco in the H.E. Huntington Library (# 45911).

Another arms block this bindery used has also got lion and unicorn supporters and is garlanded with vine branches. It decorates an elaborately gold-tooled brown morocco binding on Julius Schillerus, *Coelum Stellatum Christianum*, Augsburg 1627 at St. John's College, Oxford (b.2.6).[43] The arms block which was on occasion used for James I and for Charles II, occurs on two or possibly four more bindings for Charles I in the British Library.[44] A roll depicting curving vine branches which decorates the binding of the Schillerus at St. John's is also used on a binding with the arms block SRA V covering T. Morton's *Institution of the Sacrament*, London 1635 (C.47.k.4). However, the other tools on this binding do not seem to have belonged to the Lord Herbert/Squirrel bindery.

Variant VII of the Stuart Royal Arms block was also used by this shop and occurs on the presentation copy of Raderus, *Bavaria Pia*, Munich 1628 (C.24.c.4) and on the three copies of Davies, *Antiquae linguae Britannicae*, London 1632, all discussed above.

This leaves us with several bindings for Charles I unaccounted for. They are mostly presentation copies and four bindings, though not attributable to any specific bindery, are worth a brief description. Three were made for Charles as Prince of Wales and belong to the Old Royal Library. A 1622 London *New Testament* in Greek, dedicated to James I, is bound in brown morocco and has the arms of Charles, Prince of Wales—on a block also used for Prince Henry—tooled in gold on a semis of small flowers (C.27.e.11). Aelfric, Abbot of Eynsham, *A Saxon Treatise concerning the Old and New Testament*, London 1623, dedicated to Prince Charles, is bound in red velvet and tooled in blind with curved tools in the border, fleurs-de-lis in the corners, and the Prince of Wales's feathers

---

43 *Ibid.*, p. 58, n. 16.
44 G. Coperario, "Instrumental Fantasias", early 17th-century manuscript in gold-tooled dark brown morocco (R.M. 24.k.3, see also note 13) and F. Mason, *Vindiciae Ecclesiae Anglicanae*, London 1625, in gold-tooled brown morocco (C.18.b.15) could both have been bound for James I. The other two examples are: H. Hugo, *De Militia equestri antiqua et nova libri*, Antwerp 1630, in gold-tooled brown calf (C.46.k.2) and J. Stow, *Annales*, London 1631, 32 in gold-tooled brown calf (C.21.e.11) decorated with the same corners as are found on a *Bible* (1609) [and] *Prayer Book* (1636) illustrated by G.D. Hobson, *English Bindings 1490-1940 in the Library of J.R. Abbey*, London 1940, n. 23. The binding for Charles II covers "Compositions for Consorts . . . made by Matthew Locke", a 17th-century manuscript presented to Charles II in 1672 (Add. MS. 17801).

with the initials CP in the centre (C.65.l.1). A very splendid red silk binding embroidered with spangles, pearls, and gold and silver threads showing floral motives in the border, a large flower in each corner, and the Prince of Wales's feathers within a wreath in the centre, covers "Cinquante emblemes chrestiens premierement inventez par la noble damoiselle Georgette de Montenay", the drawings and verses copied by Esther Inglis in Edinburgh, 1624, with a dedication "To the thrice illustrious and most excellent Prince Charles" (Royal MS. 17 D.XVI).[45]

The last binding was a New Year's gift to Charles I from Francis Stewart, Earl Bothwell, with a long presentation inscription dated 1 January 1636 (Eg. MS. 1140). It covers a collection of treatises by Sir Nicholas Halse collected by Stewart under the title "Great Britains Treasure", and bound in black morocco, tooled in gold with several borders built up of small tools, the King's arms and initials on a semis of quaterfoils and the inscription "TIBI SOLIO REX CHARISSIME": a suitable sentiment for a presentation, and one that with a single alteration could well serve to grace this birthday gift.

---

[45] Illustrated in W.Y. Fletcher, *op. cit.*, pl. XLVI. Could this be the "Booke in french verse on sevrl Noble Ptr [Portraits] fol" mentioned in a list of manuscripts and English printed books at Whitehall, c. 1641 (Bodley, MS. Smith 34, p. 107)?

A JONSON PROOF-SHEET — *NEPTUNES TRIUMPH*

Johan Gerritsen

It has long been known that in the British Library copy (press-mark 644.b.57) of Jonson's masque for Twelfth Night 1623/4, *Neptunes Triumph*[1] (STC 14779, Greg 407(a)), the outer forme of the last sheet, C, is uncorrected. The corrected state may be seen in the Bodleian (Malone 233(7)) and Huntington (62110) copies. Greg merely notes that copies "are known to differ in a few readings in C(o)", but Herford and Simpson (vol. VII, p. 677) record four variants.

It therefore comes as something of a surprise when, on inspecting the BL copy, one discovers that not one but *both* formes are variant, with nine changes in the outer forme and six in the inner (and more if one counts in, as one really should, displacements in the type consequent upon the correction of the forme). In fact, Herford and Simpson record the four variants that might be called textual, and ignore all others. Presumably, then, the BL copy was collated quite early in the history of the Oxford *Jonson*, and Greg never inspected the sheet at all. For one would like to think that if either the author of *Proofreading in the Sixteenth, Seventeenth and Eighteenth Centuries* (1935)—and of the earlier *Proof-reading by English Authors of the Sixteenth and Seventeenth Centuries* (1928)—or the bibliographer of the English printed drama to the Restoration had personally set eyes on the sheet, they would have recognised it for what it is, a proof-sheet, with twelve corrections marked in pen and ink by, there is reason to think, Ben Jonson himself. And since for several reasons the matter is important enough to be reasoned carefully, we may perhaps begin by investigating the question begged by the preceding paragraph: are the corrections genuine?

A number of considerations prompt us to say that they are. To those who might think that they could not have been there when the scholars above named saw the volume we may answer that we do not know that it was Simpson (rather than Herford, or an amanuensis) who collated it (living as he did at Oxford, he ought to have used the—corrected—Bodleian copy in preparing his edition), and that if Greg had collated it

---

1 Collation: 4to, A-C^4. The BL copy lacks A2.3, the blank C4 is absent in BL and Bodley. The BL copy is on pot paper, the other two on arms.

he, of all people, would certainly have turned up the variants in *both* the formes, whether or not they had already been marked for him. Greg only recorded textual variation when it happened to be known to him; he "made no special investigation with a view to discovering it" (vol. I, p. xviii). Simpson, in recording only the four variants that can be regarded as corrections of textual errors of omission or commission,[2] conforms to what was common nineteenth-century practice; and in any case the Oxford *Jonson* has always remained weak in matters of bibliographical analysis. And finally, in spite of Simpson's categorical "Our text is based upon the Quarto" (VII, 678), there is the incontrovertible fact that his text was prepared from F2 (1640) and then brought, somewhat carelessly, into conformity with Q.[3] This is indeed a method of long standing, but it does not belong to a generation that worries about proof-sheets and press-corrections. If we now look for more positive evidence, we may begin by noting that the ink of the corrections is of a brownish yellow colour that accords well with age, and that it has run just a little here and there, as it might if the paper had not quite lost its printing-house dampness. Moreover, there is no running of the ink along the fore-edge of C2^v where that edge terminates two corrections. In other words, the corrections will already have been there when the sheet was last trimmed, and this must have taken place before the advent of either Greg or Simpson, for they both note the resultant cropping of the side-notes.

The next point that should be established is that, whatever the standing of the corrections may be, the sheet is in any case a proof-sheet, i.e. a "trial or preliminary impression taken from composed type, in which typographical errors may be corrected and alterations and additions made" (*OED*). The definition (which embraces first proofs as well as revises) is emphasized, because it allows us to distinguish the sheet clearly from two other categories, the trial formes (pages, sheets) composed as the first stage of book production and intended for deciding on the type, lay-out, etc. and as a basis for calculations and casting off, and the variant states of a particular forme (or sheet) intended as integral elements of the completed book. The matter is emphasized here because Hellinga, in his authoritative and invaluable *Copy and Print in the Netherlands* (1962), introduced a binary division into "trial proofs" and

---

2 Both in the textual (foot)notes and in the Introduction (p. 677: "Four corrections were made in the text during the printing"), viz those in ll. 435, 527, 532, 544.

3 This appears plainly from the opening of the masque, the line arrangement of most of the descriptive directions, the failure in four cases (339, 455, 471, 514-15) to convert the Folio's use of italic and roman in them correctly to that of the Quarto, and some thirty unacknowledged Folio spellings. Besides these, there is a sprinkling of independent errors, of which the most disturbing is "where" for "whence" in side-note k.

"corrector's proofs", identifying the latter as being "in the nature of things, recognisable by the corrections marked on them" (p. 146, footnote 1) but concluding this section by what is in fact a discussion of variant states of which no marked corrections are known at all (pp. 150-51).

That the last sheet of the finished book should have been set up as a trial sheet is in itself extremely unlikely. In the present case it can be ruled out since sheet C is short: its text ends on C3, leaving three blank pages.

That it is indeed a proof-sheet, and not a sheet from the normal print run showing the uncorrected forme on both sides is demonstrated by the fact that the type for it had not yet been properly imposed. The two sides are completely out of register in both directions, as a result of which the final headline is almost wholly trimmed away. All other sheets in the three known copies make good register. Though it was eventually bound up in a complete copy of the masque,[4] the sheet cannot therefore have been produced with that intention, and since it will also not have been produced as a preliminary trial sheet, it can only have been produced for proof-reading purposes. In other words, it is precisely the type of sheet on which one would expect to find marks of correction, as in fact we do, and this in turn implies that the onus of proof would lie with whoever should wish to claim that they are not genuine.

It has already been indicated that the marks must have been in the book for a considerable time, well before it was used for the Oxford *Jonson*. At the time it was so used they were not brought to Simpson's attention (or alternatively were ignored by him) and in the later twenties or early thirties that would have been hardly thinkable, even though Simpson's interest was not so much in proofs as in proof-reading authors at first. But who could there have been at any earlier time who could have been interested in forging correction marks for the printer? For, as we shall see, the marks are plainly of the kind one inserts when there is still the possibility of getting the errors corrected in the type, not of the kind one makes either with a view to a new edition or in order to make the text easier to read.

To appreciate this, let us examine, in order, all the corrections in the sheet, both those that are marked and those that are not. They fall into three groups (cf. plates):

---

[4] It seems unlikely that the missing A2.3 should have lacked from the start.

NEPTVNES TRIVMPH.

CHORVS.
'Tis incense all, that flames!
And these materials scarce haue names!

PROTEVS.
My King lookes higher, as he scorn'd the warres
Of winds, and with his trident toucht the starrs.
There is no wrinkle, in his brow, or frowne,
But, as his cares he would in nectar drowne,
And all the (l) siluer-footed Nymphes were drest,
To waite upon him, to the Oceans feast.

Or, here in rowes upon the baskes were set,
And had their seuerall bayres made into net
To catch the youths in, as they come on shore.

SARON.
How! Galatea sighing! O, no more.
Banish your feares.

PORTVNVS.
And Doris dry your teares.

PROTEVS.
And (m) Haliclyon, see,
That kept his side, as he was charg'd to do,

SARON.
—And the Syrens haue him not.

PORTVNVS.
Though they no practise haue, nor hearts forgot
That might haue wonne him, yet by charme, or song.

PROTEVS.
Or, laying forth their wasses all along
Vpon the glassie waues,

POR-

NEPTVNES TRIVMPH.

PORTVNVS.
Then diuing:

PROTEVS.
Then,
Vp with their heads, as they were made of some.

SARON.
And there, the high-=going billowes crown'd,
Whilst some lusty Sea-god pusb'd them downe.

CHORVS.
See! He is here!

PROTEVS.
Great Master of the mayne,
Receiue thy deare, and precious pawne againe.

CHORVS.
SARON, PORTVNVS, PROTEVS bring him thus,
Safe, as thy Subiects wishes gaue him vs:
And of thy glorious Triumph let it be
No lesse a part, that thou their loues dost see,
Then, that his sacred head hath return'd to thee.

This sung, the Iland goes backe, whilst the
vpper Chorus takes it from them, and the
Masquers prepare for their figure.

CHORVS.
Spring all the Graces of the age,
And all the Loues of times;
Bring all the pleasures of the stage,
And relishes of rime;
Adde all the softnesses of Courts,
The lookes, the laughters, and the sports.

G   And

NEPTVNES TRIVMPH.

The Reuels follow.

Which ended, the Fleete is discouered, while the three Cornets play.

POET.

'Tis time, your eyes should be refresh'd at length
With something new, a part of *Neptunes* strength
See, yond, his fleete, ready to goe, or come,
Or fetch the riches of the *Ocean* home,
So to secure him both in peace, and warres,
Till not one ship alone, but all be starres.

A shout within followes.
After which the *Cooke* enters.

COOKE.

I haue another seruice fer you, Brother *Poet*, a dish of pickled Saylors, fine salt Sea-boyes, shall relish like *Anchoues*, or *Cauiare*, to draw downe a cup of *nectar*, in the skirts of a night.

SAYLORS.

Come away boyes, the Towne is ours, hay for *Neptunes*, and our *young Master*.

POET.

He knowes the *Compasse* and the *Card*,
While *Castor* sits on the maine yard,
And *Pollux* too, to helpe your sayles;
And bright *Leucothoe*, fils your sayles:
Arion sings, the Dolphins swim,
And, all the way, to gaze on him.

The *Antimasque* of Saylors.

The last Song to the whole *Musique*, fiue Lutes, three Cornets, and ten voyces.

Song.

PROTEVS.

Although we wish the Triumph still might last,
For such a Prince, and his discouery past,
Yet now, great Lord of waters, and of isles:
Giue Proteus leaue to turne vnto his whiles:

PORTVNVS.

And, whilst young Albion doth thy labours ease,
Dispatch Portunus to thy ports,

SARON.

And Saron so thy Seas?

To meete old Nereus, with his fiftie girles,
From aged Indus laden home with pearls,
And orient gummes, to burne vnto thy name.

CHORVS.

And may thy Subiects hearts be all on flame:
Whilst thou dost keepe the earth in firme estate,
And, mongst the winds dost suffer no debate.
But both at sea, and land, our powers increase,
With health, and all the golden gifts of peace.

The last Dance.

The end.

NEPTVNES TRIVMPH.

And wing la all their sweets, and salts,
  That none may say, the Triumph halts.

Here, the *Masquers* dance their
  Entry.

Which done, the first prospectiue of a ma-
ritime Palace, or the house of *Oceanus* is
  discovered, with lowd Musique.
And the other aboue is no more seene.

POET.

Behold the Palace of *Oceanus*!
Hayle Reverend structure! Boast no more to vs
Thy being able, all the Gods to feast;
We haue seene enough: our *Albion* was thy guest.

Then followes the Maine Dance.
After which the second prospect of the Sea,
is showne, to the former Musique.

POET.

Now turne and view the wonders of the deepe,
Where *Proteus* heards, and *Neptunes* orkes do keepe,
Where all is plough'd, yet still the pasture greene
The wayes are found, and yet no path is seene,

There *Proteus*, *Portunus*, *Saron*, goe vp to the
Ladies with this Song.

PROTEVS,
Come noble Nymphs, and doe not hide

NEPTVNES TRIVMPH.

The ioyes, for which you so prouide:
SARON.
If not to mingle with the men,
  what doe you here? Go home agen.
PORTVNVS.
Your dressings doe confesse,
By what we see so curious parts
of Pallas, and Arachnes arts,
  That you could meane no lesse.
PROTEVS.
Why doe you weare the Silkewormes toyles;
  Or glory in the shellfish spoiles?
Or striue to shew the graines of ore
That you haue gather'd on the shore,
  whereof to make a stocke
To graft the greener Emerald on,
Or any better-water'd stone?
SARON.
  Or Ruby of the rocke?
PROTEVS.
Why doe you smell of amber-gris,
Of which was formed Neptunes Neice,
  The Queene of Loue; vnlesse you can
  Like Sea-borne Venus loue a man?
SARON.
  Try, put your selues vnto't.
CHORVS.
Your looks, your smiles, and thoghts that meete,
Ambrosian hands, and siluer feete,
  doe promise you will do't.

C 2 The

1) a group of three variants not marked in pen and ink.
outer forme
   C1 :   7 427 highest   the long ligature *st* has, in both Bodley and Huntington,[5] been replaced by a different, properly kerning type, eliminating the excess space between *e* and *st*.
   C2^v: 14 517 fer   corrected to *for*; room for the wider *o* was found in this (prose) line set to the full measure by taking out the word-space in *Poet, a*.

inner forme
   C2 : 24 497 Likǝ   the turned italic *e* has been corrected.

2) a group of twelve variants marked in pen and ink.
outer forme
   C1 : 15 435 SAKON   The *K* has been struck through vertically and an *R* placed in the right margin. Corrected as indicated.
   C2^v: 6 509 *Neptunes*   the first *e* rises above the baseline; a bow has been placed under it and repeated in the left margin (partly trimmed). Correction has resulted in an *e* nearer the baseline and excess white between it and *p*.
        24 527 sayles   the initial long *s* has been struck through vertically and an *h* written in the left margin. The corrected forme reads *hayles* (and see further (3) below).
   C3 : 1+ 532 Λ   following line 531 *Then* has been interlined in pen and ink in the proof and has been set up in type to print in the corrected forme.
        3+ 534+ ⎤
        4+ 535+ ⎦   a short horizontal pen-stroke has been placed centrally in the wide interlines between *Song.* and the lines above and below. In the corrected forme the interlines have been reduced, and so have those above and below *The last Dance.* at the bottom of the page.
        14 544 SAROV.   the *V* has been struck through vertically, and an *N* placed in the right margin. Corrected as indicated.

inner forme
   C1^v: 15 463 sea,   the long *s* has been struck through vertically and an *S* placed in the left margin. Corrected as

---

5 Since Bodley and Huntington differ only in the variant specified under (3) their agreement will not be further noted.

	19 467 *orkes*	indicated, the extra space for the capital being found by removing the word-space between *of* and *the* preceding it. the *o* has been struck through vertically and an *O* placed in the left margin. Corrected as indicated, the space for the capital being found by replacing the preceding *and* by &.
C2 :	6 479 *confesse*	a bow under *ess* indicates that the excess space between the first *e* and the double long *s* should be closed up; a similar bow is in the right margin. In the corrected forme the double long *s* has been replaced by a properly kerning ligature long-short *s*.
	confesse	a vertical pen-stroke has been placed after this word and has been repeated in the margin with a comma before it. The corrected forme shows a comma after the word.
	7 480 *see*	a comma to follow this word has been marked by the corrector in precisely the same way as for the preceding word and has been inserted accordingly.

3) a correction marked in pen and ink, ignored in the corrected forme, but carried out by stop-press correction.[6]

outer forme

C2ᵛ:	24 527 *sayles*	the word has been underlined for italics; the marginal *h* (see above under 2) has been firmly underlined and the line extended to the right; it is trimmed at the margin. The corrected forme as represented by Huntington retains the roman type; Bodley has corrected to italics, inadvertently turning the colon below.

There do not appear to be any further intentional changes distinguishing the three states, but there is the usual crop of accidental differences in the print that do not represent changes in the type it was printed from.

If we now try to evaluate our findings, it seems clear that the corrections listed under (1) and (2), carried out in both Bodley and Huntington, must represent either two successive proofing stages (of which the first is then not represented in our copies), or a single proofing stage in which two proofs were sent out for either forme, and then presumably one to the printing-house corrector and one to the author. In trying to decide

---

6 By stop-press correction because the forme had been imposed.

between these alternatives we should begin by observing that the proof-sheet we have bears every appearance of being a first proof. For five quarto pages set in english to a measure of nine ems, with interspersed great primer for directions, the text being largely verse punctuated by centred speech-headings and with very few lines set to the full measure,[7] a crop of errors like that listed above is in no way remarkable for a first proof, but would be somewhat large for a revise. But if our sheet is a first proof and the corrections listed under (1) should represent a revise, it is rather strange that of the three errors mended at the revise stage two should be purely typographical faults of the type that a printing-house corrector is likely to catch on a first reading, while only two such errors were caught in the putative first proof (*Neptunes* and *confesse*).[8] They are technical, not textual. Yet they must represent a proof-reading, for since the compositor has to correct his errors at his own expense, he does not correct errors that have not been marked against him; and none of the three occur in a line which he had to touch again in any case. This argues that we do not have successive stages of revision (whether at the proofing stage or by stop-press, for the stop-press correction we have is the correction of an error marked in the proof that we also have), and it indicates that in fact we are faced with a case of concurrent proofing by two independent agents.

If one of these was the author, the technical nature of most of the corrections listed under (1) argues that our proof is the author's. Of course the corrections listed under (1) only represent, then, the difference between the two concurrent proofs. The proof we do not have will have listed, in addition, at least a number of those errors that we also find marked on the sheet we do have, but there is nothing in the corrected formes that causes us to suspect that they were not corrected on the basis of the known proof-sheet where it runs. The initial failure to italicize *hayles* is hardly remarkable in this context, since another correction was made in the word.

But can the proof indeed be Ben Jonson's? If so, it would be the only one known so far, and so we have no material for comparison. Comparing the handwriting offers little hope. We have a reasonable sample of Jonson's handwriting, it is true, but the longest word our proof corrector inserts is *Then*, and that is not written currently but, for good reason, lettered. On seeing the over-sloping *h* we may indeed think we recognize a frequent and characteristic feature of Ben's usual hand, but the next character, *e*, is the italic form, and except in *œ* and *œ* Ben

---

7 14 out of 136, of which 4 are corrected (463, 467, 509, 517).

8 There can have been no special attempt to catch such faults, as several remain; the type, moreover, is not of a quality to make such an attempt rewarding.

always employs either the Greek or the secretary form. By way of consolation we may then observe that the *h* in the correction for *sayles* is a very different, careful, upright and complete form, and conclude that, in fact, the handwriting can tell us little except that it is a hand of the general type that Ben Jonson wrote. He *could* have corrected proof like that.

Another line of enquiry, and one that must remain similarly unfruitful, is an examination of the method for marking proof. It was plainly done by a person of some experience in the matter, but for a professional it would seem surprising that not a single caret is used to indicate an omission (it would have been in order for *confesse*ˏ and *see*ˏ). But the range of correction marks needed is too small for a decision, and in any case our knowledge about practical proofreading of the time is too limited. We do not even know which printing-house was responsible for our masque. It may have been Stansby's, but even if it was, we have no other Stansby proofs.

In the final resort we are therefore thrown back once more on the proof correcting itself. Could an author have overlooked the error *Which* for *With* in line 509?[9] He could, and easily: literature is full of examples. The other corrector missed it too, and it was only corrected in 1640. Could a printing-house corrector have supplied all the corrections we find carried out? Of course he could, if they stood in the copy, and if the copy could be made available to him. With C being the last sheet, and the proof a proof on both sides, he obviously could have had the copy. The crucial question is, therefore, if all these corrected readings were in it. In other words, is there any reason to think that among the corrections we find marked on the proof-sheet there are changes of matter which the compositor may be presumed to have set correctly from copy? The greater part of the corrections concern technical blemishes and simple literals, but there are three that do not. To begin with, there are the comma's after *confesse* and *see*. It is possible that they were overlooked. But it seems far more likely that they are an afterthought in proof, to mark off *By what we see* as a parenthesis. The compositor might have overlooked one comma, but hardly a pair, the more so as he seems to have omitted no others.

The remaining correction that should be discussed in this context is the inserted *Then* on C3. The compositor made no comparable error elsewhere, the word, if in the copy, would have stood prominently by

---

[9] Simpson suggests that "the pasture greene" in line 468, where the Folio reads "the pasture's greene" is another Quarto error, but this is not so obvious. The Quarto reading is good contemporary grammar, and the corresponding passage in *The Fortunate Isles* has "pastures" in both Quarto and Folio and has changed the singular "path is" of the next line to the plural "paths are". It is therefore less than certain that Simpson is right in reading "pasture's greene" in both masque texts.

itself in a position (centred) where he had to look throughout the masque because it is the position for the speech prefixes. Its function is to indicate that two successive directions indicate successive, not simultaneous business. As such it could again have been quite easily an afterthought prompted by the printed proof. But the marker of the proof must then have known that they were successive.[10]

It is time to sum up. That the correction marks are genuine proof-reader's marks of 1623 seems beyond cavil.[11] That they were not placed on the sheet by the printing-house corrector seems a reasonable hypothesis. That the sheet is a proof on both sides argues that it was pulled to be sent outside. Where else could it have been intended to go than to the author? It was, after all, a masque for Court performance, printed for private distribution. The author will have paid for it, so he must have seen proof. That the proof-sheet we have was corrected by Ben has not, in the strict sense, been proved, and it is doubtful if it can be. But all lines of argument seem to lead, without forcing, to the same conclusion: there is reason to think that the proof is his.

    10 It is relevant to note that *The Fortunate Isles* also places *By what we see* in commas, and that the direction corresponding to ll. 531-3 is a simple "Then the last Song.".
    11 In view of the date aimed at for production it seems likely that the printing was done in 1623 either style.

BETWEEN TWO LANGUAGES: CAXTON'S TRANSLATION OF REYNAERT DE VOS

Wytze and Lotte Hellinga*

" . . . Once upon a time there was an Englishman who learned a little Dutch and then, due to his arrogant lack of self-criticism, had the temerity to translate a classic of Dutch literature, which he understood only vaguely, into not too fluent English; subsequently he committed this to print, with even worse lack of judgment . . . " Thus one may summarize, with only moderate exaggeration, the received critical opinion of William Caxton's translation of the Dutch prose version of *Van den Vos Reynaerde*, which he completed in 1481. Critical judgment was first passed in the text edition of the Dutch prose version by J.W. Muller and H. Logeman (1892), where a whole chapter (probably written by Logeman) was devoted to Caxton's translation (pp. XLI-LVII). "There are many instances where Caxton failed to understand the Dutch text", Logeman declared (p. XLVII), and "with Caxton's scant knowledge of Dutch his translation was a risky enterprise" (p. XLIX). The most recent editor of the English text, N.F. Blake (1970), is somewhat more cautious but in the end also condemns Caxton: "The accuracy of the translation leaves much to be desired" — and, even more redolent of a school report: " . . . he was not concentrating on his translation as he ought to have been"; " . . . by no means unintelligent". But Blake allows Caxton "a fairly competent working knowledge of the language" in spite of "many examples of an imperfect command of Dutch" (p. liii).

Did Caxton deserve this? We propose to examine the question in this paper, written for Tom Birrell who, like William Caxton, like ourselves, knows what it is to live with more than one language.

There are two elements, at the very least, by which Caxton's translation must be judged: not only his knowledge of the original language but also his familiarity with the text. As for the language, in the thirty years of his life which Caxton spent in the Low Countries, "in the contres of Braband, flandres, holand and zeland", Caxton seems to have lived mostly in areas that were preponderantly Dutch-speaking, but with a bilingual element that was socially determined. In Flanders French was

*We are grateful to Miss Helen Smith for correcting our English.

the language for the Court when it resided there, Flemish the language of most of the ordinary people. Bruges, the city where Caxton lived for a considerable time, was then, as now, a Flemish-speaking city, but a French speaker would have had no difficulty in finding inhabitants readily fluent in his tongue. The French-speaking world was nearby, and it was the centre towards which social and cultural aspirations tended to gravitate. French vocabulary mixed happily with the Dutch understructure, as it will mix now: "Moeder gij zijt een embêtanterik" — a cry from the heart, recently overheard, at a time when the two languages do not tolerate each other with the same ease as in the fifteenth century, but still blend.

Anyone living in the geographical area indicated by Caxton, and at the social level which we may assume Caxton's to have been, would communicate in Dutch in his everyday contacts, on the quayside, in his workshop, in the lower law-courts, not only with his servants but with his peers. They would switch to (effortless) French when speaking to anyone at a higher level of officialdom, or when enjoying literature, or encountering anyone who had been attracted to this active centre of world trade and had no Flemish or Dutch. The scribe Colard Mansion, who worked in Bruges, was one such, and it is noteworthy that when dean of the guild of St John he kept the records in French, as did his colleague Jean le Clerc, while all the other scribes who had this office from 1454 on wrote in Flemish.[1] Perhaps the current English view of Caxton's years in the Low Countries needs some correction as far as the linguistic situation is concerned, especially since Caxton's knowledge of French has left so many traces in English literature. A man of two worlds he was,[2] but also a man of three languages.

Anyone living in the Western part of the Low Countries, and in particular anyone living in the great Flemish cities, must have felt at home with the setting of *The History of Reynard the Fox*. It is a landscape that began immediately outside the city gates (and even now, with more effort, can be found there). The village beside the stream and its inhabitants, the farmyards, the copses and sandy paths, they are all depicted in *Reynard* with the utmost reality until the half-realistic, half-imaginary animal world takes over. In its sense of realism, and of space, we can hardly escape associating it with the world of Breughel, but it is more true to historical sense, and also to form, to think of the Flemish

---

1 W.J. Weale, "Documents inédits sur les enlumineurs de Bruges", in: *Le Beffroi*, 2 (1864-65), pp. 298-319.

2 This characterization is the striking opening sentence of D.F. McKenzie's "Printing in England from Caxton to Milton" in: *The Age of Shakespeare. Volume 2* of *The New Pelican Guide to English Literature*, edited by Boris Ford. Penguin Books, 1982, pp. 207-226.

miniatures of Caxton's own time, where Jason appears amid the civic buildings of a Flemish city, John the Baptist is half immersed in the meandering Leye and David plays the harp in a landscape of poplars.

Besides, anyone who had lived for thirty years in this geographical area, and had only the slightest literary sense must have known at least part of the *Reynard* in one of the versions in verse, either by oral or by manuscript tradition. Caxton, therefore, is bound to have known the poem, but wisely refrained from translating it in his own doggerel. Only when a prose version became available did he translate it — probably wasting little time once he had acquired this source. This brings us to the next question, one that requires a technical answer: what was Caxton's source? This question has often been posed, and has never met with an entirely conclusive answer. It is quite obvious, even from a fairly superficial collation, that Caxton's translation must be very closely related to the Dutch prose version printed by Gheraert Leeu in 1479, but as to the degree of relationship editors differ in opinion. There are minor variant readings between Caxton's text and the Gouda edition, which led Muller-Logeman to postulate that Caxton must have worked from a manuscript, possibly a good deal earlier, that was also an ancestor of Leeu's version.[3] Blake rejected the idea of an earlier manuscript, and ascribed the variant readings to Caxton's haste and to his misunderstanding the Dutch text.[4] Donald B. Sands, the editor of a modern-spelling edition (1960) took an altogether milder view of Caxton, credited him with emendating the Gouda text where it was faulty, and did not hesitate to decide that Caxton used the Gouda text of 1479.

Since these publications appeared the relationship of the various printed versions of the prose *Reynaert* has been the subject of several studies. This has served to clarify connexions which cannot come to light from a comparison between *Leeu* and *Caxton* alone. In the first place there is the relation between Leeu's edition of 1479 and the later edition in Dutch, printed at Delft in 1485. This was discussed in an article by the present authors;[5] to the evidence quoted by them more examples were added by their former student Paul Vriesema, which supported their original thesis.[6] The translation into Low-German, entitled *Reynke de*

---

[3] Muller-Logeman, pp. XV, XXIX.
[4] Blake, p. xlviii.
[5] Lotte and Wytze Hellinga, "De betekenis van de incunabelkunde voor de Neerlandistiek", in: *Dietse Studies. Bundel aangebied aan Prof.Dr.J. du Plessis Scholtz bij geleentheid van sy vijf-en-sestigste verjaardag, 14 mei 1965*, Assen 1965, pp. 52-74, especially pp. 57-61.
[6] In an unpublished thesis and in P. Vriesema, "Gheraert Leeu en *Die hystorie van Reynaert die vos. De Reynaert* als prozaroman", in: *De letter doet de Geest leven. Bundel opstellen aangeboden aan Max de Haan*, Leiden, 1980, pp. 73-84.

Vos, of which the *editio princeps* appeared in Lübeck in 1498, was studied by W. Krogmann, who paid a great deal of attention to the earlier phases of transmission of the text.[7] With perhaps surprising unanimity these various studies all led to the conclusion that Leeu's edition of 1479 must have been preceded by another edition which had page-endings identical to the edition of 1479 (a page-for-page-reprint is quite common in this period) and which was probably printed by the same printer. The evidence for the existence of this edition, which has otherwise completely vanished, is simple: the 1479 edition begins with a quire signed 'a' with a Table of contents which refers to the foliation of the part that was to follow. If this had been the *editio princeps* this quire would in the normal course of events have been printed last and would have remained unsigned. The plausible explanation for the form in which it now exists is that the book was a reprint. There are other examples of this procedure in Leeu's printing of this period. However, as the sole argument for the existence of an edition this would be unsatisfactory. Fortunately there is much textual evidence to support the theory. One can demonstrate that the Delft edition must have used a copy of this first edition as *exemplar*. Gouda 1479 and Delft 1485 would therefore have had a common ancestor. The line of argument is that variants between these two can be understood as independent emendations of obvious corruptions in the earliest Gouda edition, especially corruptions that are familiar as simple typographical errors. The ancestry of the Low-German edition can likewise be traced to the first (hypothetical) Gouda edition, via the version in verse, edited by Henric van Alcmaer which Leeu printed in Antwerp and for which a few fragmentary leaves are the only witness. The only divergence in opinion is as to the number of intermediate phases one should postulate. Sometimes the human mind, in the *persona* of a translator or editor, is able to achieve all at once several stages of thinking which can appear as distinct phases in a long stemma (such as Krogmann's). This is a difference in interpretation that is beginning to be familiar to students of Caxton's translations, where this problem is repeatedly encountered. Before we can attempt to solve this problem we shall need far more experience with editing methods of the late fifteenth century than is at present available. It seems therefore fruitless to try to decide the (academic) question whether Caxton used the Leeu edition of 1479 or the one that must have preceded it. It is certain that he used one of the two. The proof lies in a printing-house joke which can bear to be retold, although it has been told before.

One of the subordinate characters in the *Reynaert* is the ram, named

---

7 W. Krogmann, "Die Vorlage des 'Reynke de Vos'", in: *Jahrbuch des Vereins für niederdeutsche Sprachforschung*, 87, 1964, pp. 29-55.

Bellyn, who in Leeu's text (followed by Delft, so it must have occurred in the earliest edition) suddenly assumes in some places the name *Bellart*, a form that had never occurred in the manuscript tradition of the text.[8] But the name *Bellart* (or *Bellaert*) has a connexion with Leeu's printing house: it is the name of Jacob Bellaert, who started a printing house of his own in Haarlem in 1483 with material that a little later appeared also in Leeu's Gouda printing house. There are other typographical connexions which also point to a link between these two printers.[9] The sudden appearance of the name Bellart in a Leeu edition is therefore too much of a coincidence to be ignored. Moreover, its relevance to the person of Jacob Bellaert finds confirmation in the fact that in a series of names of important cities Leeu's version of *Reynaert* substitutes "Zierikzee" for "Douai",[10] and this small town in Zeeland is known to be Bellaert's birthplace: he styled himself "Meester Jacop Bellaert gheboren van zerixzee" in the only colophon he ever published.[11] (He never stopped talking about Zierikzee, of course, when he was a young apprentice.) This variant can therefore be easily understood in the ambiance of the printing house — a mild practical joke to raise a smile in an intimate circle. Caxton, quite rightly, removed it from his text, substituted more appropriately *London* for *Zierikzee* and reinstated Bellyn — except in one place where he forgot to do so (See figures).[12] A moment's lack of attention, certainly, on Caxton's part, which caused Leeu's compositors to leave their mark even in another language. This puts paid to any doubts that Caxton's translation is based on one of Leeu's printed editions.

The text printed by Gheraert Leeu is not a prose version of the earliest Reynaert (known as *Reynaert I*), which is famous as one of the great poems of European literature, but the version known as *Reynaert II*, written in the fifteenth century. Here the original poem was expanded from *circa* 3400 lines (the length of the sources varies between 3393 and 3469 lines) to 7805 lines. This expansion has obscured to some extent the theme of the original poem, and the results are unfortunate.

The theme of *Reynaert I*, to which the poet adhered rigorously, is the battle of wits between the small fox with his superior intellect and the lion Nobel who ruled the animal kingdom and had therefore all the advantages worldly power can give. The clash of wills between the two

---

8 P 2559, 4565.

9 Wytze and Lotte Hellinga, *The Fifteenth-Century Printing Types of the Low Countries*, Amsterdam 1966, pp. 38, 73-74. *De Vijfhonderdste Verjaring van de Boekdrukkunst in de Nederlanden*, Brussels, 1973, pp. 286-87.

10 P 1947.

11 In: Bartholomaeus Anglicus, *Vanden proprieteyten der dinghen*. Haarlem, 24 December 1485. GW 3423.

12 Blake 84:13.

conste vroet Ende om dat mi dese iuwelen veel
te goet waren te houden daer om had icse dē
conincē eñ mijnre lieuer vrouwen d͂ coninghin
nen te heple gesant Waer sijn si nv die sulcke
presenten in trouwē horē herē geuē· dē rouwe
die mijn twee kind om den spiegel dzeuen die
was veel te groot·want si hem daer dicke mꝫ
groter ghenoechten in plaghen te spieghelen
ende daer voer te springhen·ende besaghen hē
hoe dat hoer bereptsel hem stōt ende voert alle hoer lijf Och arme knecht my was onbekē
lic dat ky waert die hase alsoe nae sijnre doot
was Doe ic hem op groter trouwen die ma
le mitten iuwelen gaf ic en wist niet wie dat
icse bat beuelen mochte al had dat ocek mijn
lijf ghegouden·dan hem ende bellaert dan rā
Het waren my twee alsoe ghetrouwe vrien-
de als ic v̄mermeer waene te ghecrighen Wa
pen ouer den moer denser Ick sal daer noch
dat waer of weten Al soude ic alle die werlt
daer omme door dwalen · want moerdaet
dye en bleef nye verholen Het mach licht dz
hij hier onder onsen hoop is ende bi ons staet
Ende dye daer wel of weet waer kyewaert
ghebleuen is Al en seyt hijs niet·want men-
nighe scalcken die loesheyt pleghen die wan-
der en dicke mitten goeden·daer hem nyemāt

   lxxx   ſ ʒ

I. 'Bellaert dan ram' in Leeu's edition of 1479.
  British Library, G. 10495, leaf 3 recto, 1. 16.

and make amendes them self. Therfore it is said and trowthe it is, Who that wyl chyde or chastyse, see that he be clere hym self.

Alle this and moche more than I now can wel remembre was made and wrought in this glasse. The maister that ordeyned it was a connyng man and a profounde clerk in many sciencis. And by cause thise Jewells were ouer good and precious for me to kepe & haue/ Therfore I sente them to my dere lord the kynge and to the quene in presente/ Where ben they now that gyue to theyr lordes suche presentes/ The sorowe that my ij chyldren made whan I sente away the glasse was grete for they were woned to loke therin and see them self how theyr clothyng and arraye bycam them on their bodyes. O alas I knewe not that kywart the hare was so nygh his deth whan I delyuerd hym the male with thise Jewellis/ I wiste not to whom I myght better haue taken them, though it shold haue coste me my lyf. than hym & bellart the ramme, they were two of my best frendis/ Oute alas I crye vpon the murderar/ I shal knowe who it was, though I shold renne thurgh al the world to seke hym. ffor murdre abydeth not hyd, it shal come out perauenture he is in this companye that knoweth where kywart is bicomen, though he telleth it not. ffor many false shrewys walke wyth good men, fro whom noman can kepe hym, they knowen theyr craft so wel & can wel couere their falsenes. but the most wondre that I haue is that my lord the kyng hier saith so felly, that my faure

II. 'Bellart' taken over by Caxton as 'bellart the ramme', showing direct influence of Leeu's printing house on Caxton's translation.
British Library, G. 10545, leaf 6 verso, 1. 19.

protagonists leads to a complicated outcome in which to some extent each is loser *and* winner. It is beyond doubt who the real victims are: the king's friends and vassals, the wolf Ysengrim and Bruyn the bear who had conspired to expel him. The king's own power, however, was broken by Reynaert, and the king sensed that he had lost not only his friends but his honour as well. His way out of this was to have Reynaert condemned to death by the Court; but the fox escaped by choosing voluntary exile from king Nobel's realm in a secret country with plenty of game. The king's reconciliation with the wolf and the bear causes the downfall of one of his loyal subjects, the ram Bellyn, a personification of the Church, who himself, by guilty negligence, had caused the death of the character-less (or even soul-less — a moot point) hare Cuwaert. But highest in the hierarchy, and altogether the victor in the struggle for power is the panther Firapeel, who prompted the king's machinations. He is an anti-king who commands the forces of Evil and, in a sense, he is an antichrist.

In *Reynaert II* an entirely different kind of conclusion was found to end the story. The king and Reynaert were reconciled, the fox submitted to the power of the crown and was rewarded with high honour and a consultancy. It sounds true to this day. In order to save his life the fox sold his independence and corrupted his superior intellect. It is a conclusion which gives a dismal view of the freedom of the individual, celebrated in *Reynaert I*. In the final scene the whole clan of foxes congregates to approve the happy outcome: collectively they surrender their independence. Clearly, in the fifteenth century concepts of morality were entertained — and therefore shaped a fitting end to Reynaert's story — which differed widely from those of the wicked twelfth century. In spite of these adaptations to suit contemporary taste Caxton must have been aware of the underlying tone of independence (or immorality) and rebellion against established order, a remnant of the original story which can be discerned even in the watered-down version, for in a short epilogue he added a disclaimer, and admonished any reader who might take offence: "blame not me, but the foxe, for they be his wordes and not myne". This in itself is a charming piece of proof of Caxton's sensitivity to the tone and contents of the text he translated.

The prose version as it survives in Leeu's Gouda edition must derive from a source closely related to the manuscript source for *Reynaert II*, known as the "Brussels Codex", which was written circa 1475, probably in the County of Holland. The Brussels Codex (and presumably Leeu's source as well) had peculiar linguistic features, since it was written using two distinct sources: a version of *Reynaert I*, which must have been written in West Flanders, and in addition another manuscript of *Reynaert I*, but one that was close to the "Dyck" Codex, which itself was commissioned by a patron who, late in the thirteenth or early in the fourteenth century, required modernization of the language and adaptation to usage of the Utrecht region. It was commissioned for members of a noble family with connexions both in Utrecht and Guelre-Cleve. A feature of the Brussels Codex is therefore that it is a linguistic mixture, determined by which verses were chosen from either of the two sources. The north-netherlandish characteristics prevail. Gheraert Leeu and the other printers of this period strengthened this element. Even at this early stage of printing in Holland (which began in 1477) it can be observed that the printers tried to establish a universally acceptable use of Dutch, without too many local or regional features although the "northern" Hollands character dominated. When Gheraert Leeu, to take the best investigated printer, re-issued texts in Dutch, even with an interval of only one or two years after the earlier edition, his attempts to achieve a balance can be followed by comparing the two versions on spelling and vocabulary. The printers in Holland succeeded in this attempt, much as Caxton succeeded in exercising a similar influence by imposing a self-devised standard in the use of English. The usage as found in Leeu's books became the language of vernacular printing in the Western part of the Low Countries. In the South this area ended where the French language took over. Eastward the transition began at the river IJssel: after crossing this linguistic border one immediately enters the printing centres of Zwolle, Hasselt and Deventer, where the language had "Eastern" features, a distinction which lasted well into the nineteenth century.

The language of Leeu's *Reynaert* in the surviving edition can therefore be best defined by the general term "Diets" (a term which is not adequately covered by the English "Dutch") without any qualification. The few regional features do not affect it sufficiently to call it otherwise. The slightly earlier version from which Caxton may have translated may well have had a somewhat more regional colour, if a parallel with other Leeu editions which appeared in rapid succession in the same period is anything to go by. A particularly good example is the Dutch translation of Jacobus de Voragine's *Golden Legend*, printed by Leeu in 1477 and 1479, where this linguistic evolution is obvious.

However this may be, the few regional forms do not seem to have formed an obstacle to the translator, or even to have had much influence. Caxton, with his multi-linguistic adaptibility, and his sensitivity for regional and social nuances which appears from his own observations on his mother-tongue, seems to have taken in his stride the variability of the Dutch language in the process of consolidation.

We present here only a small selection from many possible examples of Caxton's *Reynaert*-translation. Our intention in discussing these instances is only to show how close comparison may lead to a new assessment of Caxton's competence as translator.

Caxton's work has all too often been scrutinized in the atmosphere of an examination board: a great deal of frowning when a word has escaped, and tut-tutting provoked by even the slightest variation from the original. It seems needless to point out that an omission, used judiciously, may be an improvement in context or in the pace of the story. Our first examples will discuss such simple omissions (nos. 1, 2, 3, 4). Moreover, some of these highlight a very positive feature of Caxton as translator/narrator: his vivid visual imagination. His divergences from the original text can in several instances be shown to depict a situation with greater precision (nos. 2, 3, 4). The preference for a simple form need not necessarily be caused by lack of linguistic versatility, but by the desire to find the concrete image, as opposed to the abstractions to which the Dutch text sometimes inclines. The best demonstration of this is Caxton's simple disclaimer, quoted above, where the longer Dutch epilogue rambles vaguely on about "exempelen", "wise lere", "doghet" and "ere". Confirmation can be found in nos. 4 and 6 of our examples. Also Caxton seems sometimes to have preferred not to aim for a colourful equivalent in English where the Dutch had a striking word (nos. 5, 7) but to find his own stylistic means; in other instances, as is well known, he was led by the Dutch form. And finally, just to show that we are not blindly defending Caxton, we add an example of what can only be understood as an error, albeit a minor one (no. 8). We have not thought it necessary to concentrate on Caxton's shortcomings, alleged or real. Low marks given by his editors have carefully been assembled elsewhere.[13]

The Dutch text is quoted from the edition by W.Gs Hellinga (as P), for Caxton's text we quoted from N.F. Blake's edition, with a page and line citation.

(1) Panther the beaver speaks before the Court:
P 91-92   Iae onsen here den coninck *of wye dat hij sy*
C 8:8   our lord the kyng here

Caxton omits the words, evidently denigratory "the king or whoever he may be", which were an addition in the prose version. Apparently he judged that the moment had not arrived to let scorn for Nobel be expressed. There would be plenty of opportunity later on. It seems to have eluded Muller-Logeman that Caxton shows insight here into the dramatic unfolding of the text that is superior to the Dutch prose version: Nobel's downfall is prepared step by step. We should not imagine that Caxton made careful comparisons between sources, but in this instance

---

13. Muller-Logeman, pp. XLIV-LVII. Blake, pp. lii-liv, lviii-lix.

we must conclude that he spotted an arbitrary addition in the prose version and discarded it.

(2) Reynaert had stolen plaice for Ysengrim:

P 142   ... die u vander karren werp doe ghi *vast van verres nae volghede*

C 9:4-5   ... whiche he threwe doun fro the carre / whan ye folowed *after fro ferre*

A translation of *vast* is omitted here. In Dutch it may have had an ironical sense: "bravely", or "steadily", or even "safely" (see Buitenrust Hettema's glossary s.v. *vaste*). Was this too vague for Caxton? Perhaps his "after fro ferre" with its suggestion of trailing behind, at a safe distance, a little more specific than the Dutch "van verres nae", was considered sufficient. To all appearances Caxton tried above all to be clear in this highly graphic description of a situation. Thus he also simplifies with good effect:

P 157   ... enen sack daer hi nauwelic uut quam *hi en was eerste by nae doot*

C 9:3   ... a sacke / that he scarsely cam out *wyth his lyf*

(3) Grymbart's defence speech for the court is interrupted:

P 221-224   ... So saghen si neder ten dale waert ende saghen daer comen gevaren Cantekleer die haen met eenre baer met eenre doder hennen *ende die hiet coppe*

C 10:18   so saw they comen doun the hylle *to hem* chauntecler the cock and *brought* on a biere a deed henne

A good example of give and take: Caxton omits the name of Coppe, but takes care over details of the actions of the mourning fowl: the direction of their procession, and their carrying of the *corpus delicti* on the bier. He adds "to hem", "in the direction of the observers", and transfers the direction of their gaze "neder ten dale waert" to the direction of the procession, "doun the hylle". In Caxton's view the court-session is therefore held in a low (sheltered?) spot instead of on top of a hill (as the Dutch version would have it) and is approached from surrounding hills — an altogether more likely site.

(4) Chauntecler's procession arrives:

P 242-243   Aldus soe quamen si samelijck voer den coninc *inden gedinghe*

C 10:31-32   thus cam they to gydre to fore the kynge

Caxton will have considered *inden gedinghe* a superfluous specification. It has an abstract connotation: "in the dispute" which would distract again from the visual presentation: the moaning procession arrives and Chauntecler starts crowing his complaint without any preliminaries.

(5) Bruyn the bear is shocked that honey is not Reynaert's favourite food: the fox even complains of flatulence. Bruyn reacts:

P 438-441   Bruijn die sprack ter stont *Help* reynaer *doer den doot* maec di dat honich aldus onweert. Men waert sculdich te prysen ende te minnen boven alle spyse.

C 14:14-15   Bruyn tho spack anone / *alas* reynart *what saye ye* / sette ye so lytyl by hony / me ought to preyse and love it above all mete

Bruyn, a somewhat unpolished character, has strong feelings about honey, which are expressed in a very forceful exclamation: "Help ... doer den doot". This cannot be translated literally. Caxton has a much milder rendering: "alas ... what saye ye ... ". The question is here whether he misunderstood the value of the expression, or deliberately mitigated it. We venture to surmise that Caxton did know the expression, from the pithy language he must have heard in Bruges. When we turned for information to Professor Willem Pée, expert on West-Flemish and himself born in Bruges he commented (letter 14 Nov. 1982) "I know this exclamation and use it myself as an answer to the question 'Would you have done that?': 'Neen ik, voor de dood nie(t)!'" ("Never, not for the life of me!") Could perhaps English of the fifteenth century have tended to make scarcer use of expletives than Dutch, as is certainly true of modern usage? This does of course not mean that Dutch expletives are not understood by English-speakers. Caxton may therefore have betrayed a preference in this translation: Bruyn speaks more in sorrow than in anger.

(6) Grymbart defends Reynaert to the Court:

P 139-140   Doch soe wil ic somme punten seggen die *bewiseliken* sijn
C 9:3   yet wil I telle some poyntes that I *wel knowe*

Caxton must have understood *bewiseliken* as "which I can prove with material evidence", and both simplifies and enforces: that I know well. This is not a matter of Dutch but of entering into the spirit of the narrative. Caxton seems also to eschew the abstract, judiciary notion, which is perhaps to be taken only half-seriously in the Dutch text.

(7) Grymbart discusses Ysengrim's appetite:

P 143-157   ende ghi *aet* die goede pladdyse allene in v gherief ende en gaeft hem daer niet of sonder die grate ende dat gy selver niet en mocht Aldus soe dede ghi hem oec vanden vetten bake die alsoe wel smakede. ende die ghi allene in uwen buuck *hemelde*

C 9:5-8   And ye *ete* the good plays allone/and gaf hym nomore than the grate or bones/whyche ye myght not *ete* your self / In lyke wyse dyde ye to hym also of the fatte vlycche of bacon/ whiche savourd so wel / that ye allone *ete* in your bely

This passage concerns two of Ysengrim's tricks played on Reynaert: those concerning the plaice and the bacon which Reynaert stole for Ysengrim at grave personal risk. Muller-Logeman quote this passage as an example of

Caxton not understanding the Dutch text, in particular his rendering of "hemelen" by "ete" (p. xlvii). The verb *hemelen* means "to clear out", "to put away" and still quaintly survives in the language with connotations of spring-cleaning. Caxton may not have hit on an equally picturesque equivalent in English, but he seems to have found his own means of transmitting the irony in the passage: by repeating *ete* three times Caxton effectively mocks Ysengrim's gluttony, and uses the repetition stylistically as an intensification.

(8) The end of Grymbart's plea:

P 219-221   Recht onder dese woerde dat grymbert aldus *van sinen* oem stonde en predicte

C 10:16-17 Thus as grymbert *his* ome stode and preched thise wordes

Blake observed that Caxton must have mis-translated, for in P the badger speaks of his uncle, whereas in Caxton's translation the badger appears to be his (Reynaert's) uncle. Caxton had entitled this chapter "How grymbart the dasse the foxes susters sone spack for reynart . . . " and continued: "Tho spack Grymbart the dasse / and was Reynart's suster sone . . . " (C 8:27-29). A serious misunderstanding of the relationship can therefore be ruled out, but not a momentary lapse of attention. It seems, however, much more likely that C 10:16-17 should be emended by simply inserting *of*: "Thus as grymbert *of* his ome stode and preched". The question of course is why the word should have been omitted either by Caxton or by his compositor. Louis Havet, *Manuel de critique verbale* (Paris 1911) has wise words relevant here: " . . . en principe, un mot quelquonque peut toujours être omis, sans que nous parvenions à supposer d'autres conditions que celles qui nous l'échappent par essence . . . Les mots dont l'omission parait inconditionnée sont ordinairement des mots courts et, d'ailleurs, peu significatifs" (p. 126 sub 420). And finally: "L'opinion qu'un critique aura d'un passage dependra . . . moins du texte lui-même que de l'état d'esprit du critique . . . " (p. 29 sub 127).

THOMAS BAKER'S *REFLECTIONS UPON LEARNING*

F.J.M. Korsten

Among the members of the republic of letters in the first half of the eighteenth century Thomas Baker (1656-1740) was widely known as a distinguished antiquary. Like other nonjurors of note Baker played an important part in the revival of antiquarian learning at the end of the seventeenth and the beginning of the eighteenth century. His extensive knowledge and his large collections of manuscript material were at the service of every one who approached him for help, and numerous prefaces to scholarly works written in the first half of the eighteenth century contain expressions of gratitude to Baker for his valuable advice and cooperation. After he had resigned the rectory of Long Newton near Durham on 1 August 1690 and became a nonjuror, this shy and gentle man lived a quiet, regular and very industrious life at his rooms in St. John's College Cambridge for half a century.[1] For a number of years Baker assiduously collected material for a work on Cambridge and its university on the model of Wood's *Athenae Oxonienses*, but he gave it up in the end because he found the Cambridge registers inadequate.[2] Baker's own productions, apart from the forty-two manuscript volumes of transcripts now lodged at the British Library and the Cambridge University Library, are few in number. He published only two books, *Reflections upon Learning* and *The Funeral Sermon of Margaret Countess of Richmond and Derby*,[3] both of them anonymously, which was typical of

---

1 The one event in Baker's long life at Cambridge that seriously disturbed his peace was his being expelled as a Fellow of St. John's College on 21 January 1717, because he refused to comply with the abjuration oath after the accession of George I. He was allowed to keep his rooms in the college, but his feelings about his expulsion clearly appear from his regularly styling himself "socius ejectus" in his writings after this.

2 See letter Baker to Thomas Rawlins, 23 Aug. 1735 (Bodleian Library, MS. Ballard 30, f.3r).

3 *Reflections upon Learning; Wherein is shewn the Insufficiency Thereof, in its several Particulars; In order to evince the Usefulness and Necessity of Revelation* (London, 1699); *The Funeral Sermon of Margaret Countess of Richmond and Derby, Mother to King Henry VII and Foundress of Christ's and St. John's College in Cambridge. With a Preface, containing some further account of her charities and foundations. Together with a Catalogue of her Professors both at Cambridge and Oxford, and of her Preachers at Cambridge* (London, 1708). Baker also wrote, but never published, a history of St.

this cautious and unassertive man. His voluminous correspondence is a storehouse of information on the antiquarian milieu and the state of antiquarian scholarship in the first half of the eighteenth century.

The *Reflections upon Learning* is not an antiquarian work; it was written by Baker to show the insufficiency of learning "In order to evince the Usefulness and Necessity of Revelation", and to this end he tackled the development and present condition of seventeen branches of learning in an equal number of chapters.[4] According to the *Cambridge History of English Literature* the *Reflections upon Learning* brought Baker "considerable credit at the time, but is now happily forgotten".[5] In spite of this discouraging verdict there seems to me to be sufficient reason for having a closer look at this work which, while being clearly opposed to the prevailing trends of the day, achieved great popularity. In Paul Hazard's view Baker's *Reflections* can be seen as presenting opposition to the idea of progress and the idolization of science at the expense of religion at the end of the seventeenth century.[6] In this paper I will try to show that the *Reflections* provides the interesting reaction of a conservative and pious scholar to the spirit of the new age after the Glorious Revolution. Before doing so I will pay some attention to the way in which the book was received and also to Baker's reaction to this, because it will help to throw some light on the personality of the author and indirectly on the character of the work as well.

The *Reflections upon Learning* by a "Gentleman" was announced in the Term Catalogue for Trinity Term 1699 and it was entered into the Stationer's Register on 21 August 1699.[7] The book was immediately successful; it went through eight editions between 1699 and 1758, and it was moreover translated into French, Italian and Latin. In the "Preface" Baker writes: "I hope to take effectual Care to be in the Dark", and this attitude can first of all be attributed to his innate shyness and self-distrust, but there was certainly also the consideration that he had written a book directed against the "Humour of the Age". Although Baker's

---

John's College; it was edited from Baker's manuscripts by J.E.B. Mayor in 1869 (*History of the College of St. John the Evangelist, Cambridge*, 2 vols., Cambridge, 1869).

4 The references in this article are to the text of the seventh edition of the *Reflections upon Learning* (London, 1738).

5 Sir A.W. Ward and A.R. Waller, eds., *The Cambridge History of English Literature* (XV vols., Cambridge, 1932), vol. IX, p. 354.

6 Paul Hazard, *La Crise de la Conscience Européenne 1680-1715* (Librairie Arthème Fayard, Paris, 1961), p. 298.

7 Edward Arber, ed., *The Term Catalogues 1668-1709* (III vols., London, 1903-1906), vol. III, p. 135; *A Transcript of the Registers of the Worshipful Company of Stationers 1640-1708* (3 vols., London, 1913), vol. 3, p. 488.

authorship of the book was soon surmised and virtually known in the circle of his friends and acquaintances at Cambridge, he remained very wary and secretive about it even long after its publication. When, in 1728, nearly thirty years after the book appeared, Thomas Hearne asked Baker to give him a list of the books he had written, Baker did not admit to being the author of the *Reflections*, which was rather odd in view of the fact that Baker and Hearne had been corresponding for more than fifteen years and were on very friendly terms with each other. Baker's answer to Hearne's inquiry shows that he in a way felt ashamed of his first publication: "To your other Enquiry I can say no more then that I onely owne the little Book I sent you [*The Funeral Sermon of Margaret Countess of Richmond and Derby*]: If common fame will give me more, I cannot help it. I wish, I had engag'd in Antiquities as early as you did, I set out too late (wch I now repent of) after I had spent my time in other Studies".[8] The "other Studies" is clearly a reference to the subject-matter of the *Reflections*, and one can safely assume that during the last decade of the seventeenth century he spent much of his time on these subjects, and that his studies took a clearly antiquarian direction only after 1700. Baker's disposition was such that he naturally took to antiquarian studies, but I think that the adverse reactions of some people to the *Reflections* were also responsible for his later concentration on antiquarian subjects and this also explains Baker's life-long reticence about the authorship and his rather dismissive attitude towards the book.

The second and the third editions of the *Reflections* both appeared in 1700, and this fact by itself testifies to the appeal of the book. In a letter of 9 September 1699 Anthony Twyman, student at St. John's College Cambridge,[9] wrote to his cousin Anthony Hammond, Member of Parliament for the University of Cambridge and M.A. of St. John's College,[10] that Thomas Baker had just, anonymously, published a book called *Reflections upon Learning* and that the first impression was already sold out.[11] On 19 September Anthony Hammond replied: "Yesterday Dr Birch[12] put into my hands M^r B -'s Reflections upon Learning, it had

---

8 Letter Baker to Hearne, received 24 Oct. 1728 (Bodleian Library, MS.Rawl.Lett. 27^b, f.67^r (new numbering: f.40^r); see also C.E. Doble et al., eds., *Remarks and Collections of Thomas Hearne*, vol. X, p. 58).

9 Anthony Twyman (? - 1722), admitted to St. John's College in 1693, B.A. 1696-7, M.A. 1700, Fellow 1701-1707 (see J. Venn and J.A. Venn, eds., *Alumni Cantabrigienses*, 4 vols., Cambridge, 1922-1927).

10 Anthony Hammond (1668-1738), poet and pamphleteer; in July 1698 he was returned for the university of Cambridge and became a member of St. John's College; in November 1698 he was elected F.R.S.

11 Letter Twyman to Hammond, 9 Sept. 1699 (Bodleian Library, MS.Rawlinson D174, f.16).

12 Probably Dr. Peter Birch (1652-1710); he was appointed chaplain to the House

been recommended to him by my L. Dorset,[13] as a thing extremely well writ, & with this particular Observation, that tho he did not know the Author yet he cou'd not be long private, for in his L^{ps} opinion there was not ten Men in England cou'd have writ such a Booke. I read it once over at one time without stirring from it & am now reading it again".[14] It is evident from this that the book which had been written with such pious intentions made an impact also in worldly circles, and certainly the high praise for it by the former Restoration rake and wit Lord Dorset is remarkable. At the end of October Twyman informed Hammond that he had thanked Baker for the book on Hammond's behalf, and upon that occasion Baker apparently showed the same evasiveness about the authorship, which we have seen in the letter to Hearne quoted above: "he desired me to return his humble service; he doth not yet acknowledge himself to be the Author, nor doth he deny it; however he bad me tell you he was glad you had rec'd it, saying, your commendation had done the Book no small Kindness & that himself was unworthy your thanks, yt tis more than is due to him".[15] The second, corrected, edition of the *Reflections* contained an appendix in which the author thanked the many people who had complimented him on the work, and in the course of the first half of the eighteenth century the book received several other enthusiastic tributes.

Yet the reception of the book was not equally favourable on all sides. Much to his surprise and embarrassment Baker was, on account of a certain passage in the *Reflections*, drawn into a very unpleasant controversy with Dr. John Woodward, the geologist and physician, which lasted for almost a year, from July 1699 to the end of May 1700.[16] As this controversy has been dealt with at some length by Joseph M. Levine in his book *Dr. Woodward's Shield*,[17] I will here limit myself to giving the main facts. Woodward, who had been appointed professor of "physic" at Gresham College in 1692 and was one of the promising eager young men wholeheartedly devoted to the new science, published in 1695 his

---

of Commons and prebendary of Westminster in 1689, and he became vicar of St. Bride's Fleet Street in March 1695.

13 Charles Sackville, 6th Earl of Dorset and Earl of Middlesex (1638-1706), poet and courtier, friend of Dryden, Butler and Wycherley.

14 Letter Hammond to Twyman, 19 Sept. 1699 (Bodleian Library, MS.Rawlinson D174, f.32).

15 Letter Twyman to Hammond, 28 Oct. 1699 (Bodleian Library, MS. Rawlinson D174, f. 43).

16 The correspondence between Baker and Woodward is to be found in the Cambridge University Library (MS. Add. 7647, nos. 26-44, and MS. Add. 8286, nos. 2-3).

17 Joseph M. Levine, *Dr. Woodward's Shield. History, Science and Satire in Augustan England* (Univ. of California Press, 1977), pp. 58-62.

geological work *An Essay toward a Natural History of the Earth.* In it he offered a new explanation of the origin of the earth, maintaining that at the Deluge the earth had been generally dissolved and that the Deluge was responsible for the formation of fossils which, as he alleged, were not whims of nature, but the remains of living beings. In the first edition of the *Reflections* Baker had spent about half a page on Woodward's *Essay*, stating that Woodward's so-called theory was no more than a hypothesis for which there was as yet far too little proof. One John Gualter[18] drew Woodward's attention to the offensive passage in the *Reflections* and wrote, with Woodward's approval, a letter to Baker, which started the long controversy. As the ensuing letters between Woodward and Baker make clear, the latter had not only scientific objections but he believed Woodward's hypothesis not to be in accordance with the text of the Scriptures on this point. This angered Woodward exceedingly because he, completely in the spirit of the modern scientifically-minded believer of the day, had proudly claimed that his explanation of the origin of the world fitted in exactly with the Mosaic account, so that he had proved the truth of the revealed Scripture-text. Woodward's reaction to Baker's objections was disproportionately vehement, certainly if one takes into account that Baker was after all only an amateur and not at all of Woodward's scientific calibre. Woodward retaliated by calling Baker "a Stranger both to Nature and Mathematicks",[19] and he completely turned the tables on Baker by charging him with being a sceptic and with undermining religion in the *Reflections*. Very soon the controversy became a dispute about the *Reflections* instead of the *Essay*, and Baker was driven more and more into the defensive. Obviously intimidated by his touchy and overbearing opponent, who moreover threatened to publish the letters that had so far been written between them, Baker became more and more apologetic. He promised to leave out the most offensive part of the passage in the *Reflections* if the book was to have a second edition,[20] and in the end he even agreed to giving Woodward satisfaction by writing a letter of retraction to be published in any work Woodward would care to name. The dispute was not yet at an end, however. The before-mentioned John Gualter thought that the draught of the letter of retraction which Baker had sent, did not give sufficient

---

18 I have not been able to identify John Gualter.

19 Letter Woodward to Baker, 13 Nov. 1699 (Cambridge University Library, MS. Add. 7647, no. 34).

20 Baker actually did leave out the following passage from the second edition of the *Reflections*: "And tho Dr. W.'s *Theory* be very natural and so pious as to incline a good man to wish it true, yet I am affraid the Dr. will never be able to prove it so, for want (amongst other things) of such a Menstruum as shall dissolve all things except his Shells" (*Reflections upon Learning*, London, 1699, pp. 83-84).

satisfaction, and he drew up a long letter himself which would bring Baker completely to his knees. This was too much even for the gentle Baker, who had already conceded so much. He indignantly refused to agree to it, and his last letter to Woodward is one of great bitterness and disgust.

The acrimonious tone of Woodward's letters was certainly in part due to Baker's odd behaviour throughout the controversy. All the time Baker stubbornly refused to admit that he was the author of the *Reflections*. Baker had written the first two letters as the anonymous author of the *Reflections* and he had tried to use a disguised hand to prevent discovery.[21] In the rest of the letters, which he signed with his own name, he claimed to be a friend of the author, whose views, he said, he was familiar with. From the start Woodward refused to believe this, and after some time he grew so nettled at Baker's rather transparently devious ways that he took the papers he had received from Baker so far to Alexander Bosvile, the publisher of the *Reflections*, who confirmed that they were all in Baker's handwriting and thus also implicitly confirmed Baker's authorship.[22] When, even after this, Baker persisted in denying that he had written the book, Woodward understandably became increasingly furious. It will be clear from the foregoing that Baker did not come off very well in this affair and he was obviously well aware of this. Woodward had made him realize sharply that for him as an amateur the field of modern science was very dangerous ground. Moreover, to a person so little contentious as Baker, the whole dispute must have been very distasteful. Baker also knew that all the while Woodward had been publicly criticizing the *Reflections*. As he was not the man to shrug off an experience of this kind, it probably left him feeling awkward about the *Reflections*. All this goes, I think, a long way to explain Baker's almost neurotic wariness and reticence about the book for the rest of his life.

The dispute between Woodward and Baker is in a sense illustrative of the growing gap between the latitudinarians and the orthodox, which began to manifest itself in the Church of England after 1689. The *Reflections* was the outcome of an increasing anxiety on Baker's part about this and other developments in late seventeenth-century England, and as this is the background against which Baker's book has to be seen, I will briefly sketch some of these developments before proceeding to a discussion of the book itself.

In 1667 Thomas Sprat, when defending the work of the Royal Society

---

21 Letter Baker to Woodward, 1 Aug. 1699 (Cambridge University Library, MS.Add.7647, no. 28).

22 Letter Woodward to Baker, 13 Nov. 1699 (Cambridge University Library, MS.Add.7647, no. 34).

against doubts on the part of the orthodox believers as to whether the new science could be reconciled with religion, confidently asserted: ". . . the Church of England will . . . be safe . . . amidst the consequences of a Rational Age".[23] However, by the end of the 1690s, when Baker wrote his *Reflections*, the age was decidedly more rational and there was sufficient ground for orthodox believers to be seriously concerned about the safety of the Anglican Church and its doctrines. A major threat to orthodoxy and to the Christian religion in general was posed by the views of the early Deists. People like John Toland, Charles Blount and Charles Gildon struck at the roots of traditional Christianity by rejecting the existence of miracles and mystery in religion, by discarding revelation and by refusing to acknowledge any other form of authority in religious matters but the individual reason. All this was enough cause for alarm to the orthodox, but within the Church of England itself a development was taking place which presented a less conspicuous but more insidious threat to orthodoxy. After 1689 the latitudinarians, whose views were greatly affected by the new spirit of rationality, rapidly increased in number and strength. The great advances made by science in the second half of the seventeenth century, and especially Newton's astonishing achievements, had brought about a growing optimism about the possibilities of the new science and a high regard for man's rational capacities. One of the important effects of the rationalistic outlook on the part of latitudinarian Churchmen was an increasing tension and even opposition between the claims of natural and revealed religion, and in this process the writings of John Locke certainly played an important part. In his *Essay concerning Human Understanding* and *The Reasonableness of Christianity* Locke minimized the importance of revelation by insisting that human reason should be the judge of revelation. The Boyle Lectures, instituted in 1691 to defend Christianity against the dangers of atheism and freethinking, provide a good illustration of the way in which rational argumentation and the findings of the new science came to be employed in the cause of religion. Latitudinarian clergymen like Richard Bentley and William Wotton enthusiastically made use of the new science in their eagerness to prove the truth of Christianity. Religion was shown to be demonstrable by reason, and revelation was, though not rejected, often explained as something which had been far more necessary in the less enlightened past. The latitudinarian wing of the Church of England became very influential during the 1690s and especially in 1695 many important posts in the Church were taken up by latitudinarian divines. These developments largely explain why by the end of the century orthodox believers of

---

23 Thomas Sprat, *History of the Royal Society* (ed. Jackson I. Cope and Harold Whitmore Jones, London and St. Louis, 1959), p. 370.

Baker's stamp felt that the Church and indeed traditional Christian faith itself was endangered by "the consequences of a Rational Age".

Baker wrote the *Reflections upon Learning* in the first place to emphasize the vital importance of revelation, but the book is also clearly related to the controversy over the Ancients and the Moderns. This controversy had been going on for some time in the seventeenth century and in England it came to a head in the 1690s with Sir William Temple's "An Essay upon the Ancient and Modern Learning" and William Wotton's answer *Reflections upon Ancient and Modern Learning*.[24] The title of Baker's book is clearly a deliberate variation on Wotton's title, implying that, where Temple and Wotton had mainly concentrated on the merits of respectively ancient and modern learning, he, Baker, would view the whole field of learning in order to show that human learning as such was inherently deficient. Baker was well aware of the awkwardness of his position in undertaking such a task, as appears from the "Preface". If he performed the task expertly and convincingly, he could be said to have defeated his own purpose; if, on the other hand, he were to mismanage his case, he could be blamed for being ignorant. Moreover, Baker knew that he was on dangerous ground in decrying human reason. After all, did he not run the risk of appearing to adopt the position of the Catholics, who were in the habit of depreciating human reason as a guide in religion only to insist the more strongly on the infallible authority of their Church?[25] This is, I think, one of the reasons why in the "Preface" Baker explicitly states that he had written the book from an anxiety that people in England, after having found natural religion inadequate, would find themselves at a loss and would then be tempted to seek certainty in the Church of Rome. As appears from the "Preface", he studied several works that also aimed at showing the inadequacy of learning, but he found none of them very useful for his purpose. The French book *La Vanité des Sciences*, published anonymously in 1688, was not considered very helpful by Baker because it was "rather a sermon, than a Treatise of Science". In fact its emphasis was different from what Baker wanted, for it set out to show that learning was not at all necessary for a happy life, whereas Baker wished to treat the subject in the context of the reason-faith opposition. His comment on the French book also indicates that he intended to write a book that would have to be taken seriously by

---

24 Temple's "Essay" appeared in 1690 in the second part of his *Miscellanea*, Wotton's reply was published in 1694 (in the "Preface" Wotton remarks that he would never have written the book "if the importunate sollicitations of my very ingenious Friend, Anthony Hammond Esq., had not at last prevailed upon me to try what might be said upon it").

25 Cf. Louis I. Bredvold, *The Intellectual Milieu of John Dryden* (first pbd. 1934, Ann Arbor Paperback, 1962), Ch. IV "Roman Catholic Apologetics in England".

scholars and scientists and that would prevent the accusation that he had launched a primitive attack on knowledge and learning.

Immediately after the appearance of the *Reflections* Woodward accused Baker of being a sceptic, because by postulating the uncertainty of history and the imperfection of science he implied that no complete historical or scientific proof could ever be given of the truth of the revealed text. This criticism by a scientist who held that there are "Historyes y^t are solid, perfect, & true" and who believed that "ye Study & Contemplation of Nature carryes us directly to ye Knowledge not only of his Being, but of his Power, & his Providence"[26] is understandable, although part of it was, I think, due to his being piqued about Baker's strictures on his own *Essay*. However, we also find a modern scholar characterizing Baker as a sceptic. In his "Thomas Baker: A Sceptic's Attack on Rhetoric" Gerald R. Miller states that "Baker's *Reflections upon Learning* is an example of English sceptical thought".[27] Yet it seems to me that this view is not tenable, because there is sufficient proof in the *Reflections* and elsewhere that Baker was not really a sceptic. In his correspondence with Woodward Baker denied the charge of scepticism, and in the *Reflections* itself there are several negative references to scepticism and sceptics. In the chapter on Moral Philosophy Baker dismisses the principles of Greek Pyrrhonism as "imaginary", and when discussing Malebranche's views on rhetoric and eloquence Baker's comment on Montaigne, a reputedly sceptical author, is that he is "not worth the mention".[28] On the other hand the *Reflections* provides enough evidence of Baker's esteem for learning. First of all, in the chapters on history, chronology and law Baker strikes one as the interested and well-informed scholar who expounds his views with evident zest. He is critical of Gratian's low opinion of human learning, and he is scathing in his remarks on the Quakers with their contempt for traditional knowledge and their claim to an inner light, and on the book-burning of the German Anabaptists. Furthermore, in the "Conclusion" Baker admits to having deliberately overstated his case against learning for tactical reasons.

In his brief and on the whole sympathetic "Life of the Rev. Mr.

---

26 Letter Woodward to Baker, 13 Nov. 1699 (Cambridge University Library, MS.Add.7647, no. 34).

27 Gerald R. Miller, "Thomas Baker: A Sceptic's Attack on Rhetoric", *Western Speech*, XXVII (1963), pp. 69-76. Miller's procedure of comparing Baker's views on rhetoric to Plato's theories strikes me as a clear case of over-interpretation.

28 Baker does not mention Montaigne explicitly, but he refers to Malebranche's treatment of Seneca and "two other Authors", that is Tertullian and Montaigne, in his *La Recherche de la Vérité* (Paris, 1674, Livre Deuxième, Troisième Partie, Chapitres III, IV, V).

Thomas Baker of St. John's College", written in 1778, Horace Walpole also discusses the merits and demerits of the *Reflections*.[29] In his opinion the book "wanted a logical conclusion", for "how does revelation supply the defects of knowledge, except in what it was to reveal? I will mention a few of Mr. Baker's topics, to which revelation seems a very inadequate supplement. In fact, except morality, I see not what revelation was intended to improve, has improved or could improve". In giving this comment Walpole showed that he did not realize Baker's unconditional acceptance of the literal meaning of the Scripture-text, also where it dealt with questions like the origin of the world. Walpole also failed to see that Baker's real intention with the work was to assert emphatically the absolute necessity of a belief in revelation in the face of the diminished esteem for it as a result of the growing feeling of self-confidence and self-sufficiency among many of his contemporaries. Baker's book is an attack on the pride of reason, on human presumptuousness in making such high claims for reason and learning; frequently phrases like "a Check to Man's Pride" and "some Check upon our Ambition" occur in the book. Therefore the *Reflections* can also be seen as belonging to the anti-pride wave discernible at the end of the seventeenth and the beginning of the eighteenth century.[30] In the "Conclusion" Baker writes that learning and the Word of God "may well consist" as long as reason is kept within its proper sphere, and that learning "being only a hand-maid to Religion, wherever it usurps upon that, is to be taken down and taught its Duty".

Within the scope of this paper it is impossible to discuss in detail all the subjects dealt with by Baker in the *Reflections*. Neither will this be necessary for our purposes, for if one regards Baker's book as a reaction against the spirit of the new times, it is only natural to concentrate mainly on those parts of learning where this spirit manifested itself, in Baker's view, most clearly and alarmingly. Generally speaking this applies to the subjects that together can be said to constitute the field of science and philosophy.[31] In his discussion of the more traditional branches of humanist learning Baker emerges as a scholar dealing with congenial subjects and speaking with a fair amount of authority; and although here Baker is also critical and tries to show how imperfect the state of learning in these fields is, his fear about the undermining effects on religion is far less conspicuous. Throughout the book Baker applies to all products of learning the strict criteria of their congruity with the Bible-text and their

---

29 *The Works of Horace Walpole* (9 vols., London, 1798-1825), vol. 2, pp. 339-363.

30 Cf. A.O. Lovejoy, "Pride in Eighteenth-Century Thought", *Essays in the History of Ideas* (Johns Hopkins Press, 1948), pp. 62-68.

31 Ch. V "Of Logic", ch. VI "Of Moral Philosophy", ch. VII "Of Natural Philosophy", ch. VIII "Of Astronomy", ch. IX "Of Metaphysics", ch. XV "Of Physic".

possible danger to religion. His comment on Samuel Bochart's *Geographia Sacra* is telling in this respect: "I am unwilling to oppose this Author for the sake of his Title . . . and shall readily grant, nay, it is what I contend for, that as far as it is Sacred, it is likewise true; but where he leaves *Moses*, he forsakes his Guide . . .".[32] Baker firmly holds that ecclesiastical history, in contrast to profane history, is always and unquestionably true. He accuses many modern critics of being far too free with the text of the Scriptures, and especially Le Clerc is singled out for attack by him.[33] Baker's animus against Le Clerc was, I think, caused by a combination of anger and contempt for Le Clerc's inadequacy as a scholar and fear about his unorthodox views on religion. Baker clearly values Simon's critical work more highly, although it is remarkable that he does not appear to regard Simon's biblical criticism as particularly dangerous.[34] Apart from the field of science and philosophy I will pay some attention to Baker's views on language and rhetoric,[35] because these will make clear that Baker, however far removed from the spirit of the new age, was also a child of his time and shared a number of assumptions current in Restoration and early eighteenth-century England.

Some later eighteenth-century writers blame Baker for not once mentioning John Locke or his works in the *Reflections*. In his *Life of Erasmus* J. Jortin sarcastically remarks that this is just "as if a man should write the lives of the Greek and Latin poets, and only omit Homer and Virgil",[36] and in the second edition of the *Biographia Britannica* this omission is attributed to Baker being "too much prejudiced against the new philosophy".[37] It seems to me first of all that Locke, although he is not mentioned explicitly by Baker, is clearly present in some places in the

---

32 Baker does not mention Bochart by name, but his reference to the author's research into "Phoenician Antiquities" makes it clear that he is speaking about Bochart's book (first pbd. 1646, extended edition 1674), and not about Nicolas Sanson's *Geographia Sacra* (Paris, 1662).

33 Le Clerc was greatly offended by Baker's reproach that his strictures on Erasmus in his *Ars Critica* (1696) were unjustified and that he was not sufficiently at home in the Greek language. In the index to the fourth edition of the *Ars Critica* (1712), under the word "Erasmus", Le Clerc angrily tried to refute Baker's charges (the English translation of Le Clerc's answer is to be found in the second edition of the *Biographia Britannica*, ed. Andrew Kippis, London, 1778, vol. 1, p. 519; for an account of this see also J. Jortin, *The Life of Erasmus*, 2 vols., London, 1758, vol. 1, pp. 550-551).

34 Cf. Bredvold's comment on Richard Simon's *Histoire critique du Vieux Testament* (1678): "What made his book so dangerous to the Protestants was the immense and impressive learning with which Simon demonstrated his thesis of the *unreliability* of the Biblical text" (*The Intellectual Milieu of John Dryden*, pp. 99-100).

35 Ch. II "Of Language", ch. III "Of Grammar", ch. IV "Of Rhetoric and Eloquence".

36 Jortin, *op.cit.*, vol. 1, p. 550.

37 Kippis, *op.cit.*, vol. 1, p. 519.

Reflections, and secondly that it was not so much Baker's prejudice against the new science, but his extreme caution and fearfulness which made him leave out the name of Locke. In the chapter on language Baker discusses Wilkins's *Essay Toward a Real Character and a Philosophical Language* and he says that if Wilkins were to write the book now, he would have to "suit his Design to the Philosophy in vogue ... and instead of Accidents must take in Modes", which is, I think, a reference to Locke's theories in the *Essay concerning Human Understanding*.[38] When dealing with logic and commenting upon the nature of ideas Baker writes: "Clear and distinct Perception has been given us for a Rule, and the Conformity of our Ideas with the Reality of Things has been given as another", which reminds one very much of Locke's words in the *Essay*.[39] Baker had read Wotton's *Reflections upon Ancient and Modern Learning* carefully, and in this work Wotton shows himself to be a great admirer of Locke, and he mentions him frequently. Then why did Baker not mention Locke and why did he refer to him only in a roundabout way? I think that a clue to the answer to these questions can be found in Baker's discussion of the work of the German philosopher von Tschirnhausen.[40] There he says that "It is not safe to censure an Author of so establish'd a Reputation". There can be no doubt that by 1699 Locke's reputation was greater than that of von Tschirnhausen, for the *Essay* had won him an enormous prestige in the 1690s; and one can easily imagine that to a person with Baker's make-up, who moreover did not feel himself to be on very safe ground, fear of possible negative consequences of an open attack on Locke—in fact fear of precisely such difficulties as he got involved in with Woodward—made him decide to refrain from mentioning Locke in his book. In this respect it is also striking that he does not mention Newton by name, but only refers to him briefly and cautiously.

Although Baker had tried to prepare himself well for his task and had read several of the most important works in the field of the new science and philosophy, it is obvious that he cannot in any way be called a scientist. Baker's attitude towards Bacon is one of qualified praise: he admits Bacon's importance in having made a clean sweep of the scholastic cobwebs and having invented a new method of inductive arguing based on observation and experiment, but he does not believe that Bacon's plan to discover the working of the world in this way is

---

38 For Locke's introduction of the term "modes" see the *Essay*, Book II, ch. XII, 4; see further also Book III "Of Words".
39 Cf. *Essay*, Book III, ch. XI, 9.
40 Ehrenfried Walther von Tschirnhausen (1651-1708); the two works discussed by Baker are *Medicina Corporis* (Amsterdam, 1686) and *Medicina Mentis* (Amsterdam, 1687).

feasible. Moreover, he blames Bacon for employing a needlessly intricate jargon and thus relapsing into the mistake of the scholastic philosophers. Typically enough Baker praises the majority of the members of the Royal Society for their modesty, and he maintains that the vanity of some of its members like Wilkins and Glanvill who have put forward such fantastic hypotheses, has injured the reputation of the Society. More than once Baker asserts that observation and experiment should be the basis of scientific theorizing, but this seems to be rather the due repetition of a general demand that was in the air at the time than the expression of a really personal conviction. Baker's chapter on astronomy shows that he had ventured into dangerous paths. He rejects the Ptolemaic theory of the heavens as far too contrived, for nature "acts in a more simple manner", but he also criticizes the Copernican system as assuming far too great constancy and regularity, for after all there is nothing so uncertain as fluctuating matter, "the most unstable thing in the World". Astronomers like Kepler, Hevelius and Riccioli are charged with presumption by Baker in their new theories of the moon. It is perhaps not surprising that Baker should only mention anatomy and botany, sciences that were relatively accessible to the non-expert and of no immediately apparent danger to religion, as the fields where considerable progress had been made of late.

Baker's severest criticism is reserved for Descartes. Evidently Baker regarded Descartes's theories as both largely wrong scientifically and extremely dangerous for religion, and it is interesting to find several of the charges levelled against Descartes at the end of the seventeenth century together in Baker's book.[41] Baker holds that Descartes is wrong in postulating matter and motion as the two basic principles and he remarks that most of Descartes's laws of motion have proved to be incorrect. He rejects Descartes's plenum and in general accuses him of framing hypotheses "without consulting Nature". He thinks Descartes's methodical doubt an arrogant and unnecessary procedure and in this he illustrates Lamprecht's point that many Englishmen were unwilling to apply doubt to the views of common sense.[42] However, what alarmed Baker most in Descartes's system of science was its mechanistic character and the consequent reduction or virtual dismissal of God's role in the working of the world, and here again Baker's attitude was like that of many other Englishmen at the time.[43] Baker calls Descartes's proof of the

---

41 For an account of the reception of Descartes's theories in seventeenth-century England see Marjorie Nicolson, "The Early Stage of Cartesianism in England", *Studies in Philology* (vol. 26, 1929), pp. 356-374 and S.P. Lamprecht, "The Role of Descartes in Seventeenth-Century England", *Studies in the History of Ideas* (vol. III, Columbia U.P., 1935), pp. 181-240.

42 Lamprecht, *op.cit.*, p. 211.

43 Lamprecht, *op.cit.*, pp. 223-224.

idea of God "the abstrusest and least conclusive Argument that has been brought". Malebranche's effort to reconcile Cartesianism with orthodox religion is viewed with approval by Baker but rather for the piety of the attempt than for its conclusiveness. Baker takes up the commonsensical attitude that Malebranche's theory of ideas as ultimately founded in God, is too abstracted and ethereal. Similarly Newton's assertion of the principle of attraction receives the comment that probably Newton's intentions were pious but that the theory itself is "not . . . so Philosophical".

In the chapter on natural philosophy Baker states that a scientist, no matter how deep and extensive his researches are, will always find in the end that "the ways of Nature, like those of God, are past Man's finding out". Baker's attitude towards God's creation is one of reverent wonder and he frequently remarks that we should be contented to admire God's power and wisdom, without being so arrogant as to meddle with things that are too deep for us. Against Descartes's mechanism Baker argues the constant and direct presence of God in the world. Again and again Baker emphasizes "the shortness of our Reach"; the very fact that we need a discipline like logic is itself a sign of the imperfection of our understanding. Subtle matter and intestine motion escape the closest scrutiny, and in medicine we will perhaps never exactly understand the working of the "Humours and Spirits and Blood". Baker feels that modern science disparages man as God's creature, as appears from his discussion of Fontenelle's *Plurality of Worlds* and of the view that there existed vast other worlds besides the earth. He contends against this view that if it were true, we would have found more about it in the Bible, and he accuses these "World-mongers" of undervaluing the earth. Did not Christ after all redeem it by his death? At the end of his chapter on astronomy Baker claims that there is "more Perfection in one Rational Immaterial soul, than in the whole Mass of Matter, be it never so bulky". This remark, clearly revealing Baker's fear of the materialistic implications of the new science, reminds one strongly of the same assertion of the importance of man's spiritual side by that very pious seventeenth-century scientist Robert Boyle,[44] who "strongly opposed the tendency to

---

[44] "I am by these considerations disposed to think the soul of man a nobler and more valuable being, than the whole corporeal world; which though I readily acknowledge it to be admirably contrived, and worthy of the almighty and omniscient author, yet consists but of an aggregate of portions of brute matter...", *The Excellency of Theology...*, London, 1674 (Thomas Birch, ed., *The Works of the Honourable Robert Boyle*, 6 vols., London, 1772, vol. 4, p. 19).

depreciate man's importance in the world and to relegate him to the condition of a spectator".[45]

It was good tactics of Baker to place the discussion of language at the beginning of his book, for, using terms and arguments that strongly resemble Locke's,[46] Baker scores a point by maintaining that language as the necessary channel for the conveying of knowledge, is essentially imperfect, and will thus always be rather an obstacle than a help to knowledge and learning. But whereas Locke insisted that this situation could be remedied if only people would use language more accurately and consistently, Baker states that language, being largely the effect of chance, will always remain so uncertain a medium that the advancement of learning will be hindered by it. He grants that if there were only one language, uniform and unambiguous, "Men might then immediately apply to Things, whereas now a great part of our Time is spent in Words", and the distinction he here makes between words and things was a typical feature of the post-Restoration discussions about language.[47] In his treatment of rhetoric and eloquence Baker also voices the common views of the period. He condemns Puritan rhetoric and associates the use of rhetoric with political and social unrest. It is interesting to see, by the way, how much the criterion of reason is invoked by Baker in his attack on eloquence. He says that eloquence does not persuade "from Rational Arguments, which ought to be the proper Means of convincing a reasonable Man . . .", and that eloquence "is usually a Cheat upon the Understanding; it deceives us with Appearances, instead of Things; and makes us think we see Reason, whilst it is tickling our Sense . . .". Baker criticizes the metaphysical style of the early seventeenth century for its affectation, its "fantastick Dress and Jingle of Words". Speaking about style Baker makes a remark that could have come from the pages of the *Spectator*: ". . . a decent Negligence is often a Beauty in Expression as well as dress". Yet as a scholar, who moreover had his roots in Restoration England, Baker himself does not aim at politeness in the first place; he does not really object to "Rough language and barbarousness of Expression, that were made so great Objections upon the Reviving of Learning and are yet so with polite Men whose Ears can bear nothing without Ornament and Smoothness". All in all it will be clear that in his views on language and rhetoric Baker in no way distinguished himself

---

45 Frederick Copleston S.J., *A History of Philosophy, vol. 5, Modern Philosophy: The British Philosophers: Hobbes to Paley* (Image Books, 1964), p. 156.
46 *Essay concerning Human Understanding*, Book III, ch. X "Of the Abuse of Words".
47 Cf. A.C. Howell, "*Res et Verba*: Words and Things", Stanley E. Fish, ed., *Seventeenth Century Prose* (OUP, 1971), pp. 187-199.

from the average educated person in Restoration England.[48]

The *Reflections upon Learning* could in a way be seen as the side-step of a traditional scholar who from the start felt insecure about venturing into the field of the new science and whose insecurity was considerably strengthened by especially Woodward's reaction to the book. The reason why he wrote the book in the 1690s was his growing alarm about the arrogant optimism of many of his contemporaries about man and the world. He himself was convinced of the moral and intellectual imperfection of man, and his *Reflections* was a plea for humility because man by himself is too small and constantly needs God's help. Baker's book was not an isolated instance of the reaction against the overvaluing of human reason and the depreciation of revelation. Some of the writings of John Dryden, Jeremy Collier and Peter Browne can be seen as clearly springing from a similar anxiety.[49] I have said before that Baker's book stood out against the prevailing spirit of the time, and this is of course largely true, but on the other hand it has to be borne in mind that the popularity of the book in the first half of the eighteenth century points to an appeal that went beyond the circle of the nonjurors. In fact the book's popularity could be said to be an illustration of Leslie Stephen's point that, whereas early eighteenth-century theology was often deistical in spirit, "the commonsense of the country was entirely on the side of Revelation . . .".[50]

---

48 Cf. R. F. Jones, "Science and English Prose Style, 1650-75", in Fish, *op.cit.*, pp. 53-89; R.F. Jones, "Science and Language in England of the Mid-Seventeenth Century", in Fish, *op.cit.*, pp. 94-111.

49 Cf. John Dryden, *Religio Laici* (1682), Jeremy Collier, *Essays upon Several Moral Subjects* (1697), Peter Browne, *Letter in Answere to a Book entitled Christianity not Mysterious* (1697).

50 Leslie Stephen, *History of English Thought in the Eighteenth Century* (first pbd. 1876, 2 vols., New York, 1962), vol. 2, p. 314.

ENGLISH VIRTUE IN BAVARIAN BAROQUE LITERATURE: MARY WARD AND HER BIOGRAPHER MARCUS FRIDL

Hans Pörnbacher

To speak of national virtues or, for that matter, of vices is not unproblematical. After all it was the English philosopher Johannes Duns Scotus who warned against false generalizations and the prejudices they give rise to. So when I speak here tout court of "English virtue" I refer to great figures in English intellectual history whose virtuous life and work have found expression in the literature of Bavaria. I shall present one single instance, however tempting it would be to conduct an exhaustive investigation of English examples in Bavarian baroque literature.[1]

It was after all in Bavaria that Maria Ward (1585-1645),[2] the subject of this article, found support for her idea to further the education of young women. The necessity, the urgency, and the novelty of this idea need no elaboration here. For the purposes of this small contribution it is sufficient to keep in mind that Munich became very early on the centre of Maria Ward's English Ladies ("Englische Fräulein"), and indeed, until 1929, was the generalate of this order. When in 1630 a decree issued by the Roman authorities (without the knowledge of Pope Urban VIII) ordered the suspension of all establishments of Maria Ward's English Ladies, the Munich foundation continued, and so was able to celebrate its 350th anniversary in 1977.

While Maria Ward had already been in contact with Wittelsbacher princes in Liège earlier on, she made her first acquaintance with Munich

---

1 Many examples could be found in the Jesuit plays: in Jean-Marie Valentin's inventory (Stuttgart, 1983) or in Elida Maria Szarota's soon to be concluded edition of play summaries, the so-called "Periochen" (Munich, 1979 etc.). A very fine example in lyric poetry is Jacob Balde's Ode *Thomas Mori Constantia* (Lyricorum Lib. I, 3). See also Eckart Schäfer, *Deutscher Horaz. Conrad Celtis. George Fabricus. Paul Melissus. Jacob Balde* (Wiesbaden, 1976, pp. 205-212).

2 For information about Maria Ward, see Peter Guilday, *The English Catholic Refugees on the Continent 1558-1795* (London 1914, pp. 163-214 [VI. The Institute of the Blessed Virgin Mary]); *Lexikon für Theologie und Kirche* [2] vol. 10, 955 f. (by J. Grisar); about Bavaria in particular: M. Theolinde Winkler, *Maria Ward und das Institut der Englischen Fräulein in Bayern* (Munich, 1926); Joseph Grisar, *Maria Wards Institut vor römischen Kongregationen* (Rome, 1964); *350 Jahre Englische Fräulein in München* (Festschrift, Bayerland, Sonderausgabe, March, 1977).

and Bavaria at the end of 1626.³ As poetic legend has it this occurred on the feast of her countryman, the saintly Thomas of Canterbury on the 29th of December. She soon obtained the sympathy and the full support of the Elector Maximilian, who was deeply impressed by the personality of this distinguished, determined but modest English woman. He did everything in his power to enable her to put into effect her ideas about the education of young women in his capital and territory.

Maria Ward did not stay long in Munich. In 1631 she once more travelled to Rome to defend her enterprise there. Six years later she returned to her English birthplace where she died on the 30th of January 1645 at the age of sixty, and was buried in the cemetery at Osbaldwick. But her idea had taken root in Bavaria and remained alive there, and with it her memory. In the 17th century the very successful Jesuit author Tobias Lohner from Neuötting (1619-1680) wrote a life of Maria Ward which never appeared in print but is preserved in manuscript in the archive of the English Ladies in Munich.⁴ Soon after the centenary celebration of the order in Bavaria a life of the founder appeared in Augsburg, entitled:

*Englische Tugend-Schul | Mariae | unter denen von Ihro Päbstlichen Heiligkeit | Clemente XI. | gutgeheissnen | und bestättigten Reglen | dess | von der Hochgebohrnen Frauen, Frauen | Maria Ward, | Als Stiffterin aufgerichteten Edlen | Instituts Mariä, | insgemein unter dem Namen | der Englischen Fräulein |*⁵

The author of this work in two fat volumes, the simple village priest Marcus Fridl, is one of the many forgotten writers of baroque Bavaria. He is a quite fascinating person whose career sheds much light on the ardent spiritual life of the rural Catholic South of the Holy Roman Empire.⁶ Except for a few dates we learn little about Fridl from his

---

3 Towards the end of 1626 Maria Ward was apparently so disheartened that she wanted to give up her plans and return to England. Her last resort was the Bavarian Elector Maximilian. Therefore Maria Ward made a detour via Munich. At the time Maximilian was at the height of his power and enjoyed great esteem both at the Emperor's court and at the Holy See. Besides, Maximilian took a strong interest in religious conditions in England. After all, it was Maximilian who had founded a college at Liège for the English Jesuits to train English Catholics. For more details about Maria Ward's journey to Munich and about Maximilian's English interests, see: Joseph Grisar, "Das erste Verbot der Ordensgründung Maria Wards (1628)", *Stimmen der Zeit*, 113 (1927), pp. 34-51 (about Maximilian, pp. 49 f.). For the college in Liège, see *Florus Anglo-Bavaricus* (Liège, 1685; reprint, with a new introduction by T.A. Birrell, Gregg International Publishers, 1970).

4 For Tobias Lohner, see *Allg. Deutsche Biographie*, vol. 19; the title of his biography is: *Gottseeliges Leben, Vnd fürtreffliche Tugendten Donna Maria Ward, der Hochlöblichen Stiffterin der so genanten Engländischen Gesellschafft*.

5 Bayerische Staatsbibliothek, Munich, 4° V. SS. 589 and 4° H. Mon. 231.

6 For intellectual history, see Benno Hubensteiner, *Vom Geist des Barock. Kultur und Frömmigkeit im alten Bayern* (Munich, 1967; 2nd ed., 1978); for literary history,

biographers. Klement Alois Baader mentions him in his encyclopedia *Das gelehrte Baiern*[7] and reports that he was well versed in Latin, French, English and Spanish. This suggests varied interests and a certain degree of education. He published a series of edifying books, often without putting his name to them, because they were translations from other languages, primarily Spanish and Italian.[8] More recent authors' dictionaries no longer mention him.

Marcus Fridl hailed from the Augsburg region. He was born in Burgstall, a hamlet belonging to the parish of Mering to the south of Augsburg. His parents owned the "Amplbauerhof", so called, because the farm, which was otherwise unencumbered, was taxed for the lights ("Ampel") at the tomb of Emperor Ludwig the Bavarian's wife. Fridl studied at Dillingen and Ingolstadt (see note 7). Early on, in 1711, he took up his duties as a priest in Moorenweis, a village close to the Cistercian monastery of Fürstenfeld, and followed his calling there till 1744. During his last years at Moorenweis he also played a decisive part in the foundation of the new seminary for priests in Pfaffenhausen, somewhat to the north of Mindelheim, which, in the early 18th century (1705-1714), belonged to the Dukes of Marlborough and consequently is perhaps not unknown to English readers. In the end he moved to Pfaffenhausen where he served as *Regens* until, at the age of 78, he withdrew from the administration of the seminary to spend the rest of his days in his birthplace. There, in Burgstall, he built a chapel modelled on Loretto, joined a small hermitage and till his death led a life of prayer and

---

see Hans Pörnbacher in: *Handbuch der bayerischen Geschichte*, vol. II (ed. Max Spindler, Munich, 1977); for art history, see John Bourke, *Baroque Churches of Central Europe* (London, 1958).

7 Klement Alois Baader, *Das gelehrte Bayern oder Lexikon aller Schriftsteller, welche Bayern im achtzehnten Jahrhundert erzeugte oder ernährte*, vol. I (Nürnberg and Sulzbach, 1804, Col. 350); J.A. Stegmayr, *Studenten der ehem. Universität Dillingen*, vol. I (Dillingen, 1941, typescript): Fridl is mentioned under theologians of 1698; Goetz v. Pölnitz, *Matrikel der Universität Ingolstadt-Landshut-München*, vol. III, 1941, Col. 43. On Pfaffenhausen, see Th. Specht "Geschichte des ehemaligen Priesterseminars Pfaffenhausen (1743-1804)", *Jb Hist. Verein Dillingen* XXX (1917), pp. 1-78.

8 Inventory of his writings in Stadtbibliothek Augsburg, in Studienbibliothek Dillingen und in der Bayer. Staatsbibliothek München:
S. Francisci vest-stehende Demuth, Augspurg 1731;
Evangelische Tugend-Schul, Theil 1.2. Augspurg 1732;
Jesu Christi Unsers Lieben Herrn Ruhe, Augspurg 1732;
Beste Bruderschafft, Augspurg 1734;
Lieb mit Bestand in Leid und Freud, Friedberg 1734;
Der hl. Antonius von Padua, Augspurg 1735;
Grosse Klag ohn alle Klag, Augspurg 1741;
Allerreichstes Erbtheil, Mindelheim 1753;
Vindeliciae Sacrae, vol. III, Aug. Vind. 1756.

good works, performing modest priestly duties and teaching the young. He died in 1754. His tombstone in the chapel bears this inscription:

> Parva haec fossa capit virum, in quo omnia magna, cujus nomen ob zelum ac scientiam etiam Romae inclaruit. Fuit is pl[urimum]. r[everendus]. ac cl[assissimus]. D[ominus]. Marcus Fridl SS[Sanctissimae]. Th[eologiae]. et J[uris]. U[trivsque]. C[andidatus]., | in Burk, Bayrn ac Mohrnweis par[ochus]. et cam[merarius]., I. Regens Pfaffenh., sacelli hujus fundator. Postquam etiam inter nubila semper effulsit, hic tandem, echeu, 12.Kal.Dec.
> soL Iste In Morte oCCIDIt, (=1754)
> VbI orIens LaetantI MVnDo ILLVXIt. (=1675)[9]

Pastor Fridl is recalled in Moorenweis on account of the parish church which he built there. Considering it is sited in a mere village, this church is exceptionally beautiful, of note if only because of its size, distinguished because of its harmonious proportions. Pastor Fridl managed to persuade the famous master-architect from Wessobrunn, Joseph Schmuzer,[10] to build the church because Moorenweis was a parish of this venerable monastery in the Pfaffenwinkel, a region in the south-west corner of Bavaria. But apparently the parish had to bear most of the construction costs. It is only much later (c. 1775), when the church was finally decorated with murals by the famous painter Matthäus Günther and with plasterwork by Thassilo Zöpf that the monastery was able to make a more substantial financial contribution. Building was started in 1717. To alleviate the shortage of money that soon made itself felt Pastor Fridl, in the tradition of the village, made a pilgrimage to the Holy City.[11] But both Marcus Fridl and his mother also made a very considerable personal contribution. They sold their farm in Burgstall and used the

---

9 Quoted in *Chronik von Moorenweis* (1875) by Franz Seraph Wecker (mayor of the village); the translation reads:

> This small tomb houses a man who was great in everything he did. Because of his industry and his knowledge his name was well-known even in Rome. This man is the very venerable and famous Father Marcus Fridl, Candidatus in holy theology and both systems of jurisprudence, pastor in Purk, Beuern and Moorenweis and first *Regens* in Pfaffenhausen, the builder of this chapel. After he has always shone, also in dark times, may he here find peace.
> This sun set in death,
> Here where it started to light up and gladden the world.

10 Gabriele Dischinger, *Johann und Joseph Schmuzer. Zwei Wessobrunner Barockbaumeister* (Sigmaringen, 1977, p. 144 [Moorenweis] and p. 147 [Pfaffenhausen]).

11 The inscription on the tomb also seems to point to a journey to Rome. The aim of the journey could have been the request for recognition of a pilgrimage or of the privileges of a fraternity in Moorenweis. Two paintings were presented on the occasion of the centenary celebrations of the consecration of the church in 1842; the first shows Pastor Fridl at his audience with the Pope, and the second shows him on his return to Moorenweis. Today both paintings hang in the choir of the church.

Englische Tugend-Schul
MARIÆ
unter denen von Ihro Päbstlichen Heiligkeit
CLEMENTE XI.
gutgeheißnen/ und bestättigten Reglen
deß
von der Hochgebohrnen Frauen, Frauen
Maria Ward,
Als Stiffterin aufgerichteten Edlen
Instituts Mariä,
insgemein unter dem Namen
der Englischen Fräulein
Erster Theil.
das ist;
Wunder-volle Lebens-Beschreibung diser hoch-
gebohrnen Englischen Frauen Stiffterin/ und Seelen-
eiffrigen Dienerin GOttes.
Aus verschiedenen glaubwürdigen Schrifften zusammen getragen/
und durch eingestängte Stellen der Heil. Schrifft/ Geschichten der Heiligen/
Sitten-Lehr/ auch denckwürdige Sprüch anderer Wissenschafften erkläret/
und zum Druck gegeben von
A. R. D. Marco Fridl, SS. Theol. & J. V. Cand.
Pfarrer in Morenweiß/ dann des Land-Capitls Schwab-
hausen Camerario.
AUGSPURG/ In Verlag Martin Happachs seel. Erben und Consort.
Anno 1732.

Bayerische Staatsbibliothek, Munich, 4° V. SS. 589;
Frontispiece see p. 156

proceeds for the church.[12] On the north wall of the church a tablet commemorates the magnanimous woman who until her death lived in the parsonage at Moorenweis:

> Maria Fridlin
> Amplbäuerin auf dem befreiten
> Kaiserlichen Amplhof in Burgstall,
> starb anno 1736 den 24. März im
> 85. Jahre.

So it is thanks primarily to the beautiful church that Marcus Fridl is remembered in the village where he worked as a parish priest for more than thirty years. But little is known about his books there. Let us here at least consider his bulky, two-volume *Lebens-Beschreibung der Hochgebohrnen Frauen Maria Ward, diser hochgebohrnen Englischen Frauen Stiffterin | und Seeleneiffrigen Dienerin GOttes.* This work appeared in Augsburg in 1732 and is dedicated to the Bavarian Electress Maria Amalia. Like all biographies of saintly men and women Fridl's representation of the life of Maria Ward is a true *Tugend-Schul*, *i.e.* a mirror of the Christian life in which every reader can and should recognise a reflection of his own life. *Englische Tugend-Schul* appears on the title page of the book, where "englische" does not merely refer to Maria Ward's country of origin but also offers the suggestion of "angelic" virtue.

To be sure, Fridl made a thorough study of his subject, and it would not be surprising if he had also consulted letters and documents in Rome about Maria Ward and her work.[13] He mentions many sources, quotes from letters and conversations, and presents a wealth of interesting cultural and historical particulars, for instance about Maria Ward's diet or about her use of mineral springs in the vicinity of Rome. But above all the book is distinguished by its beautiful and lucid use of language, by its clear composition and by profound thought. Of course the individual virtues play a large part. Next to perseverance and steadfastness, humility and charity, patience has an especially important place. In volume II, in a chapter on Maria Ward's patience, the author even quotes one of her pronouncements in the original English: "there is no remedy but patience" (p. 196). In volume I he speaks of her patience in suffering. Here follows a short sample, which will also serve to give an impression of his style:

> ...Ich erinnere mich von den Chinesischen Kayseren gelesen zu haben / dass sie zuweilen mit Million-weiss Soldaten wider ihre Feind ins Feld gezogen. Das ware vil Volck. Aber die fromme Frau Maria hat die Gewalt-leidende Himmels-Vestung

---

12 Cf. *Chronik von Moorenweis*, p. 15.

13 No doubt the institutes of the English Ladies, especially the institute in Augsburg, provided him with materials for his biography.

mit noch weit mehr Schmertzen bekriegt / und gestürmet. Also / dass man von ihrem Leyden und Gedult gar füglich singen könte / wie folgt:

>Gross war sie in der Gedult
>Wenig Freud / lauter Leid
>War ihr gantze Lebens-Zeit.
>GOtt hat sie aufs höchst gelibt /
>Und durch alle Creutz geübt /
>Dass ihr Herz offt in Schmerz
>War versenckt / und sehr betrübt.

Of course Maria Ward's arrival in Munich plays a special part in this biography.[14] And if Marcus Fridl calls the reigning Elector Maximilian I, admittedly a great and important ruler, a "teutscher Salomon", he does not hesitate to compare Maria Ward to the Queen of Saba either, "welche zu unserem teutschen Salomon gantz gewiss weit grössere Schätz der Tugend mit sich gebracht / als jene Schätz von Gold und Edelgestein". Although Maria Ward appears before the Elector in a pitiful cortege Maximilian recognises "die Fürtrefflichkeit dieser seiner auslandischen Gäst gleich bey dem ersten Anblick sattsam: Er wusste auch gar wohl gut / wie die Schrifft sagt / das kostbare von dem schlechten [schlichten, einfachen] auszusöndern / das ist / den innwendigen herrlichen Geschmuck der Tugend von dem / schlechten äusserlichen Aufzug" (pp. 264-5). Therefore it was not long before an establishment of the English Ladies was founded in Munich in a house donated and generously endowed by the Elector.

In accordance with the spirit of innovation after the Council of Trent, the education of the young had initially been taken up primarily by the Jesuits; but now the English Ladies applied themselves to the education of girls and to the care of orphans who were the sad legacy of the Thirty Years' War. When Maria Ward, in "ihrer Grund-losen Demuth / ihrer grossen Bescheidenheit / Höflichkeit und Weissheit" (p. 270) endeavours to express her gratitude, the Elector answers:

>"Nicht sie / sondern er / seye schuldig zu dancken / wie er ihr auch würcklich Danck gesagt hat / dass sie das Hauss und Stiftung angenommen / mit dem Beysatz: Er wisse wohl / was CHristus der HERR gesagt: dass nemlich der Tagwercker seines Lohns werth seye. Zu dem sagte Seine Churfürstliche Durchläucht ferner / ist uns gar wohl bekannt / was massen die Engländer die erste gewesen / welche die Völcker in Teutschland in dem Catholischen Glauben unterwisen haben / hoffen also auch wir / dass unserer Unterthanen Töchter gleichfalls von euch in gutem und Christlichem Wandel aufs beste werden unterrichtet werden. Also redete bey Uebergebung der Stifftung der grosse Held und Fürst Maximilianus der Erste Chur-Fürst in Bayern. Dessen letzter Wort sonders wohl zu mercken seynd / als durch welche klar angedeutet wird / dass die fleissige Anführung der jungen Töchteren zu einem guten Christlichen Wandel nicht nur

---

14 Vol. I, Book II, chapter X: "Frau Maria wird zu München wohl empfangen / richtet ein Hauss auf / und gehet manches mit ihr vorbey" (pp. 263-273).
15 Matthäus Rader, *Bavaria Sancta et Pia* (Munich, 1615-1628).

das Zihl und End / sondern auch die Grund-Veste diser Stifftung seye . . . Andere Umständ der Aufrichtung und Fortsetzung dises fürtrefflichen und der Zeit ansehnlichsten Instituts-Hauses werden wir an einem anderen Ort anhandeln. Allda haben wir nun fürnemlich von der Frauen Stiffterin zu reden.

Und bisshero zwar haben wir von ihr als einer Ausländerin geredet, nunmehro aber müssen wir sie als eine Landsmännin / Burgerin / und Hausgenossne erkennen . . . Mitbürger der Heiligen seynd sie / allermassen sie eben wie vil andere ausländische Heilige / insonderheit verschiedene heilige Engelländer / wie der gelehrte Raderus[15] schreibet / ihren beständigen Wohnsitz in Bayerländischen Landen genommen . . ." (pp. 270-1)

Like the English Walburga and her brothers Wunibald and Willibald in Eichstätt, like many other English missionaries in Bavaria, Maria Ward had earned the "rights of citizenship" and was a foreigner no longer: this sympathetic thought of Fridl's must serve as a conclusion to these pages. They have been concerned with English virtue in Bavarian baroque literature. But what the industrious and scholarly village priest Marcus Fridl described in the early 18th century does not merely belong to the past. Much of it lives on today, not only through the memory of Maria Ward and the name "Englische Fräulein", but also through the virtues and ideals which we associate with this great woman and her order.

THE ENGLISH ACTORS IN THE LOW COUNTRIES, 1585 - c. 1650: AN ANNOTATED BIBLIOGRAPHY

J.G. Riewald

> [*The English actors*:] ". . . sy suysebollen, en draeyen als een tol: / Sy spreeckent uyt haar geest, dees [viz., *the Rederijkers*] leerent uyt een rol".
> G.A. Bredero, *Moortje* III. iv. 1458-61

When, almost thirty years ago, I consulted Professor Birrell about the feasibility of doing some research on the English players who passed through the United Provinces and the Spanish Netherlands in the late sixteenth and the first half of the seventeenth century, he wrote me: "Your suggestion of work on the English actors in the Netherlands sounds excellent—this is a subject for which in general there is usually a lot of interest. I don't know how large your work . . . is going to be, but an article on the subject certainly *ought* to find a home in one of the learned journals". And he followed this with some suggestions for tracing their steps in England. The article appeared in 1959, a second one in 1960, both in *English Studies* (91, 92).[1] In grateful recognition of Professor Birrell's generosity in sharing his learning with others, I now venture to offer to fellow investigators an annotated bibliography of the subject, together with a tentative survey of unexplored or underexplored sources, both Dutch and English.[2]

I

Undoubtedly one of the reasons for the interest of theatre historians and Shakespeare scholars in the English travelling actors is the fascinating possibility that Shakespeare himself may have been one of them. In *TGV*, Valentine, on being questioned by the second outlaw: "Have you the

---

1 The numbers refer to the serial numbers of the entries in the Bibliography.
2 I should also like to thank H.W. Crundell, Bristol; Dr. D. Grosheide, Utrecht University Library; James McManaway, Folger Shakespeare Library; Professor W. Schrickx, University of Ghent; and Mgr. Th.H.J. Zwartkruis, Haarlem, for various kindnesses. I am particularly indebted to Ph.H. Breuker, of the Fryske Akademy, Leeuwarden, for permitting me to use the evidence he has found for the presence of English actors in Leeuwarden and Harlingen.

tongues?", answers: "My youthful travel therein made me happy, / Or else I often had been miserable" (IV.i.33-35). In this context it has been suggested that a number of topical allusions in certain Shakespeare plays seem to prove that he visited France and Italy.[3] It has also been argued that the dramatist had practical sea experience and that this accounts for his knowledge of seamanship and the astonishing range of his nautical vocabulary.[4] There is, furthermore, the scene of the players on tour in *Ham.*, which might reflect Shakespeare's own experience.[5] These and similar conjectures are certainly tantalizing, but they are no proof that Shakespeare himself ever acted on the Continent. His name does not occur among the hundred or so names of English players that have been recorded in Germany and surrounding countries. In itself this is not at all surprising since he would have been too young an apprentice to have his name carried on the pay-roll: normally only the leader or leaders of the troupe are mentioned in the official documents. Yet, perhaps somewhere, buried in a forgotten record, there may be evidence of when and where Shakespeare acted in Europe.

As has been implied, the subject of the English strolling actors in the Low Countries cannot be studied in isolation. The vast geographical extent of their itineraries in Germany and the rest of Europe is strikingly illustrated in the diagrams published by Herz (48), Price (63), and Stahl (81). As compared with the Netherlands, the wealth and quality of the German archival material is absolutely superior. No wonder then that German scholars played such a prominent part in opening up this field of study.[6] The aforementioned diagrams also show that the importance of the Netherlands lies in the fact that most of the English companies passed through this country on their way to the great German cities, where they can be traced periodically, and to the German princely courts, where they used to practise their art for many years in succession, probably by invitation. Consequently, with very few exceptions, the Netherlands was the first European country to experience the refreshing impact of a completely new style of acting.

English players crossed the North Sea for various reasons, but the principal motive was always the economic one: "We can be bankrupts...

---

3 Georges Lambin, *Voyages de Shakespeare en France et en Italie* (Genève: E. Droz, 1962).

4 A.F. Falconer, *Shakespeare and the Sea* (New York: Frederick Ungar, 1964) and *A Glossary of Shakespeare's Sea and Naval Terms, including Gunnery* (London: Constable, 1965).

5 Three of the actors who played at Elsinore in 1586 afterwards became members of the Chamberlain's men, Shakespeare's company; see Jacob A. Riis, "Hamlet's Castle", *Century Magazine* (New York), 61 (1901), 388-98.

6 For a survey of their work see 92, pp. 67-69.

on this side, and gentlemen of a company beyond the sea: we burst at London, and are pieced up at Rotterdam".[7] Their principal ports of arrival were the rapidly growing Amsterdam; Antwerp, which had just passed the zenith of its prosperity; Dordrecht, afterwards the seat of the English Court of Merchant Adventurers; Flushing, where an English garrison was stationed; Middelburg, next to Amsterdam the principal seaport of the United Provinces in the sixteenth century; Rotterdam, which was then outstripping Dordrecht as a commercial centre; Veere, the residence of many Englishmen and Scotchmen; and Calais. From the passport issued by the Lord High Admiral on 10 February 1592 on behalf of Robert Browne, John Bradstreet, Thomas Sackville, and Richard Jones, it appears that these actors intended to travel to Germany via Zeeland, Holland, and Friesland (see 110).

What was the repertory of these strolling players? A catalogue of the pieces acted by them in Dresden between 1 June and 4 December 1626 contains the names of forty-one plays, including Shakespeare's *Rom.*, *JC*, *Ham.*, and *Lr* (21, pp. cxiv-cxvi). On the basis of the available evidence Lawrence Marsden Price (75, pp. 15-16) has been able to itemize sixty plays as having been performed in Germany. In his list practically all the major Elizabethan, Jacobean, and Caroline dramatists are represented, except Jonson, Middleton, and Webster. At first (i.e., till about 1608) the actors performed in English, but unfortunately not a single scrap of the original dialogue has survived. The garbled texts of a number of their plays have come down to us in early printed German versions (1), and in manuscripts. The titles—authentic or otherwise—are recorded, but the names of the dramatists are never given. In a few rare cases contemporary documents and publications contain details about the theatres, the stages, the scenery, and the costumes. We also have one or two (rather crude) pictures of the actors themselves (see, e.g., 74 and 95).

In contrast with the German archives the public records in the Low Countries are a pretty barren source. No original English or Dutch texts have survived, nor have details about stages, designs, or costumes. At best the municipal archives contain some general indication of the *sort* of play to be acted: comedies, tragedies, histories, pastorals, &c. (cf. Polonius' presentation of the strolling actors in *Ham.* II.ii.415-18), but not a single *title* has emerged from the records. The only one I have been able to discover occurs in a book, the *Disputationes Theologicae Selectae* (1667) by that notorious theatrophobe Gisbertus Voetius. In Pt. 4 of this work he writes: "Agatur *tragico comoedia Jobi* (quam ego adolescens

---

[7] *The Run-awayes Answer* (1625), as quoted in J. Payne Collier, *Memoirs of the Principal Actors in the Plays of Shakespeare* (London: Shakespeare Society, 1846), p. 143, n. 1.

FRANS HALS: MONSIEUR PEECKELHAERING, or DER LUSTIGE ZECHER
c. 1628-30
Staatliche Kunstsammlungen, Kassel

Leidae è circumforaneis histrionibus Anglis actam memini)" (2, p. 361). Voetius studied divinity at Leiden from April 1604 to April 1611. The play he saw may have been *Job*, a lost biblical history by Robert Greene (?), first performed between 1586 and 1593 (?), or a descendant from *De Iobi Iusti Afflictionibus*, a lost tragedy written by Ralph Radcliffe (1519?-1559), a schoolmaster at Hitchin, and first performed at his school between 1546 (?) and 1556.[8] William Peadle's characterization of his pantomimes—"fraeye ende eerlicke spelen"—,which he performed at Leiden in the church of the Bagijnhof (then part of the university buildings) in November 1608, seems to re-echo Radcliffe's "jocunda & honesta spectacula". However, since at least five English companies performed in Leiden when Voetius was there, it is impossible to determine which of them acted *Job*. Unfortunately it cannot be proved that the "comedy" of *The Murder of the King of France* ("De moort van de Coninck van Vranckrijck"), acted at Flushing in 1610-11, was performed by Englishmen. The entry in the city records may refer to a performance of Abraham de Koning's *Tragi-Comedie over de Doodt van Henricus de Vierde, Koning van Vrancrijck en Naverrae*,[9] written in 1610.

But while the archival and printed evidence in the Low Countries is very meagre indeed, Dutch art has made a magnificent contribution to the pictorial record which surpasses anything that has emerged from contemporary manuscripts and publications. I am referring to that lively model by Frans Hals, "Monsieur Peeckelhaering", or "Der Lustige Zecher" (see Plate), now in the Staatliche Kunstsammlungen, Kassel. The same man posed for the so-called "Mulatto", now in the Museum der Bildenden Künste, Leipzig.[10] The two portraits, both dating from c. 1628-30, represent Robert Reynolds—"Meester van de Engelsche Commedianten", as he is styled in an Amsterdam notarial act of 1636 (61, p. 142)—, who made a considerable reputation on the Continent under the clown-name Pickleherring. They are a masterly evocation of the dizzying naturalistic vein of Bredero's improvising, spinning and twirling English comedians, as opposed to the wooden histrionics of the Dutch *Rederijkers*. We know that Reynolds had been in Amsterdam before 1621 (1, sig. Zz2^v). As I have shown elsewhere (92, p. 84), he probably resided in

---

8 See Alfred Harbage, *Annals of English Drama, 975-1700*, rev. S. Schoenbaum (London: Methuen, 1964), pp. 28-29, 52-53, and *CHEL*, V, p. 103.

9 Ed. G.R.W. Dibbets (Zwolle: W.E.J. Tjeenk Willink, 1967); see N. Wijngaards, *LT* 242 (Dec. 1967), 722.

10 For a description of these paintings see Seymour Slive, *Frans Hals*, National Gallery of Art: Kress Foundation Studies in the History of European Art, III (London: Phaidon Press, 1974), pp. 39-41. In the so-called "Mulatto" painting Pickleherring's pointing forefinger is a gesture traditionally given to fools, and generally implies scorn or derision.

Utrecht and The Hague in 1629. Hals, who was an associate of a local Haarlem Chamber of Rhetoricians (*Rederijkerskamer*), may have seen him act on some unknown occasion.

II

Almost four hundred years after Fynes Moryson (50) and Arend van Buchell (55) first noticed the presence of English actors in Holland, the time has come to review the published evidence up to now. The following bibliography covers books, dissertations, theses, and articles containing details about the activities of the English strolling players in the United Provinces and the Spanish Netherlands. It includes the relevant material published between 1620 and 1982, but does not claim to be exhaustive. Thus publications with cursory references only to the Low Countries are not usually listed. However, in view of the lack of play titles in Dutch and Belgian documents, I have added a couple of items which, though not dealing with the Northern or Southern Netherlands, contain German texts of the plays performed by the English actors in Germany (29, 39); they may give us some idea of the kind of play likely to have been seen in the Low Countries. Much of the material is repetitive, leaning heavily as it does on the work of older authors. The arrangement is chronological by publication dates so as to illustrate the gradual development of this field of study. The bracketed numbers after book titles refer to the page(s) where the subject is discussed. Acronyms are used in accordance with the 1981 MLA International Bibliography.

1. *Engelische Comedien vnd Tragedien Das ist: Sehr Schöne... Comedi vnd Tragedi Spiel Sampt dem Pickelhering Welche ... von den Engelländern in Deutschland ... seynd agiret vnd gehalten worden ...* N.p.: 1620 [n. pag.]; rpt. Leipzig, 1624, and in *Spieltexte der Wanderbühne.* Ed. Manfred Brauneck. Vol. I. Berlin: Walter de Gruyter, 1970.

    Contains ten plays and five interludes; three of the plays and four of the interludes have Pickleherring in their cast.

    Pickleherring: "zu Ambsterdam bin ich gewesen" (*Aliud*, sig. Zz2^v).

2. Voetius, Gisbertus. *Selectarum Disputationum Theologicarum Pars Quarta.* Amstelodami: Johannes Janssonius à Waesberge, 1667 [p. 361].

3. Hasselt, G. van. *Arnhemsche Oudheden.* Vol. I. Arnhem: J.H. Moeleman Jr., 1803 [p. 244].

    See also [G. van Hasselt], *Kronyk van Arnhem* (Arnhem: W. Troost en Zoon, 1790), p. 241.

4. Tieck, Ludewig [sic]. *Deutsches Theater.* Vol. I. Berlin: Realschulbuchhandlung, 1817.

"Als in London die Theater bluehten und selbst im Auslande beruehmt waren, gingen zuweilen Schauspielertruppen nach den Niederlanden, um dort zu spielen" (p. xxiii).

See H. Lüdeke, *Ludwig Tieck und das alte englische Theater: Ein Beitrag zur Geschichte der Romantik* (Frankfurt a. M.: Moritz Diesterweg, 1922); Edwin H. Zeydel, *Ludwig Tieck and England: A Study in the Literary Relations of Germany and England during the Early Nineteenth Century* (Princeton: Princeton Univ. Press, 1931), pp. 1, 30, 129; and Harvey W. Hewett-Thayer, "Tieck and the Elizabethan Drama: His Marginalia", *JEGP*, 34 (1935), 377-407.

5. Flensburg, J.J. Dodt van. *Archief voor Kerkelijke en Wereldsche Geschiedenissen inzonderheid van Utrecht.* Vol III. Utrecht: N. van der Monde, 1843 [p. 271].

6. Thoms, William J. "Old English Actors in Germany". *Athenaeum*, 25 Aug. 1849, pp. 862-63.

7. Scheltema, P. *De Graaf van Leicester, te Amsterdam, in de jaren 1586 en 1587.* Amsterdam: P.N. van Kampen, 1851.

1586: Payment made by the City of Amsterdam to certain "trompetters ende andere speelluyden" in Leicester's suite (p. 62); see also pp. 70-71, and 96, pp. 83-87.

8. M., J. "Engelsche tooneelspelers in de Nederlanden". *Navorscher*, 2 (1852), 27.

The note concludes with the query: "Weet ook iemand eenig nader berigt te geven omtrent zoodanige Engelsche tooneelspelers als waarvan Heywood en Tieck gewagen; waar, wanneer en wat zij in ons land hebben gespeeld?"

9. [W.I.C. Rammelman] Elsevier. "Engelsche tooneelspelers in de Nederlanden". *Navorscher*, 3 (1853), 17.

10. ———, "Engelsche tooneelspelers in de Nederlanden". *Navorscher's Bijblad*, 3 (1853), xl-xli.

11. ———, "English Comedians in the Netherlands". *N&Q*, 9 April 1853, pp. 360-61.

12. N., V.D. "Engelsche tooneelspelers in de Nederlanden". *Navorscher*, 3 (1853), 17.

13. V., W.D. "English Comedians in the Netherlands". *N&Q*, 29 Jan. 1853, p. 114.

14. Bergh, L. Ph.C. van den. *'s-Gravenhaagsche Bijzonderheden.* Vol. I. 's-Gravenhage: Martinus Nijhoff, 1857 [pp. 20-22]. See 19.

15. [W.I.C. Rammelman] Elsevier. "Engelsche tooneelspelers in de Nederlanden". *Navorscher*, 8 (1858), 7.

16. Lennep, J.H. van. "English Comedians in the Netherlands". *N&Q*, 8 Jan. 1859, p. 36.
17. Cohn, Albert. "English Actors in Germany". *Athenaeum*, 25 June 1859, pp. 842-43. See 18.
18. Thoms, William J. "English Actors in Germany". *N&Q*, 9 July 1859, pp. 21-22.

    A lengthy extract from the preceding item.
19. Lennep, J.H. van. "English Comedians in the Netherlands". *N&Q*, 21 Jan. 1860, pp. 48-49.

    English translation of the relevant passages in 14.
20. Ruelens, Ch. "Notes pour l'histoire du théâtre à Anvers". *Revue d'histoire et d'archéologie* (Bruxelles), 4 (1864), 405-07.

    Brussels 1605: "une compagnie royale anglaise" (p. 405, n. 1).
21. Cohn, Albert. *Shakespeare in Germany in the Sixteenth and Seventeenth Centuries: An Account of English Actors in Germany and the Netherlands and of the Plays performed by them during the same period.* London: Asher & Co., 1865; rpt. Wiesbaden, 1967.

    A carefully researched study. Ch. iv (pp. lxxv-civ) contains the first comprehensive record of the English actors in the Netherlands. Prints the text of six plays. See 22 and 35.
22. C[itters]., J. d[e]. W[itte]. v[an]. "De Engelsche Comedianten op het vaste land". *Ned. Spectator*, 22 April 1865, pp. 125-27.

    Review of 21. "Onwaarschijnlijk is het niet, dat in de archieven van nog andere steden . . . berigten schuilen, die het opzoeken waard zijn" (p. 127).
23. Feith, H.O. "Eenige Comedianten te Groningen in 1597". In *Bijdragen tot de Geschiedenis en Oudheidkunde, inzonderheid van de Provincie Groningen.* Ed. G. Acker Stratingh, et al. Vol. II. Groningen: J.B. Wolters, 1865, p. 162.
24. Loffelt, A.C. "Nederlandsche Navolgingen van Shakespeare en van de oude Engelsche dramatici in de zeventiende eeuw". *Ned. Spectator*, 25 Jan. 1868, pp. 30-31; 2 May 1868, pp. 138-41; 9 May 1868, pp. 148-51; 23 May 1868, pp. 162-64.

    "Is het mogelijk . . . dat de Engelsche Comedianten, die in de 16e en 17e eeuw Nederland zoo dikwijls bezochten, en op verschillende plaatsen voorstellingen gaven, geen ander spoor hebben achtergelaten, dan hier en daar in muffe archieven een '*item voor de Engelse Comedianten*'? Hoe is dat mogelijk, terwijl in Duitschland de invloed van diezelfde comedianten op de dramatiek vrij belangrijk mag heeten, en er oude Duitsche navolgingen van Sh's werken bestaan" (p. 30).
25. Genée, Rudolph. *Geschichte der Shakespeare'schen Dramen in Deutschland.* Leipzig: Wilhelm Engelmann, 1870 [pp. 9, 18].

26. Hellwald, Ferd. von. *Geschichte des holländischen Theaters.* Rotterdam: Van Hengel & Eeltjes, 1874.
    Ch. i, "Englische Schauspieler in den Niederlanden", pp. 7-10.
27. Moltzer, H.E. *Shakespere's Invloed op het Nederlandsch Tooneel der Zeventiende Eeuw.* Groningen: J.B. Wolters, 1874 [pp. 35-38].
28. Boeles, W.B.S. *Frieslands Hoogeschool en het Rijks Athenaeum te Franeker.* Vol. I. Leeuwarden: H. Kuipers, 1878 [p. 290].
29. Tittmann, Julius. *Die Schauspiele der Englischen Komödianten in Deutschland.* Deutsche Dichter des sechzehnten Jahrh., 13. Leipzig: F.A. Brockhaus, 1880.
    Prints seven plays from *Engelische Comedien vnd Tragedien* (1).
30. Mentzel, E. *Geschichte der Schauspielkunst in Frankfurt am Main von ihren ersten Anfängen bis zur Eröffnung des städtischen Komödienhauses: Ein Beitrag zur deutschen Kultur- und Theatergeschichte.* Archiv f. Frankfurts Gesch. u. Kunst, NS 9. Frankfurt a.M.: K.Th. Völcker's Verlag, 1882 [pp. 22, 55]. See 47.
    Contains a description of "ein alter Holzschnitt, der eine Bühne englischer Komödianten, vielleicht in Cassel, Nürnberg oder gar in Frankfurt selbst, aus dem Jahre 1597 darstellt, giebt genauen Aufschluss, wie die Einrichtung derselben beschaffen gewesen" (pp. 38-39). Unfortunately the woodcut is not reproduced, nor is there any clue as to its whereabouts.
31. *Musique et Musiciens au XVIIe siècle: Correspondance et oeuvre musicales de Constantin Huygens.* Ed. W.J.A. Jonckbloet and J.P.N. Land. Leiden: E.J. Brill, 1882 [p. ccxxv, n. 1].
32. Velthuis, K.R. *De Opkomst van het Tooneel te Groningen: Eene Bijdrage tot de Geschiedenis van het Nederlandsch Tooneel.* Groningen: P.L. Folmer, 1883 [pp. 9-10].
33. Meissner, Johannes. *Die englischen Comoedianten zur Zeit Shakespeares in Oesterreich.* Beitr. z. Gesch. d. deutschen Lit. u. d. geistigen Lebens in Oesterreich, 4. Wien: Carl Konegen, 1884 [pp. 30, 34]. See 36.
34. Sorgen, W.G.F.A. van. *De Tooneelspeelkunst in Utrecht en de Utrechtsche Schouwburg. Met Bijlagen van A.G.A. van Rappard en L.W.R. Wenckebach.* 's-Gravenhage: A. Rössing, 1885 [pp. 13-15, 17, 75, 78, 79].
35. Cohn, Albert. "Englische Komödianten in Köln (1592-1656)". *JDSh*, 21 (1886), 245-76.
    Contains additions to 21. The author concludes that the English actors "wohl ohne Ausnahme über die Niederlande nach Deutschland zogen" (p. 245).
36. Worp, J.A. "Engelsche Tooneelspelers op het vasteland in de 16de

en 17de eeuw". *Ned. Museum*, 2nd ser., 3, I. Gent: Ad. Hoste, 1886, pp. 65-113.

Review of 33.

37. Creizenach, W. *Die Schauspiele der englischen Komödianten.* Deutsche Nat.-Lit., 23. Berlin: W. Spemann [1889] [pp. III-V, IX, XI-XII].

    Lists forty plays performed in Germany and prints the German text of five of them, including *Der bestrafte Brudermord.* The author concludes that "das Repertoire der wandernden Komödianten den ganzen Reichtum und die ganze Mannigfaltigkeit der englischen Bühne jener Epoche widerspiegelt" (p. LIX).

38. Claeys, Prosper. *Histoire du théâtre à Gand.* 3 vols. Gand: J. Vuylsteke, 1892 [I, pp. 47, 183; II, pp. 7-10].

    Some of the author's statements are unreliable.

39. Bolte, Johannes. *Die Singspiele der englischen Komödianten und ihrer Nachfolger in Deutschland, Holland und Skandinavien.* Theatergesch. Forschungen, 7. Hamburg: Leopold Voss, 1893.

    Contains some information about English musicians (pp. 3-4). Discusses the extant "Singspiele" and prints a dozen select texts and the extant melodies.

40. Hauwaert, O. van. *Historisch en Critisch Overzicht van het Vlaamsch Tooneel in de XVIIde eeuw.* Gent: A. Siffer, 1893 [p. 20].

41. Veen, S.D. van. "Iets naar aanleiding van de comediën te Groningen in de 17de eeuw". In *Groningsche Volksalmanak voor het jaar 1894.* Groningen: B. van der Kamp, 1893, pp. 56-80.

42. Bolte, Johannes. *Das Danziger Theater im 16. und 17. Jahrhundert.* Theatergesch. Forschungen, 12. Hamburg: Leopold Voss, 1895 [p. 34].

    Contains the text of two hitherto unpublished plays performed by the English actors.

43. Kalff, G. *Literatuur en Tooneel te Amsterdam in de zeventiende eeuw.* Haarlem: Erven F. Bohn, 1895.

    ". . . acht ik het niet onwaarschijnlijk dat [Theodoor Rodenburgh] in Amsterdam of elders stukken als *Hamlet* en *Macbeth* heeft zien vertoonen" (p. 170).

44. Schevichaven, H.D.J. van. *Penschetsen uit Nijmegen's Verleden.* 2 vols. Nijmegen: H. ten Hoet, 1898, 1901.

    Nijmegen 2 April 1619: ". . . dat eenige officieren vant Engelsche guarnizoen . . . hem gelieften te laeten een comedie te ageren . . ." (I, p. 166).

45. Bolte, Johannes. "Englische Komödianten in Münster und Ulm". *JDSh*, 36 (1900), 273-76.

46. Feith, J.A. "Wandelingen door het oude Groningen, XI. Bestaande en verdwenen gebouwen: Het Raad- en Wijnhuis". In *Groningsche Volksalmanak voor het jaar 1901.* Groningen: B. van der Kamp, 1900, pp. 130-59 [p. 143].
47. Mentzel, E. *Das alte Frankfurter Schauspielhaus und seine Vorgeschichte.* Frankfurt a. M.: Rütten & Loening, 1902 [p. 18].
    Includes material from 30.
48. Herz, E. *Englische Schauspieler und englisches Schauspiel zur Zeit Shakespeares in Deutschland.* Theatergesch. Forschungen, 18. Hamburg: Leopold Vosz [sic], 1903 [pp. 7, 11, 27, 30, 44, 53, 56, 59-60].
    Contains five maps showing the routes of the various companies through the Low Countries and central Europe (pp. [144]-[153]).
49. Hoog, Az., W. de. *Studiën over de Nederlandsche en Engelsche Taal en Letterkunde en haar wederzijdschen invloed.* Vol. II. Dordrecht: J.P. Revers, 1903 [pp. 63-64].
    Dutch plays possibly based on texts used by the English actors (pp. 64-86); Jan Jansz Starter (pp. 92-99).
50. Hughes, Charles, ed. *Shakespeare's Europe: Unpublished Chapters of Fynes Moryson's Itinerary. Being a Survey of the Condition of Europe at the end of the 16th Century.* London: Sherratt & Hughes, 1903; rpt. New York, 1967.
    "So as at the same tyme [c. 1593] when some cast Players of England came into those parts [viz. the Netherlands], the people not vnderstanding what they sayd, only for theire Action followed them with wonderfull Concourse, yea many young virgines fell in louve with some of the players, and followed them from Citty to Citty, till the magistrates were forced to forbid them to play any more" (p. 373).
51. Scheurleer, D.F. *Het Muziekleven van Amsterdam in de zeventiende eeuw.* 's-Gravenhage: Martinus Nijhoff [1904] [p. 23].
52. Worp, J.A. *Geschiedenis van het Drama en van het Tooneel in Nederland.* Groningen: J.B. Wolters. Vol. I, 1904; vol. II, 1908.
    Survey of the appearances of the English actors in Holland, with some observations on the language, the texts, and the influence of their plays (I, pp. 311-15). Further references in I, pp. 173, 264, 359, 362; II, pp. 29, 78, 80, 257, 403.
53. Kaulfusz-Diesch, Carl Hermann. *Inszenierung des deutschen Dramas an der Wende des sechzehnten und siebzehnten Jahrhunderts: Ein Beitrag zur älteren deutschen Bühnengeschichte.* Probefahrten, 7. Leipzig: R. Voigtländer, 1905 [pp. 34, 35].
    "Die Bühne der Englischen Komödianten", pp. 58-84.

54. Zuylen van Nyevelt, Suzette. *Court Life in the Dutch Republic 1638-1689.* London: J.M. Dent; New York: E.P. Dutton, 1906 [p. 104].
55. Brom, G., and L.A. van Langeraad, eds. *Diarium van Arend van Buchell.* Amsterdam: Johannes Müller, 1907.

    Utrecht 1594: "Angli histriones hic agunt" (s.v. 10 Feb. 1594, p. 360).
56. Lefebvre, Léon. *Histoire du théâtre de Lille de ses origines à nos jours.* Vol. I. Lille: Imprimerie Lefebvre-Ducrocq, 1907 [pp. 135-37, 139].
57. Grabau, Carl. "William Kempe". *JDSh*, 45 (1909), 311.
58. Kossmann, E.F. *Das niederländische Faustspiel des siebzehnten Jahrhunderts (De Hellevaart van Dr. Joan Faustus). Mit einer Beilage über die Haager Bühne 1660 bis 1720.* Haag: Martinus Nijhoff, 1910 [p. 104, nn. 2 and 5].
59. Worp, J.A. "Die englischen Komödianten Jellifus und Rowe". *JDSh*, 46 (1910), 128-29.

    Biographical details about George Jolly and William Roe.
60. ———, "Hollandsche of Engelsche Tooneelspelers te Neurenberg?" *TNTL*, 29, NS 21 (1910), 261-62.
61. Kossmann, E.F. *Nieuwe Bijdragen tot de Geschiedenis van het Nederlandsche Tooneel in de 17e en 18e eeuw.* 's-Gravenhage: Martinus Nijhoff, 1915 [pp. 141-42]. See s.v. 78.

    Leiden c. 1614: this item refers to English artisans, not to players.
62. Niessen, Carl. *Dramatische Darstellungen in Köln von 1526-1700.* Veröffentlichungen d. Kölner Geschichtsvereins, 3. Köln: Verlag des kölnischen Geschichtsvereins, 1917 [pp. 74, 98].
63. Price, Lawrence Marsden. *English-German Literary Influences: Bibliography and Survey.* UCPMP, 9. Berkeley: Univ. of California Press, 1919-20. See also 75.

    The diagram inserted between pp. 136 and 137 records the following appearances in the Netherlands: The Hague 1605, 1606, 1607, 1629, 1644-45; Leiden 1604, 1605, 1608; Utrecht 1597, 1613, 1620, 1645 (for which also see p. 138), 1659.
64. Winkel, J. te. *Geschiedenis der Nederlandsche Letterkunde van de Republiek der Vereenigde Nederlanden.* Vols. I and II. 1922-27; rpt. Utrecht: Hes Publishers; Leeuwarden: Uitgeverij "De Tille", 1973.

    Brief survey of the appearances of the English actors in the Netherlands, based on published sources (I, pp. 214-16); discussion of contemporary Dutch plays written under English influences (II, pp. 223, 270-74).
65. Chambers, E.K. *The Elizabethan Stage.* 4 vols. Oxford: Clarendon Press, 1923 [I, p. 342; II, pp. 272-74, 284, 285, 288, 291, 292].

The alphabetical list of actors (II, pp. 295-350) contains biographical data about many of the English strolling players in the Low Countries.

66. Liebrecht, Henri. *Histoire du théâtre français à Bruxelles au XVIIe et au XVIIIe siècle.* Pref. Maurice Wilmotte. Paris: Édouard Champion, 1923 [pp. 12, 13, 17].
67. Bense, J.F. *The Anglo-Dutch Relations from the Earliest Times to the Death of William the Third, being an historical Introduction to a Dictionary of the Low-Dutch Element in the English Vocabulary.* Diss. Amsterdam 1924. 's-Gravenhage: Martinus Nijhoff, 1924 [pp. 199-200].
68. Fransen, J. *Les comédiens français en Hollande au XVIIe et au XVIIIe siècles.* Bibliothèque de la Revue de Littérature Comparée, 25. Paris: Honoré Champion, 1925.

    Survey of the English actors in the Netherlands (pp. 11-12).
69. Ent, W. van den. "Bredero en de Engelse Toneelspelers". *NTg,* 20 (1926), 255-58.
70. Lefèvre, J. "La Cour de l'Archiduc Léopold-Guillaume 1647-1652". *Archives, Bibliothèques et Musées de Belgique: Bull. Mensuel de l'Assn. des Conservateurs d'Archives, de Bibliothèques et de Musées* (Brussels), 15 May 1928, pp. 65-77.
71. Renieu, Lionel. *Histoire des théâtres de Bruxelles depuis leur origine jusqu'à ce jour.* Pref. Auguste Rondel. 2 vols. Paris: Duchartre & Van Buggenhoudt, 1928.

    "Les spectacles anglais furent rares et leur ensemble ne constitue pas une série représentative de l'art dramatique en Angleterre" (I, p. 143).
72. Nungezer, Edwin. *A Dictionary of Actors and of Other Persons Associated with the Public Representation of Plays in England before 1642.* CSE, 13. New Haven: Yale Univ. Press; London: Oxford Univ. Press, 1929.

    An attempt "to collect and organize all the discovered facts now scattered in widely separated places" (p. v). Contains biographical data about most of the English strolling players in the Low Countries.
73. Fijn van Draat, P. "Graaf Leicester die te Utrecht het feest van St. George viert, 23 April 1586". *Maandblad van "Oud-Utrecht",* 15 Jan. 1930, pp. 2-6.

    See also *ibid.,* pp. 12-14 and 81-83.
74. Flemming, Willi. *Das Schauspiel der Wanderbühne.* Barockdrama, 3. Leipzig: Philip Reclam jun., 1931; rpt. Darmstadt, 1965.

    Prints a number of German texts, including *Niemand und Jemand* (1608), and reproduces the "Niemand" (John Green) from the early 17th-century Graz MS. (frontispiece); cf. Johannes Bolte, "Niemand und Jemand: Ein englisches Drama aus Shakespeare's Zeit, übersetzt von Ludwig Tieck", *JDSh*, 29-30 (1894), 4-91, esp. the woodcut on p. 4. The "Einführung" (pp. 5-69) contains a few scattered references to the Netherlands.

75. Price, Lawrence Marsden. *The Reception of English Literature in Germany.* Berkeley: Univ. of California Press, 1932. [First rev. ed. of 63.] [p. 12].
76. Dalen, J.L. van. *Geschiedenis van Dordrecht.* Vol II. Dordrecht: C. Morks Czn., 1933 [i.e., 1936] [p. 874].
77. Hartleb, Hans. *Deutschlands erster Theaterbau: Eine Geschichte des Theaterlebens und der Englischen Komödianten unter Landgraf Moritz dem Gelehrten von Hessen-Kassel.* Berlin: Walter de Gruyter & Co., 1936 [pp. 14-17].
78. Junkers, Herbert. *Niederländische Schauspieler und niederländisches Schauspiel im 17. und 18. Jahrhundert in Deutschland.* Haag: Martinus Nijhoff, 1936.

    "Kossmann hat in seinen 'Nieuwe Bijdragen' [61] die letzte und wohl gültigste Zusammenstellung der Züge der englischen Komödianten in Holland gegeben, der wir hier folgen" (p. 19). Follows, on pp. 20-22, a brief summary of the data supplied by Kossmann.
79. Bentley, Gerald Eades. *The Jacobean and Caroline Stage.* 7 vols. Oxford: Clarendon Press, 1941-68.

    The section on the actors (II, pp. 344-628) provides the English background of a number of players well known on the Continent. Departing from the method of Chambers, Nungezer, and other biographers of the Elizabethan actors, the author quotes for each actor "every scrap of biographical evidence (except for the careers of English actors in Germany)" (I, Pref., p. [v]).
80. Bald, R.C. "Leicester's Men in the Low Countries". *RES*, 19 (1943), 395-97.
81. Stahl, Ernst Leopold. *Shakespeare und das deutsche Theater: Wanderung und Wandelung seines Werkes in dreiundeinhalb Jahrhunderten.* Stuttgart: W. Kohlhammer, 1947.

    The diagram showing the wanderings of the English actors in Germany [*sic*] includes The Hague, Leiden, and Utrecht (p. 2).
82. Hoppe, Harry R. "English Actors at Ghent in the Seventeenth Century". *RES*, 25 (1949), 305-21.

    For "Lerecque" (p. 311) read "Screcque" [private communication from Professor W. Schrickx, dated 7 July 1965].
83. Dart, Thurston. "English Music and Musicians in 17th-Century Holland". In *Kongress-Bericht Intern. Gesellschaft f. Musikwissen-*

schaft, Utrecht 1952. Amsterdam: G. Alsbach & Co., 1953, pp. 139-45.

About *The Forces of Hercules* (Utrecht 1586).

84. Feldman, Abraham B. "Playwrights and Pike-Trailers in the Low Countries". *N&Q*, May 1953, pp. 184-87.
85. Gelder, H.E. van. *Het Haagse Toneel-leven en de Koninklijke Schouwburg 1804-1954.* 's-Gravenhage: Gemeentebestuur [1954] [pp. 13, 15].
86. Hoppe, Harry R. "George Jolly at Bruges, 1648". *RES*, NS 5 (1954), 265-68.
87. ———, "English Acting Companies at the Court of Brussels in the Seventeenth Century". *RES*, NS 6 (1955), 26-33.
88. Bachrach, A.G.H. "Jan Starter, Engeland en Nederland in de XVIIe eeuw". *LT*, 188 (Feb. 1957), 55-73.
89. Mithal, H.S.D. "Will, My Lord of Leicester's Jesting Player". *N&Q*, Oct. 1958, pp. 427-29, and *ibid.*, March 1959, p. 112.
90. Bald, R.C. "Will, My Lord of Leicester's Jesting Player". *N&Q*, March 1959, p. 112.
91. Riewald, J.G. "Some Later Elizabethan and Early Stuart Actors and Musicians". *ES*, 40 (1959), 33-41.
92. ———, "New Light on the English Actors in the Netherlands, *c.* 1590 - *c.* 1660". *ES*, 41 (1960), 65-92.

Addenda et corrigenda: On *The Murder of the King of France* (p. 77) see s.v. I; pp. 78-80: I suggest that "Thomas Berghel", "Thomas Borel", and "Thomas Barrett" are the same person; p. 90: "Wm. Corkin" must, I think, be William Corkine, a minor composer and lutanist (probably), who published books of "Ayres" in 1610 and 1612; p. 91: the "Commedianten van den Coninck van Inghelandt" were all Frenchmen; see W. Schrickx, "French, Italian, Spanish and German Actors and Other Artists at Ghent (1575-1700)", *RBPH*, 44 (1966), 871-72, and item 105. See also 93.

93. George, J. "English Actors in the Netherlands 1600-1610". *ES*, 41 (1960), 255-57.

Addendum to preceding item. "I now think that my last sentence is perhaps too categorical; it is certain that a member of Green's company was in England in 1609, I think, but not so certain that it was Green himself, though I think that probable" [J. George, private communication, dated 24 Aug. 1960].

94. Hotson, Leslie. *The Commonwealth and Restoration Stage.* Cambridge, Mass., 1928; rpt. New York: Russell & Russell, 1962.

Contains a comprehensive account of the continental wanderings of George Jolly, the "last member of the great line of Elizabethan strollers", pp. 167-76.

95. Brennecke, Ernest and Henry. *Shakespeare in Germany 1590-1700: With translations of Five Early Plays.* Chicago: Univ. of Chicago Press, 1964 [pp. 2-3].

   English translations of five German plays [*Tit.*, *MND*, *MV*, *TN*, *Ham.*], "each of which represents Shakespeare as his work first captured the imagination of Continental audiences in the seventeenth century" (p. v); reproduction of "Pickelherring, the Clown of the English Comedians", from the songbook, *Pickelhärings Hochzeit; oder, Der lustige singende Harlequin* (1652), facing p. 56.

96. Strong, R.C., and J.A. van Dorsten. *Leicester's Triumph.* Pubs. of the Sir Thomas Browne Inst., Leiden, Special Series, 2. Leiden: Univ. Press; London: Oxford Univ. Press, 1964 [pp. 83-87].

97. Leeuwe, H.H.J. de. "Shakespeare op het Nederlandse toneel". *Gids*, 127 (1964), 324-39.

   It was the English actors who introduced into the Netherlands the dramatic nucleus of some of Shakespeare's plays (p. 324). Early Dutch Shakespeare adaptations (pp. 324-25).

98. Begemann, Nienke. "De Engelse komedianten in de Nederlanden". *Gids*, 127 (1964), 398-412.

99. Schrickx, W. "Nederlandse en andere acteurs te Gent en elders in de XVIIde eeuw". *SGG*, 7 (1965), 25-53.

100. Bachrach, A.G.H. "Leiden en de 'Strolling Players'". In *Jaarboekje voor Geschiedenis en Oudheidkunde van Leiden en Omstreken 1968.* Leiden: A.W. Sijthoff, 1968, pp. 29-37.

   The 1592 passport, which the author believes to be unfindable (p. 30), is in the Algemeen Rijksarchief at The Hague, *Lias* England of 1591 (Staten-Generaal 5882 I).

101. ———, "Bredero en de Engelse toneelspelers". In A.G.H. Bachrach, et al., *Rondom Bredero: Een viertal verkenningen.* Culemborg: Tjeenk Willink-Noorduijn, 1970, pp. 73-89.

   An exhaustive analysis of a much discussed problem. Bredero stresses the fact that the English players were (modern) professionals, whereas the Dutch *Rederijkers* were (old-fashioned) amateurs.

102. Koster, Simon. *Van Schavot tot Schouwburg: Vijfhonderd jaar toneel in Haarlem.* Haarlem: Erven F. Bohn, 1970 [p. 100].

103. Wikland, Erik. *Elizabethan Players in Sweden 1591-92 &c.* 1962; 2nd ed. rev. and enl. Stockholm: Almqvist & Wiksell, 1971 [pp. 69, 111-12, 135-37, 187].

104. Ludvik, Dušan. "Zur Chronologie und Topographie der 'alten' und 'späten' englischen Komödianten in Deutschland". *AN*, 8 (1975), 47-65.

105. Richards, Kenneth. "The Comedians of the King of England at Ghent, 1663". *EA*, 28 (1975), 70-71.

The company in question was a French troupe rather than an English one; see s.v. item 92.
106. Schoenbaum, S. *William Shakespeare: A Documentary Life*. Oxford: Clarendon Press; London: Scolar Press, 1975 [p.89].
107. Albach, Ben. *Langs kermissen en hoven: Ontstaan en kroniek van een Nederlands toneelgezelschap in de 17de eeuw*. Zutphen: Walburg Pers, 1977.
 Contains a few scattered references.
108. Alexander, Robert J. "George Jolly [Joris Joliphus], der wandernde Player und Manager: Neues zu seiner Tätigkeit in Deutschland (1648-1660)". KSGT, 29-30. Berlin: Selbstverlag der Gesellschaft f. Theatergesch. e. V., 1978, pp. 31-48.
109. Brand, Peter. "Der englische Komödiant Robert Browne, (1563 - ca. 1621/39)". M.A. thesis Heidelberg [1978]. TS [pp. 14, 16-17, 21-22, 40-41, 64-66, 68-69, 86, 99, 100, 102].
110. Schrickx, Willem. "English Actors at the Courts of Wolfenbüttel, Brussels and Graz during the Lifetime of Shakespeare". *ShS*, 33 (1980), 153-68.
 Contains the first complete and accurate transcript of the Howard passport, 1592.
111. Limon, Jerzy. "New Evidence for the Activity of English Players in the Netherlands in the Second Quarter of the Seventeenth Century". *ES*, 62 (1981), 115-19.
112. Koster, Simon. "'Vreemde Speelders' in Gelderland rond 1600". In *Bijdragen en Mededelingen van de Vereniging tot beoefening van Gelderse Geschiedenis, Oudheidkunde en Recht*. Vol. LXXIII. Arnhem: Vereniging "Gelre", 1982, pp. 13-39.

III

From the foregoing bibliography and one or two unpublished sources it appears that, between 1585 and c. 1650, English players, including some musicians, dancers, acrobats, and fencers, were active in at least twenty-eight localities in the United Provinces and the Spanish Netherlands, with a total number of more than a hundred shorter or longer stays. Altogether forty-one names of actor-managers, actors, and other entertainers have emerged. Many of them were members of reputable acting companies in England; some were Shakespeare's fellows (see 92, pp. 66-67); most of them are more fully recorded in Germany and other countries.

In the following survey the dates given are of the official documents (permissions, prohibitions, &c.), not of the actual performances, which are imperfectly chronicled. The numbers after the dates refer to the entries in the Bibliography where the appearances in question are discussed.

AMERSFOORT 16 May 1586 (William Kempe): 96.
AMSTERDAM 1586 (Leicester's trumpeters and players): 7, 96; before 26 Nov. 1601 (John Kemp): 45, 48, 49, 60, 65, 92; between 1602 and 1612 (the "strange accident"): 6, 60, 92; 11 Dec. 1613: 92; before 1621 (Robert Reynolds): 1; 28 Nov. 1623: 52, 61, 92; 13 Dec. 1636 (Robert Reynolds and Edward Pudsey): 61, 92, 111; 20 March 1646 (John Payne, William Roe): 61, 67, 87, 92, 98, 99, 100, 104.
ANTWERP 1604 (Ralph Reeve): 109; 31 Jan., 24 Feb., and 8 March 1610 (John Green): 93, 110.
ARNHEM 1592 (Robert Browne, John Bradstreet, Thomas Sackville, Richard Jones, Everhart Sauss (or Sanss): 3, 52, 61, 65, 67, 77, 92, 98, 100, 103, 109, 110, 112.
BREDA 1646 (George Jolly): 78, 92, 99, 108.
BRUGES 1647-48 (George Jolly): 37, 48, 62, 82, 86, 87, 92, 94, 99, 104, 111.
BRUSSELS 1603 (Robert Browne, Ralph Reeve): 109, 110; 1604 (Ralph Reeve), 109; 1605: 20, 110; 13 Feb. 1607: 110; c. 1608: 65, 66, 87, 92; 16 Nov. 1609: 87, 93, 110; 19 Feb. 1614 (John Green): 87, 92, 110; 3 Sep. 1617 (John Waters, Henry Griffin, Robert Archer): 66, 87, 92, 110; 8 Feb. 1648: 66, 70, 71, 86, 87, 92, 111; 27 Jan. 1650 (John Wayde): 66, 70, 71, 87, 92.
DELFT Dec. 1585: 84.
DORDRECHT 10 Oct. 1656 (Archief der Gemeente Dordrecht, Resol. v. d. Kerkeraad 1656-64, fol. 5v): 12, 13, 21, 26, 36, 49, 52, 61, 67, 76, 92.
DUNKIRK 12 Nov. 1585 (William Kempe): 57.
FLUSHING (archives partly destroyed by fire in 1809) between 1 May 1610 and 30 April 1611 (Gideon Morris)?: 92.
FRANEKER 25 Oct. 1597: 28, 36, 49, 52, 61, 67, 88, 92, 109; Nov. 1645: 36, 52, 61, 87, 92, 112.
GHENT March 1604: 40, 67, 82, 92, 93, 109, 110; 18 Feb. and Oct. 1611: 38, 82, 92; 1612-13 ("Thomas Berghel"): 82, 92; 12 June 1614 (Jacques Screcque): 82, 92; Aug. 1614 ("Thomas Barrett"): 82, 92; 1 March 1617 (Robert Archer, Henry Griffin, John Waters): 82, 87, 92; 19 April 1624 (John Green): 38, 82, 92, 110; 10 May 1625 (Thomas Rogers): 38, 82, 92; 13 Aug. 1629 (William Morley): 82, 92; 22 March 1651: 82, 92.
GOUDA 26 March 1616 ("Engelsche speelluyden", Alg. Rijksarchief, The Hague, Holland 2611 f.): unpublished.
GRONINGEN 21 April 1597: 23, 28, 32, 36, 49, 52, 61, 67, 92, 98, 109; 13 Oct. 1601: 46, 52, 61, 92; 22 Oct. 1645: 41, 52, 61, 87, 92, 112.

HAARLEM Oct. 1639 (John Butler): 102; 16 March 1640 (John Butler): 102.
THE HAGUE 7-11 Jan. 1586: 96; 9 Oct. 1602: 21; 10 May 1605 (John Spencer): 14, 21, 26, 27, 36, 48, 49, 52, 61, 63, 65, 85, 92; 8 June 1606: 14, 21, 26, 27, 36, 48, 52, 61, 63, 65, 85, 92; 23, 26, and 27 April 1607: 14, 21, 26, 27, 36, 48, 52, 61, 63, 65, 85, 92; 24 and 29 Sep. 1610: 14, 21, 26, 36, 52, 61, 85, 92; 9 Oct. 1612: 14, 26, 36, 52, 61, 85, 92; c. 26 March 1616: 92; 2 May 1618 (John Waters, John Studley): 61, 85, 87, 92; 16 Sep. 1620: 61, 85, 92; 30 April, 23 May, and 24 Dec. 1629: 14, 21, 26, 36, 52, 61, 63, 85, 92; 9 Jan. 1632 (Robert Reynolds): 61, 85, 92, 111; 21 May 1638: 92; 23 Oct. 1639 (John Butler, John Payne): 87, 92, 99, 111; 24 March 1643: 92; 30 Oct. 1644 (Nathan Speede): 92; Nov. 1644 - Feb. 1645 (Jeremy Kite, William Cooke, Thomas Loveday, Edward Shatterell, Nathan Speede and son): 14, 21, 26, 27, 36, 49, 52, 61, 63, 82, 85, 87, 92, 100, 104, 112; 11 April 1646 (George Jolly): 61, 67, 85, 87, 92, 108; 6 March 1648 (George Jolly?): 61, 82, 85, 87, 92, 111; 8 Aug. 1648 (George Jolly?): 31, 52, 85, 87, 92, 108.
HARLINGEN 5 March 1612 ("[Engelsche] Commedianten vanden overste compagnie [Julius van Eysinga]", Gemeentearchief Harlingen, 303, 304): unpublished.
HEVERLEE before 18 Feb. 1611: 66, 82, 92, 110.
LEEUWARDEN 20 Sep. - 15 Nov. 1593 (Jan Andres zoon, Willem Pates zoon, Jan Maffet, Willem Joercs, Jan Jorden, "Engelsche speelluiden ende comedianten", Gemeentearchief Leeuwarden, Aktenboek 1588-1604, fols. 107-11; 16 July 1635 ("Engelsche Commedianten", Rijksarchief Leeuwarden, Staten G 10^9: unpublished.
LEIDEN 7 Oct. 1590 (Robert Browne): 15, 16, 21, 26, 32, 36, 37, 48, 52, 61, 65, 67, 77, 82, 85, 92, 95, 98, 100, 103, 109, 110, 112; 19 June 1597: 100; 30 Sep. 1604 (John Woods): 10, 11, 21, 26, 27, 36, 48, 52, 61, 63, 65, 67, 82, 92, 100; 6 Jan. 1605 (John Spencer): 10, 11, 21, 26, 27, 30, 33, 36, 37, 42, 48, 49, 52, 61, 62, 63, 65, 67, 92, 100; 30 Sep. 1605: 92; 18 Nov. 1608 (William Peadle): 9, 13, 21, 26, 36, 48, 52, 61, 63, 65, 67, 82, 92, 98, 100; 1 June 1610: 92, 100; 17 Oct. 1617 (John Jorden, "musijcijn"): 92, 100; 21 May 1638: 52, 61, 92, 98, 100; 10 June 1645 (William Ingram): 87, 92, 100; 21 Oct. 1645 (John Payne): 61, 87, 92, 99, 100, 112.
LIÈGE 1604 (Ralph Reeve): 109.
LILLE c. July 1603 (Robert Browne, John Green, Robert Ledbetter): 56, 92, 98, 109, 110; 1604, first semester: 56, 92, 93, 98, 109; 1605, first semester: 56, 92, 109; 31 Oct. 1605 (Robert Browne): 56, 92, 98, 110; 1606 (Francis Jones): 92; 8 June 1606: 56, 92, 110; 1606, second semester: 56, 92; 1614 ("Thomas Borel"): 56, 92.
LOUVAIN before 18 Feb. 1611: 66, 82, 110.
NIJMEGEN 13 June 1602: 92, 112; 2 April 1619: 44, 112.

THE UNITED PROVINCES between 1632 and the summer of 1636 (Robert Archer): 111.
UTRECHT 23 April 1586 (William Kempe): 6, 25, 26, 34, 36, 37, 65, 67, 73, 80, 83, 84, 88, 89, 90, 92, 95, 96, 98, 100, 103, 106, 112; 10 Feb. 1594: 55, 92; 31 July 1597: 5, 9, 13, 21, 27, 32, 36, 49, 52, 61, 63, 67, 92, 109; 15 Nov. 1613 (John Green): 34, 36, 48, 52, 53, 61, 63, 65, 67, 82, 92, 110; 11 Jan. 1619: 34, 36, 52, 61, 67, 92, 109; 17 July 1620 (John Green): 34, 36, 48, 52, 61, 63, 65, 67, 82, 92, 99, 104; 20 July 1630: 34, 36, 52, 61, 92; 23 Dec. 1633 and 6 Jan. 1634: 61, 88, 92; 8 July 1645 (William Roe): 34, 36, 48, 52, 61, 63, 75, 92, 98, 100, 104, 108, 112.
VEERE 1583? (L.E. de Brakke, private communication, dated 18 May 1954; evidence destroyed by enemy action in 1940).
ZEELAND, HOLLAND, and FRIESLAND 10 Feb. 1592 (Passport issued by the Lord High Admiral on behalf of Robert Browne, John Bradstreet, Thomas Sackville, and Richard Jones): 17, 21, 25, 27, 32, 33, 36, 37, 47, 49, 51, 52, 53, 54, 61, 65, 67, 77, 85, 92, 95, 98, 100, 103, 109, 110, 112.
ZUTPHEN 29 May 1610: 112; 17 Aug. 1610: 92, 112; 14 Aug. 1613: 112; 10 Nov. 1613: 92, 112.

IV

The story of the English actors in the Northern and Southern Netherlands has not been completely told. In recent decades the researches of Professors Hoppe, Schrickx, and others in Belgian and Dutch as well as in British archives have proved that it is still possible to make interesting discoveries in this field.

In Holland most of the relevant material is to be found in the record offices of the principal cities (especially in the "vroedschapsresoluties" and the notarial dossiers), the general and provincial record offices (*Rijksarchieven*), and the archives of the Dutch Reformed Church. More specifically, a systematic search in the following sections of these archives (municipal, unless otherwise stated) might be rewarding: AMSTERDAM: Notarieel archief; Stadsrekeningen; Vroedschapsresoluties; ARNHEM: Stadsrekeningen; *Rijksarchief*: Archief van de Gelderse Rekenkamer; BREDA: Resolutieregisters van de Magistraat; BRIELLE: Stadsrekeningen; Stadsresoluties; DEVENTER: Concordaten Schepenen, Raad, en Gezworen Gemeente; Rekeningen van de Lebuïnuskerk; Resolutieboeken Schepenen en Raad; *Herv. Gemeente*: Acta Classis Deventer; Kerkeraadsakten; DORDRECHT: Resoluties van de Kerkeraad der Herv. Gemeente; GOUDA: Kamerboeken; Stadsrekeningen; Vroedschapsresoluties; GRONINGEN: Rechterlijke archieven; HAARLEM: Memoriaal van Burgemeesters en Regeerders; Resoluties van Burgemeesteren; THE HAGUE: Notarieel archief; Notulen van de Kerkeraad; Resoluties van Baljuw, Burgemeesters, en Schepenen; Rechterlijk archief: Verbalen; Wettelijke akten; *Alg. Rijksarchief*: Archief Hof van Holland; Archief van de Nassause Domeinraad; Ordonnantieboeken; Archieven van de stadhouderlijke secretarie; Archieven van de Staten-Generaal; HARDERWIJK: Resoluties van de Magistraat; *Herv. Gemeente*: Handelingen van de Kerkeraad; 's-HERTOGENBOSCH: Archief van het Heilige Geesthuis; Notulen van de stedelijke Magistraat; Rekeningen van de "Arme Gevangens"; *Rijksarchief*: Archieven van het Gereformeerd Burgerweeshuis; Archief van het Leprozenhuis; LEIDEN: Notarieel archief; Secret. archief 1575-1851 (Burgemeestersdagboeken, Gerechtsdagboeken, Ordonnantieboeken, Tresoriersrekeningen); MAASTRICHT: Raadsresoluties; ROTTERDAM: Resolutieboeken van de Kerkeraad der Herv. Gemeente; SCHIEDAM: Certificatieboeken; UTRECHT: Rekeningen van de Aalmoezenierskamer; Secretaris; Stadsrekeningen; Vroedschapsresoluties; ZUTPHEN: Resolutieboeken van de Magistraat; *Herv. Gemeente*: Protocollen van de Kerkeraad.

Allardyce Nicoll, of the Shakespeare Institute, Birmingham, once wrote me that it would be most unlikely that the names of the English actors who went abroad would be recorded in any *English* documents.[11] The evidence from English archives unearthed so far contradicts this view. Which is not to say that nothing remains to be done. Feeling confident that a thorough examination of the proper English documents will add to our knowledge of the subject, I conclude with a few suggestions for future work in this area.

For tracking down the English actors in their own country the various printed records, such as those of the British Record Society, the Harleian Society, the Historical Manuscripts Commission, and the individual county record publications will prove useful. Other obvious sources are the State Papers of the reigns of Elizabeth, James I, and Charles I, the Acts of the Privy Council, the Chancery proceedings and depositions, the Remembrancia of the City of London, the court proceedings, the Books of the Livery Companies of London, the London parish registers, and the registers of passengers from England to the Low Countries. Of course the Lord Chamberlain's Records, the documents relating to the Office of the Revels, and similar dramatic records are bound to yield valuable information. The Cecil Papers and the Marquess of Salisbury's mss at Hatfield, the Marquess of Downshire's mss, and the Longleat Papers have already brought to light interesting details.

Finally, the published and unpublished papers and diplomatic reports of the English ambassadors and agents in the Low Countries, among

---

11 Letter dated 21 Aug. 1954.

them Thomas Sackville, Sir Henry Wotton, William Trumbull, Sir Dudley Carleton, and others, and of military commanders and soldiers who served there (Robert Dudley, Earl of Leicester, Robert Devereux, second Earl of Essex, Sir Francis Vere, Sir Henry Percy, ninth Earl of Northumberland, Sir Philip Sidney, Robert Sidney, first Earl of Leicester, Thomas D'Oylie, Sir Edward Cecil, Edward Herbert, first Baron Herbert of Cherbury, Sir John Ogle, Thomas Herbert, et. al.) are equally promising, not least because their household accounts may contain payments made to travelling companies. Further research in the correspondence of visiting noblemen, in private diaries, letters, and family papers which may not have been already calendared or otherwise noticed in print, and in other contemporary documents and writings that have never been panned for nuggets before, will certainly fill a number of gaps in the vast jigsaw puzzle of the English strolling players in the Low Countries—and beyond.

ANTHONY BATT: A FORGOTTEN BENEDICTINE TRANSLATOR

David Rogers

An unsigned note, contributed in 1943 to a former running feature in the *Downside Review* called "Odds and Ends", describes[1] a copy of an English Recusant book printed in 1633 and believed to be unique. The writer of this note is easily identified as the late Dom Raymund Webster, whose remarkable knowledge of such books finds its abiding monument in the very extensive collection of recusant literature which he was largely responsible for putting together in the Library at Downside, a library he did so much to build up (in many other fields besides) during the forty years when he was its librarian. In the years just prior to the Second World War he enjoyed access to the immense private collection of Sir Leicester Harmsworth, so much of it now one of the glories of the Folger Shakespeare Library in Washington. It was in Sir Leicester's collection that he examined the work entitled: *A three-fold mirrour of mans vanitie and miserie. The first written by . . . Iohn Trithemius . . . Abbot of Spanhem. The two others by Catholicke Authors unknowen: Faithfully Englished by the R. Father Antonie Batt, Monke . . .* Printed at Doway by Laurence Kellam, . . . 1633.

With characteristic precision, Dom Raymund gave useful particulars derived from a somewhat brief inspection of the volume and drew attention to the propensity of the book's translator to break into verse—the whole of the third "Mirroir" consists, indeed, of verse translations. In a later note in the same volume of the *Downside Review*[2] Dom Raymund was able to announce the existence of another copy, this time at Ampleforth, though unfortunately, like the Harmsworth-Folger copy, it is slightly imperfect. By 1956, when "A&R"[3] was published, a third copy was recorded; this had belonged to Belmont Abbey and is now in the Bodleian Library. It unfortunately lacks the title-leaf. As Dom Raymund knew, this work had escaped the first *Short-Title Catalogue of*

---

1 *Downside Review* (1943), p. 56.
2 *Ibid.*, p. 125.
3 Throughout this article I use 'A&R' to mean A.F. Allison and D.M. Rogers: *A Catalogue of Catholic Books in English printed abroad . . . 1558-1640*, originally published in 1956 as two consecutive issues of *Biographical Studies*, 3, nos. 3-4. The Trithemius is their no. 830.

... *English Books* ... *1475-1640*[4] published in 1926. It is one of 220 items in the original A&R which are not to be found in the 1926 edition of STC, but the second edition of that work (Vol. 2 only) which came out in 1976, records, under number 24285.5, the above three copies. A fourth copy, likewise imperfect, is known to me, in private hands. Finally, in 1978, a complete facsimile of this very rare book, made from the Bodleian copy with the titlepage reproduced from the Folger copy, formed volume 386 of my facsimile series *English Recusant Literature*.[5] So does knowledge progress.

Although Dom Raymund writes that "Antony Batt's name is fairly well known as a translator and editor of little books of devotion", he goes on to deny this, in effect, by remarking that "his works are so scarce and so little known that this side of his activity has escaped notice". Though not literally unnoticed, the writings of this English Benedictine have not been even properly listed hitherto, so that an attempt to set the record straight may, I hope, prove of interest, especially to Professor Birrell, who is not only a distinguished Professor of English but also a recusant historian of note, and a very dear personal friend.

Aside from his writings there is little to tell of Antony Batt himself. Of his birth, education and early life nothing has yet been discovered.[6] The first we hear of him is, therefore, his profession as a monk of the recently-founded English Benedictine priory of St. Laurence's at Dieuleward in Lorraine. This was in the year 1615 or 1616.[7] He was still there in 1621, as is shown by the dedication of his first book, described below, and ten years later, on 13 February 1631, he dedicated his second book, again from Dieuleward. In the meanwhile, no doubt at the third General Chapter of the Congregation, held at Doway in 1629, Batt was made Secretary to the Congregation.[8] This must have taken him, on business visits at least, to St. Gregory's, Doway, where the President was residing. In 1633 he was appointed Cathedral Prior of Peterborough,[9] a title he

---

4 Hereinafter abbreviated 'STC'.

5 Hereinafter abbreviated 'ERL'; volumes are numbered serially over a period of years as they were issued and many contain two or more different A&R items reprinted in facsimile.

6 G. Anstruther, *The Seminary Priests*, vol. 2, p. 18 separates for the first time the William Batt who was ordained a secular priest at St. Omers in 1604 and then worked for many years as a missionary in England, from the Benedictine professed in 1616, who is thus left with no known origins. Cf. notes 22-23 below.

7 Earlier authorities say 1615, but Dom Basil Whelan, *A Series of Lists* (Stanbrook, 1933), p. 51 corrects this to 1616.

8 He is described as "Secretary of our Congregation" in all the three Approbations by the President given to Batt between 1 March 1631 and 11 July 1633, cited here in the text.

9 On the cathedral priorships see D. Lunn, *The English Benedictines 1540-1688* (1980), pp. 110-112.

resigned in 1642. According to the annalist Allanson,[10] he was at St. Edmund's, Paris, by 1640 and in the following year, 1641, he went from Paris to La Celle-en-Brie, the noviciate for St. Edmund's, where he was superior and novice-master. But in 1642 at his own request he returned to St. Edmund's, Paris, and lived there as a simple monk until his death on 12 January 1651.[11]

The list of Batt's writings given in the *Dictionary of National Biography* is incomplete, while that of Gillow is, like his life of Batt, both incomplete and erroneous, and has even misled my good friend Dom Yves Chaussy, who furnishes a fuller, but still inaccurate, list on page 202 of his 1967 study, *Les Bénédictins anglais réfugiés en France*. Both writers err, for a start, in ascribing Batt's earliest publication to the year 1624, though Dom Yves could have corrected Gillow's mistake by reference to A&R, which appeared in 1956 and is quoted by him on the very same page. In fact, the 1624 St. Omers edition of Batt's translation of (pseudo-) Augustine actually *reprints* the Latin approbation from the original edition, given by the then President of the Congregation, the redoutable Dom Rudesind Barlow, at Doway on 27 December 1621, and preceded by another from the Doway University censor of books, Georgius Colvenerius, dated 18 March 1622. The true first edition in fact bears the titlepage date of 1621 though, since Colvenerius was obviously using new-style dating (bringing the March date of his imprimatur close to that of Barlow's, given at the end of December 1621), the book must actually have been published early in 1622 by modern reckoning.

The titlepage of this, Batt's first appearance in print, reads, in a style typical of the age and of the man himself: *A heavenly treasure of confortable meditations and prayers written by S. Augustin, Bishop of Hyppon in three several treatises of his Meditations, Soliloquies, and Manuel; faithfully translated into English by the R.F. Antony Batt Monke of the holy order of S. Bennet of the Congregation of England.* Printed at Doway, by Laurence Kellam, 1621.[12] The knowledge that Augustinian scholarship since Batt's time has decided against the authenticity of these works (which had already circulated under his name for many centuries) need not spoil our enjoyment of Batt's genuine admiration of the Saint and of these his supposed writings.

Between the titlepage and the two Approbations already quoted is a lengthy dedicatory letter by the translator to his former fellow-monk,

---

10 Allanson's enormous manuscript compilations have now been published by the Congregation in microfiche form.

11 N. Birt, *Obit Book of the English Benedictines* (1913), p. 32.

12 A&R 47; ERL 256; not in STC. This elegantly printed little volume is not, as A&R states, an 18mo but a 24mo gathered in 12's and 6's. Each of the three opuscules has its own titlepage and pagination.

Gabriel (a Sancta Maria) Gifford, by now become Archbishop of Rhemes, and therefore Premier Peer of France. Written "From my Cell in Dieulewart, your Lordshipps beloved monasterie", it is warm in affection and praise of Gifford, manifesting, behind the formalities of contemporary addresses to patrons, the true joy and pride of the writer at his friend's new dignity. It also shows that Batt stands four-square within the English Benedictine historical tradition of that time, as massively expressed in Dom Edward Maihew's *Trophoea* and culminating in the *Apostolatus Benedictinorum in Anglia* in 1626, for which Dom Augustine Baker furnished important source-materials. This tradition stressed (understandably at a time when these English monks felt themselves fighting for their rights) the rôle the Benedictines had played in the first evangelization of England and in the subsequent government of its church. Batt also makes interesting references to recent Benedictine champions, including Abbot Feckenham and Dom Sigebert Buckley. He further finds space in his dedication to attack a predecessor, Thomas Rogers. Rogers had in 1581 published in London a translation (several times reprinted thereafter) of the same three works of "Augustine",[13] and Batt rebukes him for daring quite openly to "mangle & maime" the saint's writings in the interests of Protestant doctrine.

The 1624 edition (A&R 48) is then, after all, a straight reprint of this 1621 original, though its three parts are given a single pagination throughout. But so far from being a product of the press of the English Jesuits at St. Omers,[14] this reprint of Batt's version was actually in competition with a Jesuit English one, also first published in 1621, and reprinted more fully at Paris in 1631 (A&R 49-50). The unnamed printer of the 1624 edition can be shown on typographical grounds to have been Charles Boscard, a St. Omers printer who frequently worked for its publisher, John Heigham, an English layman who wrote, edited and translated many Catholic works of devotion and controversy for his countrymen.[15] Batt himself *may* have had nothing to do with this reprint, though Heigham did publish Batt's next work.[16] Nevertheless this second

---

13 STC 944 + 950 + 938.

14 Thus, Dom Yves' suggestion that Batt at least was free from the prevailing anti-jesuitism because his 1624 Augustine was published at St. Omers, rests on a mistake. Further in the same line of argument he has accepted Gillow's guess that Batt was the "A.B." who translated from Bellarmine *The Mourning of the Dove* which was printed at the College Press in 1641 (T.H. Clancy, *English Catholic Books 1641-1700* (1974), no. 89). The real translator, Thomas Everard SJ, also used "A.B." for two other slightly earlier translations made by him from Bellarmine (A&R 98, 99; see Allison in *Biographical Studies*, 2, pp. 206-207).

15 On Heigham see A.F. Allison, "John Heigham of S. Omer", *Recusant History*, 4, pp. 226-242.

16 At this time, only *some* books were given copyright by a special privilege,

appearance is testimony to the popularity of his translation.

A whole decade passed before Batt had ready in print his second book: *A hive of sacred honie-combes containing most sweet and heavenly counsel: taken out of the workes of the Mellifluous Doctor S. Bernard... Faithfully translated ... by the R. Fa. Antonie Batt Monke... of the Congregation of England.* Printed at Doway by Peter Anroy, for Iohn Heigham. Anno 1631.[17] This book carried two approbations: (1) of Dom Sigebert Bagshaw, who in 1629 had succeeded Barlow as President of the Congregation, given at St. Gregory's, Doway, 1 March 1630 (old style); (2) of the bishop's censor, dated 21 February 1631, given on the testimony of the Prior of Doway, the learned Dom Leander Jones, since clearly the censor had no English himself. Batt's own "epistle dedicatorie" addressed to the Queen of England, Henrietta-Maria, was written "From Dieuleward in the countie of Verdune the 13 of Februarie, 1631". Though small in format, Batt's little octavo is a lengthy compilation, running to over 600 pages of small type and embracing his translation of eighteen different treatises. Although none of these is today ascribed to St. Bernard himself, they commonly went under his name in the Middle Ages and were believed to be genuine writings of the saint, for whom Batt repeatedly shows his deep admiration. Typical of his personal mode of presentation is that he prefaces the text with what he calls "An Epigramme, wherein the contents of the ... Treatises are most amplie expressed in verse". This is signed at the end "Bro. Leander Neville"[18] and is followed by three further pages of verse, evidently Batt's own, in form of a dialogue imagined between St. Bernard and his reader.

The two books which follow next after the *Hive* in Batt's literary output were both printed at Doway by Kellam, (as had been the 1621 Augustine) and both are dated 1633. It is only through their Latin approbations that we can establish that one came off the press slightly before the other.[19] The earlier proves to be the one entitled: *A rule of good life: written by the mellifluous Doctor S. Bernard... especiallie for Virgins, and other Religious woemen* [sic]; *and may profitably be read likewise by all others, that aspire to Christian perfection. Faithfully translated ... by the R. Father Antonie Batt...*[20] This has an approbation by President Bagshaw,

---

granted by royal or other authority; most were not, so reprinting without leave was therefore very commonly practised.

17 A&R 104; STC 1922; ERL 194.

18 Professed at Dieuleward in 1628, he perished five years after these verses were printed, being hanged, with a fellow-monk, from a tree by protestant soldiers near S. Mihiel in Lorraine, early in 1636. Birt, *Obit Book*, p. 18.

19 The titlepage and preliminaries (which would include, as here, dedication and licence to print) were generally the last sheet or sheets of any book to leave the press.

20 A&R 105; STC 1923; ERL 79.

dated 6 June 1633, and another, dated 17 June, from the same episcopal censor (and via the same intermediary) as had the *Hive*, already described. The later of the two 1633 books is the *Three-fold mirrour,* having its two approbations dated in July.

The *Rule of good life*, translated from St. Bernard's *Modus bene vivendi*, has the very small page-size[21] of the 1621 Augustine by the same printer, but the text runs to 483 pages. The translation is dedicated "To the Venerable, Religious, and deuout sister, Dame Francis Gawen, . . . first Abbesse of the cloister . . . in Cambray". The foundation at Cambray was made in 1623, so as to include contemplative nuns within the English Benedictine Congregation, and Dame Frances Gawen, with two other mature nuns, was lent, by the English Benedictines already established at Brussels, to help train the infant community, which was then only a group of nine postulants; she became the first Abbess, though she was not still in office when Batt addressed his dedication to her.[22] It is possible that the two were known to each other earlier in life, since the dedication ends "Vouchsafe to receive it as a remembrance of an old servant and well-willer of your familie, particularlie obliged to your worthy brother . . ."[23] Between this dedication and the approbations already quoted are four sets of verses. Only the last of these is signed by him, but the other three are surely also the translator's own.

The second of the two books of 1633 is the *Threefold-Mirrour* with which this article began. It carries two approbations, the episcopal one (again by Colvenerius) dated 15 July 1633, and that of President Bagshaw, dated four days earlier. These follow a short, undated dedication "To my noble and vertuous patronesse Maistresse Anne Arondelle the elder, of Chedioke".[24] The choice of members of noted recusant families, one in Wiltshire and the other in Dorset, as his dedicatees for the two books of 1633, allows us to infer that at least at one stage he had been a West Country man; this must have been in earlier life, for he was never sent to England as a missioner. In choosing to translate Trithemius for

---

21 Like the 1621 Augustine (see note 12, above) this is really also a 24mo, but gathered this time in quires of eight.

22 She resigned in 1629 but instead of returning to Brussels she chose to stay on at Cambray, where she died in 1640 (Catholic Record Society, *Miscellanea VIII*, p. 76).

23 This brother has not been identified; according to Gillow (*Bibl. Diction.* II, p. 407) the father of Frances was Thomas Gawen of Norrington, member of a family prominent in Wiltshire recusancy.

24 Identified by F.B. Williams, *Index of Dedications* (London Bibliographical Society, 1962), p. 6 as the Anne Jerningham who married John Arundell of Chideock. It sounds from this dedication as if the connection between her and Batt had been a fairly long one and might possibly furnish a further clue to his whereabouts before he left England. Cf. note 23, above.

the first of his three "mirrours" (Batt's mind evidently rejoiced in triads) he was being soundly Benedictine; his author was a great scholar and reforming abbot, who died at the Scots monastery in Würzburg in 1516. Batt describes his second and third mirrors as written "by Catholicke Authors unknowen". In fact, in his third choice he was, unwittingly, again under the influence of St. Bernard, in so far that what he translated into English verse as *A Doleful Dialogue or disputation, betweene the soule and bodie of a damned man* was popularly attributed to St. Bernard. Indeed, another verse translation from the same Latin original had been published under the saint's name in London in 1616.[25] The second of Batt's "mirrors", the one he termed *A godly short treatise, intituled, the Golden Mirrour of a sinne-full soule* was actually the very work (by that fifteenth-century Flemish prodigy, Denis the Carthusian) of which the celebrated Lady Margaret Beaufort, mother of Henry VII, had published (about 1506) her own translation under almost the same English title.[26] Finally, Batt appended to his third mirror three (!) further short verse translations of his own making. In the first of these he renders, in the dactylic metre of the Latin original, an anonymous poem, sometimes falsely ascribed to St. Bernard under the title *De contemptu mundi*, which begins "Cur mundus militat sub vana gloria".[27] The next poem is ascribed by name to Denis the Carthusian himself, while the final one is (as Dom Raymund had time to note) Batt's English rendering of the *Dies irae*, though this is not stated in the book itself.

An English 'Approbatio', given at Doway on 27 August 1639 by the then President, Clement Reyner, licenses for printing "This threefold treatise contayning the Life and Rule of our Holy Father St. Bennet, and the Confraternity of his holy Order".[28] The first two of the three works so licensed would seem to have been already in print by the date of the president's license, if we are to believe the date 1638 on the titlepage of *The second book of the Dialogues of S. Gregorie the greate . . . containinge the life and miracles of our Holie Father S. Benedict. To which is adioined the Rule . . . translated . . . by C.F. priest & Monke.*[29] This book has no imprint apart from "Permissu superiorum. Printed Ann. 1638", but

---

25 STC 1909, translated by William Crashaw, Puritan father of the Catholic poet Richard Crashaw.

26 There were four editions, STC 6896-6898; of these the undated one by Pynson is the earliest.

27 The original was identified for me by my Bodleian colleague Dr. Barker-Benfield, to whom I am most grateful. I would like to thank other friends, too, for help in need: A.F. Allison, Dom Daniel Rees and Clive Hurst, who all aided me in making this article.

28 Quoted from *A short treatise*, facing p. 1.

29 A&R 368 (369); ERL 294.

typographically it belongs to the printing-house of the widow of Mark Wyon at Doway. The titlepage initials "C.F." are those of Cuthbert Fursden, who was a disciple of Augustine Baker. He died, however, on 2 February 1638,[30] leaving his translation uncompleted, and it was Batt who finished the work and saw it through the press. The dedicatory epistle, signed "B.E.T."[31] is addressed to "the Honorable Mistresse Anne Carie daughter to the Lord Vicount [sic] of Faukland". This lady was the eldest of four Cary sisters who, with two younger brothers, became Catholics themselves following the conversion of their mother, the learned Elizabeth, wife of the first Viscount Falkland; later all six children became Benedictines.[32] Anne entered the Order at Cambray on 8 March 1639,[33] so Batt's letter of dedication was at least penned earlier than that, otherwise he would have alluded to her becoming a nun, which he does not do. It seems likely, since Batt writes to her as "you for whom" the work "was principallie done", that Fursden, who had been one of the priests in Lady Falkland's household in London, had begun this translation at Anne's request.

Most copies of the Fursden/Batt translation also have, bound in, the following booklet: *A short treatise touching the Confraternitie of the Scapular of St. Benedicts Order . . . Permissu Superiorum. Anno Do. 1639.*[34] Although apparently anonymous, it is Batt's own work, a fact revealed in the preface to the reader, and was intended to form the third part of that "threefold treatise" approved by the President in August 1639,[35] which Batt was thus bringing to completion. In his preface to the reader he tells how "some of the most ancients [sic] of the Fathers" of the Congregation, hearing that the English texts of the Life and Rule of St. Benedict were about to be printed, "desired me (to whom the care of having them printed was committed)" to add the text of the Congregation's Letters of Confraternity with a "verie briefe, yet cleare declaration" which should clear up any difficulties which might be felt by

30 Birt, *Obit Book,* p. 19.

31 Congregational records identify Batt as the editor, so the initials "B.E.T." must somehow indicate him. Dom Raymund could only solve the puzzle of the last two initials (B. is clearly B[rother]) by assuming they stand for the *final* letters of the author's name, viz. (Antoni)E (Bat)T. This may well be correct; a number of other contemporary examples of such "telonyms" (as our editor named them) were revealed by work on the new (STC period) revised volume of Halkett and Laing, recently published.

32 See Lunn, *op. cit.,* pp. 176-177, and note 33, below; Cath. Rec. Soc., *English Benedictines,* XXXIII, p. 254.

33 Catholic Rec. Soc., *Miscellanea VIII,* pp. 44-5, gives the entry of all four Cary sisters at Cambray.

34 A&R 75; reprinted as part of A&R 369 in ERL 294.

35 See note 28, above.

those who "understand not the sayd letters rightly". Reading between the lines, we may well ascribe to Batt himself the initial suggestion to add some explanatory and apologetic treatment to the Letters of Confraternity, though for obvious reasons his bretheren, or the President, to whom Batt carried the proposal for his sanction, may have added the proviso that it should be both clear and very brief. In the event the President ordered Batt himself to carry out the plan "without delay and to dispatch it out of hand".

The result was this little tract of 62 pages, Batt's first published writing of his own original composition. In its seven chapters he treats of the text of the letters of Confraternity,[36] the ceremony of admittance, the historical basis of the practice of admitting confraters, the right of the English Congregation to confer confraternity (derived from the papacy, through the Spanish Congregation), the doctrine of sharing another's merits, and answers to objections raised (e.g. by Wycliffe) against that doctrine. There is little opportunity in such a work for Batt's customary versification, but on page 32 he does translate a Latin tag by an English rhyming couplet.

Although designed as a pendent, his treatise can stand on its own and separate copies survive today which are still in their original bindings and obviously have never formed part of the triple volume.[37] Furthermore, Batt provided it with a dedication of its own, initialled "A.B.", which is integral to this work and is additional to the one addressed to Anne Cary which Batt prefixed to the Life by St. Gregory. This dedication is "To the right honorable Thomas Lord Windesor", namely Thomas, 6th Baron Windsor. To judge from the number of books by different authors on a variety of topics which were dedicated to him,[38] Lord Windsor must have enjoyed a wide and continuing reputation as a patron of letters, while volumes inscribed with his name and motto suggest he owned a considerable library. Batt's letter refers to him, guardedly, as the obvious patron for this confraternity book, which suggests that he was already a prominent confrater and benefactor of the English Congregation. Certainly his Benedictine connections can be documented from other

---

36 An imperfect example of such a letter of admission, printed on one side of a leaf, was recorded as A&R 292. That copy was used, according to its manuscript dating, on 26 November 1625. A perfect copy has since been found and is reproduced as ERL 162(2). It shows that the document was issued in the name of Alphonsus Barrantes, the Spanish President General 1613-1617. The new copy is dated in manuscript 26 February 1626.

37 Hence its independent appearance as A&R 75. Batt does not figure in the 1926 STC, but the Harmsworth copy of *A short treatise* was recorded (no. 1020) under "A.B.".

38 F.B. Williams, *Index*, p. 201 lists fourteen.

sources: for example, in 1632 Dom Jerome Porter's *The flowers of the liues of the . . . Sainctes of . . . England Scotland, and Ireland*[39] had been dedicated to him, and he had a Benedictine chaplain living with him at his home at Bradenham in Buckinghamshire.[40]

In the same year as the *Short treatise*, another small devotional work, of 68 pages only, was published anonymously, with no imprint except "Printed with license of Superiors" and the date 1639. Its title runs: *A poore mans mite. A letter of a Religious man of the Order of Saint Benedict, vnto a Sister of his, concerning the Rosarie or Psalter of our blessed Ladie, Commonly called the Beades.* Corresponding to a dedication is the first letter, the "Poor man's mite" itself, from the author to his sister, as described on the titlepage. This is unsigned and serves to explain and justify generally the use of the Beads, a pair of which accompanied the letter. It also serves to introduce a method of saying the rosary which the writer explains thus (page 14): "I lighted of late vpon certaine most devout and ancient Meditations in latine, called *Rosarium aureum* . . . These have I translated into English meeter". The *Golden Rosary* is translated into fifty 4-line stanzas of English verse, numbered in tens, and one was intended to be interpolated into the recital of each of the fifty *Aves* of "once round the beads", to aid meditation.[41] The translation of the *Golden Rosary* occupies 15 pages and is followed in turn by "Another letter to his Sister, concerning the Office of our blessed Lady commonly called the Primmer", and by yet a third letter to his sister, "concerning the Order of Saint Benedict, together with a little Office of Saint Benedict. According to the houres of the Primmer, as aforesaid". The rest of the book is occupied by this little Office, in English, including seven hymns in honour of the Saint's life and virtues.

This book was first described by A&R,[42] which attributes it (without a query) to Batt and to the press which also printed the *Short treatise* in the same year. The immediate grounds for the attribution were that the only copy hitherto known was discovered bound with a copy of Batt's tripartite *Life, Rule* and *Short treatise*. It is in one of the copies of that work belonging to Colwich Abbey, Staffordshire, the community which before the French Revolution was the English Benedictine convent of Our Lady of Good Hope at Paris, founded from Cambray in 1651. But

---

39 A&R 658; STC 20124; ERL 239.
40 Cath. Rec. Society XXXIII, p. 217; Lunn, *op. cit.*, p. 227.
41 I have not identified the original *Rosarium aureum*; there is some resemblance to the Franciscan Crown (or Seraphic Rosary) in the breaking of the *Ave* at the word "Jesus" for meditation on the mystery.
42 A&R 74; not in STC; ERL 133(2). I am not now certain that the printer was widow Wyon at Doway, but (as will be shown in discussing his *Hidden treasure*) a change of printer need not be an argument against Batt's authorship.

the announcement of a second copy of the 1639 *Poor man's mite*, now in the library of the University of Texas, weakens the *prima facie* evidence of the Colwich copy. Yet the Colwich library also possesses one of the rare copies of the close reprint made in 1674 (Clancy 82) which perhaps restores somewhat their claim to some association with the author. Because Batt has as yet no identified family, we do not know whether he had a real sister; this one could be a literary fiction, for passages in the letters to her are defensive and apologetical, as if written to a non-Catholic, while others are explanatory and hortatory, as if to a devout Catholic. Whether she be fictional or real does not prove or disprove Batt's claim to authorship. There seems to be no case against such authorship, and the work bears several marks of his style and attitudes.[43] In the absence of any other candidate this booklet is probably best left under Batt's name until further evidence comes to light; it is more easily overlooked if left to lurk under 'anonyma'.

To judge from its appearance in three different languages, and ultimately in a total of five editions, Batt's last published[44] work was in a sense his most ambitious and his most influential. All the three versions, Latin, French and English, were undoubtedly issued by the compiler himself, being published each with a separate dedication addressed by him to a different patron. Even though the French text, *Le thrésor caché au champ du Seigneur nouuellement trouué*, bears the titlepage date 1640, whereas the Latin *Thesaurus absconditus in agro Dominico inventus* and the English *A hidden treasure of holie prayers and deuout meditations newly found out in holie Scripture*.[45] are each dated 1641, it would seem certain that the work was originally put together in its Latin dress, woven by Batt as far as possible out of the actual wording of the Vulgate, and that the French and English are his own translations from the Latin.[46] The assembled passages from the Old

---

43 Besides the amount of verse, there is much of Batt's gentle antiquarian pride in Benedictine history, turned to practical use for his reader's spiritual benefit. And on page 47 he actually refers to "this holy Fraternitie [not previously mentioned] . . . ordayned for lay people, that are devoutly affected vnto the Order, as I understand you are one". This suggests a real sister (at a distance, perhaps in England) and also an unconscious disclosure that this is a sequel to the confraternity treatise, as well it may be.

44 The English Benedictine chronicler Weldon, who died in 1713, saw in manuscript at La-Celle a Catechism, commissioned from Batt by the Chapter of 1641, but never printed for lack of funds.

45 Clancy, no. 82.

46 That the French is a translation is stated in the Privilege (which was a legal instrument) appended to the Latin, as described further on. Evidence that the English is also translated from the Latin is satisfactory though indirect; for example, the Sorbonne censors' Approbation was obviously granted in Latin and the English one (which adds the name of a third censor, itself a mark of posteriority) translated verbatim from it, rather than *vice versa*.

and New Testaments which he brings together with only such occasional adaptations and such changes of grammatical construction as he found necessary to make up his short but consecutive units, are divided into prayers for various occasions (the 59 chapters of part 1) and meditations (the 39 chapters of part 2). It is obviously a just claim that he makes, in an address to the Christian Reader prefixed to his Latin text and translated word for word in his English version of the book, "to select and collect all these things together out of diverse places of the holy Scripture, to have reduced each one to his several Chapters and to have ranged them into that order, in which they are, could not be done without much labour, diligence and care". This was recognized by the censors, two Doctors of the Sorbonne, whose Approbation, dated 22 February 1641, he likewise translates verbatim from the Latin original for his English book; they characterize his work as "compiled of the text of holy Scripture with great labour and industry, and that with excellent coherence" [i.e. of subject-matter and arrangement].

In fashioning his "chapters" as far as possible out of whole passages and verses of the bible, Batt made a book of biblical prayers quite different from that of an earlier and more famous English recusant writer. This was the *Psalmi et precationes* of St. John Fisher, which enjoyed extraordinary popularity for almost a hundred years in various different languages.[47] Fisher, though he uses nothing but the vocabulary and phraseology of Scripture, writes a text of his own and apparently does not cite any single verse of the bible in its entirety.

Batt's original Latin book has on its final page a royal privilege (in French) giving its author copyright in getting printed "un Livre intitulé, *Thesaurus absconditus in Agro Dominico, &c.* avec la Traduction Françoise". This privilege, dated 21 January 1641, is to be valid for five years from the day printing should be completed; as so often in French-printed books of this period, this led to a statement (in this instance below the Privilege on the final page) "*Achevé d'imprimer le 8. Mars 1641*". The publisher of the Latin was Pierre Rocolet, who describes himself on the titlepage as "Royal Bookseller, at the Palace", but the name of the printer, who worked for him here, is not recorded. For fully a century before 1640 it had become common practice (as it still is today) especially in great centres of book production such as Paris, Lyons, Rouen, Antwerp and (more latterly) London, for the name in titlepage imprints to be that of a bookseller/publisher only, with no necessary clue

---

[47] Besides the numerous editions in Latin or English which were printed in England, sometimes openly, sometimes with false imprints (as the new STC will reveal), Fisher's work was published abroad at least six times in Dutch and German translations.

to the owner and operator of the press or presses which carried out the actual printing. While this makes precise identification difficult for the printing historian, it means that we need feel no surprise that the same author, in this instance Batt, should have issued books almost simultaneously under three different publishers' names. Rocolet was certainly a publisher only; Jean Laquehay, whose name stands on the titlepage of the French *Thrésor*, was certainly a printer/publisher, who on this occasion risked little, since Batt's French was printed "Aux depens de l'Autheur". Whether Guillaume Baudry, who issued the English *Hidden Treasure*, was his own printer I have not established, but it is probably no coincidence that he should have published, barely a twelvemonth earlier and also for the English Benedictines, the only other work printed under his name directly for English clients.[48] The other work is an English translation of St. John Fisher's *De orando Deo*, issued in 1640.[49] On its titlepage and at the end of the dedication to Elizabeth, wife of Percy Herbert later second Baron Powis,[50] the translator uses the initials "R.A.B.", and it needs mention here for it has also been claimed as Batt's work.

But President Clement Rayner, who gave the translation his approbation on 6 February 1640, there describes it as "a Reverendo Patre R.A. eiusdemque Ordinis & Congregationis nostrae . . . traductum", so the attribution of an 1887 reprint of this Fisher translation to "(R.A.B. [i.e. Reverend Anthony Batt?])", made in the printed catalogue of the British Museum library,[51] cannot stand. Whoever the R.A., B[enedictine?] was,[52] there remains no evident reason to connect him with Batt, though some association with the English Benedictine community of St. Edmund's, Paris, where Batt lived in 1640 and again from 1642, seems likely in view of the common patronage of the same publisher.[53]

Batt's original Latin *Thesaurus absconditus* was dedicated by him, in

---

48 Baudry had already, in 1636, published at his own costs the Latin of Mersenne's celebrated *Harmonie* with a dedication and a preface, both signed by the publisher himself, addressed to Sir George Cavendish, Kt.

49 A&R 305; STC 10890; ERL 11(2).

50 F.B. Williams, *Index*, p. 93.

51 This attribution is made also in STC, no. 10890. The British Library had no copy of the 1640 edition until recently.

52 The candidate proposed by A&R was Dom Robert Anderton, *vere* Ashton, professed at St. Edmund's, Paris, in 1635 (Birt, p. 55), but this was only a conjecture. A long-standing ascription to St. Alban Roe probably has more to recommend it; he was in England in prison continuously from 1625 till his martyrdom in 1642.

53 A volume at Downside has Part 1 of Batt's *Hidden Treasure* which, although wanting its preliminaries, forms a suitable partner to the copy of the 1640 Fisher which it follows in a single seventeenth-century binding. It serves to underline their affinities, including their common origin from the same printing-house.

the formal language then employed by clients addressing important patrons, to Dominique Séguier, bishop of Meaux since 1637, Grand Almoner to the French king and brother of the Chancellor, Pierre; the dedication does not convey any suggestion of a personal link, whereas with the dedicatee of the English version, named as "the right worshipfull John Preston of Manner Esquire",[54] Batt had had some slight personal connection, since he writes of "such smal acquaintance, as I had with you, whiles you liued heere in Paris". The dedication of the French text to Françoise de la Châtre, Abbess of Faremoutiers, is the most personal gesture of the three; expressed though it is by means of two (not quite perfect) French/Latin anagrams on her name and title accompanied by a sonnet in French which Dom Yves (who quotes it in full)[55] rightly terms "high-flown"; it is at least typical of the period and of the man himself. No doubt, as Dom Yves suggests, it was the abbess, who was already a benefactress of the English Benedictines and at Faremoutiers was a near neighbour to their house at La-Celle-en-Brie where Batt was superior, who had made it financially possible for him to publish his French version "aux dépens de l'Autheur" and so enabled him to reach another public, above all of "dévotes" — French women of piety who might not find his prayerbook useful in its Latin form. It evidently did have some appeal, for even after he and his patroness both were dead, another edition of the French "traduites en forme de paraphrase, par messire François Doujat" was published in Paris by D. Foucault in 1669 in two twelvemo volumes.

Though Batt's other works were undertaken with the needs of his own fellow-countrymen principally in mind, and though there is nothing in his literary output to suggest that he was touched by any of the strong tides of new spirituality which were flowing through France during the long period — not far short of forty years — during which he lived there as a monk, we may take our leave of him with pleasure in the thought that by his final publication, both in the Latin (of which his publisher Rocolet issued a second edition in 1647, to which were added some short works of Thomas à Kempis) and especially in its French form, Batt established a place among the few Englishmen who attempted — not without some success in his case — to reach a French public directly and thereby

---

54 "John Preston of the Manner" (the Manor, near Furness, Lancs.) was listed sixth in a "note of Papists and priests assembled at St. Winefred's Well, on St. Winefred's day, 1629" quoted from the State Papers by Foley (*Records*, IV, 534). This document also states that he kept two priests at his house. He was created a Baronet in 1644 for his loyalty to the king in the Civil War, and died of wounds. His son Thomas, 3rd Bt., became a Jesuit (*ibid.*, V, 358).

55 Chaussy, *op. cit.*, p. 203.

witnessed to what Dom Yves describes as "those relationships of trust and friendship which linked at least some of the English exiles to their French hosts, and made France their second spiritual homeland".[56]

Postscript

An unpublished translation by Batt survives in a manuscript at Ampleforth (MS. 86) transcribed by Augustine Baker's own hand in 1632: *A Spirituall Looking-glass, written by ... Abbot Blosius ... made into English by the Rd. fa: fa: A. Batte.* See *American Benedictine Review*, 25 (1974) p. 314.

---

56 Chaussy, *loc. cit.*

STILLINGFLEET'S SERMON PREACHED BEFORE THE KING ON THE ANNIVERSARY OF THE EXECUTION OF CHARLES I 30 JANUARY 1668/9

Irène Simon

The sermons preached by Anglican divines after the Restoration on the anniversary of the execution of Charles I, as well as those commemorating the "providential" discovery of the Gunpowder Plot,[1] have special interest for students of the period because of the close association between religion and politics which they reveal. While 5th-November sermons had been, and continued to be, aimed at the Church of Rome, those delivered on 30 January were bound to be directed against the Puritans and their heirs, the Dissenters. Although the Act of Uniformity ensured unity of doctrine and discipline and although the doctrine of passive obedience was accepted by all the Anglican clergy,[2] the diversity of men within the clergy—from old Laudians like Sheldon to former Presbyterians like Tillotson—made for a variety of attitudes towards recent events.

Given Stillingfleet's irenicism,[3] one may expect him to display less anti-fanatic zeal than did such High-Churchmen as Robert South, "the scourge of the fanatics". Preaching on the same occasion six years before, South had launched into a passionate attack against the rebels, particularly against the Presbyterians, who, as signatories of the Covenant,[4]

---

1 The 5th of November was commemorated by the C.o.E. from 1606 until well into the 19th century. The order for the service for the 30th of January appeared in the revised Liturgy after the passing of the Act of Uniformity and survived until 1859; from the time of the 1688 Revolution, however, Whigs clamoured for its suppression for the sake of political and religious peace. With the accession of the Hanoverians the clergy was invited to speak with moderation so as not to revive old quarrels.

2 The Act of Uniformity imposed on the clergy "subscription to a doctrine of non-resistance, together with a repudiation of the view that the Solemn League and Covenant had binding force on any one, including those who had sworn to observe it". David Ogg, *England in the Reign of Charles II*, Oxford, (1934), 1962, I, 201.

3 His *Irenicum* (1659), an attempt to resolve the differences about Church government between Anglicans and Presbyterians so as to lay a foundation for peace and union, ranged him among the more broad-minded Anglicans like Jeremy Taylor and Bishop Ussher. The book was reprinted in 1662, the very year marking the failure of such attempts towards a comprehensive Church.

4 Both Houses adopted the Solemn League and Covenant in September 1643.

had first dared to question the duty of obedience to the magistrate by making it conditional upon his acceptance of their claims. *They* had dealt the first blow against their lawful sovereign, so that the execution of Charles I was only the last stroke against his prerogatives in a rebellion that had begun as an attack against the clergy. From his text, *Judges* 19.30,[5] South had shown that "the *Sceptre* was judged by God himself most concerned to assert the Privileges of, and to revenge the injuries done the *Crosier*; the *Crown* to support the *Mitre*".[6] He had inferred from this that it would be both foolish and sinful to grant a Declaration of Indulgence to these late rebels, whatever their "postdated" loyalty in condemning the execution of Charles I, or to seek accommodation with them in the Church. Not only had he charged the Puritans with the foulest of crimes, but he had presented the trial of the King in terms evoking the Passion of Christ, so that Charles appeared as the Lamb of God sacrificed by false doctors of the Church for his devotion to the true Church and his steadfast adherence to the laws of the land. The sermon was clearly a tract for the times,[7] reminding the King that, as Defender of the Faith, he was expected to protect the Established Church. The violence of South's language is only equalled by the pregnancy of his wit, the violence and prejudices against the Dissenters being an index of the temper of those Royalists in the Cavalier Parliament who supported the measures known as the Clarendon Code.

Stillingfleet chose for the text of his sermon[8] *Jude* 11 : *And perished in the gainsaying of Corah*, i.e. the end of a verse from an Epistle warning Christians against the false teachers who are crept in unawares to seduce them, and reminding them of the judgment of God against Corah for his revolt against Moses and Aaron (*Num*. 16). The slow pace and measured cadences of the opening suggest not only the solemnity of the occasion but the seriousness of the crime to be denounced, a crime against the honour of the nation, against the King, and above all against religion. For while the Christian religion has always made resistance to the

---

5 I.e. the conclusion of the story relating the destruction of the tribe of Benjamin for their crime against a Levite, a revenge entrusted by God to the other tribes under the leadership of the *royal* tribe of Judah.

6 For the text of this sermon, see my *Three Restoration Divines: Barrow, South, Tillotson. Selected Sermons*, Paris, I, 1967; II, 1976; II i, 281-309.

7 Just over a month before the sermon was preached Charles II had tried to secure freedom of worship for non-Anglicans. In the early months of 1663 attempts were made to grant him dispensing power in religious matters. See David Ogg, *op. cit*, I, 203-4, 352-4.

8 Sermon VII, in *The Works of ... Dr Edward Stillingfleet*, 6 vols. 1707-10, I (Fifty Sermons), 83-103 (Unless otherwise indicated, the place of publication is London). All further quotations refer to this edition.

magistrate unlawful,[9] these wicked men used a pretence of it for things contrary to its nature and design in order to show themselves "Christians of a higher rank than others".[10] Stillingfleet limits himself to the explication of the nature of the ungodly teachers (vv. 4 and 8), but he amplifies in such a way as to evoke the claims of the "wicked men" at home: they pretend to inspiration and impulses; they destroy "all usual difference between good and evil"; they deny the power of the magistrate over the Saints; they consider themselves as the only Saints, and they regard temporal government as "the contrivance of some evil spirits to abridge men of that liberty which God and nature had given them": not only do they speak contemptibly of it, but they openly resist it. In short, as the text says, they are charged with the same sin as Corah and are threatened with the same punishment.

In his explication Stillingfleet already glances at the doctrines of the Saints and at the debate on Christian liberty[11] which had ultimately led to the destruction of the Church and of the monarchy. It may be noted at this point that such a paraphrase of "ungodly teachers" reminds one of the Independents and the Sectaries more than the Presbyterians, in other words, of Puritans of the Left.[12] Going over to his other text, Stillingfleet once more expands far beyond the verses dealing with the rising proper (*Num.* 16, I-3, 13-14). The point of this long development is to show the devious means used by ambitious and factious men to achieve their aim, in this case, to lay aside Moses and share the government among

---

9 St. quotes the usual texts: *Matt.* 22.21 and *Rom.* 13.1,2.

10 The original meaning of the term "Puritan".

11 As interpreted by Puritans on the basis of such texts as: *Rom.* 8.15-21; *Gal.* 5.2.; and *Jas.* 5.2.

12 The term "Puritan" is used here all through to refer to those who, whatever their differences, held "in some form the idea of the 'holy community'". See *Puritanism and Liberty, Being the Army Debates (1647-9)*, Selected and edited with an Introduction by A.S.P. Woodhouse, (1938), 1965, Introduction, p. 36. When speaking of the years following the King's defeat, it is easiest to keep to the distinction Woodhouse draws between four groups among the opponents of the King: (1) the Erastians, guided by secular principles, and (2, 3, 4) Puritans as defined above, i.e.: (2) Puritans of the Right, the Presbyterians; (4) Puritans of the Left, i.e. Sectaries descended from earlier Separatists, but falling into 2 sub-groups: (i) those whose aim was ultimately secular and democratic, such as the Levellers, and (ii) those who, on the contrary, emphasized the privileges of the Saints and looked forward to the Millennium such as the Fifth-Monarchy Men; (3) Puritans of the Centre, the Independents, who distrusted Presbyterian clericalism and supported religious toleration, but who also fell into 2 sub-groups: (i) those who were prepared to remain within the Church provided they were granted some accommodation, and (ii) the separating Independents, who supported—or were supported by—the group on the Left and were less attached to Parliament since by then Parliament had taken over from the King, just as the Presbyter meant to take over from the Priest. *Op. cit*, Introd., pp. 14-20.

themselves. He lists the means by which such men usually insinuate themselves into the good opinion of the people and set up as their champions against so-called usurped power; once this has been achieved, he says, "groundless suspicions and unreasonable fears and jealousies will pass for arguments and demonstrations".

By shifting from the past to the present tense Stillingfleet succeeds in drawing a vivid picture of the ways in which sedition spreads and of the response of the people once their "affections" have been gained. The reader's interest is absorbed by this shrewd, though biassed, analysis of popular response to what we would call demagogues, for Stillingfleet supports his general statements with specific examples of the people's behaviour, showing that, once they have been incited to criticize their governors, they *will* grumble whatever these do. The wording suggests that the shift is not only to sedition in general, but from Biblical times to the present or recent past. For instance, he says that the people are ready to cry up these factious men "as true *Patriots* and Defenders of their liberties", or as "Men of honesty, because they are farthest from being *Flatterers* of the *Court*" so that the earlier praise of Moses somehow redounds to the credit of Charles I. Speaking next of the sedition raised against such an excellent prince as Moses (v. 4), he accuses the faction of making "a *Remonstrance*, asserting the Priviledges of the *people* against Moses and Aaron". This may refer to the *Grand Remonstrance* of 1641, but, as appears from what follows, it probably refers also to the *Remonstrance of the Army* to Parliament in defence of the people (Nov. 1648), since Stillingfleet is deliberately wording the explication of his text so as to evoke the progress of the Puritan opposition to the King until Charles was brought to trial on the ground that he was an enemy of the people and had to account to them for his behaviour. Such phrases as: "we appear only in behalf of the *fundamental Liberties* of the people both civil and spiritual", "retrenching the exorbitancies of power and some late innovations", "power offensive to *God's holy people*", "the *Cause of God's people*", "dying in so good a *Cause*", "making votes of *non-Addresses*", "breaking off treaties with Moses" for exercising an "arbitrary and tyrannical power over the people" and for being "guilty of breach of the trust committed to him", and, particularly the final sentence: "So that now by the ill management of his *Trust*, the power was again devolved into the hands of the people and they ought to take account of his actions" (93)—such phrases show that Stillingfleet is conflating arguments used in the early months of the Long Parliament by the defenders of the Common Law with some others used by the Presbyterians since both these groups were out to curb the power of the Crown, as well as language proper to the former with language specifically used by the Puritans. Moreover, he is implicitly taking a leap from 1641 to the period between 1646 and January 1648, thereby putting the emphasis on the more revolutionary aspects of Puritanism. While "votes of non-Addresses" clearly refers to the vote by the Commons, now the Rump, in January 1648 and unanimously approved by the Council of the Army, the "breaking off treatises" skilfully links the rebellion of men who, in signing the Covenant, had sworn to maintain the King—albeit conditionally—yet had revolted against him ("for exercising an arbitrary and tyrannical power over the people"), with the breach of law committed by the remnant of the House of Commons under pressure from the Army in declaring itself alone a true Parliament, erecting itself as supreme power, and setting up a High Court of Justice to try the King ("for breach of the trust committed to him").[13] Stillingfleet is thus directing the attention of his public to events following the First Civil War, i.e. to a time when the power of the Presbyterians was dwindling and when the fight was "being transferred from Parliament to the street and the camp".[14] His parting shot is to brand the rebels as hypocrites, who took good care to make it appear that they had been driven to revolt by "*Necessity* and *Providence*". "Necessity" was not only pleaded by Parliament when it raised its standard against the King, but by the depleted Parliament of 1646 when asking the Scottish Covenanters to surrender the King to them, as well as in all the Remonstrances or Engagements of the people submitted to Parliament by the Army;[15] most important, it was pleaded by the High Court set up to try the King. As to "Providence", though a frequent word on the lips of Puritans of all colours, it was used with greater significance by those who drew on personal religious experiences to justify, or confirm, their decisions through divine inspiration and who, believing in special providences, were apt to see the hand of God in their own victories.

The Puritans' objection to encroachments on their spiritual liberty in "matters indifferent" was grounded in the liberty of Christians as children of God, a doctrine first asserted by Luther, notably in his

---

13 In early January 1649 "the Commons declared 'that the people are, under God, the original of all power' and 'that the Commons of England, in Parliament ... have the supreme power in this nation'". In March the House of Lords was abolished and from then until April 1653 the Commons exercised both executive and legislative power. See Blair Worden, *The Rump Parliament*, Cambridge, 1974, p. 2.

14 C.V. Wedgwood, *The King's War, 1641-1647*, (1958), 1967, p. 581.

15 See *A Solemn Engagement of the Army* (5th June, 1647) and *An Agreement of the People* (3 Nov., 1647), in Woodhouse, *op. cit.*, p. 401 and p. 445. Cf. "So spake the fiend, and with necessity, The tyrant's plea, excused his devilish deeds", *P.L.*, iv, 393-4. Cromwell's many invocations of Providence and necessity were usually interpreted after the Restoration—and also at the time—in the way Milton here speaks of Satan. For a more favourable view, see Christopher Hill, *God's Englishman*, 1970, especially Ch. IX, "Providence and Oliver Cromwell", pp. 215-250.

Commentary upon *Galatians*, and canvassed in England since the days of the Elizabethan Settlement by those who found the Church of England insufficiently reformed. The resistance to Laud's "innovations" brought forth a spate of pamphlets in defence of reform of the Church's discipline — as well as many in defence of episcopal order — the best remembered among students of literature being Milton's *Of Reformation* (1641). It was argued that the civil magistrate has no right to force conscience, and the most powerful group of Puritans in Parliament, the Presbyterians, set out to reform the Church according to *their* principles. It was not long, however, before the form they proposed, and contemplated imposing, was found to restrain the liberty of others, notably of those whom not even accommodation within a national Church (which, in any case, the Presbyterians were not willing to grant) could satisfy because they held to the principle of gathered Churches: in their case no form of worship imposed by the magistrate could be acceptable; among these were the separating Independents and the Sectaries. The doctrine of Christian liberty thus posed the problem of obedience to the magistrate, for the Christian's freedom from bondage to the Law could have application beyond the religious sphere. In the *Westminster Confession of Faith* (1644) the Presbyterians had set clear limits to inferences from Christian liberty to civil liberties.[16] All the same, through its insistence on liberty Puritanism was a revolutionary force: as Woodhouse said, "Nothing could dissipate the divinity that hedged a king save the divinity of religion itself when religion was ranged against him",[17] and in the Long Parliament, religion was so ranged. Since the Church discipline that the Presbyterians tried to enforce through Parliament—then functioning as the magistrate—satisfied neither the Congregationalists nor the Sects, it was inevitable that the doctrine of Christian liberty should be pressed further, and, ultimately, be enlisted by revolutionary forces in support of their own secular arguments.

In the passage discussed above it is clear that Stillingfleet is lumping together claims put forward in the early days of the Puritan Revolution and others that became loudest after the King's defeat in 1646, when Independents and Sectaries were gaining ground in the Army, which, being at odds with Parliament, gradually became the main revolutionary

---

16 "the *Westminster Confession of Faith* concludes its chapter (chiefly devoted, in the manner of Calvin, to explaining what the doctrine [*viz.* of Christian liberty] is not) with the declaration that 'they who, upon pretence of Christian liberty, shall oppose any lawful power ... whether ... civil or ecclesiastical, resist the ordinance of God', while whoever disturbs the peace of the church may be proceeded against not by ecclesiastical censures only, but by 'the power of the civil magistrate'". Woodhouse, *op. cit.*, Introd., p.66.

17 *Ibid.*, Introd., p. 61.

force and the spokesman for "the people". Stillingfleet is thus building up to the committing of the King for trial, i.e. to power devolving into the hands of the people. This is indeed the "false principle" against which he will direct his argument. Yet even before reaching this point, i.e. when considering the men Corah drew to his faction, he reiterates the accusation that the "discontented Levites" like the "sons of Reuben"[18] who joined the rebellion, though prompted by ambition, concealed their purpose by talking of religion and public interest. The discontented Levites who first threw in their lot with Corah cannot but be the Presbyterians, yet Stillingfleet seems to avoid laying the blame too clearly on them by once more elaborating on the nature and ways of sedition in general and on its ruinous effects on simple people. The picture he draws of the rebels at the end of this section is the stereotype "character of a Puritan" after the Restoration, one which blurs the differences between the various groups and tends to emphasize the characteristics of the extreme Sects, such as "deep sighs and extatic motions", which in no way can apply to the Presbyterians. The two hundred and fifty "princes of the assembly" whom Corah drew to his side, Stillingfleet calls "Members of the *Great Council* of the *Nation*", and, adapting the text of *Num.* 10.3, he says that they sat in "*Parliament at the door of the Tabernacle of the Congregation*" without having been called by Moses. Though the Long Parliament *was* summoned by the King, it did refuse to be dissolved at the King's pleasure; but the full phrase—though largely from Scripture—also seems to suggest the meetings of the Army after the King's defeat, when it practically laid siege to the depleted Parliament, then forcibly excluded from it those members who opposed the King's trial (and was to help Cromwell dissolve the Rump in April 1653). This interpretation seems to be correct in view of what follows, i.e. that

> the *Faction* had gained so great strength by the accession of so great a number of the most leading men among the *People*, we may expect they should soon declare their intentions. (95)[19]

Stillingfleet finally turns to the "intentions" of the rebels, and this

---

18 Reuben was Jacob's first-born (*Gen.* 35.23). St. may be thinking of such members of the aristocracy as Lord Brooke or Lord Saye and Sele, or the Earl of Manchester, who supported Pym and, during the First Civil War, was General of the Eastern Association.

19 Possibly a reference to men like Cromwell, both an M.P. and later Lord General of the Army, and Ireton, also an M.P. and an officer in the Army; in accordance with the Self-Denying Ordinance (1644)—which deprived Essex and Manchester of their command in the army—they had been away fighting in the New Model Army, but returned to Parliament after the King's defeat. In the next sentences St. goes out of his way to stress the difference between Israel's Assembly (which he calls "the great Council of the Nation") and the Sanhedrin; the reason may be to avoid confusion between Parliament and Convocation, which was also summoned by a King's writ.

constitutes the core of his argument against rebellion. The pretences he infers from vv. 4 and 13, without being wire-drawn, recall the political and religious theories put forward during the Interregnum; these are of two kinds:

> 1. *The asserting of the Rights and Liberties of the people in opposition to the Government of Moses.*
> 2. *The freeing themselves from the encroachments upon their spiritual Privileges, which were made by the Usurpation of Aaron and the Priesthood.* (95)

Given the occasion, the first point will be dealt with at greater length. First, Stillingfleet explains what Moses was accused of, i.e. of having "taken upon himself the Government of the people *without their consent*" (my italics) and of having thereby "debarred the people of that *Liberty* which God had given them". In the circumstances, Corah acted "as though he had been already *President* of a *High-Court* of *Justice* upon *Moses* their King" (96). The principles implied in Corah's accusation are two: first, that "*Liberty* and a *Right to Power* is so inherent in the *People* that it cannot be taken from them", and second, that "in case of *Usurpation* upon that *Liberty* of the people, they may resume the exercise of *Power*, by punishing those who are guilty of it" (96). The theory that Stillingfleet will have to confute is thus that of contract, i.e. that all power resides in the people, is delegated by them to the magistrate for the defence of their liberty, and may be resumed by them in case of usurpation.

Contrary to South, Stillingfleet chooses to attack the principles of the Rebellion at the ultimate stage, when the doctrine of Christian liberty had been extended to the civil polity, and the right to resistance for conscience sake was used to justify rebellion of the subjects against the magistrate. Although the Presbyterians had been ready to make limited inferences from the doctrine in their struggle against the King,[20] they were by no means ready to grant this right to the people when, from 1646 onward, Parliament came into conflict with the Army, who asserted with greater and greater force the sovereignty of the people and their right to power. For this position the men of the Army found support among, or were incited by, Puritans of the Left like the Independent John Goodwin[21] as well as from Sectaries arguing from secular principles, like some Levellers. Milton's tracts on liberty show how the basic notion of Christian liberty could develop under the pressure of events, in his own life as well as in the nation at large. While in *Of Reformation* and in his defence of

---

20 See for instance the Scottish Presbyterian Rutherford's *Lex, Rex* (1644), in Woodhouse, *op. cit.*, p. 199.
21 In *Right and Might Well Met* (1649), written in defence of Pride's Purge, *ibid.*, p. 213.

Smectymnuus he only deals with "matters indifferent", in the Divorce tracts and in *Areopagitica* he both extends the concept to civil liberty and argues from reason as well as from Scripture; in *The Tenure of Kings and Magistrates, Eikonoklastes* and the two *Defenses of the English People* he defends the right of the people to call the magistrate to account,[22] while in *The Ready and Easy Way* he is as much an authoritarian as the Millenarians and is ready to impose on the unregenerate the liberty which his own illumined reason regards as beneficial to them.[23] His appeal to the law of nature (besides a host of Scriptural authorities) is perhaps most striking in the Divorce tracts.[24] Among Puritans of the radical Left the latter position is best represented by the Levellers; for instance, Lilburne, though sometimes using the language of Puritanism, grounds his claims, for manhood suffrage among others, on the rights of man. The Levellers were no less influential among the men of the Army than the separating Independents, and in the final resolutions of the Army debates the argument is from the natural rights of man or the law of nature. This is not incompatible with the Independents' conception of Christian liberty as extended to civil liberties, and the—temporary—convergence[25] of these two trends of thought is an index of the kind of political radicalism the Puritans' zeal for God's people could foster.[26] In this sense South was

---

[22] The clearest and shortest statement is in *The Tenure*: "It follows, lastly, that since the king or magistrate holds his authority of the people, both originally and naturally for their good in the first place, and not of his own, then may the people, as oft as they shall judge it for the best, either choose him or reject him, retain him or depose him, though no tyrant, merely by the liberty and right of freeborn men to be governed as seems to them best" (John Milton: *Complete Poems and Major Prose*, ed. Merritt Y. Hughes, New York, 1957, p. 757). In *The Tenure* M. accuses the Presbyterians of regarding those who wish to bring the King to account as "no less than Korah, Datham, and Abiram" (*ibid.*, p. 753); as Merritt Hughes reminds us (n. 31), "royalist divines often compared the leaders of Parliament to the rebel Levites" of *Num*. 16. In the same tract, M., like South, argues that, in fact, the Parliament's "oaths of subjection broken, new supremacy obeyed, new oaths and covenants taken ... have in plain terms unkinged the King much more than hath their seven years' war" (*ibid.*, p. 767).

[23] In this respect Christopher Hill is right to stress Milton's kinship with the extreme Left. See *The World Turned Upside Down*, 1972, *passim*. For the evolution of Milton's thought and the conflict in him between Puritanism and Christian humanism, see A. E. Baker, *Milton and the Puritan Dilemma*, Toronto, 1942.

[24] Milton justifies the expansion, in *Tetrachordon*, of the Scriptural commentary he had given in *DDD* by saying that some thought the latter tract "had of reason in it a sufficiencie" but required "that the Scriptures there alleged, might be discuss'd more fully" (*Tetrachordon* in *Complete Prose Works of John Milton*, ed. Don M. Wolfe, *et al*. [New Haven]; II, 1959, p. 582).

[25] Lilburne, Overton and Walwyn were arrested in March 1649; Lilburne was, however, acquitted by a London jury on 26 October.

[26] As Woodhouse aptly remarks: "The Presbyterians, not without chapter and

right to blame the execution of Charles I on the Presbyterians as the *fons et origo* of this heinous crime. In the Army debates the theory that "power is inherent in the people" with its corollary, their right to resume power and to call the magistrate to account, is asserted again and again: in the Putney Debates (Oct. 1647), for instance by Colonel Rainborough arguing from the law of nature; in the Whitehall Debates (Dec. 1648), for instance by John Goodwin arguing from the principle of segregation;[27] and in the *Agreement of the People* (Nov. 1647), which even extends the people's power to the making of war and peace.[28] One may note with a wry smile that the Rump, which the Army had brought into being by force, repudiated the *Agreement* in March 1649; one may note, too, that the tug of war between the Army and the Rump eventually ended in the victory of Cromwell and the Protectorate. This, however, is immaterial to our purpose, since the background evoked by Stillingfleet is the period ending with the execution of Charles I. But it is his reference to the background, particularly to the theories of government canvassed at the time, that makes the sermon so interesting, while the perspective from which he views it—one wholly different from South's—tells us something of his own conception of government.

From what he has said so far we may expect Stillingfleet to go on to show that the changes of government resulted, not, as South stated, in the arbitrary power of One (the Protector), but in another form of arbitrary power, lawlessness. Rather than tackle the problem of the original state of man living in society, he broaches that of the *function* of government by asking his public to consider what sort of happiness men would enjoy if every man was free to do as he pleases without any restraint from any kind of government whatsoever. This, indeed, "were a desirable *Liberty* if a man could have it alone"; but though a man living in society have equal freedom with all other men, "his *Power* is not equal to theirs". This

---

verse from the *Institutes*, had sown the wind; the year 1647 [when the Army Debates began] marks the beginning of the whirlwind" (*op. cit.*, Introd., p. 63).

27 Rainborough: "it's clear, that every man that is to live under a government ought first by his own consent to put himself under that government; and I do think that the poorest man in England is not at all bound in a strict sense to that government that he hath not had a voice to put himself under" (in Woodhouse, *op. cit.*, p. 54); John Goodwin: "Magistrates [I say], have so much power as the people are willing to give them" (*ibid.*, p. 159).

28 Especially Point IV: "That the power of this, and all future representatives of this nation is inferior only to theirs who choose them, and doth extend, to the enacting, altering, and repealing of laws; to the erecting and abolishing of offices and courts; to the appointing, removing and calling to account magistrates and officers of all degrees; to the making war and peace; to the treating with foreign states; and generally whatever is not expressly reserved by the represented themselves" (*ibid.*, p. 444).

inequality of power will put each man's security in jeopardy unless "a more just proportion" of power can be maintained. Failing this, men would live in "a *state* of *confusion*, which some improperly call a *state* of *nature*"; it follows that it is worth sacrificing *some* power for a great deal of security (96). Since some government there must be, the obvious conclusion is, first, that laws, far from being instruments of slavery, are safeguards of liberty; and second, that "what *Liberty* is inconsistent with all *Government* must never be pleaded against any sort of it"(97). And Stillingfleet asks what greater liberty or security the people of Israel (England) may have expected under the 250 men of Corah (Parliament, or perhaps the depleted Parliament of 1646, which numbered about 250 members) than under Moses, and adds: "and if one is thought troublesome, what *Liberty* and ease is there when their name is *Legion*"(97), thereby implying that the men wielding power were a pack of devils like those Christ cast out of the Gadarene.[29] In all late seventeenth- and eighteenth-century discussions of government three forms were usually considered: monarchy, aristocracy, and democracy—in the then sense of the word —, plus, especially after the 1688 Revolution, mixed government, i.e. limited monarchy. Stillingfleet is, in fact, arguing that any form of government—excluding democracy, where people may resume power when they list—*can* guarantee any man security and a measure of freedom. Implicit in this is what he has posited at the beginning of this section: that *all* government involves some compact whereby both liberty—though not utmost liberty — and security are guaranteed to every man, the alternative to such a compact being "a state of confusion". So much, then, for the rights of the people as derived from the law of nature.

Stillingfleet has not shown, however, how government does ensure "a more just proportion of power"; he has thus bypassed the argument for liberty, whether grounded in the law of nature or in Christian liberty. Instead, he reiterates that:

> There can be no principle imagined more destructive to civil *Societies* and repugnant to the very nature of Government [than the right of the people to resume the exercise of power]. For it destroys all obligations of Oaths and Compacts, it makes the solemnest bonds of obedience signifie nothing *when the people shall think fit to declare it*. (97, last italics mine)

The last clause probably gives us the reason for Stillingfleet's wholesale dismissal of all theories vesting power in the people. Indeed, events had shown that once the acknowledged representatives of the people, Parliament, had asserted their right to curb the King's prerogatives, they had unleashed forces that they could no longer control, nay that turned the

---

29 *Mark* 5.9.

same weapon against them. What Stillingfleet can and does demonstrate is the ruinous effects such doctrines *will* have both on the people and on the governors they choose: government will be fraught with danger for any prince since the people, though unable to judge of his actions, will ever be ready to misconstrue them; the possibility for the prince to be called to account will "keep up a jealousie between him and the people", and will drive him to use all means to increase his power at the expense of the people and to keep them "as unable to resist as may be"; all mutual confidence between the two will be destroyed, and this is the surest way to bring in an arbitrary government;[30] besides

> This must necessarily engage a Nation in endless disputes about the forfeiture of power into whose hands it falls: whether in the people in common, or some persons particularly chosen by the people for that purpose. (98)

In an "established government", on the contrary, the king himself is the true representative of the people. Stillingfleet gives no justification for this, and we may take it that he is merely echoing old English constitutional theory, which vested all power in the head of the body politic. Further, he says, there is no danger to the people "in supposing the persons of *Princes* to be *sacred*", that is, in supposing them to derive their power from God[31] since this does not

> give Princes the liberty to do what they list; for the *Laws* by which they *govern*, do fence in the *rights* and *properties* of Men. (98)

This may have been a cautious but salutary reminder to Charles II not to insist on having dispensing power granted him in religious matters. Laws, Stillingfleet believes, are more likely to keep princes from abusing their power than can "the *Peoples* holding a Rod over them", for such a threat can only make the best princes suffer and the bad desperate.

At this stage we realise how important is Stillingfleet's insistence from the start that a community of men *qua* community must have some kind of "government". His premiss implies what jurists call a *contract of society*, that is, some agreement among a body of men "cohering in virtue of a common social will" so as to constitute a community (*societas*).[32] The role of laws is all important in any community since they alone guarantee each man's security, the prince's no less than the people's. What Stillingfleet does repudiate is a *contract of government*, that is, a

---

30 It is worth noting that St.'s argument does not exclude the possibility of the prince becoming an arbitrary ruler.

31 Cf. *Rom.* 13.1; in view of what follows it would be unfair to interpret "sacred" as implying the divine right of kings as expounded in James I's *Basilikon Doron*.

32 Ernest Baker, in Introduction to *Social Contract: Essays by Locke, Hume and Rousseau*, (1947), 1960, p. xiii.

contract between the governor and the people governed, which creates power (*potestas*).[33]

The objection of Corah to the order of priesthood was that all the Lord's people are holy (*Num*.16.3), that there is no need of an order "distinct from that of the Levites",[34] particularly of a "High-Priest above all the people", and finally, that the revenues used to maintain Aaron might serve equally well for public uses; this last, Stillingfleet adds, has "always been the quarrel at *Religion*, by those who seldom pretend to it, but with a design to destroy it"(99). The explication of this verse from *Numbers* is little more than a summary of the main attacks against the episcopal order in the preceding period. Since Stillingfleet lists the complaints without elaborating on any—except a little on tithes—there is no point in relating each specifically to a particular group among the Puritans, except to note that once again the objection that is given *some* consideration here is one that the Presbyterians did not raise: quite the contrary, they were staunch supporters of tithes (hence, indeed, South's sarcasm in his sermon about their turn-about face when their revenues were threatened). Besides, the one point he stresses is that religion is apt to be despised all the more if it is "rendred more *mean* and *contemptible* by the *Poverty* of those who are devoted to it", thus again implicitly exonerating the Presbyterians.

As a matter of course Stillingfleet amplifies on the punishment inflicted by God on Corah in order to stress the remarkable judgments God "had left on record to all ages, that all the world may be convinced how displeasing to him the sin of faction and sedition is" (100). The most impressive examples he quotes being from the Old Testament, he must also show that, whatever claims are made from Christian liberty, the Gospel too condemns rebellion: this appears from Jude's epistle, which by now we had almost forgotten. Stillingfleet once more reminds us that the false teachers Jude denounces are men who act "under a pretence of Christian liberty" and who may "please themselves with the greater light".[35] According to him it is quite clear—as he said at the beginning of the sermon—that the Gospel teaches obedience to the magistrates, so clear indeed that he calls this precept "a great part of Christianity", quoting to the effect from *Tit*.3.1: "Put them in mind to be subject to principalities and powers", a text that serves as an apt transition to his

---

33 The full significance of St.'s stress on laws was to appear at the time of the 1688 Revolution: he seems to have had no difficulty in reconciling his subscription to the doctrine of passive obedience with allegiance to William III. South, on the contrary, did hesitate.

34 The Root and Branch Bill, abolishing ecclesiastical ordinations above that of minister, was passed in May 1641.

35 A reference to the Saints' belief in the inner light.

final exhortation to his audience to bless God for their deliverance and to avoid "the curse of Meroz".[36]

The peroration builds up to a forceful denunciation of the Rebellion in England: Stillingfleet rehearses the crimes of the "Sons of Violence", who "trampled under foot the *Laws* both of God and men", crimes that were all the greater as the Lord's Anointed refused "to betray his *Trust* for the saving of his life":

> Thus fell our *Royal Martyr*, a sacrifice to the fury of unreasonable men; who either were so blind as not to see his worth, or rather so bad as to hate him for it. (103)

The praise of Charles I, which so far had been only implied in the parallel with Moses, is now spoken openly the more to shame his murderers. Just as he refrains from high eulogy of the victim, so Stillingfleet refrains from violence in his final accusation: obviously, his purpose is not to stir hatred or revenge but to exhort to obedience to God as well as to the King. He therefore concludes by expressing thankfulness to God for his mercy "in the miraculous[37] preservation, and glorious restoration of our Gracious Sovereign", and by warning his audience to reform their ways and not to abuse God's mercies lest He should be provoked again.

It will have appeared from the examination of the sermon that Stillingfleet's appeal is primarily to the understanding of his audience, although at each point he makes sure, through topical references to recent history, that their feelings will also be engaged. By stating the position at the outset he has prepared his audience for a demonstrative oration: he chooses to argue rather than arouse passion; for this reason his criticism of the motives and justifications of the rebels seems the more convincing, even though the modern reader may find some of the arguments lame.

The sermon is built on the pattern usual with Anglican preachers after the Restoration, i.e. Explication, Confirmation, and Application. Stillingfleet duplicates the Explication owing to what we might call the text within the text (*Jude* implying *Numbers* 16), and also the final part of the

---

36 *Judges* 5.23. Although the curse of Meroz was often referred to by preachers in any period, St.'s words are the more telling if it is remembered that on 23 Feb. 1641, when Laud was already in the Tower and Pym was calling for Strafford's blood, the Presbyterian Stephen Marshall, the most violent contributor in the petition for a Root and Branch Bill, preached a fast sermon before the House of Commons on this particular text and in the course of it quoted with evident relish *Jer.*48.10: "Cursed be he that keepeth back his sword from blood" in a slightly different version: "Cursed is everyone that withholds his hand from shedding blood". St. does not, of course, draw attention to this Presbyterian's contribution to the Rebellion (did he remember it?).

37 A reference to Charles II's lucky escape—hidden in an oak tree—after the battle of Worcester (1651); hence the celebration, after the Restoration, of Royal Oak Day, i.e. the anniversary of Ch. II's restoration on 29th May, 1660.

Confirmation (from the Old, then from the New Testament), without, however, checking the development of the argument. It is to his credit that, while dividing his sermon into several heads or subheads — like all preachers of the period—his divisions are not stressed, nor are there many subdivisions. As usual with him, the steps and links are clear without obtruding on the reader or listener: this certainly contributes to the smooth flow of the sermon and to its clarity. So does the style, as will have appeared from the quotations.

Indeed, Stillingfleet makes his point in clear though complex sentences without any kind of ornament, unless one considers as such his use of terms appropriate to the Puritan Revolution when explicating his Biblical texts: this may indeed be regarded as a means of persuasion. In this sense the whole sermon, playing as it does on two registers, *is* rhetorical all through; but then, the texts of sermons were meant to express points applicable to the contemporary audience. Anagogical interpretations of Scripture were of long standing, and preachers made frequent use of this method (within limits after the Restoration). What is distinctive in Stillingfleet's use of the revolt of Corah as a type of the Puritan Revolution is that he mixes terms from both contexts, making the old sound new and the recent old (e.g. the assembly of the Levites "sitting in Parliament at the door of the tabernacle of the congregation"); only in such juxtapositions does he achieve a kind of pregnancy or wit. Otherwise, his style is plain, as befits a demonstrative oration, and rhetorical devices are few: occasional anaphora in the reiteration of sentences built on similar syntactic patterns, some rhetorical questions, again on similar patterns, and balanced members at the beginning and at the end of the sermon.

Another distinctive feature of this sermon is that, though the occasion lent itself to high encomium of Charles I and to invective against the Puritans, Stillingfleet praises the King indirectly all through, and only refers to his martyrdom in the last paragraph. It is almost as though his temperate language hedged in the power of the martyrdom of Charles I to arouse excessive devotion. Equally striking is Stillingfleet's care—if my reading is correct—to spare the Presbyterians. Not that he distorts history to whitewash those he is still hoping to bring back into the fold, but he mutes those aspects of the revolt that might have pointed unambiguously to their part in it. This is understandable since the Puritans of the Left were the staunchest opponents of the King;[38] besides, they had propounded doctrines of government which threatened to turn the world upside down, while Stillingfleet is pleading that nothing justifies upsetting the stability of government. We may also assume that

---

38 Lilburne, however, did not agree to the execution of the King.

one reason why he refrains from including the Presbyterians in his condemnation of the rebels —besides his wish not to deal too harshly with brethren who may still be persuaded to join in communion with the Established Church—is the fact that their Church discipline, like that of the Church of England, was based on the idea of a national Church. As he said in his sermon on *The Mischief of Separation*:

> the true notion of a *Church* is no more than of a society of men united together for their Order and Government according to the Rules of the Christian Religion

so that

> National Churches are National Societies of Christians, under the same Laws of Government and Rules of Worship. (I, 283)

Such a definition implies a conception of the Church completely different from that of gathered Churches, but one that accords with the national covenants of the Presbyterians in Scotland.[39]

Another point of interest to the modern reader is what we may call the theory of government Stillingfleet adumbrates in this sermon. Clearly, he was not only an erudite man and a good controversialist; he was a thinker of a high order who could apply his learning to problems of his time. That he was of his time appears from the ease with which he can reconcile his belief that kings are vice-gerents of God with the stand he takes on laws as the surest safeguards of amicable relations between the king and the people. It is worth noting that, for all his adherence to the doctrine of passive obedience, he grounds the security of men living in society in what he calls "government", that is, laws. It is worth noting, too, that he clearly does not countenance a system of absolutist monarchy or of enlarged royal prerogatives, *and* that he did not hesitate to say so before the King. It is even more remarkable that he expressed such views on the anniversary of the execution of Charles I, which no doubt recalled the contempt for the laws of the land manifested in the procedure of the trial of the King, but which was also an occasion for exalting the sacredness of kings. On all these counts Stillingfleet deserves to have been called by Professor Birrell "the most intelligent, the best read, and the least inhibited" of all Restoration divines.[40] Our final impression of him as a preacher is certainly one of seriousness; for this, as well as for his other achievements, he earned the respect of his contemporaries, as he has earned the respect and admiration of his modern readers.

---

[39] The difference in discipline may be paralleled with that between Puritan experiential faith and the Restoration Anglican's rational assent to the truths of the Christian religion.

[40] *English Studies*, L, Feb. 1969, p. 121.

JOHN WODROEPHE'S *SPARED HOURES*

Anna E.C. Simoni

I will maintain the word with my sword to be a good soldier-like word
(II Henry IV)

Sage mir, mit wem du umgehst, und ich will dir sagen, wer du bist
(German proverb)

The name of John Wodroephe is known only to specialists nowadays and even to them he is not much more than a name. The STC assigns two editions of his French grammar to him and suggests his name as solution to the initials I.W. of the translator of César Oudin's Spanish grammar published in London in 1622.[1] So much for his real and presumed literary output, none of which has got him into the NCBEL or the OED. Brunet[2] knew the first edition of his grammar; Gratet-Duplessis[3] gives a reasonably correct account of it and other writers on proverbs have copied from him. Not surprisingly, Gratet-Duplessis judges the collection of proverbs contained in Wodroephe's French grammar to be its best part, although he does not mention its derivation, expressly stated by the compiler, from Mathurin Cordier. Still, he allows the whole work a certain interest for the variety of its contents. On his poems he is devastating: "Je ne dirai rien des poésies; elles sont au-dessous du médiocre", denying him any knowledge of French or even English versification. Well, maybe, we cannot all be Ronsards or Shakespeares. This essay will try to build up a somewhat clearer picture of the man and his work in the hope of restoring him to a place among authors who are read, and read with pleasure.

---

1 STC² 25939, 25940, 18897. The solution suggested for the initials is erroneous. This article will show that John Wodroephe could not easily have prepared the translation of Oudin's Spanish grammar for publication in London in 1622, nor, had he done so, would he have refrained from alluding to it in his French grammar. This subjective rejection of the identification is confirmed by Dr. Robin Alston who in the forthcoming vol. XII of his *Bibliography of the English language* will assign the translation of Oudin's *Arte breve* to James Wadsworth. I thank Dr. Alston sincerely for giving me this valuable information.

2 Jacques Charles Brunet, *Manuel du libraire*, Paris, 1860-1880, tom.V, col. 1468.

3 Pierre Alexandre Gratet-Duplessis, *Bibliographie parémiologique*, Paris, 1847 (reprint Nieuwkoop, 1969), pp. 165, 166, no. 269.

THE SPARED HOVRES OF A SOVLDIER IN HIS TRAVELS.

OR

THE True Marrowe of the French Tongue, where in is truely treated (by ordre) the Nine Parts of Speech.

Together, with two rare, and excellent Bookes of Dialogues, the one Presented to that Illustrious Prince, Conte Henry of Nassau, in his yonger Yeares, for his Furtherence in this Tongue: newly reviewed, and put in pure french Phrase (easie, and delight full) from point to point: and the other formed, and made (since) by the Authour him selfe.

ADDED yet an excellent Worke, very profitable for all the Ages of Man, called The Springwell of Honour and Vertue, gathered together very carefully, both by anciant, and Moderne Philosophers of our Tyme.

With many other Godly Songs, Sonets, Theames, Letters Missives, and Sentences proverbiales; so orderly, plaine, and pertinent, as hath not (formerly) beene seene in this most famous Ile of great Britaine.

By IOHN VVODROEPHE. Gent.

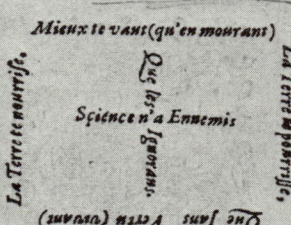

LES HEVRES DE RELASCHE D'UN SOLDAT, VOYAGEANT.

OV

LA Vraie Moëlle de la langue Françoise, en laquelle est naïfuement traité (par Ordre) des neuf Parties d'icelle.

Ensemble, deux excellens, & rares livres de Dialogues, l'vn presenté A Tresillustre Prince, Conte Henry de Nassan en Son jeunne Aage pour Son Advancement en ceste dite Langue; reveu, & mis en pure Phrase Françoise, aisée & plaisante de Point en Point; & l'autre formé, & faict (de puis) par l'Autheur mesme.

Iouxte encore vne excellente Oeuvre, fort profitable pour tous les Aages de l'Homme, appellée la Fontaine de Vertu, & d'Honneur, recueillie fort soigneusement, Si bien par les anciens Philosophes, que par ceux de ce Temps ci.]

Auecques beaucoup d'autres Chansons pieuses, Sonets, Themes, Lettres, Missives, & Sentences Proverbiales, si aises, & pertinens (par Ordre) qu'on n'a guères veu cy devant en ceste famense Isle de la grande Britagne.

IMPRIME A DORT.

Par Nicolas Vincentz. Pour George Waters, Marchant Libraire, demeurant pres le Marché aux Poissons, a l'Enseigne des Mouchettes dorées. Ano. 1623.

Fig. 1 *(by courtesy of the British Library)*

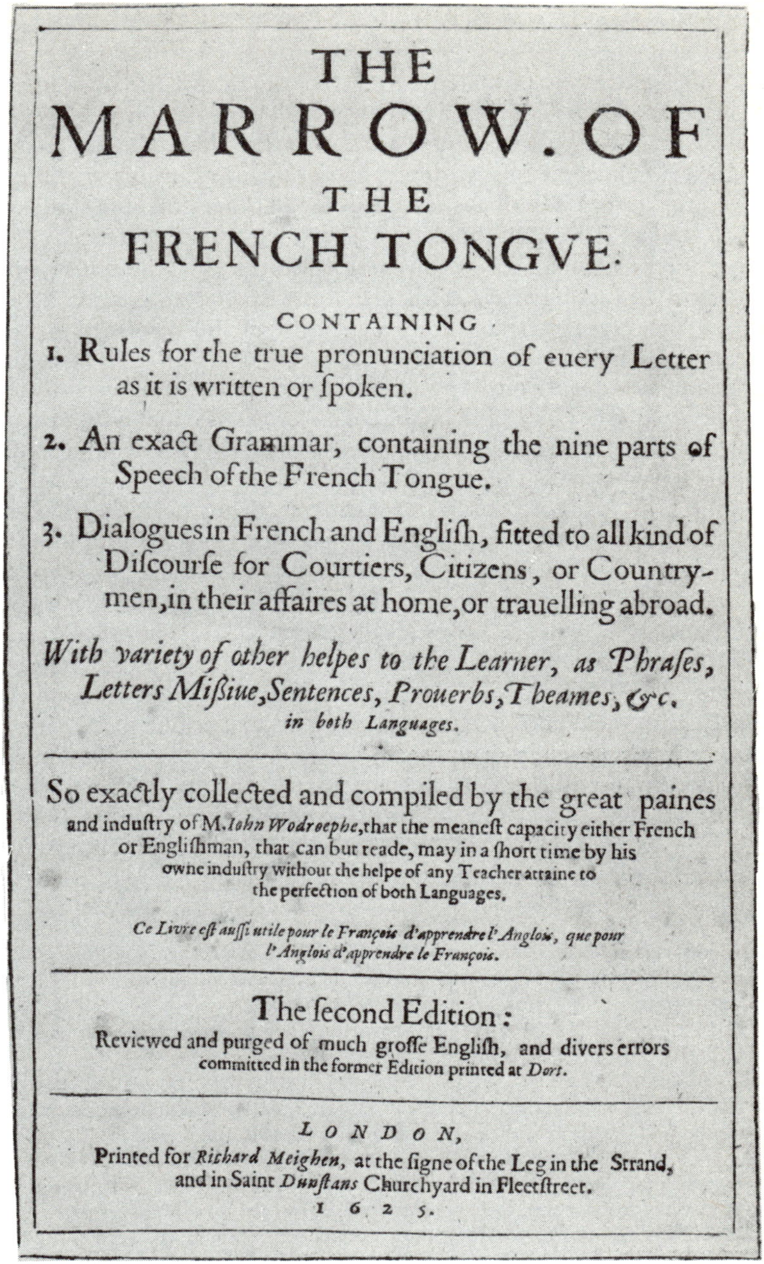

THE MARROW. OF THE FRENCH TONGVE.

CONTAINING

1. Rules for the true pronunciation of euery Letter as it is written or spoken.

2. An exact Grammar, containing the nine parts of Speech of the French Tongue.

3. Dialogues in French and English, fitted to all kind of Discourse for Courtiers, Citizens, or Countrymen, in their affaires at home, or trauelling abroad.

With variety of other helpes to the Learner, as *Phrases, Letters Missiue, Sentences, Prouerbs, Theames, &c. in both Languages.*

So exactly collected and compiled by the great paines and industry of M. *Iohn Wodroephe*, that the meanest capacity either French or Englishman, that can but reade, may in a short time by his owne industry without the helpe of any Teacher attaine to the perfection of both Languages.

Ce Livre est aussi utile pour le François d'apprendre l'Anglois, que pour l'Anglois d'apprendre le François.

The second Edition:
Reviewed and purged of much grosse English, and divers errors committed in the former Edition printed at *Dort*.

LONDON,
Printed for *Richard Meighen*, at the signe of the Leg in the Strand, and in Saint *Dunstans* Churchyard in Fleetstreet.
1 6 2 5.

Fig. 2 *(by courtesy of the British Library)*

What seems so far to have been overlooked is Wodroephe's most distinguishing characteristic, which is also the most curious aspect of his book, namely that he compiled a French grammar for British soldiers in the Netherlands, the country where it was also first published in 1623, a combination of circumstances which is rare indeed. On its first appearance in handsome folio format it had a titlepage as follows (see Fig. 1).

True, the author describes it as useful for all other potential students of French, but much of the book is specially directed at members of the British forces serving on behalf of the States General under Prince Maurice of Orange against the Spanish army in the Netherlands. More, a thin but persistent personal note runs through the first edition, to be excised from the shortened London edition of 1625. In this the military connection is hidden from view, its title now reading *The marrow of the French tongue*[4] (see Fig. 2). As the soldier no longer dominates the titlepage, so the author has deleted, or has had deleted for him, whatever appeared as a personal revelation in the first edition.[5]

Nothing is known of John Wodroephe outside his book and it is to the first edition, the *Spared Houres*, that one must look to find him. The titlepage already shows him to be a man well aware of his own merit. His book is said to be comprehensive, yet easy to follow; it will teach young or old, and do so without tears, all they need to know in order to speak and write French fluently, and it will be an education in morals and good manners as well: a book, in short, such as has never been offered before to the English speaking student. Self-advertisement of one sort or another also occurs occasionally in the body of the book, but mostly tempered with modesty and the acknowledgment of debts to other authors.[6]

What we feel we can guess from the titlepage is confirmed in the dedication to Prince, later King, Charles, in a passage[7] cut from the second edition. In it the author stresses the trouble he has taken in writing

---

4 In quotations I have transcribed u and v as modern typography prefers. I have similarly supplied the n where it is contracted and have added the accent to French à since this occurs in the book when printed in italics.

5 The London edition, also in folio format, has 340 pages whereas the Dordrecht edition had 515.

6 Cf. the sentiments expressed in the sonnet "Invocation" on sig. †2r beginning "All powers rule, that treades the purest aire", vv. 7, 8 "Poure doune a grace to grace this silly booke, that it may please its cens'rers great and small" and vv. 13, 14 "Loe, Lord I trust (who trusts, do'st not beguile) Thow'lt spreede this worke ov'r Albion many a mile". Or the "Epistre à la jeunesse", "An epistle to youth", which ends "The word is lost like smoake into the aire, but writs do dure for now, and evermaire. Reade then, and buy this booke for thine advance, if ever thou think'st to trafike into France". The French gives a better sequence for this: "Achete donc & lis soigneusement ce livre, se tu veux toujours avec le François vivre".

7 Sig. †2v; information repeated in the address to the reader on p. 7.

this book which has occupied his own "spared houres" during watches and guard duties for the past seven years. He was therefore a soldier himself. This is also abundantly proved in the text in which examples from military life are profusely used. He never betrays his rank or function, nor even which unit of the British forces he belonged to. But there are pointers. While he bursts into verse at the slightest opportunity, a special section of poems, mainly sonnets, addresses individual persons, some as close friends. A few of these are Dutchmen, but more are British officers, and of these most are in the Scottish Brigade. Dedications of parts of the work to different persons again show a preponderance of Scottish names. His Scottish origin is implicitly revealed in a complimentary sonnet to Queen Anne, consort of James I. In a conceit aimed at pleasing her Wodroephe makes her the best of the three queens under whom he has lived: a Mary, an Anne and a Margaret, whom he then describes as queens of more than one kingdom: Mary and Margaret had two each, but Anne, great Anne, has three. He was therefore born under Mary Queen of Scots, who had also been Queen of France and it puts his date of birth before her execution in 1587. Anne was Queen of Scotland through her marriage to James VI in 1589 and with him acceded to the titles of England and Ireland in 1603. At some time he must have lived in France where Margaret was consort of Henry IV, first as King of Navarre, then of France until he was murdered in 1610. Neither his place of birth nor any account of his youth can be found in the book. It is possible that he made the journey to London attached to some Scottish courtier at the time of James's accession or returned to Britain with one of James's envoys to France. As we shall see he knew several suitable men in high places who could have brought him to court. For to court he undoubtedly came and was at one time not so far from the present writer's abode. The part of the work entitled "Springwell of honour and vertue" has a dedication to James Hay, Count of Carlisle, beginning "Monseigneur: le debvoir, & l'obligation, me font tousjours souvenir du grand plaisir que votre grandeur me fit (il y a environ seize ans) à Hamtoncour . . ." He was therefore at Hampton Court in about 1607 and may have been in London earlier. His scattered references to young men and children whom he taught are reason to believe that he was tutor and French master in noble houses.

Then we find him in the army in the Netherlands not later than 1616. Why? Nowhere does he mention any financial difficulties; he speaks of his employers, if they were his employers, with respect; but there may be a clue in his frequent bitter condemnation of women which far exceeds the conventional and fairly jocular balance between adoration and fear of ladies also found in his book, especially where he has taken material from other authors. However, he gives nothing away. Nor does he describe any fighting he witnessed although it is hardly possible that he should not have had his share of it. His relations with the officers of the Scottish Brigade were those of comradeship, and he had friends among the officers of the English Brigade as well. For himself he adopts the epithet "Gent." on the titlepage of the first edition of his grammar. Perhaps he was no regular member of the army, to be paid and, if he so deserved, promoted, but had joined as a loosely attached volunteer-gentleman,[8] free to leave if he wished. Apparently he did so by early 1625 when as already described, his book came out in a second edition, in London, and in "civvies", with his name preceded only by the polite "M.".

While in the army he occupied quieter moments, his "spared houres", with teaching and laying down his practice in writing, including the names of commanders and fellow officers in many of the examples he invented. Other names may be those of soldiers well known to those he taught, even of the pupils themselves, causing laughter in class.[9]

Such immediacy pervades much of the text. He also admonishes his students to hard work and perseverance and demands constant application and repetition of vocabulary and grammatical rules.[10] Simply picking up a language by ear has its place, but only at a very low level: to gain true command of it requires following a thorough and methodical course of instruction such as he can give and has proved with youngsters unable to speak French after some considerable time spent in France who then learnt it with him in a matter of months. Now it is the soldier's turn to make the effort. French, the general international modern language of the time, was widely used in the multinational army of the States General and its study was therefore not as esoteric an occupation for the soldier's leisure as might appear at first sight. It would also help him, as Wodroephe's titlepage immediately proclaims, on his travels, that is wherever he ventures abroad. He might be glad to know his drill in French—and Wodroephe skilfully teaches it quite early on, together with a list of his kit and other military requirements, woven into little scenes written with liveliness and humour—or so they are bound to strike the modern reader. "Mon lieutenant, ou sont mes soldats? . . . Je vous prie, donnez leur leurs gages", are sweet words to every soldier's ears, never mind that here they serve to teach the possessive pronoun. Another example, and one less likely to be found outside military manuals than

---

[8] I thank Dr. Simon Adams of the University of Strathclyde for telling me of this type of officer and the suggestion that Wodroephe was such a one.

[9] They range from the "Prince of Aurange" through "Monsieur Cecile" to Mr. Drommond and plain Roger, Walter, etc.

[10] Cf. his "Sonet instructif à la jeunesse, pour en avoir patience apprenant les langues, etc." which begins "Qui va le petit pas, la voye mieux advance".

perhaps the pay parade, consists of a series of commands during exercises which ends with the men being told to discharge their muskets, fall in and march back to barracks—because it's raining.[11] Hardly what is done at Aldershot these days. Exhorted always to remember that he is fighting for what to him is the true religion and thus to behave virtuously, the soldier is also provided with a large variety of terms of abuse applicable to horse and man. One I specially liked is the English "hedge rogue" who can be told in French or English to go and get hanged.[12] There are many other everyday situations drawn upon to illustrate grammatical points, teach useful phrases or improve the pupil's ease of expression. There are scenes of arrival and departure, a stay at an inn (where it is of course essential to be able to ask for the chamber-pot), a consultation between a hypochondriac patient and a greedy quack, a conversation between a particularly nasty bossy lady and her gardener in which the poor chap has a hard time finding excuses for all his sins of commission and omission, a teasing bout between a girl and her admirer, a friendly chat, still among the "familie" dialogues, between a king and his queen in which the talk is mainly of hunting, and so on. The job of the interpreter is extolled, an old man is reassured that he is as capable of learning French as any young fellow, and all are told to shun vice. Oh, a drink at the end of the day is all right,[13] but cards are out, and as to women, "be wise and stay away from them". The author's strong religious conviction is evident on every page. He takes it for granted that his readers share his faith. His oft repeated motto is "Vers Dieu, c'est le meilleur".

All the elementary and intermediate stages of the course are Wodroephe's own work, admittedly grounded on a good knowledge of earlier grammatical writers.[14] But whole chapters in the later part of the book are adaptations of works by other authors and Wodroephe claims no more than having "improved" the French where necessary and added the English. The section on proverbs derived mainly from Cordier[15] has

11 This is true: see *Spared Houres"*, p. 185.
12 French epithets for the relief of frustration include pestiferé, puant, eshonté, to mention only a few.
13 "Irons nous dehors boire un pot à nos amis" (p. 165).
14 He expresses surprise (on p. 46) that even an authority like Hollyband should allow contractions of verb forms such as "amerra" for "amenera" which he himself frowns on. This refers to Claude de Sainliens, a prolific and successful writer of language textbooks published in London in the 1570s and '80s whose *The French Littelton* and *The French schoolemaister* went through numerous editions.
15 It is difficult to decide which of Cordier's works Wodroephe used and then, in which edition. The *Colloquiorum scholasticorum . . . libri IIII* had so many editions that Wodroephe need not have had one of the Plantin ones although these might have been easiest to obtain in the Netherlands. There is a similar choice of editions of Cordier's other Latin textbook, *De corrupti sermonis emendatione libellus*, and its derivatives,

already been mentioned. Here Wodroephe tries to supply not only literal translations, but also English equivalents to the various proverbs or proverbial sayings which include old favourites like that of the three wise monkeys. He often explains whether it has to be understood allegorically or metaphorically and for good measure he frequently adds a short comment, a fact already noted by Gratet-Duplessis. This is generally limited to an occasional "so true" or the more common "so", with here and there an odd remark of more individual application as when he is unsure himself of the interpretation of "Bon poëte, mauvais, ou vitieux (faux)", which he translates as "A good poet, is bad, or vitious", saying "This is hard to judge"—and how right he is. Another time, dealing with a proverb on sea crossings teaching people to pray, he declares that this has indeed been his own frequent experience.[16]

When Wodroephe disapproves of an original text he avoids naming the perpetrator even if he knows his name, a gesture kinder to the earlier author than to the modern reader who wants to know. Of the two instances where this happens one book is indeed anonymous while the author of the other can be traced eventually. *La fontaine d'honeur, & de vertu*[17] was a book which Wodroephe, so he informs us, saw in the hands of a gentleman who was not only reading it, but extracting passages for further use and who might want it one day for his children's French lessons. Wodroephe borrowed it, found its morals highly acceptable, but its language in need of improvement. At the same time he added an English translation and thus the *Springwell of honour, & vertue* was born, an anthology in both languages of passages from ancient philosophers, chiefly Cicero and Seneca, and Christian writers. The incident which brought it about is more likely to have happened in the Netherlands than in Britain for the text seems to be of Low Countries origin. There exists an edition of 1607, produced at Antwerp by Guislain Janssens, entitled *De fonteyne der eeren ende der deught . . . La fontaine de l'honneur et de la vertu*, whose author has remained unknown. It is expressly stated to be a book of instruction for the young and was authorised by the Antwerp censors for use in school. It was printed once more, also at Antwerp, in 1677 by Gonzales van Heylen.[18] I know of no other editions, whether in French only or

---

especially the *Sententiae proverbiales, sive adagiales Gallicolatinae*. Jules Le Coultre, *Maturin Cordier et les origines de la pédagogie protestante dans les pays de langue française*, etc., Neuchâtel, 1926, does not mention Wodroephe.

16 "Qui veut apprendre à prier aille souvent sur la mer. Who will learne to pray let him go often upon the sea. True, for I have learned it" (p. 510).

17 The titlepage quotes it as *La fontaine de vertu, & d'honneur*, but in the text the word order is the same in French as in English.

18 See Emile H. van Heurck, *Les livres populaires flamands*, Anvers, 1931, p. 130. I never suspected such a Dutch connection and should have been quite unable to give

bilingual, although the fate of schoolbooks is such that one ought not to exclude the possibility that they existed. Wherever Wodroephe found it, he makes it quite clear that it is not his own invention and it is omitted from the London edition.

The short preface to *The second booke of court, and countrie dialogues* again mentions only the title of its original: *Le verger des colloques recreatifs*. Its author is however described as a Walloon whose French was very bad, even "scurvie", who offered his book to Prince Henry of Nassau when he was young to teach him French. Wodroephe recognised that this work was itself based on a book published in England, brought there from Italy. He does not name Giovanni Florio, but it is obvious that he refers to him. The Walloon of the scurvie French is in fact a native of Mechelen by name of Gomes de Trier. His *Jardin de recreation* was suspected by Brunet and confirmed by Gratet-Duplessis as a blatant piece of plagiarism on Florio's *Giardino di ricreazione* of 1591. Similarly, his *Verger* was found to be nothing but a translation, and a poor one at that, of Florio. Unhappily Gratet-Duplessis connects it with the famous grammarian's *First frutes* while in fact it should be his *Second frutes*, also of 1591.[19] Gratet-Duplessis pays his compliments to Brunet for his perspicacity; he does not give Wodroephe credit for having recognised it before. That Gomes de Trier should have tried to pass his French/Dutch translation off as his own creation, dishonest though it be, is perhaps understandable. It was also foolish, for if he had been able to lay his hands on a copy of Florio in the Netherlands, then so could others, including the highly educated members of the house of Nassau. He had not even taken the precaution of altering the Italian names of the characters in the dialogues. Wodroephe, having made his statement, had no reason to change them. Not having a copy of Florio at his disposal he made do with the unfortunate Gomes de Trier. His French as seen in the first edition of the *Verger* published by Zacharias Heyns at Zwolle in 1605 is indeed pitiful.[20] It is surprising to find in the book a highly laudatory

---

the above account of it had Mr. Ronald Breugelmans of Leiden University Library not sent me word of the copy of the 1677 edition in his care. For this kindness I thank him most sincerely.

19 Brunet, *op. cit.*, tom.II, col. 1659; Gratet-Duplessis, *op. cit.*, p. 163, no. 265 and p. 258, no. 421.

20 Neither Brunet nor Gratet-Duplessis knew the full history of the works of Gomes de Trier, or Gomes van Triere, on whom see *Biographie Nationale de Belgique*, Bruxelles, 1866 etc., vol. XXV, coll. 613, 614; E.W. Moes and C.P. Burger, *De Amsterdamsche boekdrukkers en uitgevers in de 16de eeuw*, Amsterdam, 1900-1915, vol. IV, p. 256; J.G.C.A. Briels, "Zuidnederlandse onderwijskrachten in Noordnederland", *Archief voor de geschiedenis van de katholieke kerk in Nederland*, vol. XV, 1973, pp. 276, 277; the same author's *Zuidnederlandse boekdrukkers en boekverkopers in de Republiek der Verenigde Nederlanden omstreeks 1570-1630*, Nieuwkoop, 1974 (Biblio-

poem by the publisher who recommends it to Dutchmen wanting to learn French. Heyns must have known that language very well: his own father had taught it for many years and had himself written textbooks which Zacharias also published.[21] The *Verger* is dedicated to Henri Frederic, Comte de Nassau, the youngest son of William the Silent and eventual successor as stadholder to his halfbrother Maurice. He had no need to learn French from Gomes de Trier, of all people, nor did Trier presume to make him do so. Rather was the book intended to help him with his Dutch which the author implies he once taught him. Wodroephe improved the French, rightly, and also removed what he claims to have been passages of lascivious character, then adds his own English version based on the French. This metamorphosis of Florio's work makes amusing reading. It was alas unknown to Dame Frances Yates.[22] In the 1625 edition of Wodroephe's grammar the dialogues are retained under new titles. His own "The first booke of familie dialogues" becomes "The little orchard of recreation" and "The second booke of court, and countrie dialogues" becomes predictably "The great orchard of recreation", titles immediately recalling Florio although neither he nor Trier is mentioned by name or description.

Another author whom Wodroephe had studied was Philippe Desportes. His most famous poem, *O nuict, jalouse nuict*, was a popular song in the Netherlands in the early seventeenth century, to judge from the many poems set to its tune. Wodroephe's "Chanson spirituelle de la vie des vertueux hommes, & princes illustres du jadis, dediée au Prince Charles..." is written to this tune, but lest the reader imagine that Wodroephe only follows the fashion secondhand he supplies the actual page number in Desportes's *Oeuvres* where the poem is printed.[23] This reference again

theca bibliographica neerlandica, vol. 6), pp. 358, 359; J.Th.W. Clemens, *Italiaanse boeken in het Nederlands vertaald*, Groningen, 1964 (Studia litteraria Rheno-Traiectina, vol. 8), no. 114. Dutch archives may yet reveal some interesting data concerning the Walloon writer of scurvie French. I am greatly indebted to Mevrouw Désirée Vreke of the Royal Library, The Hague, for answering my queries on the *Verger*.

21 For the works by Peter Heyns published by Zacharias at Amsterdam, see Moes-Burger, *op. cit.*, vol. IV, pp. 178-208. One of them, *Cort onderwijs van de acht deelen der Françoischer talen*, of 1587, was in fact republished by Zacharias at Zwolle in 1605, the same year as the *Verger* by Gomes de Trier, see *id. ib.*, p. 256.

22 In her *John Florio*, London, 1934, Dame Frances Yates gives a long account of the *Second frutes*, its more lighthearted approach when compared with the *First frutes* and those passages in it which on the surface were likely to cause offence. The 1591 edition, printed for Thomas Woodcock by Richard Meighen who was to publish Wodroephe's *Marrow* in 1625, has been reproduced in facsimile at Gainesville, Florida, in 1953.

23 Wodroephe's words are "... Sur l'air d'une chanson faicte par le Sieur de Portes, en son livre fol. 385. & qui commence, O nuit jalouse nuit contre moy conjurée &c.".

enables us to determine the edition Wodroephe used: it is Arnout Coninx's Antwerp edition of 1592.[24]

Finally among the books Wodroephe knew there is Sir William Alexander of Stirling's long poem *The foure hours*, which he says he admired greatly. He adds his own translation of the "First hour" and some to him memorable parts of the remainder of the poem to his *Spared Houres*, admitting all the while that his French cannot do the piece justice, but hoping that his attempt will spur some one else on to translate the whole of it and do it so well that it will rank in France itself with Du Bartas's famous *La sepmaine*.[25]

These scant details on Wodroephe's life, his character as a teacher and his literary background gleaned from his book can be rounded off with a survey of the people whom he respected, admired or just liked. We find them in his dedications and prefaces and above all in his poems, predominantly those "occasional" ones he brought together in the chapter "Godly sonets and Godly songs". They are written in French or English, are elaborate in design, with acrostics and anagrams and all manner of artifice, redolent more of sweat than of inspiration. Even so they should not be brushed aside as of no interest: has not one of them already declared his Scottish birth to us?

Far off on his horizon are the great stars of the royal family. The book is dedicated to Charles in both prose and verse; King James and Anne receive their poetic due in several sonnets; Frederick, King of Bohemia, and his wife, the Princess Elizabeth, follow their royal parents. There is no clue in any of them to the date or occasion that gave rise to these expressions of loyalty and piety other than a few references to Christmas. Nor do the poems make it clear whether Wodroephe handed them over in person or had them conveyed by some friend at court. They could have been written at the time of the wedding of Frederick and Elizabeth in the winter of 1612/13, for although Frederick is given his Bohemian title in the superscription, there is no hint in the verses themselves of the misfortunes which by 1623 had overtaken the young couple. The poem to Elizabeth is in English, all the others in this royal group are in French. So is the "Sonet doné à la queue d'une petition, presentée à Messeigrs. les Estats Ge. &c". It is a compliment to the States General and to Prince Maurice, but the matter of the petition which it accompanied and Wodroephe's part in it remain obscure.

---

24 There on p. 385 the poem has the title "Contre une nuict trop claire".

25 By one of those strange coincidences, Zacharias Heyns, who published the *Verger des colloques recreatifs* which John Wodroephe then adapted for his *Spared Houres*, also valued the popular work by Guillaume de Saluste du Bartas so highly that he wrote a sequel to it in Dutch entitled *De tweede weke vijfde dag* which he added to his translation of that author's *Wercken*.

Still on an exalted level in the social scale, but less inaccessible to the schoolmaster-soldier, are several members of the Scottish aristocracy whom he names.[26] A place of honour in the "Godly sonets", between those to the royal family and that to the States General, is occupied by a sonnet in French to the "Duke of Lenox". The poem is almost word for word the same as one of those addressed to James I, proof of the platitudinous nature of the composition. The recipient here was Ludovick Stuart, second Duke of Lennox and Duke of Richmond. He was a special favourite of King James and at the early age of 15 was already made President of the Council while James was absent in Denmark to marry his queen. The King never forgot his services during the Gowrie conspiracy when his quick action had saved James's life. In 1601 he was James's envoy to France and on the way was entertained by Queen Elizabeth. He accompanied James to England in 1603 before being sent north again to fetch the young prince Henry. He was naturalised in England, made a gentleman of the bedchamber and a privy councillor. More embassies to France followed in 1604/5 and honours were rained upon him. He was married three times, but left no issue.

"Iehan de Ramsay, Count of Holdernesse etc." gets a sonnet in French. Sir John Ramsay, Viscount Haddington and Earl of Holderness, who was born around 1580 and died in 1626, was a great favourite of James, to whom he had been a page of honour as a boy. For his services at the time of the Gowrie conspiracy James gave him lands and knighted him in 1600. Once in England he made him Viscount Haddington and Lord Ramsay of Barns in 1606 and Lord Melrose in 1609. Around 1619 he took offence at not being granted the title of Earl of Montgomery and retired from court to France. Thereupon James proffered him a present of £ 7000, which brought Ramsay back to court in 1620 to be created Baron of Kingston-upon-Thames. He married Elizabeth, daughter of the Earl of Sussex, for whom Ben Jonson wrote a masque. Their two sons James and Charles both died young. His second wife Margaret was the daughter of Sir William Cockayne. They had no children.

---

26 For the biographical notes that follow I have made use, except where otherwise indicated, of DNB; Sir Robert Douglas, *The Scots peerage,* ed. Sir J.B. Paul, Edinburgh, 1904-1914; Francisque Michel, *Les Ecossais en France,* Londres, 1862; William Forbes-Leith, *The Scots men-at-arms and lifeguards in France,* Edinburgh, 1882; John Hill Burton, *The Scot abroad,* Edinburgh & London, 1864; William Steven, *The history of the Scottish Church, Rotterdam,* Edinburgh & Rotterdam, 1832, 1833; and above all, vol. I of *Papers illustrating the history of the Scots Brigade in the service of the United Netherlands, 1572-1782,* edited by James Ferguson, Edinburgh, 1899-1901. For his help and advice I wish to thank Mr. William Kelly of the National Library of Scotland. There is no comparable literature on the English regiments in the Netherlands.

"Iaque de Hay" is the subject of a dedication already mentioned and also has a sonnet addressed to him, again in French. This is James Hay, first Earl of Carlisle, Lord Hay of Sawlay and Viscount Doncaster. He was another Scottish nobleman to come to England with James in 1603. From gentleman of the bedchamber he rose to become master of the King's wardrobe in 1613. He had himself been brought up in France and went there on several embassies for James in 1601, 1616, 1621 and 1622,[27] was sent to Germany in 1619 and visited Brussels on his way to Heidelberg, residence of Frederick until his move to Prague, and was in France again in 1623 to ease the way for Charles's journey to Spain. He opposed the Spanish marriage and acted again as envoy to France to arrange the marriage with Henrietta. He would have liked both James and Charles to resist Richelieu's demands for the repeal of the English laws against Catholics and supported the Huguenot cause. Political failure caused him to retire from court and he died in 1636. He had married Honora Denny in 1607, an occasion for which Campion supplied a masque. His second wife was Lucy Percy, whom he married in 1617 and who became an influential figure, famous for her beauty, at the court of Charles. He had one son. He was known for his lavish hospitality and generosity and we know that Wodroephe knew him at Hampton Court.

A sonnet follows "A la louange de preux, & valeureux Britons. & principalement du tres renommé Colonel Messire Guilleaume Edmond, Chevalier, etc.". It praises the great deeds performed by the Scottish Brigade in the Netherlands in the years leading up to the Twelve Years Truce, feats of arms which by the time Wodroephe joined it had become legendary. Sir William Edmond was a native of Stirling. He was a captain of cavalry serving in the Netherlands in 1588 and led a squadron which took part in a notable action at Turnhout. He succeeded to the command of the infantry with the rank of colonel in 1599. He distinguished himself in various battles, gaining special glory for his daring capture of Count Bucquoy. In 1600 he was with Count Louis of Nassau at the conquest of Wachtendonk in Gelderland and in June that same year was one of the few officers of the Scottish Brigade to escape with their lives after the defeat at Snaaskerke which preceded the victorious battle of Nieuwpoort. Of this action there exists a print, now at the Prentenkabinet at the University of Leiden (see Fig. 3), which is described as the defeat of the Zealanders and Scots under Ernest Casimir of Nassau before the battle of Nieuwpoort, with a four line Latin inscription: "Nobilissimo ... viro Guil. Edmontio, equiti aurato ... Scotorum ... in Belgio militantium praefecto ... typum hunc

---

27 In 1601 Henry IV expressed his appreciation of "le chevalier de Hez" in a letter to James. His repeated missions to Louis XIII prove that he was agreeable to that monarch also.

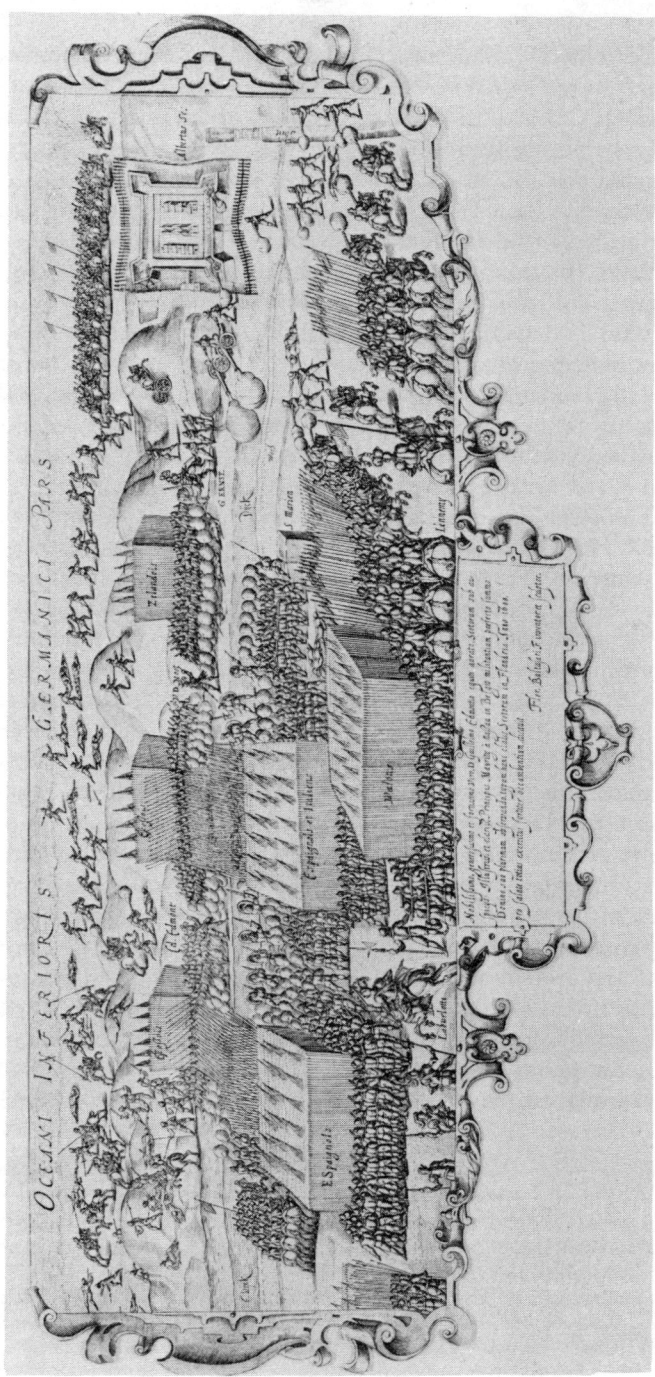

Fig. 3 (by courtesy of the Prentenkabinet at the University of Leiden)

cladis Scotorum in Flandria pro salute totius exercitus fortiter occumbentium dicavit Flor. Balthasari f. inventor et sculptor".[28] It is moreover as true a document of the battle as it was possible to produce since Floris Balthasarsz van Berckenrode[29] was the equivalent of an official war artist with a privilege of the States General for the making of maps and prints depicting the campaigns especially of Prince Maurice. Col. Edmond took part in the siege of Ostend in 1602 and defended the position which became known as the Schottenberg. In the same year he accompanied Count Louis on a foray into Luxembourg. In July 1606 he defended the river Waal and in August commanded the forces defending Rijnberk against the Spanish commander Spinola. He was mortally wounded on 3 September that same year. It is known that he was in correspondence with Prince Henry about a suit of armour which arrived after Edmond's death, a fact his widow communicated to the Prince. An anecdote recorded in Peacham's *Compleat gentleman*, published in 1634, tells of a recently arrived Scotsman informing Edmond that "my lord his father and the noble gentlemen his cousins" were well, to which Edmond is said to have replied before the assembled crowd that his father was "but a poor baker of Edinburgh whom this knave would make a lord to curry favour with me". No wonder that the troops worshipped this officer and kept his name alive for Wodroephe to glorify.

"Colonel & Chevalier Guilleaume Brog" is the next recipient of a poem in French. William Brogh is another distinguished officer in the Scottish Brigade. He was sergeant-major in 1588, captain in 1590. In 1594 he took part in an unsuccessful attempt to relieve Maastricht. In 1599 he was at Bommel, achieving fame with the capture of a Spanish captain. In 1600 he became lieutenant-colonel. He survived Snaaskerke, but in 1601 he was wounded at Ostend in a particularly grisly manner, being hit by fragments of the skull of the Comte de Châtillon, who was killed beside him. In 1604 he received the instructions on first holding and then abandoning the town. In 1606 he rose to be colonel, in succession to Sir William Edmond, of Sir Henry Balfour's regiment. In 1617 Colonel "Brock" was thought ripe for retirement and offered a pension by the King, but would have none of it. In 1623 rumour had it that he was dead, but the old man belied it and carried on until his death in March 1636.

---

28 Frederik Muller, *De Nederlandsche geschiedenis in platen*, Amsterdam, 1863-1882, no. 1133.
29 See Ulrich Thieme & Felix Becker, *Allgemeines Lexicon der bildenden Künstler*, Leipzig, 1907-1950, Bd. 3, pp. 375, 376; F.G. Waller, *Biographisch Woordenboek van Nederlandsche Graveurs*, 's-Gravenhage, 1938 (reprint Amsterdam, 1974), p. 22; *Nieuw Nederlandsch Biografisch Woordenboek*, ed. P.C. Molhuysen, P.J. Blok, Leiden, 1911-1937, vol. II, coll. 82, 83. For plates attributed to him see F. Muller, *op. cit.*, no. 1093, 1127, 1133, 1136, 1137, 1179, 1204, 1205, 1210, 1241, 1281.

His portrait by Crispijn van Queboren dated 1635 was published in 1638.[30]

"Colonel & chevalier Robert Henderson" next receives a French sonnet. Sir Robert Henderson was the second son of James Henderson of Fordell and Jean, daughter of William, 10th Baron of Tulliebardine. From a document of 1618 in which he declares that he has served in the Netherlands for twenty-four consecutive years it is evident that he took service there in about 1594. In 1599 he took over the company previously commanded by Alexander Murray, who succeeded Sir Henry Balfour as colonel and was himself succeeded in that rank by William Edmond. In 1600 he fought at Nieuwpoort. In 1607 and 1608 he served with Sir William Brogh in Gelderland, in 1609 with Buccleuch in Holland and Zealand. In 1610 he commanded the Scots in a mixed regiment made up from Scottish, English and Dutch troops, sent to Cleves and Juliers where he earned praise for his valuable services. In 1612 he was described as the States General's first choice to succeed Lord Buccleuch as colonel of the latter's regiment. In 1619 he was employed, much less gloriously, in the suppression of the Remonstrants at Alkmaar. He was killed at Bergen-op-Zoom in 1622 and succeeded as colonel by his brother Francis. The States General decided in December that year on a generous pension for his widow in recognition of his exceptional services and noble example. Wodroephe's poem was written before his death.

Captain Roger Orme, described as "Gentilhomme Anglois", gets two sonnets, remarkable for their intricate acrostics. He is affectionately called "mon capitaine", and the poems are obviously Christmas or New Year presents in which Wodroephe wishes his friend many more years of good health and happiness. Alas, it seems that this was not to be. The poems must predate the captain's death in late 1621, for such a date is noted in manuscript on a list of English officers in the service of the States General preserved in the Public Record Office[31] where this date is used as terminus ante quem for the undated record. In it Captain Orme appears as an officer in Sir John Ogle's regiment.

"Iehan de Monteith, ensign to Colonel Brog" receives a sonnet in

---

30 It is part of *Eenige formen van slach-ordens . . . van de legers der Geünieerde Provincien . . . geordineert by . . . Mauritius en . . . Frederik Hendrik*, 'sGravenhage, Hendricus Hondius, 1638. See F. Muller, *op. cit.*, no. 1136, where it is also stated that two captains Brog were among the officers killed at Snaaskerke and commemorated in the print described under no. 1133.

31 P.R.O.-S.P. 84 (Holland) 104, ff.189, 190. The pencil note dating the document by reference to his date of death is signed J.R.C., initials explained to me at the P.R.O. as being those of Mr. J.R. Crompton, a highly respected member of staff there before the Second World War. I am greatly indebted to Dr. Simon Adams of the University of Strathclyde for drawing my attention to this document.

French which, to judge from the first line's reference to "ma Muse, & mon pinceau", must have been accompanied by a drawing, perhaps in an album amicorum. The same friend is later presented with two more sonnets, one in English, the other in French, "To my very kinde Captaine Iohne Monteith: together with his . . . Lady, Marie Brogue, &c.". Marie is praised for her virtue and her descent from a valiant father, now joined to an equally brave husband, both of whom have gained laurels as only the Scots have done in these fields . . . Is she perhaps the daughter of Sir William Brogh? The English sonnet employs the word "love" or "loved" no fewer than fourteen times. Was it written for their wedding? I have been unable to find out anything about John Monteith.

A sonnet in French, addressed to "Guilleaume Drommond, enseigne du capitaine Edmond", was written long before this young officer achieved very much higher rank. The "capitaine Edmond" may be Thomas, son of Sir William and later himself a colonel. Sir William Drummond was the fourth son of John, second Earl of Perth, and Lady Jean Ker, daughter of the first Earl of Roxburgh to whose title William was to succeed in 1650. It seems he joined the army in the Netherlands out of a spirit of adventure, acquired a great reputation for gallantry and rose in rank to the colonelcy of the Earl of Buccleuch's regiment in 1646, having previously taken the younger Edmond's place as lieutenant-colonel in 1625. He was still colonel of his regiment in 1649 when he returned to Britain to join the loyalist cause. For his pains Oliver Cromwell fined him £ 6000. When he wanted to rejoin his old regiment in the Netherlands in 1652 the States General rejected his petition because they had meanwhile appointed Walter Scott. "Mr. Drommond" is often named in the exercises set down by Wodroephe, which can be taken as a sign of their good comradeship.

"Adrianus Lord of Hoyncop, Low Germanie" gets a sonnet in English whose acrostic reads, I regret to say, "To Adrien Winsen this verse I do pen". It was originally added to an emblem which is mentioned in the poem, but not explained further, and was probably also inscribed in an album. Adriaen van Winssen was born in 1583 or 1584 as son of Johan van Winssen, lord of the manor of Hoenkoop near Montfoort under the bishopric of Utrecht. In 1612 he married Christina van Schoordyck van Rynauwen, lady of Vleuten to the west of Utrecht which she inherited and thus brought to her husband in 1636. In 1616 he was invested by the States of Utrecht with the manor of Heemstede south of Utrecht, bequeathed to him by an uncle. In 1628 he was granted tithes of Jutfaas, a village to the south of the city. He died in 1639 leaving three sons and two daughters. The seventeenth-century antiquary Arend van Buchell mentions Adriaen van Winssen as an ardent amateur historian, owner of medieval manuscripts and compiler of memoirs. The latter, according to

Van Buchell, were buried with him. Whether he had this done from modesty, jealousy or sheer eccentricity is not known. Nor have I been able to discover what, if any, official function he held.[32] A little later we get "A Christmasse carolle in french presented to my Lady Hoyncop at Utrecht", sung to the tune of that ubiquitous "O nuit, jalouse nuit".

The French sonnet that follows has a better known recipient: "Jehan Cameron, Ministre . . . dans Bordeaux". He has a place in the *Mémoires* of Philippe Du Plessis-Mornay and in Bayle's *Dictionnaire*.[33] His life has been described[34] as affording an excellent example of the vagrant Scottish scholar. He was born in Glasgow in 1579, came to Bordeaux in 1600 where he astonished the French with his facility in speaking Greek. He was professor of philosophy at Sedan, then at Paris, Geneva and Heidelberg. In 1608 he took up the ministry at Bordeaux. He lectured in public on religion in 1615 and after various other vicissitudes succeeded Jacobus Gomarus as professor at Saumur when Gomarus moved to Leiden. But Cameron soon returned to Bordeaux once more. In 1620 Cameron was in England, in 1621 he preached at Leiden. In 1622 he followed Robert Boyd as principal of Glasgow University, which post he speedily resigned to return to Saumur. He died at Montauban in 1625. Wodroephe's poem was written at a time when Cameron was at Bordeaux or Wodroephe at least believed him to be there. In it he emphasises the pastoral care his parishioners enjoyed through him: had he ever been one of them?

Ensigns "Fairefax" and "Tucke" each get a French sonnet next. It seems highly probable that the former is Ferdinando,[35] father of the famous Thomas Fairfax who himself went to fight in the Netherlands in his turn, being present in 1629 at the siege of 's-Hertogenbosch. Ferdinando gave up soldiering for the law, wisely, since too many

---

32 All the information I could provide here was supplied to me after a cry for help and at exceedingly short notice by Drs. Pierre Pesch and Drs. A.D.A. Monna of Utrecht University Library. They traced it in Baron E.B.F.W. Wittert van Hoogland, *Bijdragen tot de geschiedenis der Utrechtsche ridderhofsteden en heerlijkheden*, Den Haag, 1909, and in *Jaarboekje van "Oud-Utrecht". 1951,* Utrecht, 1951. My thanks to them are profound. Warm thanks also go to Drs. Arie-Jan Gelderblom who on a mild November afternoon in 1982 enchanted me by taking me completely by chance for a walk to Heemstede. The present house, newly restored and glittering, is dated 1645 and therefore not the one known to Wodroephe's friend whose home was probably a much more modest, if not already delapidated structure, ready to be pulled down and replaced with a more fashionable building as soon as peace became visible on the horizon.

33 *I.e.* Philippe de Mornay, Seigneur du Plessis-Marly, *Mémoires*, first published, at least in part, at Amsterdam, 1652, and Pierre Bayle, *Dictionnaire historique et critique*, first published at Rotterdam, 1697.

34 By John Hill Burton, *op. cit.*, vol. 2, p. 104.

35 See C.R. Markham, *A life of the great Lord Fairfax*, London, 1870, p. 12.

Fairfaxes of his generation were killed on active service in the Low Countries. Ensign Tucke remains unrecorded outside the *Spared Houres*: ensigns did not qualify for inclusion by name in official pay records, as lieutenants did not either, and poor Tucke probably never rose to a higher rank. The sonnet gently teases him for his love of dancing: dance rather to the glory of Christ at this time of His birth.

The civilian to whom the next sonnet goes is called "mon ami, Msr van Beest, gentilhomme Flamen". But the poem says nothing about him except that he was virtuous and erudite, nor how Wodroephe came to know him. No person of this name listed in the Dutch dictionary of national biography fits the date of Wodroephe's stay in the Netherlands.

Of "Captain Praude" to whom the following sonnet, in praise of virtuous maidens and thus fit to be given by him to his mistress, is addressed, a record does exist, but only in the shape of his name on the list of the English officers in Dutch pay which is preserved at the PRO.[36] There are in fact two men of this name, one Captain Proude among the officers in Sir Horace Vere's regiment and a "Captain Proude, seriant Maior" in "Col. Cecyll's" regiment. My preference is for the former, the plain captain. When Wodroephe collected his poems for his book, the "bien vaillant Cap. Praude" was no longer alive, being described as "vu [i.e. feu] cap. Anglois".

After the "Christmasse carolle" to Lady Hoyncop which has been mentioned before Wodroephe has set down "A French song . . . presented to . . . Girard van Berckell, Counsellor of Rotterdam", with another "Godly French song . . . yet to M. van Berckell" both very long and to be sung to the tune of psalms. Of him it is said[37] that he maintained in 1628 that no one could say he heard him make any proposal regarding Hugo de Groot, which is no great claim to glory. In 1631 however he and his fellow burgemeester Cornelis Hartigsvelt proved themselves at least sympathetic to Grotius.

A highly ambitious piece follows, "A thankes giving unto God for the Delivrance of Bergen-up-zome . . . presented to . . . his very kind Friend, Iszack Beekeman . . . Rectour of the Latine Schoole at Rotterdam". It is again in French and sung to a psalm tune and in spite of a good deal of mythological and arcadian stuffing brings in some reality of the Dutch landscape and people in the poet's appeal to all the land and its inhabitants to rejoice in the great victory won by Prince Maurice in October 1622. He calls for example on the sailors and bargemen, the ministers of religion and the artists, the peasants and the burghers, the fields abounding in corn and the rivers producing "jolis frais poissons".

---

36 See note 31 above.
37 See Jo Melles, *Ministers aan de Maas*, Rotterdam, 's-Gravenhage, 1962, p. 90.

Let even widows and orphans lay aside their grief for this while. It is a poem full of affection and joy. Isaac Beeckman[38] was born at Middelburg in 1588, studied at Leiden for the church, but for family reasons abandoned the university and took up a technical trade at Zierikzee which included the laying of water pipes for breweries. He devoted himself to science, especially the problems of flow and inertia. He was in correspondence with Lansbergen and Snellius, and after visiting Brussels and London in 1616 he got his doctorate in medicine at Caen in 1618 with theses on air pressure and tertiary fever. That year at Breda he met Descartes who later wrote his *Compendium musicae* for him, printed in 1650, in which Descartes thanked Beeckman for his encouragement. In 1619 Beeckman was appointed conrector at the Latin school of Utrecht. In 1620 he married a lady from Middelburg and moved to Rotterdam where his brother Jacob had meanwhile become rector of the Latin school. Isaac had no proper appointment there but taught intermittently until 1624 when he became conrector. Wodroephe evidently confused him with his brother, calling him rector of the Rotterdam grammar school. At Rotterdam he was a friend of burgemeester van Berckel, founded the Collegium Mathematicum in 1623 and the Collegium Mechanicum in 1626. In 1627 he became rector of the Latin school at Dordrecht which he is said to have made famous. He died at Dordrecht in 1637. He is considered the most important Dutch scientist between Stevin and Huygens. His father Abraham was born at Turnhout in 1563 and had fled to London before settling at Middelburg where he died in 1625. Isaac's connection with England may well have contributed to his friendship with Wodroephe.

The preface to the translation from Sir William Alexander's *Foure Hours* contains Wodroephe's apology for including his incomplete and unworthy version at all: he has done so at the urging of "John Dowglas, Minister to the English and Scottish troops at Utrecht". Utrecht was a regular garrison town for the British regiments where they spent the winter months. A parallel garrison was at Gorcum. The army chaplain also provided services for the British civilians resident there, at least during the winter, until a combined approach by army and burghers led to the employment of a full time minister for their needs. The first such clergyman was the ill-fated Thomas Scott, who was murdered in Utrecht in 1626. Scott's predecessor, still only as army chaplain, had been a Mr. Clerk and he succeeded Mr. John Douglas. Douglas is mentioned as early as April 1607 when he inducted Mr. John Paget as minister to the British Presbyterian Church at Amsterdam for which the city had allowed the

---

38 See NNBW. dl. 7, coll. 84-88; J.G.C.A. Briels, "Zuidnederlandse onderwijskrachten, etc.", *Archief voor de Geschiedenis der Katholieke Kerk in Nederland*, vol. 14, 1972, p. 284.

chapel in the Begijnhof. His colleague at Gorcum was Samuel Bachiler, whose *Miles Christianus, or The Camp Royal*, published at Amsterdam in 1625, is dedicated "to all my deare countrymen in service to the States of the United Provinces" and contains laudatory verses in Latin by Johannes Spiljardus and in English by Thomas Scott. Scott appeared too late on the scene for Wodroephe's book, but neither Clerk nor Bachiler is mentioned in it either.

Finally two men whom Wodroephe must have come to know well: his printer and his publisher.[39] Both were well established at Dordrecht by this time. The latter had connections with England which may be the reason that Wodroephe took his manuscript to him. Joris Waters, or George Walters as he also called himself, was in fact born in London of Flemish descent ca. 1575. By 1607 he was in Dordrecht where he married and settled for life. Like Niclaes Vincentsz, whose surname Spierincxhouck was rarely used by him, Waters was one of a number of local printers who got permission to produce all the official documents issued by the Synod of Dort. In 1620 Waters and Zacharias Jochums signed a contract for the supply of five hundred copies of the Latin edition of the proceedings of the Synod to the London booksellers William Fisher and Robert Martin. He also published several editions of the Dutch book of martyrs, the *Historien der vromer martelaren*, which, like the acts of the Synod, cannot have failed to provide him with a handsome income. He remained a member of the English community at Dordrecht all his life and published a number of English works in the original or in translation. Among them were religious tracts and such books as Patrick Gordon's *The famous historie . . . of Prince Robert, surnamed the Bruce, King of Scotland* and the same author's *The first booke of the historye of Penardo and Laissa,* both in 1615, William Bradshaw's *The unreasonablenesse of the separation*, 1614, and perhaps of even more interest to Wodroephe, several works of Henry Hexham. It was Hexham who translated several religious pamphlets from English into Dutch for Waters to publish in 1611, and as a military man himself with interests in philology he may have alerted Wodroephe to the suitability of his own one-time publisher. Little is known of Hexham's career, but his own books describe him as captain in the English army in the Netherlands and as quartermaster to Colonel Goring in 1643 when he felt so strongly about abuses in military life in England that he translated Frederick Henry's rules of discipline into English, had them printed at The Hague and sent them to cousins of his in England with a recommendation to have them adopted in his own country.[40] In 1637 he published an eye-witness account of the siege of

---

39 See J.G.C.A. Briels, *Zuidnederlandse Boekdrukkers, etc.*, pp. 457-459 s.v. Spierincxhouck and pp. 543, 544 s.v. Watersz.

40 See the dedication in his *An appendix of the lawes, articles, & ordinances,*

Breda, printed at Delft by James Moxon, "and to be sold at Hendricus Hondius neere the gevangen Port in the Hagh".

Spierincxhouck was born at Rotterdam of Flemish parents. The *Spared Houres* is his only book in English as far as I know, and he may have had the responsibility for the French while Waters supervised the English. The book they produced for John Wodroephe in 1623 is a stately folio, not really suitable for the soldier's knapsack, but fair enough for use in his winter quarters. It has wide enough margins to scribble on if the reader felt such a need for vandalism. It is not a beautiful book, but is carefully arranged as a textbook and not tiring to the eye. Misprints however abound in both the English and French. But "grosse English"? Hardly that, and the London edition of 1625 does not really make much of a difference to the English, retaining even words of Dutch overtone such as "frolicke" and "saghtly". Rather does it emasculate the book by removing so many little personal statements, not to mention all the "Godly sonets" and most of the other poems. The military examples remain, including those which name the supreme commanders Prince Maurice and Prince Frederick Henry, the States General, and the like, wholly incomprehensible for the student who was not aware of the author's participation in the Dutch wars. All the new titlepage told him was that the book had first been printed at Dordrecht, but not why. The new version is slimmer, it is perhaps more businesslike and to the point of teaching without so many frills and fancies, but with the elimination of those passages from dedications and prefaces and all the personal poems it has got rid not only of the smell of sweat, but also of the smile that lurks in *The Spared Houres of a Souldier*.

The picture that has emerged of John Wodroephe is perhaps no more than an identikit one, if that, but where previously he had been wholly hidden in the shadows I trust he is now visible at least in outline. If I have failed in presenting him as an interesting personality and lively author, let me quote his own words with which he ends his labours: "Will ye I tell you? there is no man to whome it happens not to faile, as also (may be) it hath in mee".[41]

established for marshall discipline, in the service of the Lords the States Generall of the united Provinces ... Printed in the Hagh by Isaac Burchoorn, 1643. He is given a brief entry with a list of his books in A.J. van der Aa, *Biographisch Woordenboek der Nederlanden*, Haarlem, 1852-1878, dl. 8, pp. 764, 765.

41 The French is "Voulez vous que je vous dise? Il n'y a homme auquel il n'advienne de faillir, qu'aussi peut estre de moy". This incorporates the final proverb in the 1559 edition by Gabriel Buon of Cordier's *Sententiae*. It is actually not truly the end of Wodroephe's book, but it is the end of his grammar. He still signs the French column with his motto and fills the verso of the last leaf with a poem "A thanksgiving (of the author) unto God for his helpe in the finishing of this worke", which, if not great poetry, is an unexceptionable sentiment.

SOSPETTO D'HERODE: A NEGLECTED CRASHAW POEM

D.R.M. Wilkinson

Richard Crashaw was not a poet who was exactly central to the Metaphysical tradition; he was in fact something of a fringe figure in spite of the fact that he is usually placed with Donne, Herbert and Vaughan.[1] His poetry, by and large, is less dramatic than Herbert's, less witty than Donne's, he tends to be more committed to sensations, to the senses, than to thought, and is perhaps a little too liable to nurse emotions[2] that are rather sickeningly sweet or cloyingly erotic or tortured. Of his best poetry it has been argued that he is baroque rather than metaphysical, that in his use of paradox and symbol he is not "exploring the nature of some metaphysical problem" but rather employing "the Baroque conceit" in order to view "the same paradox or symbol from various angles, reviewing and revising and restating and expanding the issue until some truth of emotion gradually grows out from all that glittering elaboration".[3] His tendency is to repeat, then, from different angles, rather than to develop an explorative argument. Whether this makes him baroque or not is another matter—the term seems difficult to apply to poetry—but the implication is that he is not quite a metaphysical. As he is clearly not of the tribe of Ben—he is no courtier, is not urbane or detached—one might well ask where exactly he belongs in the rich turmoil of literary activity that makes the earlier seventeenth century so rewarding a period. Nor does the question seem simply academic, for in trying to place Crashaw one comes to see all the more clearly how many "traditions" were at work creatively in that rather fabulous half century.

To those who believe that the cloying element in his poetry is the essential Crashaw note, and to those who find that he is little more than

---

[1] A common view is that "Crashaw's poetry remains an anomaly in English literature, an example of a continental importation which never struck a firm hold upon the English scene, and in the end had to seek its proper nourishment in exile", from Louis L. Martz, "The Action of the Self: Devotional Poetry in the Seventeenth Century", in *Metaphysical Poetry,* Stratford-upon-Avon Studies, No. 11, London, 1970, p. 117. The present essay is an attempt to confute this view.
[2] Joan Bennett, *Four Metaphysical Poets*, 2nd ed., Cambridge, 1953, particularly pp. 92-93.
[3] Louis L. Martz, *The Wit of Love,* Univ. of Notre Dame Press, 1969, pp. 127-28.

"a kind of sport in English literary history, an exotic Italian import like pasta or castrati",[4] there is this to be said: take a careful look again at an early poem of his, *Sospetto d'Herode*. The aim of this present essay is to examine this poem which, for all its weaknesses, is certainly rich in exploiting some of the most powerful "traditions" of the time, and furthermore could show that the current view of Crashaw's work, as sketched above, is hardly adequate. I remember reading this poem as a student and being very excited by the Miltonic element which I could find nowhere mentioned in the commentaries I consulted, only to learn much later that though seldom referred to, the connexion has long been known.

Crashaw's *Sospetto d'Herode* (Herod's Suspicion, or Fear, it might be translated) is very much a European Renaissance poem in the sense that it is Biblical in origin, richly decorated with classical references and is in the tradition of "Infernal Council" literature. Furthermore the original was by the Italian poet, Marino, and translated by Crashaw into English, the first book only—but it is a complete unity in itself.

I said the poem was a translation of Marino's poem, but this is not *altogether* true. It has been pointed out that the use of literary borrowings and literary allusions was quite normal for this time—that "the demand for complete originality is a comparatively modern phenomenon"[5]—but at the same time to see the *Sospetto* as merely a translation is to miss the point that "at the beginning of the seventeenth century there seems to have been a common urge to demonstrate what the English language could do, released from the fetters of foreign originals", and that in consequence the "hostility towards literal translation was widespread".[6] It has been argued that Crashaw's poem is more an interpretation than a translation, and that it gives evidence of this "common urge". It has even been argued that Marino's influence on the English version is minimal,[7] but "a closer look at the two poems suggests that Crashaw, at the least, borrowed from Marino's original an integrated set of classical and Christian allusions, a pattern of paradoxical expansion, and the inspiration for metaphorical development".[8] Claes Schaar makes it quite clear, in his very full and fascinating account of the relationship of the

---

4 Frank J. Warnke, "Metaphysical Poetry and the European Context", in *Metaphysical Poetry*, Stratford-upon-Avon Studies, No. 11, London, 1970, p. 265.

5 Lois Potter, *A Preface to Milton*, London, 1971, p. 76.

6 Claes Schaar, *Marino and Crashaw: Sospetto d'Herode: A Commentary*, Lund Studies in English No. 39, Lund, 1971, p. 12.

7 Louis R. Barbato, "Marino, Crashaw and Sospetto d'Herode", *Philological Quarterly*, 54 (1975), 523, quoting Frank J. Warnke, "Marino and the English Metaphysicals", in *Studies in the Renaissance*, II, ed. M.A. Shaaber, New York, 1955, pp. 170-74.

8 Barbato, p. 523.

two poems,[9] the Italian and the English, to each other, that while Crashaw's poem is in the literal sense entirely dependent on Marino's (each has sixty-six stanzas and each stanza deals with the same topic, the same material), both poems lean heavily on, in fact borrow directly from, a tradition of poetry going back to Vergil and Ovid, the Bible, Dante, Boccaccio, Tasso, Vida *et al.*, so much so that this can be traced in the very details of the imagery and theme in both poems even where they differ. Schaar's book is a model of scholarly detective work that should be compulsory reading for anyone working in this field, even without a knowledge of Italian. Through his work one can come to experience the weight of the literary past that is everywhere pressing through the texture of these two poems, often compellingly, so that one understands all the more how imitation could come to be looked on as a virtue, as a requirement of literary art, and how Pope could later argue that imitating Homer was imitating nature. I imagine that the extent to which a seventeenth-century reader would have recognised and appreciated particular instances of classical borrowings or imitation can hardly be established, but the poet who deliberately exploited these resources obviously wrote for an audience he felt he could entertain in this way. He had high expectations of his reader, just as Milton must have had with all the weight of reference and allusion he crammed into *Paradise Lost.* And even in our culturally atomised twentieth century, a T.S. Eliot must have had fairly high expectations of the literacy of his readers when he produced *The Waste Land.* But agreed, there are borrowings and borrowings, and the great writer makes of them something new, and the minor writer merely echoes or repeats. The *Sospetto* is not a great poem maybe, but it does not merely echo or repeat either, and it has life enough to provide unusual entertainment, if that's the word for it.

That both poets consciously exploited their originals is plainly shown by Schaar. Before looking at their differences, a short outline of the *Sospetto* might be in place. The first half of the poem, after the brief announcement of the theme ("Hate"), the invoking of the massacred innocents and the apostrophe to the Muse and to Antonio, Duke of Alba and Viceroy of Naples,[10] consists of a description of Satan's physical and spiritual state (with authorial comment), ending up with a lengthy, defiant yet self-questioning (interior?) monologue in which Satan debates his position vis-à-vis God, clearly with the *new* threat in mind, namely the coming of the Christ-child. Stanza 33 is the turning point in that here a further important group of characters is introduced, the furies, who have apparently overheard at least the conclusion of the above-mentioned

---

9 This is the work already referred to in note 6.
10 Not St. Anthony, as previous commentators have it: see Schaar, p. 84.

monologue, and the action begins to take another turn. The furies applaud violently and in chorus protest their readiness to hurl themselves into battle to help their "impatient Prince". A brief exchange follows between them and Satan, whereupon the fourth "Erinnys", Cruelty, is selected to carry out some dark but unspecified deed. There follows a lengthy and rather overdone description of Cruelty's palace (stanzas 38-46), after which she sets off quite suddenly, arriving in Bethlehem in the 50th stanza where she finds Herod, the usurper, in charge. She approaches him in a dream, disguised as the ghost of his dead brother and makes a long speech (stanzas 53-59) inciting him to rouse himself from his lethargy and subdue and destroy the "rebels" who are gaining ground in his kingdom and are boldly proclaiming the coming of their "new King". Herod wakes, and in fear and rage begins to prepare for action, and here the narrative ends—the last two excellent stanzas again taking an unexpected turn in offering quite simply a gentle and conciliatory questioning, in the narrator's voice, of Herod's violent intentions.

Where the versions of Crashaw and Marino differ has been very fully worked out by Professor Schaar,[11] so that a few illustrations should suffice here, for it is only the English poem we are really concerned with. In stanza 57, for instance, Schaar points to the difference between the treatment of Crudeltà (Marino) and Cruelty (Crashaw) and argues that this "reflects the general tendency of the two versions, and it is substantiated by the respective analogues: the *Thebaid*, of Marino's version; the *Aeneid*, of Crashaw's".[12] That it is only a general tendency one can deduce from the fact that in stanza 49 it is Marino who is the more Virgilian.[13] In stanza 18 Crashaw humanizes Satan "by recording his feelings",[14] which is not paralleled in Marino—and there are many such small but significant differences. In a larger way, Schaar suggests that the "freer and less formal structure of Crashaw's stanza, the breathless, staccato character of the speech (in stanza 56), is part of a more vivid description extending down to the minutest details",[15] and he seems to imply that while Crashaw tends to be more dramatic and vivid,

---

11 The body of his book contains a stanza by stanza commentary and comparison. It is worth noting that Ruth C. Wallerstein in her well-known work on Crashaw, *Richard Crashaw: A Study in Style and Poetic Development,* Univ. of Wisconsin Studies in Lang. and Lit., No. 37, Univ. of Wisconsin Press, 1935, finds Crashaw obviously superior to Marino in the matter of concreteness, sensuous richness, dramatic power and intensity (p. 74).

12 Schaar, p. 264. He also shows here how a knowledge of the sources can directly affect one's reading of these poems.

13 Schaar, p. 243.

14 Schaar, p. 151.

15 Schaar, p. 260.

Marino, though more static and abstract, can be richer. This is not a view shared by Mario Praz, whose testimony cannot be taken lightly. He avers that "the English poet succeeds in imparting poetic life to certain trite metaphors and purple patches of Marino, thus relieving the flabbiness of the Italian poem, a late scion of the decayed epic tradition".[16]

Quite clearly we have not to do here with a "translation" that is simply derivative, but with a poem that is a poem in its own right. It is that peculiar thing, a free translation that both re-works the original and imitates, or works in, material from other models in the same tradition. (It is interesting to note that neither poet makes much use of Horace, the model for the tribe of Ben.) But if Crashaw is creatively involved in making a new thing, which he is, it is still a curiously mixed work, and it is at least part of my intention to show this. There is, to begin with, the heavily rhetorical mode, most noticeable in the description of Cruelty's palace (stanzas 39-46). To say, as Schaar does, that these stanzas are "thematic" (p. 206), may well be true, but they are also, alas, heavily rhetorical—as when the walls of the palace are described as hanging with

> Nailes, hammers, hatchets sharpe, and halters strong,
> Swords, Speares, with all the fatall Instruments
>   Of sin, and Death, twice dipt in the dire staines
>   Of Brothers mutuall blood, and Fathers braines.(41)

And though the traditional device of lists which Crashaw often uses may well have honourable antecedents in the Bible and in Homer, and will be employed later, impressively, by Milton, it is still difficult to believe that it can give any real life to lines like the following (we are still in Cruelty's palace):

> Whatever Schemes of Blood, fantastick frames
> Of Death *Mezentius*, or *Geryon* drew;
> *Phalaris*, *Ochus*, *Ezelinus*, names
> Mighty in mischiefe, with dread *Nero* too,
> Here are they all, Here all the swords or flames
> *Assyrian* Tyrants, or *Egyptian* knew. (46)

To track down all the significances of the italicised names in such a passage hardly answers the problem. A poet, one might say, can be expected so to use words as to create meanings, but once his words have largely lost their associations for us, why then his poetry is largely lost, though a little life be found in it still within the walls of Academe. The reader can do little with the fact that the *Geryon* in line 2 above is probably not merely "the three-bodied monster mentioned by several ancient poets", but "is rather listed here because he is said to have lured

---

16 Mario Praz, *The Flaming Heart*, Gloucester, Mass., 1958, p. 233.

strangers into his house and killed them",[17] according to Boccaccio. Granted a reader must work for it, but it is not his business entirely to *make* the poem.

That there are serious weaknesses in the *Sospetto* is clear. But there is also much to commend it. To start at the beginning, once past the "Argomento", we plunge straight into a stanza typical in one way of that other Crashaw, with the emphasis on Breasts, Babes, Blood, Sweetness, Murder and Death—in the invoking of the slaughtered Innocents:

>   and *Herod*, whose unblest
> Hand (ô what dares not jealous Greatnesse?) tore
> A thousand sweet Babes from their Mothers Brest:
> The Bloomes of Martyrdome. O be a Dore
> Of language to my infant Lips, yee best
>   Of Confessours: whose Throates answering his swords,
>   Gave forth your Blood for breath, spoke soules for words.(1)

The author communes momentarily with the Infants, out of sympathy, begging them to make him eloquent (it does not seem necessary to make Dore = wound, or Confessour = martyr),[18] and then in the last two lines develops the curiously powerful but somewhat unpleasant image of the throats speaking souls—typical of Crashaw's metaphysical-baroque ingenuity but markedly different from the rest of this poem in its tone, and certainly from the harsh description of Cruelty's palace.

The narrative itself begins—impressively—at stanza 5:

> Below the Botome of the great Abysse,
> There where one Center reconciles all things;
> The worlds profound Heart pants; There placed is
> Mischifes old Master, close about him clings
> A curl'd knot of embracing Snakes . . .

There's a kind of grandeur and dignity here that we shall see more of, the character of Satan being one of the most impressive and vital things in the poem. As Mario Praz says, in praising the poem, parts of it "Milton must have remembered while describing the appearance of his Lucifer".[19]

The next four stanzas are in the less interesting rhetorical-descriptive manner, until the poem picks up again in stanza 10, after a high moral opening, and the ironies of Satan's predicament begin to unfold, and the nature of his suffering:

> Disdainefull wretch! how hath one bold sinne cost
> Thee all the Beauties of thy once bright Eyes?
> How hath one blacke Eclipse cancell'd, and crost

---

17 Schaar, p. 231.
18 Schaar, p. 89.
19 Mario Praz, *The Flaming Heart*, p. 238.

>   The glories that did guild thee in thy Rise?
>   Proud Morning of a perverse Day! how lost
>   Art thou unto thy selfe, thou too selfe-wise
>   *Narcissus*? foolish *Phaeton*? who for all
>   Thy high-aym'd hopes, gaind'st but a flaming fall. (10)

The form of direct address and the rhetorical questions give life to the presentation; the rhymes too are pretty effective, particularly in the dramatic Old-Testament-Petrarchan "how hath one bold sinne cost / Thee all the Beauties of thy once bright Eyes?" and the rather subtler, more internal questioning of the last lines, beginning "how lost / Art thou unto thy selfe, thou too selfe-wise / *Narcissus*?" The tone of commiseration for fallen greatness is no doubt endemic to all accounts of Satan where his past, his potential, is contrasted with his yielding to the evil within him. To give him stature and significance, his angelic origin must be referred to, and this almost inevitably brings in the tragic aspect of his role, and our sympathies.[20] Here in Crashaw's poem, as in *Paradise Lost*, we tend to be a little more conscious of the "Proud Morning" than of the "perverse Day". Satan is anthropomorphized, made man, and our feelings are in consequence involved. What's more, he's the underdog. And he feels threatened, and is harassed because he cannot see into the immediate future:

>   He calls to mind th'old quarrell, and what sparke
>   Set the contending Sons of Heav'n on fire:
>   Oft in his deepe thought he revolves the darke
>   *Sibills* divining leaves: hee does enquire
>   Into th'old Prophesies, trembling to marke
>   How many present prodigies conspire,
>   To crowne their past predictions, both hee layes
>   Together, in his pondrous mind both weighes. (12)

The rhythms and rhymes again are very satisfyingly functional—"and what spárke / Sét . . ." draws the right colloquial emphasis, as does "revolves the dárke / *Síbills* divining leaves". It is a considerable achievement, too, in so long a poem to have kept the rhymes so natural and effective throughout. They are worth examining.

Satan has a lot of evidence to weigh as the next five or six stanzas show. Most important is the Annunciation and its context:

>   Heavens Golden-winged Herald, late hee saw
>   To the poore *Galilean* virgin sent:
>   How low the Bright Youth bow'd, and with what awe
>   Immortall flowers to her faire hand present.
>   Hee saw th'old *Hebrewes* wombe, neglect the Law

---

20 Schaar points out that few poems before *Paradise Lost* concentrate in this way on the *suffering* of the fallen angel (p. 114).

> Of Age and Barennesse, and her Babe prevent
> His Birth, by his Devotion, who began
> Betimes to be a Saint, before a Man. (13)

And here surely is gentle Herbert, in the grace and the wit and a sort of effortless precision.[21] Of course this is now Satan's vision, Satan's awareness, but this only increases for the reader the poignancy of his position—I mean, that it is couched in such terms of appreciation and sympathy. For several stanzas then, his vision of the "portents" develops. He comes to see (in true metaphysical manner) first how

> the poore Shepheards ran to pay
> Their simple Tribute to the Babe, whose Birth
> Was the great businesse both of Heav'n and Earth. (15)

There is a kind of qualified daring in "the great businesse"—mixing the easy colloquial with the momentous. And then he sees how

> Three Kings (or what is more) three Wise men went
> Westward to find the worlds true *Orient*. (17)

Again a metaphysical paradox, moving and witty, especially that "or what is more". It is Satan's vision, but not his phrasing. One gets the facts, as it were, objectively, but Satan is the fully conscious onlooker. He cannot understand the real significance of what he sees—

> How she that is a maid should prove a Mother,
> Yet keepe inviolate her virgin flower;
> How Gods eternall Sonne should be mans Brother,
> Poseth his proudest Intellectuall power.
> > How a pure Spirit should incarnate bee,
> > And life it selfe weare Deaths fraile Livery. (21)

In such passages, for all the metaphysical paradoxes, one is conscious of a Spenserian tone and manner, in that there is elaborate syntactical repetition with accumulation of detail; it can go on like this for several stanzas at a time—and is quite effective, largely because of the narrative and descriptive skill.[22]

At the end of the vision, Satan collapses in misery and despair—"Those stings of care that his strong Heart opprest, / A desperate, *Oh mee*, drew from his deepe Brest" (25).

---

21 Frank J. Warnke in discussing Crashaw's "The Weeper" and his "Hymne to St. Teresa" comes to conclude that "Crashaw himself felt no essential discrepancy between the wit of Marino and the, to us, very different wit of Herbert"; see "Metaphysical Poetry and the European Context", in *Metaphysical Poetry*, p. 265.

22 Ruth C. Wallerstein sees the Spenserian influence, in fact, as central: "the style as a whole manifesting the inflow of Spenserianism" (p. 78); ". . . the intensity of the sentiment, which made him turn spontaneously to Spenser" as a model (p. 79); and "Spenser is his great example" (p. 80). This seems to be an overstatement.

> *Oh mee*! (thus bellow'd hee) *oh mee*! what great
> Portents before mine eyes their Powers advance? (26)

It is a dramatic exclamation, sorrowful rather than bitter, but it is the kind of insight he cannot permit himself, and he quickly switches to the defiant note:

> Frowne I; and can great Nature keep her seat?
> And the gay starrs lead on their Golden dance?
>   Can his attempts above still prosp'rous be,
>   Auspicious still, in spight of Hell and me? (26)
>
> Hee has my Heaven (what would he more?) whose bright
> And radiant Scepter this bold hand should beare. (27)

All these stanzas (26-32) put one in mind of Milton's Satan, full of high-flown assurance and defiance, later shifting to an agonised self-questioning:

> Art thou not *Lucifer*? hee to whom the droves
> Of Stars, that guild the Morne in charge were given?
> The nimblest of the lightning-winged Loves?
> The fairest, and the first-borne smile of Heav'n? (30)

And then the despairing Faustus-like question, and the decision taken:

> Ah wretch! what bootes thee to cast back thy eyes,
> Where dawning hope no beame of comfort showes?
> While the reflection of thy forepast joyes,
> Renders thee double to thy present woes.
>   . . .
>   If Hell must mourne, Heav'n sure shall sympathize
>   What force cannot effect, fraud shall devise. (31)
>
>   what though it cost
> Mee yet a second fall? wee'd try our strengths.
>   Heav'n saw us struggle once, as brave a fight
>   Earth now should see, and tremble at the sight. (32)

His character and intentions are by definition evil, and yet, as in the case of Milton's Satan, there is something near admirable, something that we cannot accept as unqualifiedly evil in him. As Waldock once said of Milton's Satan:

> what we are chiefly made to see and feel in the first two books are fortitude in adversity, enormous endurance, a certain splendid recklessness, remarkable powers of rising to an occasion, extraordinary qualities of leadership ... What we feel most of all, I suppose, is his refusal to give in—just that.[23]

Crashaw's Satan is of course a much slighter figure, and we do not see him degraded to a snake, or hissed at by his rebellious crew. He is made

---

23 A.J.A. Waldock, *Paradise Lost and its Critics*, 1947; rpt. Cambridge, 1961, p. 77.

man, as I have said, and this is probably the only way to depict him if he is to be interesting, and if he is interesting he cannot be *purely* evil. The Furies who address him in the stanzas that follow are far less interesting in themselves because more complete in their rage, in their evil. They can have no sorrow, no doubts, no self-reproach; only bitterness. They are the committed ones:

> If all faile wee'l put on our proudest Armes,
> And pouring on Heav'ns face the Seas huge flood
> Quench his curl'd fires, wee'l wake with our Alarmes
>   Ruine, where e're she sleepes at Natures feet;
>   And crush the world till his wide corners meet. (35)

Theologically, no doubt, this Satan will not do, as he is not Evil *in extremis*; but dramatically and poetically he will do very well—as a projection of limited human evil, symbolically meaningful, the archetypal sinner rather than the Supreme Evil One; one with tragic attributes, capable, if not of repentance, at least of realising what repentance could mean: "Ah wretch! what bootes thee to cast back thy eyes / Where dawning hope no beame of comfort showes?" He is the sort of figure, to use a popular phrase, one can identify with. And if he is a little too attractive in his defiance and his sorrow, there is a certain counterbalance in the spite and vindictiveness he shows during the tender account of his Bethlehem vision (see stanza 19, for example).

Stanza 33 is the turning point. The Furies enter, and Cruelty prepares to set off for Bethlehem. The rather harsh and poetically crude description of her palace, curiously enough, also helps mark her off from Satan, the creature of ambivalence and inner conflict. When she arrives in Bethlehem, in disguise, she insinuates all the fears of Satan into the soul of Herod, who becomes in this way a kind of extension of Satan, a second satanic consciousness, with the impulsive doubts, fears and self-questionings of Mischifes old Master:

> Hee wakes, and with him (ne're to sleepe) new feares:
> His Sweat-bedewed Bed had now betrai'd him,
> To a vast field of thornes, ten thousand Speares
> All pointed in his heart seem'd to invade him:
> So mighty were th'amazing Characters
> With which his feeling Dreame had thus dismay'd him,
>   Hee his owne fancy-framed foes defies:
>   In rage, *My armes, give me my armes*, hee cryes. (60)

It is in this kind of stanza that one feels the presence of another tradition, of the Elizabethan playwrights, surely, what with the *internal* quality of the dream, the psychology—and even the comedy—in that last line. One could well regret that Crashaw did not write more narrative-dramatic poems.

The conclusion is a poetic, not a narrative, conclusion. The account stops at the point where Herod is about to summon his "Counsellours" in preparation for action, for the violence that will end in the Massacre of the Innocents. What one gets then in the two final stanzas is an intrusive comment by the narrator. It is a direct thematic answer to the fears of Herod embodied in his self-questionings. Indirectly one feels these beautiful stanzas as counterbalancing more than just Herod's anxiety; Satan too is here gently, tenderly, even wittily, answered:

> Why art thou troubled *Herod*? what vaine feare
> Thy blood-revolving Brest to rage doth move?
> Heavens King, who doffs himselfe weake flesh to weare,
> Comes not to rule in wrath, but serve in love.
> Nor would he this thy fear'd Crown from thee Teare,
> But give thee a better with himselfe above.
>   Poore jealousie! why should he wish to prey
>   Upon thy Crowne, who gives his owne away?
>
> Make to thy reason man; and mocke thy doubts,
> Looke how below thy feares their causes are;
> Thou art a Souldier *Herod*; send thy Scouts
> See how hee's furnish't for so fear'd a warre.
> What armour does he weare? A few thin clouts.
> His trumpets? tender cryes, his men to dare
>   So much? rude Shepheards. What his steeds? alas
>   Poore Beasts! a slow Oxe, and a simple Asse.

It seems to me a beautiful ending—the gentleness, the forgiveness, and the mocking that is no mocking but encouragement to alter his ways; and once again the finished rhythms and rhymes. It is these sentiments, I suggest, that really relate the evil that is in Herod (and Satan) fully to the human predicament. A perspective is given of an un-Miltonic kind in a voice that we begin to recognise as Crashaw's own—not cloyingly sweet, nor tortured, nor erotic, as we have been led to expect.

That then is Crashaw's poem: one that belongs in many traditions, having resemblances to Spenser, to the Elizabethan playwrights, to the metaphysicals and to Milton, without being weighed down by its own literariness. Into the bargain it is a "translation" from the Italian, so that we should be more than justified in finding it "European". For a young poet[24] it is a remarkable achievement even by the standards of the time, revealing a sensitiveness to the rhythms and dramatic qualities of his great forebears and contemporaries as well as an ability to create his own—while having at the same time to solve all the problems of translation. What I have said might imply that it is a kind of Jacobean

---

24 He was 24 or 25 in 1637 by which time the poem was probably completed. See Wallerstein, p. 74; and Schaar, p. 11.

missing link. Maybe it is, but it is more than that in that it is worth reading for itself. It seems to me indeed to be central to its period—not as Donne's great third and fourth *Satires* are central—but nevertheless significantly representative, and worthy of being better known. And how might this be but by being included in undergraduate programmes at universities? (And where will one get the copies?)

NO-POPERY VIOLENCE IN 1688: REVOLT IN THE PROVINCES

J. Anthony Williams

In a brilliant and influential book, *The Revolt of the Provinces, 1630-1650*[1], Dr John Morrill has analysed local reactions to an earlier English revolution: reactions first against the regime of Charles I and then against the burdens of civil war. In the rapid revolution of 1688 also, two revolts can be discerned but these, naturally, were almost simultaneous rather than successive. One was the relatively smooth transfer of power at the top from James II to William of Orange; the other, less crucial but not inconsequential, involved widespread and alarming mob-violence which appeared to be pushing the kingdom close to anarchy—though this danger was more apparent than real.

When John Evelyn wrote "It looks like a Revolution" he was referring to happenings at the top,[2] not among the lower orders, and their machinations are perhaps best seen as "a catalyst for the *acceptance* of the Revolution",[3] enabling William to be viewed as a deliverer from nationwide turmoil as well as from popery and slavery while James was seen as the deserter who had abandoned his people to chaos. "Bless God and Honour the Very Name of the Prince of Orange", the citizens of riot-torn Bury St Edmunds were urged, "for Establishing of the general Peace and greatest Tranquility",[4] prior to which the beleaguered London Catholics had been reported as yearning for the prince to come and rescue them from the attentions of the "detestable populace".[5] The comfortable adjectives which customarily qualify the Revolution—bloodless, bourgeois, aristocratic, sensible, respectable, happy and glorious (and, now, acceptable)—in no way apply to the nearly nameless contrivers of nationwide disorder who added a top-dressing of violence which most of the political nation could have done without, and few contemporaries had a good word for them. "The Mob, the Scum of a Nation", they were called, "that subsides in a Calm and mounts in a

---

1 1980 reprint, with new Preface.
2 E.S. De Beer (ed.), *The Diary of John Evelyn* (1955), 4, p. 609.
3 P.E. Murrell, "Bury St Edmunds and the Campaign to Pack Parliament, 1687-8", in *Bulletin of the Institute of Historical Research*, 54 (1981), p. 202 (my italics).
4 Cited *ibid.*
5 M. Hopkirk, *The Queen Over the Water* (1953), p. 162.

Storm" and "this Indigested Lump, the Rabble. . . who see all things double, and yet can discern no further than they can throw a millstone".[6]

The study of "no-popery" violence at the time of the Revolution has hitherto gone into most detail over London though with some mention of events outside the capital[7] and it is the purpose of these pages to look a little more closely at what occurred in the provinces and to touch on various related matters. Anti-Catholicism motivating the mob was one ingredient in the "turbulence natural to an agrarian society in which grinding poverty was the lot of most men"[8] but only occasionally did it erupt into serious violence; it was to some extent channelled fairly peacefully into organised demonstrations and ritualised pope-burnings, "the really significant point" about which "is that when they were over people went home quietly—or if not quietly, without loss of life or notable destruction of property"[9] and it is perhaps noteworthy that the wholesale opening of Catholic chapels following James II's first Declaration of Indulgence evoked verbal rather than violent opposition[10] and that major building work on prominent town sites could proceed undisturbed[11]—as could Bishop Leyburn on a protracted and extensive visitation in the summer and autumn of 1687.[12]

But in May 1688 a prescient Lincolnshire farmer noted in his journal, "If sum thing that is remarkable do not cume to pas before Mielmas next

---

6 Descriptions, respectively, by L. Echard, *History of the Revolution* (1725), p. 197, and the author of *Guido Faux Reviv'd or the Monks Late Hellish Contrivance Expos'd* (1688; printed in *The Downside Review*, 13 [1894], pp. 261-3).

7 See Macaulay, *History of England* (various editions), chap. 9; B. Magee, "The Protestant Wind", in *The Month*, 177 (1941), pp. 334-48; M. Beloff, *Public Order and Popular Disturbances, 1660-1714* (1938), pp. 40-4; J. Miller, *Popery and Politics in England, 1660-1688* (1973), pp. 259-61 and Dr Miller's "The Militia and the Army in the Reign of James II", in *The Historical Journal*, 16 (1973), pp. 673-9; R.A. Beddard, "The Catholic Fear", in the expanded version of Sir Winston Churchill's *History of the English-Speaking Peoples* (ed. Sir M. Wheeler, H. Trevor-Roper & A.J.P. Taylor, 1967-71), pp. 1866-70; W.L. Sachse, "The Mob and the Revolution of 1688", in *The Journal of British Studies*, 4 (1964), pp. 23-40 (and in G.M. Straka, ed., *The Revolution of 1688*, 2nd edn., 1973, pp. 26-41); L.G. Schwoerer, *The Declaration of Rights, 1689* (1981), pp. 129-31.

8 J.H. Plumb, *The Growth of Political Stability in England, 1675-1725* (1967), p. 19; Beloff, *op.cit.*, p. 40. See also G. Rudé, *Ideology and Popular Protest* (1980), pp. 28-9.

9 K.D. Haley, *The First Earl of Shaftesbury* (1968), p. 454.

10 One such critic was the dissenter George Trosse of Exeter; see G. Oliver, *Collections Illustrating the History of the Catholic Religion in Cornwall, Devon, Dorset, Somerset, Wiltshire and Gloucester* (1857), p. 366; also *D.N.B.*

11 E.g. by the Franciscans at Birmingham and by the Jesuits at Wigan and Durham; see W.P.W. Phillimore, J.L. Whitfield & P.E. Williams (eds.), *Warwickshire Parish Registers*, 2 (1904), pp. 4-5; Foley, 5, pp. 319, 650.

12 T.A. Birrell (ed.), *A Newsletter for Students of Recusant History*, 4 (Nijmegen, 1962), pp. 16-21: "Bishop Leyburn's Visitation in 1687", by T.B. Trappes-Lomax.

it is a sine that all that hath bene knowne befor is vain"[13] and by Michaelmas crisis-point was indeed looming. Since May there had occurred the three weeks' drama of the Seven Bishops, fuelling and re-fuelling anti-Catholic feeling, and the birth of an heir to the throne had introduced permanence into the prospect of popery-cum-arbitrary government on the French model. The continuing "regulation" of corporations violated valued local and personal prerogatives and franchises, as did royal interference with the lieutenancy and the rural magistracy; in some towns where large numbers of soldiers were quartered the citizens came to hate "both them and the cause they were embarked in"[14] and James's bringing over of Irish troops aroused dismay and disgust which reports of their unruliness reinforced. The king's belated bid for Anglican support in the face of invasion meant the disintegration of the Catholic ascendancy as he put his policies into reverse, restoring charters, assenting to a free (and Catholic-free) parliament, dismissing papists from official positions—not in every case recently usurped from Anglicans.[15] This abrupt eclipse of Catholic influence gave rise to hostile demonstrations and to official anticipation of more to come. At Norwich, where five years earlier French protestants had been attacked in mistake for papists, Sunday 14 October saw two scenes of disorder at the Catholic chapel;[16] at Cambridge, already reported by the royal agents to be of "uncertain temper", the mayor, a Catholic convert, was assaulted[17] and to Gloucester, where Brother Richard Reeve, O.S.B., had just been appointed to the Bluecoat school and a Dominican earlier spoken of as successor to a deceased prebendary,[18] there came a royal command that the Catholic chapel and its incumbent be protected.[19] The Gloucester chapel had been established in March 1687 with financial support from

13 M. Connel, "Mr Fulbeck's Journal, 1688-91", part 2, in *The Local Historian* (bi-monthly broadsheet of Lindsey Local History Society, Lincs., not the current journal of that title), no. 10 (Nov., 1936, unpaginated).
14 J. Childs, *The Army, James II and the Glorious Revolution* (Manchester, 1980), p. 87.
15 As Sir Edward Sherburne, poet and translator, complained when ejected from his ancient freehold of clerk of the ordnance which he had held, not uninterruptedly, since succeeding his father (who died in 1641) in that post; see *D.N.B.*; C.D. Sherborn, *History of the Family of Sherborn* (1901), pp. 84-6.
16 *C.S.P.D., July-Sept. 1683*, p. 363; *June 1687-Feb. 1689*, p. 316.
17 H.M.C., *12th Rep., App. 7*, p. 216; *V.C.H. Cambridgeshire*, 3, p. 213.
18 A. Wood, *Athenae Oxonienses* (ed. P. Bliss), 4 (1820), cols. 386-8 (Reeve); Luttrell, p. 405 ("Mr Littleton"; see next footnote); J. Le Neve, *Fasti Ecclesiae Anglicanae* (ed. T. Duffus Hardy, 1854), 1, pp. 449, 450 (death of Preb. Thomas Washborne and his replacement by Luke Beaulieu, 6 & 21 May 1687).
19 *C.S.P.D., June 1687-Feb. 1689*, p. 342, naming Littleton as incumbent. He was a Dominican (*vere* Gervase Pius Westcote); see W. Gumbley, *Obituary Notices of the English Dominicans, 1555-1952* (1955), p. 53.

the king; a similarly subsidised chapel existed at Portsmouth[20] where there were successive outbursts of ill-feeling between the citizens and the Irish soldiery who were reported, among other misdeeds, to have attacked the mayor, committed robberies and broken into an alehouse and one of whom laid an information against a comrade's landlady alleging that she had said of the youthful Governor (the eighteen-year-old Duke of Berwick) and of the Irish that "the Duke was a rogue and the King was a fool for sending such fellows thither".[21]

Meanwhile, November and early December saw the takeover of much territory by William of Orange and his adherents. His own entry into Exeter on 9 November was followed by the demolition of the Masshouse, the hounding, in harrowing weather, of its Jesuit incumbent, attacks on Catholics' houses and the seizure of Catholic hostages.[22] Plymouth came over to William on 24 November, its garrison-chaplain being imprisoned in the citadel, and early in December it was reported that a Devonshire Catholic mansion had been plundered.[23]

On the first of that month Bristol fell—a stubborn soil in which Catholicism had made little progress. The city's record of opposition to James II and his policies drove the Duke of Beaufort to lament "the King knows what kind of place Bristol is" and to declare that nineteen out of twenty of its citizens were hostile to the king and that it could not be held for him.[24] Early in the reign troops, formerly at Tangier, had been quartered in the city following Monmouth's rebellion, arousing much hostility by their "insolence, rapacity and debauchery";[25] in December 1685 two candidates had opposed the court's nominee in a parliamentary election and one of them had won. The other, Sir John Knight, described by Luttrell as "a violent Tory" (with the accent on "violent") earned further official disfavour and eventually arrest, when in the following Spring he stormed about Bristol with a blunderbuss "to the terrifying his

---

20 Luttrell, p. 396; J.Y. Akerman, *Moneys Received and Paid for Secret Services of Charles II and James II* (Camden Society, 1851), p. 184 (both chapels).

21 A.J. Willis & M.J. Hoad (eds.), *Borough Sessions Papers, 1653-88* (Portsmouth Record Series, 1, 1971), p. 143; H.M.C., *12th Rep., App. 7*, pp. 213-4. On civil-military relations at Portsmouth, see also Childs, *op.cit.*, p. 99.

22 Oliver, *op.cit.*, pp. 366-7; Foley, 5, p. 971 (the priest was Richard Norris, S.J.); A. Jenkins, *Civil and Ecclesiastical History of the City of Exeter* (2nd edn., Exeter, 1841), p. 188, note; Luttrell, p. 477 (the hostages were intended as security for William's supporter Lord Lovelace, captured at Cirencester on 11 November, imprisoned at Gloucester and subsequently rescued; see *infra.*, p. 251).

23 *The English Currant*, 26 December 1688 (Plymouth); H.M.C., *Hastings MSS.*, 2, p. 203 (Ugbrooke, seat of Lord Clifford of Chudleigh). The Plymouth chaplain was Christopher Turner, a secular priest (Anstruther, 3, p. 235).

24 *C.S.P.D., June 1687-Feb. 1689*, p. 325; S.B. Baxter, *William III* (1966), p. 239.

25 Childs, *op.cit.*, p. 88.

Majesty's subjects", laid an information against an Irish priest and took the lead in apprehending him and some of his congregation.[26] Ten months later, and six weeks before the first Declaration of Indulgence, Catholic worship in Bristol received royal backing in a command that premises be provided and the priest not impeded in his ministry within and around the city.[27] A chapel was indeed established and, on Bristol's transfer to the Orange camp, was gutted by the mob who also sacked Catholics' houses.[28]

This was at the beginning of December, by which time other areas had already fallen to William. On 22 November the stage-managed scare of a papist rising enabled Danby to secure York, where half a dozen Catholic chapels had sprung up and a Catholic bishop been installed (while its own archbishopric was vacant). The chapels were attacked, the bishop put to flight and priests imprisoned.[29] Lay Catholics' premises were searched for concealed priests and ransacked for arms and horses; into Danby's hands came confiscated Catholic property and intercepted Catholic correspondence, some of it mildly incriminating, including a letter, which he asked her to burn after reading it, from a priest to his aunt in Durham requesting his "cap and crucifix".[30] The priests imprisoned at York were joined by confrères from elsewhere (including two Jesuits from Lincoln), some of them doubtless the subjects of Danby's memorandum of 28 November, "The priests to be sent to the gaole to-morrow";[31] six others

26 Luttrell, pp. 377-8 (trial and acquittal of the priest, John Osyllivant), 379 (comment on Knight); *Autobiography of Sir John Bramston* (Camden Society, 1845), pp. 225-6; H.M.C., *14th Rep., App. 2*, p. 172; *C.S.P.D., Jan. 1686-May 1687*, p. 118; *D.N.B.*, sub Sir John Knight "the Younger".

27 *C.S.P.D., Jan. 1686-May 1687*, p. 373: 24 Feb. 1687 re Anthony Matthews, but whether he actually took up the Bristol incumbency seems doubtful; a priest of that name was serving as a camp-chaplain on Hounslow Heath from March 1687 to March 1688 (Akerman, *op.cit.*, pp. 169, 182, 197). At the same time as the Bristol appointment, Peter Gooden was named for Chester (*C.S.P.D.*, *loc.cit.*); in August, however the king was still pressing for the provision of "a convenient place... in the castle or elsewhere, for the Roman Catholics' devotions": *Diary of Bishop Cartwright* (Camden Society, 1893) p. 76—a provision doubtless terminated on the fall of the garrison in December 1688. For Gooden, see Anstruther, 3, pp. 79-81.

28 J. Latimer, *Annals of Bristol: 18th Century* (Bristol, 1900), p. 451; Luttrell, p. 482.

29 Earlier versions of these events are superseded by Mr John Aveling's account in his *Catholic Recusancy in the City of York, 1558-1791* (C.R.S. Monograph series, no. 2), pp. 103-6. The bishop was the Vicar-Apostolic of the Northern District, Dr James Smith.

30 H.M.C., *11th Rep. App. 7*, p. 26: from N. Colston at Mrs Hammond's, Towton, to Mrs Bridget Foster, New Elvet. For Colston, a Benedictine, see H.N. Birt, *Obit Book of the English Benedictines, 1600-1912* (1970 reprint with Introduction by D.M. Lunn), p. 68. For other matters mentioned, see A. Browning (ed.), *The Memoirs of Sir John Reresby* (Glasgow, 1936), p. 531; Browning, *Thomas Osborne, Earl of Danby* (Glasgow, 1951) 1, p. 404.

31 *Ibid.*, 1, p. 401; Foley, 5, p. 730 (Lincoln Jesuits).

perhaps forwarded from Hull, a base for "daily quest after more", and at Christmas the York mob mounted a terrifying demonstration against the prisoners.[32]

Earlier, their now precarious plight had sent East Riding Catholics flocking into Hull,[33] a garrison-town blessed with a Catholic governor, Lord Langdale, and some Catholic troops but which contained few other of their co-religionists and had an unencouraging reputation and a tense atmosphere. For an earlier governor, the Duke of Monmouth, support lingered in 1685, in 1686 the sheriff and his officers declined to accompany a Catholic assize-judge to his chapel, in 1687 a Hull bookseller was suspected of handling seditious literature and in the summer of 1688 the ministers of the two city churches were reported by Langdale for refusing to read the second Declaration of Indulgence.[34] Less episodic were mounting resentment at the billeting on its "already stretched accommodation" of over a thousand extra troops and at the requirement that a man from every household should work for at least ten days on the fortifications.[35] But the enemy was already within: Langdale was seized "at Supper, with many Gentlemen and abundance of Priests" for whom the city, after all, proved no sanctuary. A mob promptly "fell upon the Mass-house and all the houses of Papists in the Town which they Ransacked and Demolished" in the small hours of the morning; that day, 4 December, all the shops stayed shut and the Prince of Orange's colours flew upon Holy Trinity Church (near which his statue still stands).[36] The local Bench, alarmed at the excesses of "Town-taking Day", denounced the vandalism and the protestant troops were warned against any recurrence of lawlessness.[37]

Meanwhile, Lord Delamere, having raised support for William in the north-west and proceeded to the midlands, became the subject of scarifying rumours which aroused in Catholics something akin to the

---

32 *The English Currant*, 26 December 1688—possibly misleading in implying that further priests were still to be found in the Hull area; Foley, *loc.cit.*

33 *Letters of Lady Rachel Russell* (6th edn., 1801), p. 187; Aveling, *Post-Reformation Catholicism in East Yorkshire, 1558-1790* (East Yorks. Local History Society, 1960), p. 49.

34 E. Gillett, *East Yorkshire and North Lincolnshire, 1660-1688* (Hull University Department of Adult Education, Studies in Regional and Local History, no. 1, 1981), pp. 69-70; J. Tickell, *History of the Town and County of Kingston upon Hull* (Hull, 1796), p. 573 (*re* judge Allibone, for whom see *D.N.B.*); *C.S.P.D., June 1687-Feb. 1689*, pp. 166, 219.

35 Childs, *op.cit.*, pp. 110-1, 182.

36 Bodleian Library Oxford: fol. Theta 590 (43): *Great News from Nottingham the Fifth of December 1688*; *The History of the Late Revolution in England, With the Causes and Means by which it was Accomplished* (1689), pp. 165-6.

37 E. Gillett & K.A. MacMahon, *A History of Hull* (1980), p. 185.

terror later produced in protestants by the Irish alarms—of which he was reported to be circulating his own version ("French and Irish. . . to be poured into the Kingdom to massacre Protestants") three weeks before the curtain went up on Running Thursday.[38] In the hands of Catholics common-or-garden cutlery acquired a sinister aura (the procurator of a Jesuit house could not equip it with knives and forks without being arrested)[39] and the rumour that Delamere "got at one Abby 140 strange sort of knives, 60 swords and belts, as many pikes"[40] is perhaps more significant for its recording than for its content. The "Abby" is not identified but one notable sufferer from Delamere's attentions was the new Franciscan establishment at Birmingham which was "defaced and most of it burnt within" on 26 November, then finished off a week later by "the Rabble of Birmingham".[41] By that time, against a background of further Catholic fears prompted by the spurious *Third Declaration* of William of Orange, ostensibly lending his support to wholesale attacks on them,[42] Delamere's freelance revolution was coming to an end. His force was merged with the Orange army, pausing at Hungerford on its eastward advance and shortly to pass near the Eystons' chapel at East Hendred which some of the soldiers visited and vandalised.[43]

This was on 11 December, a date on which the *Universal Intelligence* listed ten places where chapels had by then been destroyed, among them York, Bristol, Birmingham and Gloucester, already mentioned. Gloucester had undergone a second upheaval following Delamere's arrival, when the liberation of William's ally, Lord Lovelace, prompted attacks on the Catholic chapel and on papists' houses. The priest took Lovelace's place in gaol, whither Brother Reeve was later conveyed after being captured in the house of the Catholic Recorder of Gloucester.[44] Meanwhile some of the Gloucester mob had visited Sir William Compton's house at Hart-

---

38 H.M.C., *12th Rep., App. 7*, p. 222; for Running Thursday, so-called, according to Brewer, because "many people ran for their lives [from the Irish] into the country", see his *Dictionary of Phrase and Fable* (revised edition, 1981, ed. I.H. Evans), p. 977. For events in the midlands and the north, see D.H. Hosford, *Nottingham, Nobles and the North* (Hamden, Conn., U.S.A., 1976) and Browning, *Danby*, chap. 17, largely superseding A.C. Wood, "The Revolution of 1688 in the North of England", in *Transactions of the Thoroton Society*, 44 (Nottingham, 1941).

39 Foley, 5, p. 732.

40 H.M.C., *15th Rep., App. 2*, p. 75 (4 Dec. 1688).

41 Phillimore, Whitfield & Williams, *op.cit.*, p. 15.

42 The *Declaration* was claimed as his own production by Hugh Speke but may "be the work of Ferguson or Johnson" (*C.S.P.D., June 1687-Feb. 1689*, p. 365, note 2). For Speke, Robert Ferguson and Samuel Johnson (1649-1703), see *D.N.B.*

43 B. Camm, *Forgotten Shrines* (1936 edition), p. 348; A.L. Humphreys, *East Hendred* (1923) p. 251; Thaddeus, *The Franciscans in England* (1897), p. 296.

44 Charles Trinder of Bourton-on-the-Water (Wood, *Ath. Oxon.*, *cit.*); *The English Currant*, 14 Dec. 1688: a lengthy report.

pury "where they destroy'd his Chappell, plunder'd the House and committed many illegal things".[45]

Of other chapels reported destroyed before 11 December, those at Wolverhampton, Bury St Edmunds and Worcester (entered by Delamere *en route* from Birmingham to Gloucester) belonged to three regional headquarters of the Society of Jesus. From Wolverhampton, where (either then or later in the month) there were fatalities when the chapel was attacked, two of the Fathers fled to Lancashire and a third was captured and imprisoned;[46] at Bury St Edmunds violence to the Society's premises in the old Abbey precincts occurred against a background of local resentment at the "regulating" manoeuvres of Lord Dover and the mayor who was rumoured to be in "an horrid Popish Plot for the burning, blowing up and destroying" of the town,[47] and at Worcester where there were three chapels, one of them a private one in Sir Isaac Gibson's house, the Carmelites' as well as the Jesuits' property was assailed.[48]

Both Narcissus Luttrell and the *Universal Intelligence* mention anti-Catholic violence in Shropshire in early December[49] and the latter adds Stafford and Cambridge. At Stafford where, as in other towns, "politics and religion became entangled" in James II's reign, there was an attack on the Catholic chapel, then in the charge of the influential secular priest Daniel Fitter on the site of the dissolved priory of St Thomas where he had also opened a school.[50] At Cambridge, unreliable politically and resentful of royal interference in university affairs, the end of November saw an onslaught on the chapel of Sidney Sussex college, obnoxiously associated with James II's nominee Alban Francis O.S.B., where vestments were burned and altar plate smashed. The mob also invaded "Bennett's College" (Corpus Christi), individuals were threatened and humiliated and an unsympathetic alderman's windows broken.[51]

---

45 *Ibid.*; the house and its owner, "Sir . . . Compton", are not there precisely identified; for Sir Henry Compton of Hartpury (and of Hindlip, Worcs.) see "G.E.C.", *Complete Baronetage*, 4, p. 141.

46 Foley, 5, p. 420; Wolverhampton constables' accounts, 1688-9 (transcript kindly provided by Dr M. Rowlands) recording expenses in connection with an inquest "on the persons killed at the chappell".

47 Murrell, *art.cit.*, p. 202 & *passim*; Luttrell, p. 483; Foley, 5, pp. 537-8; J. Rowe, *The Story of Catholic Bury St Edmunds* (Bury St Edmunds, 1959), pp. 10-11.

48 T.G. Holt, "The Residence of St George . . . ", in *Worcestershire Recusant*, 20 (Worcester, 1972), pp. 65-8; B. Zimmerman, *Carmel in England* (1899), pp. 334-6.

49 Shropshire (Luttrell, p. 484, 7 Dec. 1688); Shrewsbury (*Universal Intelligence*, 11 Dec.).

50 M. Greenslade in *V.C.H., Staffordshire*, 3, p. 107; Greenslade, *St Austin's, Stafford* (Stafford, 1962), pp. 7-8.

51 H.M.C., *12th Rep., App. 7*, p. 226 (newsletter of 4 Dec. 1688, stating that these

At Oxford, from whose colleges the Catholic appointees had fled, one of them was waylaid and beaten up in the street.[52] Catholics' windows were broken (notably those of the "Mitre" whose landlord's undiplomatic utterances had aroused fury); Catholic prisoners, including a priest, were paraded by Lovelace, some of whose "rusty ruffians" broke down an arch of Magdalen Bridge, and Catholic houses were searched for arms.[53]

Early December was also marked by anti-Catholic disturbances in Newcastle and Durham, both served by seculars as well as by Jesuits (and Newcastle perhaps by a Benedictine too).[54] One report mentions the desecration, though not the destruction, of a chapel in the latter city; the mob "pull'd down the Trinkets in the Mass-house and would have secured the Priests had they not run away" but the building itself was appropriated by a troupe of entertainers.[55] Here, as elsewhere, Catholics had been placed on the corporation by the King whose acclaiming in a Jesuit sermon before the Catholic mayor as "James the Just" may not have commanded much local enthusiasm—and whose statue was later overthrown by the mob.[56]

At Lincoln and Norwich also these days were marked by violence and incendiarism; the Jesuits' chapels in both cities were burned, as were their school at Lincoln and Catholics' houses at Norwich where the city

---

events occurred "on Friday last", *i.e.* 30 November*); *V.C.H. Cambridgeshire*, 3, pp. 213, 374. *A calendar for 1688 is printed in the Royal Historical Society's *Handbook of Dates* (ed. C.R. Cheney, corrected edn., 1970), pp. 132-3.

52 Thomas Fairfax, or Beckett, S.J., lately of Magdalen (Foley, 5, pp. 822, 956).

53 Bodleian Library: MS. Smith 141, p. 38; S.W. Singer (ed.), *The Correspondence of Edward Hyde, Earl of Clarendon and... Laurence Hyde, Earl of Rochester* (1828), p. 223; A. Clark (ed.), *Wood's Life and Times*, 3 (Oxford Historical Society, 1894), pp. 286, 287; *Universal Intelligence*, 11 Dec. 1688; also, for security-measures taken by the city council, M.G. Hobson, *Oxford Council Acts, 1665-1701* (Oxf. Hist. Soc., 1939), p. 206.

54 For Newcastle, see V. Smith, *Catholic Tyneside* (Newcastle, 1930), p. 48 and A.M.C. Forster in *Northern Catholic History*, 10 (Newcastle, 1979), p. 15 (*re* Joseph Bernard Greaves, O.S.B., for whom see also Birt, *op.cit.*, p. 80); also Foley, 5, p. 662 ("the times having been such that all papers are destroyed"). For Durham, see *V.C.H., Durham*, 2, p. 59; Foley, 5, pp. 650-1; 7, pp. c (Pearson, the Jesuit superior in 1687, misprinted as "Parsons"), 575, 578-9; J.M. Tweedy, *Popish Elvet* (Durham, 1981), pp. 63-4.

55 Bodleian Library: fol. Theta 590(43): *Great News from Nottingham the Fifth of December 1688*, also cited by Beloff, *op.cit.*, p. 41.

56 J. Gillow, *A Literary and Biographical History, or Bibliographical Dictionary of the English Catholics*, 4, p. 193 for the sermon, not an abrasive one, on the day of public thanksgiving for the Queen's pregnancy. There is a valuable account of "the intertwining of local grievance with general national policy" in R. Howell, "Newcastle and the nation: the seventeenth-century experience", in *Archaeologia Aeliana*, 5th series, 8 (1980), pp. 26-30.

fathers' ban on the erection of a stage for the sale of an "antidote against poison and other medicines...for preserving the peace of the city only", had not had the desired effect.[57]

In Kent, a county particularly edgy on account of the numerous Catholics endeavouring to escape through it, and not rendered less jittery by the assertion that the Irish would come to the rescue of those who had been captured,[58] Dover castle was seized and on 10 December a mob from Canterbury burned the house of Sir Edward Hales (the subject of the collusive case in 1686 which had opened the floodgates to Catholic appointments, and about to be the king's companion in his flight and capture) and the Rochester mob vandalised Mr Lee's house and attacked that of Mr Kingsley. The latter was chaplain to Lord Teynham of Linstead Lodge; both he and his master fled, Teynham to give himself up to the authorities, Kingsley to fall into the hands of the mob.[59]

11 December 1688, the date of the *Universal Intelligence* issue already mentioned (whose coverage of anti-Catholic activities was neither all-embracing nor, as Anthony Wood noted, particularly accurate)[60] was also the day of James II's first flight. Upon the news of this, and of the partial disbanding of his army and the turning loose of Irish troops, were superimposed nationwide rumours of Irish massacres and burnings, everywhere reported to have occurred at a place some miles distant.[61] Although some contemporaries were dismissive almost from the start (as was the Duchess of Beaufort over various Berkshire and Wiltshire alarms)[62] many took the stories seriously. The Bristol city chamberlain paid £5. 9s. "for powder when the report was that the Irish that was disbanded were coming to this city and did great cruelties wherever they goeth",[63] the Leicester accounts contain disbursements for hiring horses "to scout abroad severall waies upon the roades about the towne" and

---

57 H.M.C., *5th Rep.*, p. 198; Foley, 5, pp. 560, 621; Sir F. Hill, *Tudor and Stuart Lincoln* (1956), p. 191; J.T. Evans, *Seventeenth-Century Norwich* (1974), p. 316; W. Rye (ed.) *Depositions before the Mayor and Aldermen. . . and Extracts from the Council Books of the City of Norwich* (Norwich, 1905), p. 185: permission first granted to Cornelius Tilbourne "to erect a stage at the Halls end", then cancelled (5 Dec. 1688), because "it is feared... it will draw such a concourse of people &c". See also *C.S.P.D., 1689-90*, p. 111.

58 Sir John Knatchbull's diary, 11 Dec. 1688, cited by P.C. Vellacott, "The Diary of a Country Gentleman in 1688" in *The Cambridge Historical Journal*, 2 (1926), p. 58.

59 H.M.C., *11th Rep., App. 5*, p. 228; *12th Rep., App. 7*, p. 228; *Universal Intelligence*, 15 Dec. 1688; *London Mercury and Moderate Intelligencer*, 22 Dec. 1688; Foley, 5, pp. 309-10 (Thomas Kingsley, *alias* de Bois, S.J.).

60 *Life & Times* (ed. Clark), 3, p. 287, notes 1-6: half a dozen corrections to Oxford report.

61 For some examples, see Magee, *art.cit.*

62 H.M.C., *12th Rep., App. 9*, pp. 92-3.

63 Latimer, *loc.cit.*

for riding to Market Harborough, Northampton and elsewhere "to bring intelligence concerning the truth of the Irish marching this way"[64] and far out towards the Lincolnshire coast the constables of Hogsthorpe recorded expenditure on fitting scythe-blades into shafts, providing coal for the watch and "for going about to give all men notis to arme themselves".[65] In this highly charged atmosphere anti-Catholic violence broke out afresh: at Norwich all householders were ordered to "keep in their servants and children that they do not join with the tumult that disturb the peace of the city";[66] at Chesterfield Catholics were rounded up;[67] Carlton was invaded by a large posse who consumed quantities of Sir Miles Stapleton's food and drink before taking him "and all my Catholicke men prisoners";[68] from Lincolnshire it was reported that "the rabble plunder and affront our neighbour Catholics every day".[69] Near Kettering, however, young Joseph Perry, then still a Catholic, feared he would be killed by the mythical Irish marauders.[70]

In the days following James's withdrawal, as well as urban Catholics and their property, the country houses of persons associated with his regime were attacked, as were a few other Catholic houses with chapels recently and openly added. Such were Hoar Cross in Staffordshire where the new chapel was burned, Mr Howard's deer killed or turned loose and himself and his priest threatened,[71] and Coughton Court, Warwicks., where "the newly erected Catholic church" in the east wing was demolished by a mob from Alcester.[72]

In Northamptonshire the house and chapel of the recently converted Earl of Peterborough were pillaged and the estate searched for arms—insolence which perturbed his son-in-law the protestant Duke of Norfolk, whose vested interest in the contents of the house prompted him to

64 J.E. Stocks & W.H. Stevenson, *Records of the Borough of Leicester, 1603-88* (1923), pp. 593-4.
65 Lincolnshire Archives Office, Lincoln: Hogsthorpe Par. 12, f. 2 (kindly transcribed by Miss G.T.Y. Moyes).
66 Rye (ed.), *Depositions before the Mayor* . . . , p. 186, where also two associated indictments are noted.
67 H.M.C., *11th Rep., App. 7*, p. 28, but with "Chester" for Chesterfield—corrected in Browning, *Danby*, 2, p. 155, note 2.
68 University of Hull, Brynmor Jones Library: DDCA (2) 48/10, p. 94. See also J.C. Cox, "The Household Books of Sir Miles Stapleton, Bart., 1656-1705", in *The Ancestor*, pts. 1 & 2 (1902), pp. 17-39, 132-62 respectively (p. 31 for relevant extract).
69 Cited by C. Holmes, *Seventeenth-Century Lincolnshire* (Lincoln, 1980), p. 252.
70 *The Life and Miraculous Conversion from Popery of Mr Joseph Perry* (2nd edn., 1727), p. 15.
71 H.M.C., *Hastings MSS.*, 2, p. 211. The priest was perhaps John Bradstreet, for whom see Anstruther, 2, p. 35.
72. *Coughton Court, Warwickshire* (National Trust guide, 1967), p. 5; J. Kirk, *Biographies of English Catholics, 1700-1800* (ed. J.H. Pollen & E. Burton, 1909), p. 234.

request its protection. "Perhaps", he wrote to Sir Justinian Isham, "if the rabble knew my concern in the house, who am not, I hope, so odious to them as the present owner, they might use it a little better".[73] The weapons, however, were removed and carried into the council chamber at Northampton.[74] Local protestant zeal did not confine itself to this raid on Drayton; closer to the county town "the mobile pulled down another gentleman's house", perhaps Mr Hind's at Moulton Park with its septuagenarian secular chaplain.[75]

In Hertfordshire Lord Aston's mansion at Standon, where there was a tradition of extremely lavish housekeeping, was pillaged following news that he had "stor'd up great quantities of Provisions"[76] and in the same county an attack on Hatfield was prevented by the militia; this was the seat of the obese and unpopular fourth Earl of Salisbury, a convert whose Salisbury House complex in London had earlier been embellished with this piece of doggerel:

"If Cecil the wise
From his grave should arise
And see this fat brute in his place,
He would take him from Mass
And turn him to grass
And swear he was not of his race".[77]

At Chevely in Cambridgeshire Lord Dover's estate was despoiled by the combined mobs of Cambridge and Bury St Edmunds (where his regulating activities have already been noted)[78] and in Monmouth an important Catholic house was plundered by a gang headed by a local parson on horseback who carried off the altar furniture. This was the Vaughans' mansion at Courtfield, residence of the superior of the Jesuits' "college" of St Francis Xavier.[79]

Other Jesuit centres closed down were the urban ones at Pontefract, with a school and a chapel whose adornment and ceremonial Ralph Thoresby considered overdone (though he found the sermon "against

---

73 Cited by G. Isham, "Earl Marshals and Northamptonshire", in *Northamptonshire Past and Present*, 4 (1971), pp. 358-9; also H.M.C., *12th Rep., App. 7*, p. 230; Luttrell, p. 490; *The Universal Intelligence*, 26 Dec. 1688.

74 J.C. Cox (ed.), *Records of the Borough of Northampton*, 2 (Northampton, 1898), p. 478.

75 H.M.C., *12th Rep., App. 9*, p. 94; *Universal Intelligence, cit.* and, for a possible chaplain (Charles Cansfield), Anstruther, 2, pp. 42-3.

76 Sachse, *art.cit.*, p. 31; "G.E.C.", *Complete Peerage*, 1, p. 286.

77 Lord David Cecil, *The Cecils of Hatfield House* (1973), p. 198; Sachse, *loc.cit.*; L. Stone, *Family and Fortune: Studies in Aristocratic Finance in the Sixteenth and Seventeenth Centuries* (1973), p. 157.

78 Murrell, *art.cit.*, p. 202.

79 Foley, 5, pp. 893-5.

keeping bad company" very apt)[80] and at Wigan;[81] three chapels in Derbyshire were also affected, the one at North Lees being almost destroyed.[82] A similar fate overtook the Franciscans' "little sort of a residence" at Leominster and in Lancashire their property at Goosnargh was a victim.[83] From Portsmouth the priests fled, a yacht rumoured to be taking on board "a titular bishop and some priests" was searched and one priest was later said to have been captured on it.[84]

Continuing violence here and there rumbled on into late December and beyond. In Lancashire a papist's "good old house. . . with wainscott in several rooms" was burned, at Maidstone "a considerable quantity of money" was stolen from a Catholic; in the midlands a mob "killed the Deer and Comitted many other disorders at Sir James Simeon's house" at Aston.[85]

In this sketch of provincial "no-popery" violence the emphasis has been on urban events and this is hardly surprising. As has been suggested earlier some grievances were peculiar to towns, and the mob was largely an urban phenomenon. Moreover an ostentatious and sometimes abrasive Catholicism in a compact urban setting was a very different matter from the settled and reticent Catholicism of the countryside and while a handful of country houses was attacked the vast majority of rural chaplaincies appear to have escaped. Lords Peterborough, Dover and Salisbury were obvious targets; why others were attacked or (perhaps more often) spared is less clear. No doubt seigneurial bonds between landlords and dependents had something to do with it, and a wider good neighbourliness (such as protected Lulworth) and influential connections (like the Stonors' with the Earl of Shrewsbury).[86] Contrary factors were doubtless proximity to a sizeable town (though nearness to puritan

---

80 *The Diary of Ralph Thoresby* (ed. J. Hunter, 1830) 1, pp. 182-3; Foley, 5, pp. 726-32. Thoresby says that the service was conducted by a Father Norris and the sermon preached by another priest. For three Norris brothers, all Jesuits, see Foley, 7, pp. 549-51 (also note 22 above: Richard Norris S.J.).

81 Foley, 5, pp. 319, 405, significantly supplemented by J.A. Hilton, "Wigan Catholics and the policies of James II", *North West Catholic History*, 1 (Wigan, 1969), pp. 97-110.

82 *V.C.H., Derbyshire*, 2, p. 34; Foley, 5, p. 488.

83 Thaddeus, *op.cit.*, pp. 159, 186.

84 R.J. Kerr & I.D. Duncan, *The Portledge Papers* (1928), p. 57; H.M.C., *11th Rep., App. 5,* pp. 231, 235, 237; *15th Rep., App. 1,* pp. 70, 138-9.

85 H.M.C., *12th Rep., App. 7,* p. 231 (Lancs.); *London Mercury and Moderate Intelligencer*, 22 Dec. 1688 (Maidstone); Bodleian Library: MS.DD. Weld, c 13/8/2 (Aston).

86 See J. Berkeley, *Lulworth and the Welds* (Gillingham, Dorset, 1971), p. 81 and M.D.R. Leys, *Catholics in England, 1559-1829* (1961), pp. 112-3; R.J. Stonor, *Stonor: A Catholic Sanctuary in the Chilterns* (Newport, 1951), p. 280.

Ipswich seems not to have endangered Hintlesham)[87] or to a major highway, as one writer appreciated,[88] mitigated by the wintry weather and the sheer vagaries of mob-motivation. Whatever the reasons, numerous rural centres appear to have escaped (very few of the 250-odd private chaplaincies in existence fifteen years later were in the news in 1688)[89] though local research may well bring to light others which did not.

Nor was every town-chapel attacked; the one at Bath, founded before James II's reign, was left unmolested, perhaps because it was neither brand new nor a purpose-built Mass-house but an upper room in a lodging house—a redeeming link with the tourism upon which the resort was coming increasingly to rely;[90] and at Durham a pair of house-chapels seem to have escaped while the mob wrecked the Jesuits' new public Mass-house and school.[91]

Clearly consistency is not to be expected in the machinations of the mob; as Professor Sachse observes, "Particular local grudges and agrarian grievances must have determined mob reactions in some cases"[92] and so may the sheer desire for loot, to acquire something for nothing whether it was Sir Miles Stapleton's and Lord Aston's food and drink, venison from a deer-park, money at Maidstone or the miscellaneous plunder filched at sword-point from the Fermors' house at Tusmore ("being a papist's house"), concerning which one of the bizarre quartet of thieves confessed "that what he did was for want of money".[93] Nor did the mob confine themselves to attacks on property: Catholics might be assaulted in the street or waylaid by vigilante bands and hauled off to gaol, as were many of those seeking to escape through Kent. A much-travelled Irish priest who had arrived from Scandinavia and was hoping to return to Ireland *via* Whitehaven was seized in Cumberland and imprisoned[94] and when the Vicar-Apostolic of the Western District returned to London he was said to be suffering from an unspecified "indisposition caused by a long journey";[95] perhaps hazards supplemen-

---

[87] G.H. Ryan & L.J. Redstone, *Timperley of Hintlesham* (1931), p. 78.

[88] *The Hatton Correspondence*, 2 (Camden Society, 1878), p. 112.

[89] Even allowing for some changes in the meantime, this seems to suggest that a good many escaped. I have printed the early eighteenth-century list, of Catholic "persons of quality" who kept chaplains, in *Recusant History*, 12 (1973), pp. 42-8.

[90] See my *Post-Reformation Catholicism in Bath, 1559-1850*, pt. 1 (C.R.S., 65), pp. 43-4, 50-3.

[91] Tweedy, *op.cit.*, p. 64.

[92] *Art.cit.*, p. 31, note 42.

[93] M.S. Gretton (ed.), *Oxfordshire Justices of the Peace in the Seventeenth Century* (Oxfordshire Record Society, 1934), pp. 99-101.

[94] J. Raine, *Depositions from York Castle* (Surtees Society, 1861), pp. 285-6.

[95] G.A. Ellis (ed.), *The Ellis Correspondence* (1829), 2, p. 145. It has been doubted by some writers whether this bishop, Philip Michael Ellis O.S.B., ever visited his

tary to those normally attending seventeenth-century winter travel generated his resolve to quit the country and stay out of it as long as he lived.[96]

The anarchy of late-1688 was soon over; "the leaders of the coup slammed down the lid on the Revolution"[97] before the momentarily ungoverned came anywhere near becoming ungovernable and grew accustomed to "spoilinge and robbinge the noble and wealthy"[98] (and not merely Catholics and their priests) but if the brief no-popery panic did both make William of Orange more acceptable than he might otherwise have been and jostle "the leaders of the coup . . . into abandoning in their haste many concessions which they would have liked to have extracted from the new King",[99] then it is perhaps deserving of the glances directed at it in this paper—and of deeper investigation.[100]

vicariate, but a newsletter dated 31 July 1688 reported, "Last week Bishop Smith went for Yorke as did Bishop Gifford some time before for Oxford, and Bishop Ellis is going towards Wales, to preside in their several Districts and inspect those of the Romish persuasion" (H.M.C., *12th Rep., App. 5*, pt. 2, p. 120) and the wording of the Anglican bishops' memorial to James II in October 1688 suggests that all four Vicars-Apostolic were carrying out their functions some distance from London: "That he would *send* inhibitions *after* those four Romish bishops who . . . presume to exercise, within this kingdom, such jurisdictions as are . . . invested in the bishops of the church of England". This is printed in *Somers' Collection of Scarce and Valuable Tracts* (2nd edn., 1813) 9, p. 217; see also the version in the *Autobiography of Sir John Bramston* (Camden Society, 1845), p. 323. Italics mine.

96 James II thought poorly of his continued absence, see his letter to Ellis, 30 Oct. 1695, cited in my "Bishops Giffard and Ellis and the Western Vicariate", in *The Journal of Ecclesiastical History*, 15 (1964), p. 223 (also H.M.C., *Calendar of Stuart Papers*, 1, pp. 108-9).

97 L. Stone, in *Three British Revolutions, 1641, 1688, 1776* (ed. J.G.A. Pocock, Princeton, 1980), p. 64.

98 *Autobiography of Sir John Bramston*, p. 355, also cited by C. Hill, *The Century of Revolution, 1603-1714* (1961), p. 241.

99 Stone, *loc.cit.*

100 Since this paper was completed, a relevant article, "The Irish Fright of 1688: Real Violence and Imagined Massacre" by Professor G.H. Jones, has appeared in the *Bulletin of the Institute of Historical Research*, vol. 55, no. 132 (November 1982), pp. 148-153.

The following abbreviations are used:
Anstruther:G. Anstruther, *The Seminary Priests*, vols. 2 & 3 (Great Wakering, Essex, 1975, 1976).
C.R.S.: Catholic Record Society.
C.S.P.D.: *Calendar of State Papers (Domestic)*.
D.N.B.: *Dictionary of National Biography*.
Foley: H. Foley, *Records of the English Province of the Society of Jesus* (7 vols. in 8, 1877-83).
H.M.C., *Rep., App.*: Historical Manuscripts Commission, *Report, Appendix* (each as numbered).
Luttrell: Narcissus Luttrell, *A Brief Historical Relation of State Affairs* (1857), vol. 1.
V.C.H.: *Victoria History of the Counties of England.*

A CHECKLIST OF THE WRITINGS OF T.A. BIRRELL

1943 "The Study of Catholic Literature", *The Wind and The Rain* XI (2), 44-5.
1944 "The Tragedy of James Joyce", *Blackfriars* XXV, 303-6.
1945 "Education", *Convoy* III, 64-6.
1946 "The Reticence of Joseph Conrad", *Blackfriars* XXVII, 206-8.
1947 "The Problems of the Catholic Novelist", *The Downside Review* LXV, 139-54.
1948 "The Frontiers of Criticism: a Survey and a Plea for Classification", *The Downside Review* LXVI, 419-39.
   Review of R. Heppenstall, *The Double Image*, in *The Downside Review* LXVI, 102-4.
   Review of Pierre Danchin, *On Being a Student*, in *Unitas* III (76), 82-3.
   Review of E.G. Biaggini, *Progressive Exercises in Reading*, in *Scrutiny* XV, 160-1.
   Review of P. Claudel, *Lord, teach us to pray*, trans. Ruth Bethell, in *The Downside Review* LXVI, 351-2.
1949 "Some Notes on the Development of Franz Kafka", *Blackfriars* XXX, 63-8.
   "Dr. Leavis and Mr. Henry", *The Downside Review* LXVII, 358-62.
   Review of F.R. Leavis, *The Great Tradition*, in *Unitas* III (78), 107-8.
   Review of *Anthologies for Schools*, in *The Use of English* I (1), 46-50.
1950 *Catholic Allegiance and the Popish Plot. A Study of Some Writers of the Restoration Period.* Openbare les gegeven bij de aanvaarding van het ambt van lector in de Engelse literatuur aan de R.K. Universiteit te Nijmegen. Nijmegen/Utrecht.
   "Is Integrity Enough? A Study of George Orwell", *The Dublin Review* CXIV, 49-65.
   Review of A.C. Southern, *Elizabethan Recusant Prose 1559-1582*, in *The Tablet*, 11 November, 410.
1951 "Roger North and Political Morality in the Later Stuart Period", *Scrutiny* XVII, 282-98.
   "Where The Rainbow Ends: a Study of D.H. Lawrence", *The Downside Review* LXIX, 453-67.
   "The Figure of Satan in Milton and Blake", in *Satan*, London/New York: Sheed and Ward, 379-93.

Review of M. Petherick, *Restoration Rogues*, in *The Tablet*, 21 April, 313-4.

1952 Review of William Matthews, *British Diaries: An Annotated Bibliography*, in *English Studies* XXXIII, 264-6.

Review of F.R. Leavis, *The Common Pursuit*, in *The Tablet*, 16 February, 130.

Review of G.B. Harrison, *Shakespeare's Tragedies*, in *The Tablet*, 10 May, 378.

Review of H. Lüdeke, *The "Democracy" of Henry Adams and Other Essays*, in *Neophilologus* XXXVI, 188-9.

1953 *Non-Catholic Writers and Catholic Emancipation. An Aspect of Sidney Smith, Shelley, Coleridge and Cobbett.* Rede uitgesproken bij de aanvaarding van het ambt van hoogleraar in de Engelse letterkunde aan de R.K. Universiteit te Nijmegen. Nijmegen/Utrecht.

John Warner S.J., *The History of English Persecution of Catholics and the Presbyterian Plot.* Edited by Prof. T.A. Birrell, trans. The Reverend John Bligh S.J. London: The Catholic Record Society, no. 47-48, 1953-1955.

Review of J.B. Bamborough, *The Little World of Man*, in *The Downside Review* LXX, 109-11.

Review of T. Wood, *English Casuistical Divinity during the 17th Century*, in *The Downside Review* LXX, 111-12.

Review of R. Wallerstein, *Studies in 17th-Century Poetic*, in *Neophilologus* XXXVI, 123-4.

Review of R. Preston, *Chaucer*, in *The Downside Review* LXXI, 344-6.

Review of John Donne, *Essays in Divinity*, ed. E.M. Simpson, in *The Downside Review* LXXI, 346-7.

1954 Review of J.W.H. Atkins, *English Literary Criticism: 17th and 18th Centuries*, in *English Studies* XXXV, 25-7.

Review of Andrew Browning (ed.), *English Historical Documents, Vol. VIII: 1660-1714*, in *The Dublin Review* CXVIII, 221-3.

Review of E.M.W. Tillyard, *The English Epic and Its Background*, in *The Tablet*, 21 August, 183.

1955 "Latter-day Recusants", *The Dublin Review* CXIX, 262-74.

F. van der Meer, *Atlas of Western Civilization.* English version by T.A. Birrell. Amsterdam: Elsevier Publishing Co.

"Marvell's 'A Dialogue Between Soul and Body'", *The Downside Review* LXXIII, 174-83.

Review of F.R. Leavis, *D.H. Lawrence: Novelist*, in *The Tablet*, 1 October, 325.

Review of Eugene Vinaver (ed.), *The Works of Sir Thomas Malory*, in *English Studies* XXXVI, 332.

Review of E.N.W. Mottram, *American Studies in Europe*, in *English Studies* XXXVI, 333.

1956 "Sarbiewski, Watts and the Later Metaphysical Tradition", *English Studies* XXXVII, 125-32.

"The Animal Fable and Augustan Literature", *Handelingen van het Vierentwintigste Nederlands Filologencongres*, Groningen, p. 56.

Review of David V. Erdman, *Blake: Prophet against Empire*, in *English Studies* XXXVII, 84-5.

Review of R.T. Petersson, *Sir Kenelm Digby*, in *The Tablet*, 9 June, 544-5.

1957 Review of Claude Colleer Abbott (ed.), *Gerard Manley Hopkins. Further Letters*, in *English Studies* XXXVIII, 225-6.

1958 "English Catholics without a Bishop, 1655-1672", *Recusant History* IV, 142-78.

"The Shakespearian Mixture: Recent Approaches to Shakespeare's Handling of the Comic and Tragic Kinds", *Museum* LXIII (2), 97-111.

A Newsletter for Students of Recusant History, no. 1. Nijmegen.

A Register of Students of Recusant History. Nijmegen.

Review of Joyce Bazire and Eric Colledge (eds.), *The Chastising of God's Children and The Treatise of Perfection of the Sons of God*, in *English Studies* XXXIX, 259-61.

Review of J.A. Reynolds, *Catholic Emancipation Crisis in Ireland 1823-29*, in *The Dublin Review* CXXII, 189-91.

1959 Edition of Jacques Brousse, *The Lives of Ange de Joyeuse and Benet Canfield*. Edited from Robert Rookwood's translation of 1623. London/New York: Sheed and Ward.

"Eighteenth-Century Recusants", *The Tablet*, 31 January, 106.

A Newsletter for Students of Recusant History, no. 2. Nijmegen.

"De Verantwoordelijkheid van de Literaire Criticus", *Nijmeegs Universiteitsblad* VIII (20), 1-2.

Review of A. Gerstner-Hirzel, *The Economy of Action and Word in Shakespeare's Plays*, in *Museum* LXIV (2), 113-4.

1960 F. van der Meer, *Atlas of Western Civilization*. English version by T.A. Birrell. Second, revised edition. Princeton, N.J.: D. Van Nostrand Co.

Review of R.L. Drain, *Tradition and D.H. Lawrence*, in *English Studies* XLI, 394-5.

1961 "John Dryden's Purchases at Two Book Auctions, 1680 and 1682", *English Studies* XLII, 193-217.

Geschiedenis van de Engelse Literatuur (trans. C.E.M. Heijnen). Utrecht/Antwerpen: Spectrum.

A Newsletter for Students of Recusant History, no.3. Nijmegen.

1962 "Engelse literaire critiek op zoek naar een methodologie. Opmerkingen omtrent enige recente tendenzen in Engelse en Amerikaanse universiteiten", *Forum der Letteren* III, 166-76.

"Modern English Literary Criticism", *Levende Talen*, no.215, 342-51.

A Newsletter for Students of Recusant History, no. 4. Nijmegen.

Review of M.S. Røstvig, *The Happy Man. Studies in the Metamorphosis of a Classical Idea II, 1700-1760*, in *English Studies* XLIII, 127-8.

Review of B.H. Rasmussen, *The Transition from Manuscript to Printed Book*, in *Neophilologus* XLVI, 328.

Review of Richard Foster Jones, *Ancients & Moderns, A Study of the Rise of the Scientific Movement in Seventeenth-Century England*, in *Neophilologus* XLVI, 329.

Review of E.L. Marilla (ed.), *The Secular Poems of Henry Vaughan*, in *Neophilologus* XLVI, 330-1.

1963 *A Newsletter for Students of Recusant History*, no. 5. Nijmegen.

Introduction to Simon Patrick, *A Brief Account of the New Sect of Latitude-Men* (1662). The Augustan Reprint Society, Publication no. 100, Los Angeles.

Amerikaanse Letterkunde aan de Universiteit. Rede uitgesproken bij de openbare aanvaarding van het ambt van buitengewoon hoogleraar in de Amerikaanse en Moderne Engelse letterkunde aan de Universiteit van Amsterdam. Nijmegen/Utrecht.

De Culturele Achtergrond van Twee Wetenschappelijke Revoluties. Het Londen van Robert Hooke en het Philadelphia van James Logan. Rede uitgesproken bij de viering van de veertigste dies natalis van de Katholieke Universiteit te Nijmegen op Donderdag 17 Oktober 1963 door de Rector Magnificus. Nijmegen/Utrecht.

Review of Humphrey House & Graham Storey (eds.), *The Journals and Papers of Gerard Manley Hopkins*; Christopher Devlin S.J. (ed.), *The Sermons and Devotional Writings of Gerard Manley Hopkins*; Alan Heuser, *The Shaping Vision of Gerard Manley Hopkins*; Jean-Georges Ritz, *Robert Bridges and Gerard Manley Hopkins 1863-1899. A Literary Friendship*, in *English Studies* XLIV, 462-5.

1964 *De Katholieke Universiteit in 1963-1964.* Rede uitgesproken bij de overdracht van het Rectoraat op Maandag 21 September 1964 door de aftredende Rector Magnificus Prof. T.A. Birrell [with the assistance of Mr. C.L.A.M. Aerden]. Utrecht/Nijmegen.

A Newsletter for Students of Recusant History, no. 6. Nijmegen.

"De Studie van het Oud-Engels, 1705-1840", *Handelingen van het Achtentwintigste Nederlands Filologencongres*, Groningen, pp. 30-40.

"*The Political Register*: Cobbett and English Literature", *English Studies Presented to R.W. Zandvoort on the Occasion of his Seventieth Birthday*, Amsterdam, pp. 214-9.

1965 *A Newsletter for Students of Recusant History*, no. 7. Nijmegen.

"Dating as an Intermediary Between Literary History and Literary Criticism", *Literary History and Literary Criticism*, ed. L. Edel, New York, pp. 241-2.

1966 *A Newsletter for Students of Recusant History*, no. 8. Nijmegen.

"The Society of Antiquarians and the Taste for Old English, 1705-1840", *Neophilologus* L, 107-18.

Review of M.S. Røstvig, *The Happy Man, 1600-1700*, in *English Studies* XLVII, 149-50.

Review of T. Clancy, *Papist Pamphleteers*, in *Review of English Studies* XVII, 346.

Review of D. Wilkinson, *Enquiring Right*, in *Neophilologus* L, 294-5.

Review of P. Legouis, *Andrew Marvell*, in *Neophilologus* L, 295-6.

Review of Leo Spitzer, *Essays on English and American Literature*, in *Neophilologus* L, 401-2.

1966-1967 Contributions to *The New Catholic Encyclopedia*:
"The Oates Plot (1678-1681)"
"J.M. Corker OSB (1636-1715)"
"J. Austin (1613-1669)"
"L. Sabran S.J. (1652-1732)"
"J. Sergeant (1662-1707)".

1968 "Aspects of Dutch Catholicism", *The Clergy Review*, New Series, LIII, 759-68 (also in *Catholic Mind*, February 1969, 10-16).

"Wittgenstein en Leavis: Twee Figuren uit het Cambridge van de Dertiger Jaren", *Handelingen van het Dertigste Nederlands Filologencongres*, Groningen, pp. 101-2.

1969 *Engelse letterkunde*. Tweede herziene uitgave. Utrecht/Antwerpen: Spectrum.

1970 Robert Pugh, *Blacklow's Cabal* (1680). With an introduction by T.A. Birrell. Westmead: Gregg.

Florus Anglo-Bavaricus (Liège, 1685). With a new introduction by T.A. Birrell. Westmead: Gregg.

Joseph Berington, *The Memoirs of Gregorio Panzani* (Birmingham, 1793). With an introduction by T.A. Birrell. Westmead: Gregg.

Review of F. Refoulé, *Au Bord du Schisme? L'Affaire d'Amsterdam et l'Eglise de Hollande*; L. Roy, *Step beyond Impasse. A Chronicle of the Dutch Church*, in *Clergy Review*, New Series, LV, 69-72.

Review of D. Bush, *English literature in the Earlier 17th Century*, in *English Studies* LI, 359-61.

Review of H.C. White, *Books of Saints and Martyrs*, in *English Studies* LI, 452-3.

Review of M. Crum, *The Poems of Henry King*, in *English Studies* LI, 559-60.

"In Memoriam Prof. P.N.U. Harting", *The Times*, 8 September.

1971 *A Newsletter for Students of Recusant History*, no. 9. Nijmegen.

"Winston Churchill, Portret van een Oorlogsleider", *Bericht van de Tweede Wereldoorlog*, 6 februari, 1465-7.

1972 Review of J.M. Osborn, *Joseph Spence*, in *Neophilologus* LVI, 112-3.

Review of S.P. Zitner, *The Practice of Modern Literary Scholarship*, in *Neophilologus* LVI, 114-5.

Review of John Wilmot, *The Gyldenstolpe Manuscript Miscellany*, in *Neophilologus* LVI, 238-9.

Review of L.A. Beaurline and F. Bowers (eds.), *John Dryden: Four Comedies and Four Tragedies*, in *Neophilologus* LVI, 239-40.

Review of John R. Roberts, *A Critical Anthology of English Recusant Devotional Prose*, in *Yearbook of English Studies*, 1972, 249-50.

Review of A. Lowe, *Augustine Baker*, in *Yearbook of English Studies*, 1972, 259-60.

Review of S. Foster Damon, *A Blake Dictionary*, in *English Studies* LIII, 263-4.

Review of J.P. Kenyon, *The Popish Plot*, in *The Tablet*, 12 August, 762.

Review of J. Haswell, *James II, Soldier and Sailor*, in *The Tablet*, 2 September, 835.

1973 "James Maurus Corker and Dryden's Conversion", *English Studies* LIV, 461-9.

Review of M. Willy, *The Metaphysical Poets*; I. Simon, *Neo-Classical Criticism*, in *English Studies* LIV, 390-1.

Review of J.G. Riewald, *Reynier Jansen of Philadelphia*, in *Neophilologus* LVII, 312-3.

Review of W.L. Alderson & A.C. Henderson, *Chaucer and Augustan Scholarship*, in *Neophilologus* LVII, 426-7.

Review of B. Bevan, *Charles the Second's French Mistress. A Biography of Louise de Keroualle Dutchess of Portsmouth 1649-1743*, in *The Tablet*, 3 February, 109.

Review of J.E.N. Hearsey, *Young Mr. Pepys*, in *The Tablet*, 22 September, 898.

1974 *Engelse letterkunde.* Derde druk. Utrecht/Antwerpen: Spectrum.
1975 "Notes on the New Cambridge Bibliography of English Literature, Volume IV (1900-1950)", *Neophilologus* LIX, 306-15.
1976 "English Catholic Mystics in Non-Catholic Circles", *The Downside Review* XCIV, 60-81, 99-117, 213-31.
 The Library of John Morris. The Reconstruction of a Seventeenth-Century Collection. London: British Museum Publications.
1978 "The Greatness of *The Bostonians*", *Dutch Quarterly Review of Anglo-American Letters* VII, 242-64.
 "The New Short Title Catalogue", *Book Auction Records Quarterly*, May 1978, 5-7.
 Nawoord bij Charles Dickens, *Nicolas Nickleby*, Prisma Klassieken.
 Nawoord bij Charles Dickens, *David Copperfield*, Prisma Klassieken.
 "British Council Abroad", *The Times*, 5 August.
 Engelse letterkunde. Vierde druk. Utrecht/Antwerpen: Spectrum.
1979 Nawoord bij Charles Dickens, *De Nagelaten Papieren van De Pickwick Club*, Prisma Klassieken.
 Nawoord bij Charles Dickens, *Kleine Dorrit*, Prisma Klassieken.
1980 "A Preface to Cooper's *The Last of the Mohicans*", in J. Bakker and D.R.M. Wilkinson (eds.), *From Cooper to Philip Roth. Essays on American Literature Presented to J.G. Riewald on the Occasion of his Seventieth Birthday*, Amsterdam, pp. 1-19.
 "The Simplicity of Typhoon: Conrad, Flaubert and Others", *Dutch Quarterly Review of Anglo-American Letters* X, 272-95.
 "The Reconstruction of the Library of Isaac Casaubon", in *Hellinga Festschrift. Forty-three Studies in Bibliography presented to Prof. Dr. Wytze Hellinga on the occasion of his retirement from the Chair of Neophilology in the University of Amsterdam at the end of the year 1978*, Amsterdam, pp. 59-68.
 Nawoord bij Charles Dickens, *Oliver Twist*, Prisma Klassieken.
 Letter to the Editor of *The Times* on "The royal Talmud", *The Times*, 8 July.
1981 Review of Karl Jozef Höltgen, *Francis Quarles (1592-1644). Meditativer Dichter, Emblematiker, Royalist. Eine biographische und kritische Studie*, in *English Studies* LXII, 194-7.
1982 "Recusant Historiography", *The Tablet*, 26 June, 650-51.
 Amerikaanse letterkunde (trans. J.M. Blom). Utrecht: Spectrum.
 "In Memoriam Mario Praz", *English Studies* LXIII, 300.
1983 Review of Russell Kirk, *The Portable Conservative Reader*, in *English Studies* LXIV, 466.
 Review of Lodewijck Huygens, *The English Journal 1651-1652*, eds. A.G.H. Bachrach & R.G. Collmer, in *English Studies* LXIV, 200.

Review of J.G. Riewald & J. Bakker, *The Critical Reception of American Literature in the Netherlands 1824-1900*, in *English Studies* LXIV, 187-8.

Review of Peter Milward, *Religious Controversies of the Elizabethan Age. A Survey of Printed Sources* and *Religious Controversies of the Jacobean Age. A Survey of Printed Sources*, in *English Studies* LXIV, 502.

J.M.G.A. Aarts
  Nijmegen
Elisabeth M.A.A.J. Allard
  Vaals
A.F. Allison
  Kenley, England
J.C. Arens & E. Arens-Nijst
  Nijmegen
Mary-Jo Arn
  Groningen
A.G.H. Bachrach
  Oegstgeest
J.T.J. Bak
  Malden
A. Bardoel-v. Rijswoud
  Dongen
G.J.M. Bartelink
  Nijmegen
A.A.R. Bastiaensen
  Nijmegen
Frans Jozef van Beeck S.J.
  Chestnut Hill, U.S.A.
Mr. & Mrs. W.J.A.M. Beek
  Nijmegen
Marijke Beekelaar-De Beus
  Nijmegen
J.A.F. Bekkers
  Druten
Terry Belanger
  New York, U.S.A.
Dominic Bellenger
  Bath, England
A.P.M. van den Berg
  Limbricht
Mr & Mrs A.H.G.F. Bergmans-Engels
  Zevenaar
Hans Bertens
  Utrecht
J. van den Besselaar
  Nijmegen
S. Betsky & S. Betsky-Zweig
  Bilthoven
Jonquil Bevan
  Edinburgh, Scotland
B.H. Bichakjian
  Nijmegen

F.J.M. Blom
  Nijmegen
J.M. Blom
  Nijmegen
J.E. Bogaers
  Nijmegen
Th. Bögels
  Leiden
Th.C.G. Bongaerts
  Malden
N.A. Bootsma
  Nijmegen
T.J. Bootsma-Leereveld
  Nijmegen
J.A.H. Bots
  Mook
H.A.G. Braakhuis
  Nijmegen
Rolf H. Bremmer Jr.
  Nijmegen
A.P.A. Broeders
  Beuningen
W. Bronzwaer
  Nijmegen
R.K. Browne
  London, England
Patricia Brückmann
  Toronto, Canada
E.A.J. Bulten
  Amsterdam
G.H.V. Bunt
  Groningen
Rt. Rev. Bishop B.C. Butler OSB
  Ware, England
M.J.J. van Buuren &
E.C.J. van Buuren-Jansen
  Leidschendam
Roderick Cave
  Wellington, New Zealand
Edward P. de G. Chaney
  Uxbridge, England
Thomas H. Clancy S.J.
  Louisiana, U.S.A.
J.M. Cleary,
  Wrexham, Clwyd, Wales

J. Collins
  London, England
D.E.L. Crane
  Durham, England
Diane Crook
  Eindhoven
E. Curfs
  Zwijndrecht
Pierre Danchin
  Nancy, France
G. Debrock
  Nijmegen
M.E.A. Derks
  Groesbeek
R. Derolez
  Gent, Belgium
Mrs Michael Devas
  Chipping Campden, England
Nial Devitt
  Stanton-on-the-Wolds, England
F.N.M. Diekstra
  Nijmegen
A.I. Doyle
  Durham, England
C.L. Edwards
  London, England
C.W.A.M. Eimermann
  Breda
T.J.M. van Els
  Nijmegen
H. Ester
  Nijmegen
M. Evers
  Nijmegen
M. Faber-Hoornenborg
  Nijmegen
John Farrell
  Bristol, England
K. Fens
  Nijmegen
T.D.I. Fenwick
  Brussels, Belgium
Mario G. Fiori
  South Orange, U.S.A.
G. Flik
  Nijmegen
Mirjam Foot
  London, England

L.W. Forster
  Cambridge, England
Bert Freidus
  Rye, U.S.A.
J.F. Fuggles
  Oxford, England
G. van Gemert
  St. Anthonis
J. Gerritsen
  Groningen
A.J. Geurts
  Nijmegen
G. Giovannini
  Hyattsville, U.S.A.
Pierre Golliet
  Nijmegen
L. Gooch
  Wolsingham, England
A. Graaf
  Eindhoven
N.H. Griffin
  Manchester, England
E.F. van der Grinten
  Den Haag
Louis & Christine Grooten
  Nijmegen
Carlos Gussenhoven
  Nijmegen
P.J.M. de Haan
  Gennep
T.L. D'Haen
  Utrecht
Theodoor Harmsen
  Didam
Lars Hartveit
  Bergen, Norway
Wytze & Lotte Hellinga
  London, England
H.J.E. Hendrikx o.s.a.
  Nijmegen
C.A.J. van den Heuvel
  Geldrop
Caroline Hibbard
  Urbana, U.S.A.
Karl Josef Höltgen
  Erlangen, Germany
T.R. Howlett
  Hudson, U.S.A.

A.M.N. van den Hurk
  Tilburg
P.J.E. Hyams
  Mook
J.J. de Iongh
  Nijmegen
A.E.M. Janssen
  Nijmegen
H.M.L. Janssen
  Berkel-Enschot
Marian Janssen
  Nijmegen
Uta Janssens-Knorsch
  Nijmegen
Torvald Jansson
  Rome, Italy
Frans Kellendonk
  Amsterdam
E. Kellerman
  Beek (G)
J. Kerling
  Alphen a/d Rijn
Wallace Kirsop
  Clayton, Australia
F.J.M. Korsten
  Nijmegen
J. Kuin
  Amsterdam
David Ladner
  Whitneyville, U.S.A.
L.R. Leavis
  Nijmegen
J. Maas & V. Brok
  Valkenswaard
N.J.L.M. van der Maas
  Beek (L)
Thomas M. McCoog S.J.
  Baltimore, U.S.A.
A.A. MacDonald
  Nijmegen
David McKitterick
  Cambridge, England
J.W.H. Mali
  Ubbergen
Edward Margolies
  New York, U.S.A.
K. Meeuwesse
  Nijmegen

L.J.M. Melchiors
  Mheer
A.G.M. van Melsen
  Nijmegen
W.G.A. Mertens
  Waalre
Horst Meyer
  Bad Iburg, Germany
C. Minis
  Amsterdam
M. Moerman-Groenewoud
  Maassluis
D. de Moulin
  Boxtel
Loes Nas
  Amsterdam
Desmond Neill
  Toronto, Canada
A. Nooteboom
  Loenen a/d Vecht
Sister Marion Norman ibvm
  Toronto, Canada
J. Nuchelmans
  Nijmegen
P.F.J. Obbema
  Leiden
Th.G.M. van Oorschot S.J.
  Nijmegen
H.Th. Oostendorp
  Groningen
Very Rev. Dom Bernard Orchard
  Ealing, England
N.E. Osselton
  Newcastle Upon Tyne, England
D.L. Paisey
  London, England
John E.C. Palmer
  Harpenden, England
Katharine F. Pantzer
  Cambridge, U.S.A.
Geoffrey de C. Parmiter
  Banbury, England
David R.S. Pearson
  Durham, England
G.M. Peerbooms
  Malden
H. Penders
  Cuyk

Ian G. Philip
  Oxford, England
V. Piket
  Nijmegen
J. Plat
  Nijmegen
J.J. Poelhekke
  Nijmegen
Hans & Irmtraud Pörnbacher
  Nijmegen
Elisabeth Poyser
  London, England
A.A. Prins
  Oosterbeek
P.R. Quarrie
  Eton, England
A.F. Rasing
  Twello
Norman C. Reeves
  Leominster, England
Rosemary Reidel
  London, England
Dennis E. Rhodes
  London, England
J.G. Riewald
  Haren (Gr.)
T.N.J.A. van Rijn
  Nijmegen
Julian Roberts
  Oxford, England
David Rogers
  Oxford, England
M.Ph.H. Roomans-Merkelbag
  Venlo
C. Schaar
  Lund, Sweden
C.W. Schoneveld
  Leiden
P. Schoonenberg S.J.
  H. Landstichting
G.L.M. Schreiner S.J.
  Nijmegen
J. Schuurbiers
  Kaatsheuvel
Very Rev. Dom Geoffrey Scott
  Reading, England
S.R. Shapiro
  New York, U.S.A.

Totaro Shimamura
  Saitama-ken, Japan
I.J.J. Simon
  Liège/Luik, Belgium
Anna E.C. Simoni
  Teddington, England
J.S.F. Simons
  Kerkrade
Kristian Smidt
  Oslo, Norway
Knud Sörensen
  Hojbjerg, Denmark
Logan Speirs
  Santa Barbara, U.S.A.
M.E.B. Spiertz-Verraes
  Nijmegen
Rudolf Stamm
  Basel, Switzerland
P.G. Stanwood
  Vancouver, Canada
Otger Steggink
  Nijmegen
John Stephens
  Oxford, England
Very Rev. Dom Hilary Stewart
  Bath, England
Walter P. van Stigt
  Twickenham, England
F. Stoks
  Nijmegen
G. Storms
  Berg en Dal
F.W.J. Stronk
  Diepenheim
John Tobias
  Kingston-upon-Thames, England
H.A. Tummers
  Nijmegen
J.J. Vaissier
  Tilburg
A.G. Verdenius
  Beek/Ubbergen
A.W.J.I. Verlaan
  Arnhem
J.A. Verleun
  Haren
J.P. Verschuren
  Geldrop

R. Verwaaijen
  Gendt
Dorine de Vet
  Den Haag
A.L. Vos
  Laren (N.H.)
A.G.W.E. de Vries
  Dongen
Wally de Vries
  Overlangel
H.Chr. Wekker
  Nijmegen
Mr. & Mrs. D.R.M. Wilkinson
  Paterswolde
Gerard M. Willems
  Nijmegen
J. Anthony Williams
  Hull, England
Rev. Michael E. Williams
  Horsforth, England
W.E. Williams
  Goirle
I.R. Willison
  London, England
W.M.J. Wintjens
  Maastricht
Berthold Wolpe
  London, England
Mrs John W. Yolton
  Piscataway, U.S.A.
R.W. Zandvoort
  Amersfoort

Anglistisch Instituut,
  Groningen
The Bata Library, Trent University,
  Ontario, Canada

Biblioteca Centrale Di Magistero,
  Parma, Italy
Bibliotheek Instituut voor
  Neerlandistiek, Universiteit
  van Amsterdam
The Brotherton Library,
  University of Leeds, England
Cistercian Abbey of Our Lady of New
  Clairvaux Library, Vina, U.S.A.
College of Librarianship Wales,
  Dyfed, Wales
Foreign Accessions, Bodleian Library,
  Oxford, England
Heythrop College, University of
  London, England
The Humanities Research Center
  Austin, U.S.A.
Provinciale Bibliotheek van
  Friesland, Leeuwarden
Shakespeare Institute, University
  of Birmingham, England
Stadsbibliotheek Maastricht,
  Maastricht
St. Andrews University Library,
  Scotland
St. John's Seminary Library,
  Brighton, U.S.A.
Ushaw College Library,
  Durham, England
Trinity College Library,
  Dublin, Ireland
Werkgroep Engels-Nederlandse
  Betrekkingen/Sir Thomas
  Browne Institute, Leiden